21 世纪电子商务专业核心课程系列教材
全国高等院校电子商务联编教材

新编电子商务英语
（第 2 版）
New E-Business English
(2nd Edition)

主　编　姚国章
参　编　陈　菲　韩玲华
　　　　赵　婷

北京大学出版社
PEKING UNIVERSITY PRESS

内 容 简 介

本书是《新编电子商务英语》的第 2 版,全书结合电子商务专业教学的实际需要,从国际权威机构、知名媒体和专业网站等途径选取 32 篇较有代表性的电子商务专业课文,这些课文具有比较强的实用性、新颖性和前瞻性,比较适合学习和研究电子商务的读者阅读。全书注重培养通过英语阅读提高学习和钻研电子商务专业知识的能力,旨在通过课堂教学或个人自学,让读者能对当今国际电子商务的新理论、新应用和新趋势有一个比较全面的理解与把握,以激发读者通过英语学习电子商务的热情和兴趣,进一步拓宽电子商务的专业视野和研究视角。

本书适合电子商务本专科专业及相关专业硕士研究生教学,也适合个人自学之用,对有志于从事电子商务研究的读者同样会有较大的参考价值。

图书在版编目(CIP)数据

新编电子商务英语/姚国章主编. —2 版.—北京:北京大学出版社,2013.9
(21 世纪电子商务专业核心课程系列教材·全国高等院校电子商务联编教材)
ISBN 978-7-301-23239-2

Ⅰ.①新… Ⅱ.①姚… Ⅲ.①电子商务—英语—高等职业教育—教材 Ⅳ.①H31

中国版本图书馆 CIP 数据核字(2013)第 220577 号

书　　　　名:	新编电子商务英语(第 2 版)
著作责任者:	姚国章　主编
策 划 编 辑:	胡伟晔
责 任 编 辑:	王慧馨
标 准 书 号:	ISBN 978-7-301-23239-2/TP·1309
出 版 发 行:	北京大学出版社
地　　　　址:	北京市海淀区成府路 205 号　100871
网　　　　址:	http://www.pup.cn　新浪官方微博:@北京大学出版社
电 子 信 箱:	zyjy@pup.cn
电　　　　话:	邮购部 62752015　发行部 62750672　编辑部 62765126　出版部 62754962
印 　刷 　者:	北京鑫海金澳胶印有限公司
经 　销 　者:	新华书店
	787 毫米×1092 毫米　16 开本　25 印张　555 千字
	2008 年 6 月第 1 版
	2013 年 9 月第 2 版　2018 年 5 月第 3 次印刷　总第 5 次印刷
定　　　　价:	48.00 元

未经许可,不得以任何方式复制或抄袭本书之部分或全部内容。
版权所有,侵权必究
举报电话:010-62752024　电子信箱:fd@pup.pku.edu.cn

前　言

《新编电子商务英语》自2008年6月出版以来，取得了比较好的市场反馈，已被数十所高校选作电子商务及其相关专业的英语教材，受到了读者的欢迎。可以说，本书的出版为促进我国电子商务教学和研究事业的健康、快速发展以及电子商务专业人才的培养起到了积极的作用。

不少读者在使用该书的过程中，对存在的错误和有待改进之处提出了中肯的批评和宝贵的建议。本书是在对《新编电子商务英语》一书存在的不足之处进行完善的基础上，增加了新的课文。与原书相比，无论是在篇幅、广度，还是在深度方面都有了很大的提升，对读者更好地通过英语学习和研究电子商务有着很大的帮助。

全书分成"电子商务概述"、"电子化营销与电子金融"、"企业电子商务"、"行业电子商务"、"电子商务案例"、"电子商务技术与安全"和"电子商务综合"等7篇，每篇安排了一组课文，大致覆盖了当今国际电子商务发展的重点和热点领域，读者可根据需要进行"精读"或"泛读"。在用做本科专业的教材时，建议课堂教学以不少于32学时为宜，48学时为佳，每一大"篇"中可选择2~3篇课文在课堂讲解，其余可安排学生自学。在作为专科教学时应适当增加课堂教学学时，同时组织学生进行自学。

课文中的生词选取基本以是否超过大学英语四级词汇表作为判断依据，也就是说，对没有选入四级词汇表或词汇表中释义与文中不符的，基本上都在书中作了标注。有些标注不当或漏标的生词，期待读者批评指正。

本书是集体合作的结晶，由姚国章主编，陈菲、韩玲华和赵婷参编，惠云云、张锐、杨洁、赵生兰、郑雪琳和姜国君等收集整理了英文原稿，并进行了初步的翻译，为本书的成稿起到了不可替代的作用。早年参与《电子商务英语》编写的张震老师和陈立梅老师对本书的贡献同样是不可低估的，在书中的很多地方依然闪烁着他们智慧的光芒。

值得一提的是，在长达十余年的愉快合作中，北京大学出版社的黄庆生主任和姚成龙主任自始至终对笔者给予了热情的鼓励和大力的帮助，本书的出版可以说是我们又一次成功合作的结晶。编辑部的周伟老师、胡伟晔老师认真负责的工作态度和一丝不苟的编辑作风令我们深受感动。

电子商务是一个发展迅猛的领域，新理论、新知识、新现象层出不穷，限于时间、精力、能力和水平，笔者最大的愿望是成为一个不落伍的"好学生"，和亲爱的读者一起去探索一个又一个充满神奇的未知领地。

本书虽经多方努力，但缺点和错误仍在所难免，主要责任应由笔者承担。恳请各位尊敬的读者批评指正，并期待您能及时反馈。

姚国章（yaogz@vip.sina.com）
2013年2月

Contents

目 录

CHAPTER 1 AN OVERVIEW OF E-BUSINESS
第1篇 电子商务概述

Unit 1　E-Business Basics ··· 3
　　　　电子商务基础 ··· 9

Unit 2　E-Commerce/E-Business in the New Economy ······················· 12
　　　　新经济下的电子商贸/电子商务 ··· 17

Unit 3　Six Principles to Guide the Development of Global E-Commerce ······ 19
　　　　指导全球电子商务发展的六大原则 ····································· 26

Unit 4　The Global E-Business Environment ······································ 29
　　　　全球的电子商务环境 ·· 34

CHAPTER 2 E-MARKETING AND E-FINANCE
第2篇 电子化营销与电子金融

Unit 5　What is E-Marketing Planning ··· 39
　　　　什么是电子营销计划 ·· 46

Unit 6　A New Marketing Strategy for E-Commerce ···························· 50
　　　　一个针对电子商务的新营销策略 ·· 58

Unit 7　Customer Differentiation and Lifecycle Management of E-Marketing ······ 62
　　　　电子化营销的客户差异化与生命周期管理 ···························· 69

Unit 8　Payment Applications Make E-Commerce Mobile ···················· 73
　　　　支付应用使电子商务移动化 ··· 80

Unit 9　E-Business Strategy in an Online Banking Services:
　　　　A Case Study of Citibank ··· 85
　　　　在线银行服务电子商务战略：花旗银行的案例研究 ················ 93

CHAPTER 3　E-BUSINESS ABOUT ENTERPRISES
第 3 篇　企业电子商务

Unit 10　How SMBs Can Profit from the Internet ………………………… 101
　　　　　中小企业如何从互联网中获利 ……………………………………… 106
Unit 11　E-Business Strategy Review Report for Tesco.com …………… 109
　　　　　特易购网电子商务战略评估报告 …………………………………… 121
Unit 12　Could My Business be an E-Business ……………………………… 128
　　　　　我的业务能发展成电子商务吗？ …………………………………… 133
Unit 13　Integrating E-Business into Your Small Business ……………… 136
　　　　　将电子商务集成到你的小企业中去 ………………………………… 141

Chapter 4　E-Business about Industries
第 4 篇　行业电子商务

Unit 14　Retail "E-Procurement": Minimizing Costs and Improving Productivity …… 147
　　　　　零售业电子采购分析：成本最小化，提高生产力 ………………… 153
Unit 15　Using the Internet to Market Agricultural Exports ……………… 155
　　　　　利用互联网推销农业出口产品 ……………………………………… 161
Unit 16　Selling Products on Facebook: The Emergence of Social Commerce …… 165
　　　　　在 Facebook 上销售产品：社交商务的出现 ……………………… 177
Unit 17　Scan of E-Business in Higher Education ………………………… 183
　　　　　高等教育电子商务扫描 ……………………………………………… 191

CHAPTER 5　E-BUSINESS CASE STUDIES
第 5 篇　电子商务案例

Unit 18　Case Study of CRM: Securities Institute of Australia …………… 197
　　　　　CRM 案例研究：澳大利亚证券学院（SIA）………………………… 204
Unit 19　TDC's Implementation of E-Commerce …………………………… 207
　　　　　丹麦电信电子商务应用 ……………………………………………… 212
Unit 20　Deutsche Bank's E-Trust …………………………………………… 215
　　　　　德意志银行的电子化信任 …………………………………………… 224
Unit 21　Viral Marketing of Kettle Foods …………………………………… 230
　　　　　克特食品的病毒性营销 ……………………………………………… 239

Unit 22	Groupon Case Study	246
	Groupon 案例研究	256
Unit 23	Hitachi Group Achieves an Integrated Collaboration Environment through E-Business	262
	日立集团通过电子商务构筑起了集成协同环境	276

CHAPTER 6 E-BUSINESS TECHNOLOGY AND SECURITY ISSUES
第 6 篇 电子商务技术与安全

Unit 24	Some Technology Trends Affecting E-Business	285
	一些影响电子商务的技术趋势	292
Unit 25	Usability of the E-Business Web Site	295
	电子商务网站的可使用性	301
Unit 26	What is E-Commerce Integration	305
	何谓电子商务集成	313
Unit 27	E-Business Relies on Security	318
	电子商务依赖于安全性	325

ChAPTER 7 COMPREHENSIVE ISSUES ABOUT E-BUSINESS
第 7 篇 电子商务综合

Unit 28	E-Supply Chain Management: Prerequisites to Success	333
	电子化供应链管理：成功的先决条件	340
Unit 29	The Features, Applications and Trends of M-Commerce	343
	移动电子商务的特征、应用与趋势	352
Unit 30	International Taxation of E-Commerce	356
	电子商务的国际税收	363
Unit 31	E-Business and Government Promotion of International Trade	367
	电子商务与政府对国际贸易的促进	373
Unit 32	The Role of Knowledge Management in Building E-Business Strategy	377
	知识管理在构建电子商务战略中的作用	385

E-Business Terms Explanations
（电子商务术语解释） 389

CHAPTER 1
AN OVERVIEW OF E-BUSINESS

电子商务概述

- E-Business Basics
- E-Commerce/E-Business in the New Economy
- Six Principles to Guide the Development of Global E-Commerce
- The Global E-Business Environment

UNIT 1

E-Business Basics

Text

Introduction

This Info-Guide is designed for beginners. It will help you understand the concept of e-business and how e-business can improve your own business processes. You will be able to test your own e-business readiness and learn where to go for more information on getting started with e-business.

As we know that electronic commerce, B2C, or e-commerce refers to online sales. Electronic business or e-business, on the other hand, refers to more than just selling online.

E-business is about utilizing Internet technologies—such as simple e-mail, online banking solutions, websites, and more sophisticated applications such as web-based customer relationship management solutions—to provide superior customer service, streamline business processes, increase sales and reduce costs.

Therefore, any business owner who uses the Internet to develop or enhance their business is using e-business. This means that you may already be using e-business in your own business.

Understanding Internet Technology and Its Relation to E-Business

The Internet and the World Wide Web

The Internet is an electronic communications network that allows computers around the world to "talk" to each other. Any computer that is connected to the Internet can exchange information with other connected computers.

The World Wide Web, or simply the Web, is a subset of the Internet. It functions as the Internet's navigation system and allows users to view the Internet network through the use of websites.

How Websites Work

Websites are a collection of web pages, which are electronic pages of information linked together much like a spider's web. This spider's web-like navigational system allows users to move around the system in a non-linear fashion. This means that, unlike a book—where information is laid out for the reader chronologically, in a set order—a Web user has the power to access information online however they choose.

Websites are accessed via a web browser such as Internet Explorer or Mozilla. Web browsers are the graphical interface that enables users to view, find and interact with websites.

Websites each have their own unique address, called an IP address, through which users can find them. For example, the Alberta E-Future Centre's online address is www.e-future.ca/alberta. By typing this address into the web browser address bar, a user would be connected to our website.

But, since the Web indexes literally billions of websites, another method to facilitate finding relevant websites was necessary. Therefore, search engines that utilize "keyword searching" were created.

It is estimated that more than 98% of Internet users use search engines to find websites online. A search engine is a website whose primary purpose is to provide a search function for gathering and reporting information available on the Internet.

Search engines allow Internet users to quickly find websites related to a certain topic through the use of "keywords" and "keyword phrases", that is, words and phrases that describe the topic of interest.

For example, let's say an Internet user in the UK is looking for businesses online that sell hand carved indigenous masks and figurines from Canada. She doesn't know of any specific businesses selling these items; nor does she know any website addresses, so she uses a search engine such as Google or Yahoo to find websites whose content contains relevant keywords.

On the search engine's main page, she types into the search-box: "Canadian Native Art." The search engine returns 3,370 listings containing this keyword phrase, organized by relevancy. The user can then either start browsing the websites listed, or she can narrow the results further by searching within those results for another keyword like "mask", for example.

Search engines allow Internet users to effectively find relevant websites, making the Web's vast amount of information much easier to navigate.

Why the Internet is of Value to Business

As an instantaneous information and communication medium with global reach, the Internet is a practical and vital business tool. And, your small business can benefit from the equal footing it offers you, regardless of your size or location.

Below, we'll explore some of the efficiencies that can be achieved by small businesses using Internet technologies to further their business goals.

The Benefits of E-Business

The Internet and related technologies can change the way you develop and conduct your business processes, making them more time and cost efficient. They can diversify your marketing channels and, ultimately, help you increase your business revenue.

The Internet levels the playing field for small businesses. That is, it allows small business operators to compete on equal footing with larger businesses in the same industry.

Through the Internet, your small business can distribute information online to a global audience, immediately, with little out of pocket expense. This means you'll reach more clients or customers in a shorter period of time.

It gives you the ability to interact with your clients and customers in new ways, putting power in the hands of the buyer, giving your clients or customers more choice than they've ever had before.

And finally, the Internet gives you, the seller, the ability to readily assess your online business practices and modify them on the fly to ensure they meet the needs of your clients/customers.

In short, you can use the Internet to:

- Collect vital business information related to your customers and competitors. The Internet is a valuable research tool and, as a readily accessible information medium, its ability to allow you to remain competitive in your industry should not be under-estimated.

- Increase awareness about your company. Even if you are not considering selling online, having a website that promotes your business, provides contact information, and outlines your unique value proposition—that is, the unique collection of benefits attributed to your product or service that creates value for your customers or clients—will simply increase your reach and value in the marketplace, and make it easier for your potential clients/customers to find you.

- Streamline communications and improve customer service. E-mail communications, website FAQs and auto-responders are examples of simple and cost effective electronic techniques that can help improve communications between you

and your clients/customers.
- Improve productivity and reduce costs. Simply by streamlining communications using Internet technologies, you can improve your business productivity. And, out-of-pocket costs can be reduced further by implementing a readily updatable website, instead of printed materials that have a short shelf-life, to relay pertinent information to your customer base.
- Sell your products online. For those considering making the leap to e-commerce, selling online can lower your upfront set-up costs and operational costs, increase your reach to a global marketplace, and allow you to be "open" 24 hours per day, 7 days per week. Further, it can allow you to automate your order processing and order tracking capabilities, develop cheaper online catalogues, and update your product lists on the fly.

Adopting E-Business Strategies

Even if you're not ready to build a website just yet, you should still consider how e-business tools can help you in your business. It's important to note that not all e-strategies work for all businesses. Therefore, the best way to begin is to create a plan that outlines how you will leverage the Internet to meet your specific business needs.

Developing an Internet related business plan, or an "e-business plan", is most effectively and simply achieved when e-business aspects are integrated into your overall business plan. At each stage of your business plan, consider how you can use e-business technologies to reduce costs and improve productivity. Then only implement the strategies that make sense for your particular business.

Here are some ways to get started using e-business:
- Make your mark on the web. Build a website. Make sure that your website address is on all your marketing material.
- Leverage e-mail. Develop an e-newsletter to communicate with your clients and prospects. Make sure that it provides value to the reader.
- Embrace e-procurement. Seek out suppliers that allow you to save time and money by purchasing online.
- Investigate e-commerce. Test the online marketplace by selling through low-cost channels such as eBay.

Words and Expressions

| sophisticated [səˈfistikeitid] | adj. | 非常复杂精密或尖端的 |
| navigation [ˌnæviˈgeiʃən] | n. | 航海,航空,导航,领航,航行 |

non-linear [‚nɒŋˈliniə]	adj.	非线性的
chronologically [‚krɔnəˈlɔdʒikəli]	ad.	按年代顺序排列地
facilitate [fəˈsiliteit]	vt.	使容易,使便利;推动,帮助,促进
indigenous [inˈdidʒinəs]	adj.	本土的
instantaneous [‚instənˈteinjəs]	adj.	瞬间的,即刻的,即时的
assess [əˈses]	vt.	估定,评定
promote [prəˈməut]	vt.	促进,发扬;提升,提拔,晋升为
implement [ˈimplimənt]	n.	工具,器具
	vt.	贯彻,实现
leverage [ˈliːvəridʒ]	n.	杠杆作用;举债经营
	vt.	杠杆作用;使(某一公司)举债经营

Notes

(1) The Internet is an electronic communications network that allows computers around the world to "talk" to each other. Any computer that is connected to the Internet can exchange information with other connected computers. 互联网是允许全球计算机相互"对话"的电子通信网络。任何一台接入互联网的计算机都可以同其他联网计算机交换信息。

(2) Even if you are not considering selling online, having a website that promotes your business, provides contact information, and outlines your unique value proposition—that is, the unique collection of benefits attributed to your product or service that creates value for your customers or clients—will simply increase your reach and value in the marketplace, and make it easier for your potential clients/customers to find you. 即使你没有考虑到在线销售,也不妨建立公司的宣传网站,在网站上提供联系方式或是概述你公司的独特价值主张——即你公司为客户或顾客创造价值的商品和服务的独特集合——这将极易扩大你公司的市场份额、创造市场价值,并且能使你公司的潜在顾客/客户更容易地联系到你。

Questions

(1) What's the difference between e-commerce and e-business?

(2) How to search on the Web?

(3) Please make a comment on the e-business in small business.

Exercises

1. Translate the following sentences into Chinese:

(1) The advance of Internet technologies has enabled us to analyze the global information and distribute it to our customers.

(2) Unlike a book, where information is laid out for the reader chronologically, in a set order, a Web user has the power to access information online however they choose.

(3) When searching information online, the user can then either start browsing the websites listed, or can narrow the results further by searching within those results for another keyword.

(4) Out-of-pocket costs can be reduced further by implementing a readily updatable website, instead of printed materials that have a short shelf-life, to relay pertinent information to your customer base.

(5) Today's Internet is a powerful way for business to communicate with their customers and clients, including e-mail, instant messaging, and developing the websites of the company.

2. Translate the following sentences into English:

(1) 作为一个网站,搜索引擎的最初目的是为收集和发布互联网上可用的信息提供一种搜索功能。

(2) 互联网使小企业能够利用过去只有大公司才能获得的信息、专门知识和资金的全球储备库。

(3) 通过在线采购,企业可以省时、省钱地寻找到供应商。

(4) 网上调查高效、便捷、经济,它对于提高企业竞争力有着不可低估的作用。

Further Reading

You can read the paper with the title: How to Win the Business-to-Business Game, which will give you a better understanding about why using e-business properly can help you work more efficiently and increase business productivity.

Translation

电子商务基础

简　介

　　本信息指南为初学者设计。它将有助于你更好地了解电子商务的概念以及电子商务是如何改进公司业务流程的。据此可以检验自己是否为开展电子商务准备就绪,以及从何处获取更多相关信息。

　　正如我们所知道的那样,电子商贸,又称 B2C,或 e-commerce① 指的是在线销售。另外,电子商务,或称 e-business,不仅仅指在线销售。

　　电子商务(e-business)是利用互联网技术——如简单的电子邮件、在线银行解决方案、网站,以及更为复杂的解决基于网络的客户关系管理等问题的应用软件——来提供优良的客户服务、流线型业务流程,以及降低成本、增加销售。

　　因此,任何使用互联网来发展业务的企业主都会选择电子商务。这意味着你也可能已经准备好了要在你的企业内部发展电子商务。

了解互联网技术及其与电子商务之间的联系

互联网和万维网

　　互联网是允许全球计算机相互"对话"的电子通信网络。任何一台接入互联网的计算机都可以同其他联网计算机交换信息。

　　World Wide Web,简称万维网,是互联网的子网络。它作为互联网的导航系统,允许用户通过登录站点来浏览互联网。

网站如何工作

　　网站是网页的集合,网页是提供信息的电子页面,它们之间像蛛网一样互相连接在一起。这一蛛网样的导航系统允许用户以一种非线性的方式在系统上四处浏览。这意味着,同书籍不同——书籍中提供给读者的信息通常都是以一种固定的顺序按时间先后排列——万维网用户却无论如何选择都能获取在线信息。

　　进入网站可以使用网络浏览器,比如 Internet Explorer 或 Mozilla。Web 浏览器是允许用户浏览、搜索和互相作用的图形界面。

---

　　① 按照英文原意,"e-commerce"理解成"电子商贸"较为贴切,"e-business"理解成"电子商务"较为合适。在国内,"e-commerce"和"e-business"基本不作区分,均被译为"电子商务"。在本书中,当"e-commerce"与"e-business"同时出现时,前者译为"电子商贸",后者译为"电子商务"。其他情况下不作专门区分,均译为"电子商务"。

每个网站都有自己的唯一地址,称作 IP 地址,通过这些地址用户就可以找到它们。例如,Alberta E-Future 中心的在线地址是 www.e-future.ca/alberta。用户只需在 Web 浏览器的地址栏中键入它就可以连接到该网站。

但是,编入 Web 索引的网站差不多有几十亿家,所以有必要使用另一种方法使搜寻相关网站更便利。因此,利用"关键词搜索"的搜索引擎应运而生。

据估计,大约有 98% 的互联网用户使用搜索引擎来寻找在线网站。搜索引擎是一个网站,它最初的目的是为收集和发布互联网上可用的信息提供一种搜索功能。

搜索引擎允许互联网用户通过使用"关键字"或"关键词组",即与主题有关的字或词组,快速找到特定主题的相关网站。

例如,如果一个英国的互联网用户要在网上寻找加拿大出售当地手刻面具和小雕像的企业,可她既不清楚任何一家出售这些小物件的特定企业,也不知道任何的相关网站,于是她就可以使用类似谷歌或雅虎等搜索引擎来寻找含有相关关键字的网站。

在搜索引擎的主页的搜索框内,她键入"加拿大本土艺术"。搜索引擎按关联远近列出 3370 个含有该关键词组的选项。此时用户可以选择浏览列出的网站,也可以缩小范围,在搜索结果内键入另一个关键字,如"面具"等,进一步寻找。

搜索引擎使得用户能有效地寻找相关网站,更容易地在网络信息的浩瀚海洋中航行。

为什么互联网对企业有价值

作为全球范围的即时信息和通信媒介,互联网是一种实用而且重要的商业工具。无论规模大小、地点设在何处,小企业都能够平等地享有互联网提供的信息。接下来,让我们来探讨小企业通过使用互联网技术促进商业目标实现所能取得的功效。

电子商务的收益

互联网及其相关技术可以改变你发展和管理业务流程的方式,使你的业务流程在节省时间和成本方面效率更高。它们能使你的营销渠道多样化,最终将有助于提升你的业务收益。

互联网给小型企业提供了平等的竞争领地。也就是说,它允许小型企业以平等的关系在同一行业中与大型企业展开竞争。

通过互联网,小型企业能以很少的费用向全球用户在线发布信息,这意味着你能在更短的时间内获取更多的顾客或客户。

它还能使你以一种新的方式同顾客和客户互相交流,即将权利转交给买主,给你的顾客和客户前所未有的多重选择。

最后,互联网使你——作为卖主,能迅速容易地评估并快速修正自己的商业行为,以保证满足顾客和客户的需求。

简而言之,你可以利用互联网达到以下目标:

■ 收集你的客户和竞争者的重要商业情报。互联网是一种有价值的调查工具,作为能够快速容易地使用的信息媒介,它对于你保持在本行业的竞争力有着不可低估的作用。

- 增强你的企业意识。即使你没有考虑到在线销售,也不妨建立公司的宣传网站,在网站上提供联系方式或是概述你公司的独特价值观念——即你公司为客户或顾客创造价值的商品和服务的独特集合——这将极易扩大你公司的市场份额、创造市场价值,并且能使你公司的潜在顾客/客户更容易地联系到你。
- 简化交流方式,改进客户服务。电子邮件沟通、网站常见问题解答以及自动回应器等都是简便且耗费少的电子技术,这些技术能帮助你改善你和顾客/客户之间的交流沟通。
- 提高生产力,降低成本。仅仅依靠互联网技术简化交流方式,你就可以提高企业的生产力。同样,执行一个可迅速更新的网站代替有效期限短的印刷品来向你的客户群传递相关信息,可以进一步减少现金支付费用。
- 在线销售你公司的产品。考虑到电子商务的飞跃式发展,在线销售能降低你的前期准备成本和操作成本,增加全球市场份额,并且能够使你一天24小时,一周7天"营业"。此外,在线销售能使你的订单处理和订购追踪性能实现自动操作,开发费用更加低廉的在线目录和及时更新产品列表等。

采用电子商务策略

即使你现在还没准备好建立一个网站,你也应该考虑在商业活动中电子商务能怎样助你一臂之力。需要指出的是,并不是所有的电子化战略都适用于任何一家企业。因此,开始时,最好的办法就是先制订一项计划,概述出你在自己特定的企业内部发挥互联网影响作用的方法。

当电子商务整合进你整体的商务计划中时开发一种与互联网有关的商业计划,或称"电子商务计划",是最有效,也是最容易取得预期效果的。在你的业务计划的每一个阶段,你需要考虑如何利用电子商务技术来降低成本和提升效率,接着就需要围绕你特定的业务而执行相应的战略就行了。

以下是开展电子商务的几种方法:

- 在网络上打造标记。建立一个网站,确保你的所有销售材料上都有你网站的地址。
- 发挥电子邮件的影响作用。开发电子新闻通信来同你的客户和潜在客户沟通交流,同时确保它能给阅读者提供有价值的东西。
- 电子采购。通过在线采购,你可以省时、省钱地寻找到供应商。
- 电子商务交易调查。通过在 eBay 等一些低成本的销售渠道上卖东西来探测在线市场的情形。

UNIT 2 E-Commerce/E-Business in the New Economy

The Internet

E-commerce and e-business are both, products of the Internet. The Internet is basically a vast and ever increasing network of computers across the globe that are interconnected over existing telecommunication networks. Simply described, it is a, or the, network of networks. It is estimated that the number of persons connected to the Internet today well surpass 500 million, closing the gap on the 700 million or so connected to the telephone. It is calculated that there are over 90 million Internet hosts world-wide, facilitating a dramatic increase in the volume of trade and information available online. The economic rationale of the Internet comes from e-business and its developmental and moral platform will come from its impact in areas such as e-government.

Defining E-Commerce and E-Business

It is important to elaborate on the definitions of e-commerce and e-Business as that will help determine the scope and perspective of this analytical paper. E-commerce has been simply defined as conducting business on-line. In the World Trade Organization (WTO) Work Programmer on Electronic Commerce, it is understood to mean *the production, distribution, marketing, sale or delivery of goods and services by electronic means*. Broadly defined, electronic commerce encompasses all kinds of commercial transactions that are concluded over an electronic medium or network, essentially, the Internet. Electronic Commerce is a new way of doing business. It is transacting or enabling the marketing, buying, and selling of goods and/or information through an electronic media, especially the Internet.

From a business point of view, e-commerce is not limited to the purchase of a product. It includes, besides e-mail and other communication platforms, all information or services that a company may offer to its customers over the Net, from pre-purchase information to after-sale service and support. There are essentially two major uses of e-commerce. The first is to use it to reduce transaction costs by increasing efficiency in the use of time and procedures and thus lowering costs. The other is to use it both as a marketing tool to increase sales (and customer services) as well as to create new business through it—for example, IT enabled business, call centers, software and maintenance services, etc. as well as "digital commerce". It is thus a tool for both existing businesses as well as an opportunity for new business, both for existing companies as well as for new entrants. E-commerce is seen as being B2C (business to consumer), B2B (business to business) and B2G (business to government). Of these three, B2B has been the most successful though recent reverses in the stock market valuations of high-tech stocks and the slowing down of the U.S. economy in particular is casting doubts on this. In future perhaps the major gains and usage of e-commerce and the Internet will come from "old economy" enterprises using it, governments using it (e-government), and social sectors using it (e-education and e-health).

E-Business

E-business is the application of Internet technologies to business processes. However it is more than information technology tools or straight e-commerce. It also implies that the organization, especially its managers, are willing and receptive to radical changes that such new business techniques and tools bring. It implies organizational process and organizational culture re-engineering, for a true transition into the new economy. Its benefits come not just from the efficiencies and automation of a company's internal processes but from its ability to spread the efficiency gains to the business systems of its suppliers and customers.

An *e-enterprise* (participating in e-business) is defined as an enterprise prepared to conduct commerce in this new economy. This means it has created and embraced a business strategy informed by changing economics, new opportunities, and new threats. It has laid down the necessary technology infrastructure to support new business processes. It has used information technology to hone internal processes such as human resources, work flow management, and training. Thus prepared, the enterprise is able to conduct e-commerce: "the commercial exchange of value (money, goods, services, or information) between an enterprise and an external entity (an upstream supplier, a partner, or a down-stream customer) over a universal, ubiquitous electronic medium."

In order to appreciate the relevance of e-business and its potential to impact on business and development, it is important to understand that e-commerce and e-business are more than just electronics and commerce/business added together. They represent an entirely new way of doing business (including that of government) over a medium that changes the very rules of doing that business. They are therefore far more about strategy and management than they are about technology. In order to appreciate the importance of e-business, it is important to see it from the perspective of the transactional aspects of e-business, those that represent the business between the different players.

Therefore, e-business is taken as the extension of business on to the Internet; the re-engineering of business processes for digitizing of the transactions; the restructuring of the frameworks, both private and public to carry out the transactions seamlessly; and the development of the capacity in society and enterprises for this.

Words and Expressions

interconnect [ˌintə(ː)kəˈnekt]	vt.	使互相连接
telecommunication [ˈtelikəmjuːniˈkeiʃən]	n.	电讯,长途通信,无线电通信,电信学
surpass [səːˈpɑːs]	vt.	超越,胜过
host [həust]	n.	主机
facilitate [fəˈsiliteit]	vt.	使便利,推动,帮助,使容易,促进
rationale [ˌræʃəˈnæl]	n.	基本原理,理论基础
developmental [diˌveləpˈmentəl]	adj.	发展的
elaborate on	v.	详细说明
analytical [ˌænəˈlitikəl]	adj.	分析的,解析的
marketing [ˈmɑːkitiŋ]	n.	行销,买卖
encompass [inˈkʌmpəs]	v.	包围,环绕
entrant [ˈentrənt]	n.	进入者,新到者,新工作者,新会员,参加竞赛者
casting [ˈkɑːstiŋ]	n.	想法,手法
receptive [riˈseptiv]	adj.	善于接受的,能接纳的
radical [ˈrædikəl]	adj.	根本的,基本的;激进的
	n.	激进分子

infrastructure [ˈinfrəstrʌktʃə]	n.	下部构造,基础下部组织
hone [həun]	n.	(细)磨(刀)石,油石,抱怨,想念
entity [ˈentiti]	n.	实体
ubiquitous [juːˈbikwitəs]	adj.	到处存在的,(同时)普遍存在的
relevance [ˈrelivəns]	n.	中肯,适当
upstream [ˈʌpˈstriːm]	adv.	向上游,溯流,逆流地
	adj.	溯流而上的
seamless [ˈsiːmlis]	adj.	无缝合线的,无伤痕的

Notes

(1) It is estimated that the number of persons connected to the Internet today well surpass 500 million, closing the gap on the 700 million or so connected to the telephone. 据估计,目前互联网用户已超过5亿,快接近大约7亿的电话用户。

(2) It includes, besides e-mail and other communication platforms, all information or services that a company may offer to its customers over the Net, from pre-purchase information to after-sale service and support. 除了电子邮件和其他交流平台外,它还包括一个公司可以通过网络提供给顾客的所有信息或服务,从售前信息到售后服务和支持。

(3) The other is to use it both as a marketing tool to increase sales (and customer services) as well as to create new business through it—for example, IT enabled business, call centres, software and maintenance services, etc. as well as "digital commerce". 另一个是既把它作为增加销售(以及顾客服务)的一个营销工具,又把它看作新业务的工具。例如,信息技术推动的行业,呼叫中心、软件、维护服务及数字化商务等。

(4) In order to appreciate the relevance of e-business and its potential to impact on business and development, it is important to understand that e-commerce and e-business are more than just electronics and commerce/business added together. 为了明确电子商务的关联性和它影响企业和发展的潜能,重要的一点是要理解电子商贸和电子商务不仅仅是电子和商业/商务的简单叠加。

Questions

(1) What is the role of Internet in the new economy?

(2) What is the definition of e-commerce in the text?

(3) According to the author, how to realize e-business?

(4) What is the relationship between e-commerce and e-business?

Exercises

1. Translate the following sentences into Chinese:

(1) The Internet and e-commerce impact at different levels and therefore must be understood at diverse dimension.

(2) As an example, e-commerce is making it easier for artisans, musicians and other artists in developing countries to access business-to-consumer world markets, cutting out multiple layers of middlemen in the process.

(3) Internet entrepreneurs can take advantage of network benefits only when enough prospective customers and suppliers are online.

(4) Studies show that the most important use of the Internet in developing countries is limited to e-mail services—rather than World Wide Web services—which require minimal time online.

(5) Commercializing products electronically entails on-line credit card verification, graphic displays of the products and the capacity to generate mail orders and delivery.

2. Translate the following sentences into English:

(1) 互联网的快速发展为电子商务提供了基础,也产生了电子商贸和电子商务。

(2) 电子商贸并不是简单的在线进行的业务,它包括了采用电子化的方式进行生产、分销、营销、销售或交付货物以及服务。

(3) 电子商务意味着组织流程和组织文化的再造。

(4) 电子商务是商务向互联网的延伸。

(5) 电子商务和电子商贸是进行商业交易的新途径。

Further Reading

You can see the full paper with the title: *A Rainbow Technology for a Rainbow People: E-Business Capacity Development for the CARICOM.* By Alwyn Didar Singh.

新经济下的电子商贸/电子商务

互 联 网

电子商贸和电子商务两者都是互联网的产物。互联网其本质是一个巨大的且不断发展的全球计算机网络,它通过电信网络实现互联。简言之,它是一个由众多网络组成的网络。据估计,目前互联网用户已超过5亿,快接近大约7亿的电话用户。据统计,在世界范围内有超过9千万台的互联网主机,从而使在线交易和有效信息量显著增长。互联网的经济理论基础来自于电子商务,而它的发展和更有说服力的平台则来自于它在电子政务等领域的影响。

电子商贸和电子商务的定义

对电子商贸和电子商务定义的详细说明是非常重要的,因为它将有助于确定成本分析报告的范围和视角。电子商贸一直以来被简单定义为在线进行的业务。在WTO关于电子商贸的工作组中,它被理解为采用电子化的方式进行生产、分销、营销、销售或交付货物以及服务。广义上讲,电子商贸包含了电子化媒介或网络,实质上是通过互联网完成的各种商业交易。电子商贸是进行商业交易的一种新途径。它通过电子化的媒介,特别是互联网,实现交易或者说它使购买和销售成为可能。

从商业观点来看,电子商贸不仅仅局限于商品的购买。除了E-mail和其他交流平台外,它还包括一个公司可以通过网络提供给顾客的所有信息或服务,从售前信息到售后服务和支持。电子商贸本质上有两个方面的主要用途。第一是通过时间和程序方面的效率提高来降低交易费用,以降低总成本;另一个是既把它作为增加销售(以及顾客服务)的一个营销工具,又把它看作新业务的工具。例如,信息技术推动的行业,呼叫中心、软件、维护服务及数字化商务等。它既是开展现有业务的一个工具,又是一种开展新业务的机会,对已存在的公司和新加盟者都是如此。电子商贸被划分为B2C(企业与个人)、B2B(企业之间)和B2G(企业与政府)三种。在这三者中,B2B是最成功的,尽管股票市场上高科技股的市值下挫以及美国经济放缓使人们对此持怀疑态度。在将来,电子商贸和互联网的主要收益和用途则将来自于"旧经济"下使用它的企业、政府(电子政务)和社会部门(电子化教育和电子健康)。

电 子 商 务

　　电子商务是在业务流程过程中应用互联网技术。但它不仅仅是信息技术工具或直接化的电子商贸，它还意味着组织，特别是组织的管理者乐意并接受这些新的商业技术和工具所带来的根本性变化。为了实现向新经济的真正转变，它还意味着组织流程和组织文化的再造。它的收益不仅来自于公司内部流程的效率和自动化，而且来自于把这种效率收益扩散到它的供应商和客户的商业系统的能力。

　　一个电子化企业（参加电子商务活动）被定义为准备在新经济条件下开展商业活动的企业。这表明它创造并拥有了一个由经济的变革、新的机会和新的威胁形成的经营战略。它已经拟定了必要的技术基础设施来支持新的业务流程。它使用信息技术深化了内部流程，如人力资源、工作流管理和培训。经过准备，企业能够进行电子商贸：在一个企业和一个外部实体（上游供应商、合作伙伴或下游的客户）之间通过一个通用的、无处不在的电子媒介进行价值（资金、货物、服务或信息）的商业交换。

　　为了明确电子商务的关联性和它影响企业和发展的潜能，重要的一点是要理解电子商贸和电子商务不仅仅是电子和商业/商务的简单叠加。它们借助改变处理业务根本规则的媒介，代表了一种全新的处理业务的模式（包括政府的业务处理）。因此，相对于技术来说，它们更关注战略和管理层面。为了明确电子商务的重要性，很重要的一点是要从电子商务交易方面的视角来看它，它描述了不同竞争者之间的交易。

　　因此，电子商务表现为商务向互联网的延伸、面向交易数字化的业务流程再造、组织结构的重构、实现私人和公共部门之间的无缝化交易，并为此开发社会和企业的能力。

Unit 3 Six Principles to Guide the Development of Global E-Commerce

Text

1. Take a cautious approach to regulation: allow global e-commerce time to develop before determining which areas will require government action.

There are two major threats to global e-commerce. One is rushing to impose legal and regulatory frameworks before gaining a full understanding of the issues and needs involved. Though it is easy to imagine "any number of" problems that governments might seek to solve, to do so at this early stage could be counterproductive. Cross border business-to-consumer transactions represent a brand new form of trade; the old ways of regulating trade will not work on the Internet.

The other threat, however, is doing nothing. Global e-commerce faces many "natural" barriers, including language, currency, and cultural differences; overseas shipping costs; and national brand identification. If nothing is done, the natural tendency will be for e-commerce to become Balkanized into local zones, with consumers visiting only sites in their own country or a small number of countries with which they feel comfortable. In order to realize fully the benefits of global e-commerce, governments must lend a helping hand where necessary to reduce the risks of cross border transactions, but it will take time to determine when and where government action can be used effectively.

2. Increase global market access: maximize opportunities for buyers and sellers to come together.

Empowering consumers and sellers—especially small enterprises—by expanding market access should be the main goal of any government action (or forbearance of action) regarding global e-commerce. The reasons for this are basic, but very important. First, a larger market lowers the marginal costs associated with running Internet-based businesses, allowing the companies to spread their fixed costs over more customers, which lowers prices. E-commerce will become more efficient and less costly by gaining global economies of scale. Greater market access also gives small entrepreneurial ventures a better chance at success: a comic book store at a local strip mall selling to nearby residents may have a hard time, because comic book buyers are a niche market and the number of customers is small, whereas an online comic book store selling around the world stands a much better chance in a larger customer pool. Low cost access to global markets is especially important for ventures in developing nations, which can use the power of global e-commerce to "leapfrog" their economic development efforts and sell to an array of wealthier consumers.

Second, a global Internet provides consumers with global choice. Shopping "bots"—automated buyer agents that seek out the best price on a given item—are increasing in popularity, and promise to bring tremendous efficiency to the pricing of goods and services on the Internet. Expanding the bot's range, from national to international, will encourage competition and reduce prices. Moreover, the Internet is not just a retailing channel—diverse services and media can be delivered over ever-expanding broadband networks, creating new business opportunities for communications, information, and entertainment ventures. Greater market access gives all of these businesses, in whatever country they happen to be located, a better chance at success, and gives consumers of all nations a broader choice of goods and services.

Finally, as the infrastructure and systems to facilitate global e-commerce develop, access will also be increased in a more important market: the marketplace of ideas. History has taught us time and again that trade is the most powerful catalyst for cultural exchange and greater understanding between societies.

3. Don't use regulations for protectionism: signatories to the World Trade Organization (WTO) or other multilateral trade agreements should not be allowed to impose rules on e-commerce or the Internet with the intent of reducing online foreign competition.

The practice of protecting domestic producers through the use of subtle or seemingly unrelated regulations is an old one, but the growth of global e-commerce presents the opportunity to take it to a new level.

As global e-commerce grows, the WTO will see more disputes about regulations aimed at the Internet and designed to give advantage to domestic industries. Examples include requiring Web sites to be delivered in the country's native language, requiring transactions to occur in the country's currency, requiring certain licenses or certifications to operate or use electronic equipment within the country, or requiring the use of nonstandard security protocols. Even more troubling is the process by which some of these regulations likely will be derived: the stoking of nationalistic fears that a country is being left behind in the new world economy. Countries that use such tactics might gain in the short run, but over the long run they will limit their standard of living and hinder global e-commerce. Rather than try to create rules and regulations to limit global e-commerce, nations would be better off pursuing policies designed to build a robust digital domestic economy.

4. Enforce regulations domestically: governments cannot impose their laws on foreign companies unless their activities within the government's territory or a treaty is in effect.

In the off-line world, activities engaged in by citizens of one country don't normally affect the citizens of another country unless those activities are specifically aimed at them (such as sending international mail). The online world should be no different. An online business based in one country cannot be expected to comply with the laws of other countries—such as privacy regulations or marketing restrictions—merely because their Web site is accessible in other countries.

On the other hand, if the Internet seller targets its goods or services to citizens of another country, that seller should be prepared to comply with the laws of that country. Put another way, a government cannot "reach out" and exercise authority in another country, but it can exercise authority if someone in another country "reaches in" to consumers in its jurisdiction. Similarly, if two nations are part of a bilateral or multilateral trade agreement that imposes requirements on Web sites, then Web sites in both nations must comply with the terms of that agreement.

5. Limit restrictions on social, cultural, and political content: government restrictions on content cannot block trade in violation of WTO principles and must be enforced only within the restricting government's territory.

Given the wide variety of objectionable material available on the Internet, it is no surprise that some governments may seek to keep their citizens from accessing some content. Disputes in this vein are already arising for content that portrays or promotes racial hatred, violence, sexual activity, or drug use, to name a few. These issues go to the very heart of national sovereignty. Moreover, policies for global e-commerce should not be used as bargaining levers for these non-economic disputes over freedom and human rights; if Internet technology is made to bear responsibility for intractable social and political disagreements, it will not succeed.

But if governments choose to exercise control over the foreign Internet content that their citizens may access, every nation must demand that every other nation adhere to two conditions. The first is that such controls must apply only to cultural, social, and political content, not trade. Though the Internet will change the character of a portion of international trade transactions, there is no need to scrap the hard-won international cooperation that the WTO represents. Claims of cultural or political infringement should not be used as a back door method of discrimination against imports. If a country restricts global e-commerce on grounds that are (explicitly or implicitly) trade related rather than cultural or political, the WTO can and should take up the matter in the established dispute resolution process.

The second condition is that all content controls must be implemented domestically. In keeping with Principle 4 above, governments cannot "reach out" to shut down Internet operators that reside outside of their jurisdiction. Governments must control content through laws and regulations that apply to their own citizens, such as requiring Internet Service Providers to filter certain content or punishing individual users for downloading prohibited content. Of course, exercising control over every citizen's Internet behavior, while technically possible, requires control over the technology and communications infrastructure that only a few governments are likely to exercise. Inherent in the spread of Internet technology and the attendant economic benefits is a realization that the more time citizens spend in cyberspace, the less control their governments will have over them. This is why expansion of global e-commerce must be balanced with respect for sovereignty; if a government feels that the trade-off between commerce and social stability is not in its interest, the former is more likely to be rejected.

6. Take advantage of technology: Encourage innovation in the development of technological tools and industry best practices that solve public policy problems.

Not every problem needs to be addressed by government regulation, especially with regard to the Internet. The Internet lends itself to creative solutions to policy problems precisely because software is a powerful tool to give people the ability to manage their own transactions.

Many technological solutions are being developed to facilitate an efficient and trusted environment for both buyers and sellers. One of the best examples is the Platform for Privacy Preferences Project (P3P). The project of the World Wide Web Consortium (W3C) is creating a system that allows browsers to look at a Web page's underlying source code to determine the privacy policy that covers the page; if the privacy level is below a predetermined level set by the user, the Web browser (or other P3P implementation tool) will warn the user. This consumer-empowering technology, when fully implemented, may help alleviate the desire for strict government controls on data privacy practices and facilitate easier negotiation between nations with different privacy regimes. Technology promises other solutions as well, in areas from language translation to content control to dispute resolution.

Policymakers should turn to technology whenever possible and, more importantly, they should think in terms of what technology could do in the future rather than what it can do now. In order to facilitate the growth of global e-commerce, PPI (Progressive Policy Institute) makes the following proposals:

- stay within the current international trade framework;
- make the moratorium on tariffs for electronic transmissions permanent;

- treat digitally delivered products as intangible goods;
- eliminate tariffs on small-value transactions;
- work with third parties seeking to provide solutions;
- promote consumer education efforts;
- draft and enact global treaties governing criminal activity on the Internet.

Words and Expressions

cautious ['kɔːʃəs]	adj.	谨慎的,小心的
impose [im'pəuz]	vt.	征税;强加;以……欺骗
	vi.	利用;欺骗;施加影响
counterproductive [ˌkauntəprəˈdʌktiv]	adj.	产生相反效果的,使达不到预期目标的,适得其反的
Balkanize ['bɔːlkənaiz]	vt.	使割据
lend itself to		有助于
maximize ['mæksimaiz]	vt.	取……最大值,最佳化
marginal ['mɑːdʒinəl]	adj.	边缘的,边际的
entrepreneurial [ˌɔntrəprəˈnəːriəl]	adj.	企业家的
comic book		连环漫画册
mall [mɔːl]	n.	购物商场,商业街,林荫路
leapfrog ['liːpfrɔg]	n.	交互跃进,竞相提高
tremendous [tri'mendəs]	adj.	极大的,巨大的
diverse [dai'vəːs]	adj.	不同的,变化多的
broadband ['brɔːdbænd]	n.	宽带
facilitate [fə'siliteit]	vt.	使容易,使便利,推动,帮助
catalyst ['kætəlist]	n.	催化剂
multilateral [ˌmʌltiˈlætərəl]	adj.	多边的,多国的
subtle ['sʌtl]	adj.	狡猾的,敏感的,微妙的,精细的
nationalistic [ˌnæʃənəˈlistik]	adj.	国家主义的
bilateral [bai'lætərəl]	adj.	有两面的,双边的

objectionable [əbˈdʒekʃənəbl]	adj.	引起反对的,讨厌的
sovereignty [ˈsɔvrənti]	n.	君主,主权,主权国家
infringement [inˈfrindʒmənt]	n.	违反,侵害
discrimination [disˌkrimiˈneiʃən]	n.	辨别,区别,识别力,歧视
alleviate [əˈliːvieit]	vt.	使(痛苦等)易于忍受,减轻
negotiation [niˌgəuʃiˈeiʃən]	n.	商议,谈判,流通
moratorium [ˌmɔrəˈtɔːriəm]	n.	延期偿付,延期偿付期间

Notes

(1) In order to realize fully the benefits of global e-commerce, governments must lend a helping hand where necessary to reduce the risks of cross border transactions, but it will take time to determine, when and where government action can be used effectively. 为了充分实现全球电子商务的最大收益,在必要时政府应及时出面介入,以减少跨境交易的风险,但必须进行长期研究决定其何时何地如何介入才更加有效。

(2) Greater market access also gives small entrepreneurial ventures a better chance at success: a comic book store at a local strip mall selling to nearby residents may have a hard time, because comic book buyers are a niche market and the number of customers is small, whereas an online comic book store selling around the world stands a much better chance in a larger customer pool. 更大的市场准入也给小企业提供了更好的成功机会：一个本地商业区的漫画店只做附近居民的生意可能会很困难,因为漫画是一个很小的市场并且客户也非常少,反之一个面向全世界销售的网上漫画书店将会在一个更大的客户群中得到更多的机会。

(3) Moreover, the Internet is not just a retailing channel—diverse services and media can be delivered over ever-expanding broadband networks, creating new business opportunities for communications, information, and entertainment ventures. 此外,互联网不仅仅是一个零售渠道——多样化的服务和媒介可以为正在扩展的宽带网络所提供,并为通信、信息和娱乐业创造新的商业机遇。

Questions

(1) What are the two major threats to global e-commerce?

(2) According to the author, what should the government do to promote global e-

commerce?

(3) Why is the global market access so important? And how to increase the access?

(4) What is the relationship between e-commerce and protectionism?

(5) How to enforce regulations domestically?

(6) Why is there a restriction on social, cultural, and political content by the government? And how to handle it properly by the government?

(7) What are PPI's recommendations?

Exercises

1. Translate the following sentences into Chinese:

(1) In the coming years, the majority of e-commerce, both domestic and international, will be business-to-business transactions.

(2) The explosive growth of global B2B marketplaces has created tremendous opportunities for entrepreneurial suppliers who might otherwise go unnoticed.

(3) Business to consumer transactions, while representing a smaller volume of online trade, will provide special benefits to consumers.

(4) Prices will be reduced by eliminating exporter and importer middlemen that exist to surmount the complexities of trade bureaucracies.

(5) The revolution to succeed, however, the complexities must either be removed from the process or made transparent.

2. Translate the following sentences into English:

(1) 电子商务的发展面临着诸如语言、货币、文化等多方面的"天然"障碍。

(2) 互联网不仅是一个零售渠道,它还为通信、信息和娱乐业创造新的商业机会。

(3) 贸易是不同社会、文化间交流和理解的有效渠道。

(4) 在电子商务中采取保护主义的做法是十分急功近利的,它最终将是损人而不利己。

(5) 国家必须在全球电子商务扩展和国家主权之间寻找到一种平衡。

Further Reading

You can see the full text in *A Third Way Framework for Global E-Commerce* which is the Progressive Policy Institute Technology & New Economy Project by Shane Ham and Robert D. Atkinson March 2001.

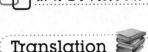

指导全球电子商务发展的六大原则

1. 对规则采取谨慎的态度：在决定哪些领域需要采取政府行为之前，应当允许全球电子商务时代的发展。

全球的电子商务面临着两大威胁。一个威胁是在完全理解相关问题和需求之前就匆忙地将法律与规范强加于它。尽管很容易想象到政府需要设法解决的一系列问题，但在早期这么做很可能适得其反。跨边界的企业和消费者之间的交易代表了一种新的交易模式，老的规范交易的规则在网上将不再适用。

另一个威胁就是不采取任何行动。全球电子商务面临着许多"天然"的障碍，包括语言、货币、文化的差异，海外运输成本以及国内品牌被认可等。如果不采取什么行动，电子商务的自然发展趋势是分割成一个个本地区域，客户只能够访问自己国家或少数让他们感到舒适的国家的网站。为了充分实现全球电子商务的最大收益，在必要时政府应及时出面介入，以减少跨境交易的风险，但必须进行长期研究决定其何时何地如何介入才能发挥作用。

2. 增加全球市场准入：使买卖双方交易接触的机会最大化。

通过扩大市场准入来增强客户和销售者（尤其是小型企业）的能力，应该是任何关于全球电子商务方面政府行为（或克制行为）的主要目的。这样做的理由虽然很基本，但非常重要。首先，更大的市场降低了运作基于网络的业务边际成本，这使公司可以把固定成本分摊到更多的客户中去，从而降低价格。通过获得全球规模经济，电子商务将变得更加有效和低成本。更大的市场准入也给小企业经营项目提供了更好的成功机会：一个位于当地狭长店铺中的漫画店只做当地居民的生意可能会度日艰难，因为漫画的购买者是一个微型的专门市场，客户非常少，而一个面向全世界销售的在线漫画书店将会在一个更大的客户群中得到更好的机会。以低成本进入全球市场对发展中国家的企业尤其重要，它可以利用全球电子商务带来的商机来实现经济的跨越式发展，并把产品出售给大量更富裕的客户。

其次，全球性的互联网给客户提供了全球性的机会。购物"搜索精灵"（按照给定的条目自动寻找最优价格的搜索精灵）在越来越普及，并有望对网络的产品和服务的价格机制形成带来显著的效率。扩大这一搜索精灵的范围，从国内发展到国际，将促进竞争和降低价格。此外，互联网不仅仅是一个零售渠道——多样化的服务和媒介可以为正在扩展的宽带网络所提供，并为通信、信息和娱乐业创造新的商业机遇。不管这些企业处在哪个国家，更大的市场准入机会都会带给它们以更大的成功，并且使各国消费者在产品和服务的选择上有更大的余地。

最后，随着推进全球电子商务发展的基础设施和系统的建立，在一个更重要的市场——概念市场上也会增加接触的机会。历史已经一再教育我们，贸易是不同社会间文化交流和更多理解的强力催化剂。

3. 不要为保护主义而使用规则：不应针对电子商务或互联网业务签订旨在减少国外在线竞争的 WTO 协议或其他的多边贸易协议。

通过使用微妙的或看起来似乎无关的规则来保护国内生产者的方式是很老套的，但是全球电子商务的发展提供了一个把保护主义推进到新水平的机会。

随着全球电子商务的发展，WTO 将会碰到更多的以互联网为目标以及专门设计为本国产业谋利的规范方面的各种争端。例如，包括要求网站使用本国语言发布，要求用本国货币实现交易支付，在一国内操作和使用电子化设备时要求有执照或证明，或要求使用非标准的安全协议。更麻烦的是，一些规则的产生可能出于这样的目的：激起一国在新世界经济中落后的民族主义的恐慌。采用那些策略的国家可能得到短期的利益，但是从长远来看，这将会限制它们生活的标准并妨碍全球电子商务的发展。因此，与其去努力制定制度和规则来限制全球电子商务，各国还不如更好地继续制定政策以建立一个富有活力的数字化国内经济。

4. 强调规则国内化：政府不能强加法律给那些外国公司，除非它们的行为在政府的管制范围或条约约束范围之内。

在离线的世界里，一个国家居民的活动不会影响到另一个国家的居民，除非这些活动就是针对他们的（如发送国际邮件）。在线的世界也没有不同，在线的企业不可能仅仅因为公司的网站与其他国家相连，就得遵守该国的法律，如隐私规则或者市场限制。

另外，如果网络销售商把产品或服务定位于另一个国家的居民，那么销售商就要准备好遵守那个国家的法律。从另一个角度来说，一个政府并不能"伸手"在别的国家建立权威，但是如果另一个国家的某人"伸手"到它管辖的消费者身上，它就可以建立这种权威了。同样地，如果两个国家是双边或多边贸易协定的成员，而且这一协定对网站提出一定要求，那么这两个国家的网站都必须符合协议规定的条款。

5. 减少对于社会、文化和政治内容的约束：政府对于内容的限制不能违背 WTO 的原则，妨碍贸易进行，并且必须在严格的政府管制范围内执行。

考虑到互联网上存在大量可以利用的反面材料，一些政府采取措施防止本国公民接触到这些内容也就不足为奇了。描述或宣扬种族残害、暴力、性行为、毒品使用等相关的内容已经产生了质疑，这些问题已经深入到国家主权的中心了。而且，全球电子商务的政策不应该被用来作为这些非经济性的关于自由和人权方面争论的一个讨价还价的筹码；如果互联网技术要为这些难以处理的社会和政治上的差异承担责任，那么它将很难成功。

但是如果政府选择对本国国民可能接触到的国外互联网内容进行控制，那么每个国家必须要求其他国家遵守两个条件。第一个条件是这样的控制必须只适用于文化、社会和政治内容，而不涉及贸易。尽管互联网将改变一部分国际交易的特征，但没必要去抛弃以 WTO 为代表的来之不易的国际间的合作。文化上的谴责和政治上的排斥不应该成为进口歧视的一个正当途径。如果一个国家以（或明或暗的）贸易为由，而不是文化和政治方面的原因限制了全球电子商务，WTO 就可以而且应该启动争端解决程序。

第二个条件是所有的控制必须在本国内实施。与上面的第 4 条原则保持一致，政府无权越界关闭不属于他们管辖范围内的网络运营商。政府必须通过适用于其国民的法律和规则来控制相关内容,如要求互联网服务供应商过滤一定的内容或者惩罚那些下载禁止内容的用户。当然,对每个国民的互联网行为实施控制,即使技术上可行,也仍要求技术和通信基础设施的控制,但这只有很少一些政府能够做到。与互联网技术扩散相伴而生、和经济利益同时出现的事实是:国民在网络上的时间将会越来越多,政府对他们的控制将会越来越少。这就是为什么全球电子商务的扩展与国家主权之间必须达到一种平衡。如果政府感到商业和社会稳定之间的权衡不符合其利益,前者更可能受到抵制。

6. 利用技术:在技术工具和产业最佳实践中鼓励创新以解决公共政策问题。

不是每个问题都需要政府的规章制度来解决,尤其是关于互联网的问题。互联网自身对政策问题就有创造性的、精确的解决方法,因为软件是一种能给人们管理自己交易能力的强大工具。

许多技术解决方法正得到开发以促进买卖双方形成有效的、信赖的环境。最著名的例子就是隐私偏好项目平台(P3P)。万维网协会(W3C)的计划是建立一个系统,这个系统允许浏览者查看隐藏了决定该网页隐私政策的源代码的网页;如果这个隐私水平低于用户预先设置的权限,网络浏览器(或其他 P3P 实施工具)将对用户发出警告。这项客户促进技术,当被完全实施时,能帮助减轻对数据隐私实践方面严格政府控制的要求并促进具有不同隐私权机制的国家之间的谈判。技术也承诺了其他的解决方法,包括从语言的翻译到内容的控制到争端的解决方法。

决策者们在任何可能时候都可以求助于技术,更重要的是,他们应该考虑的是技术在将来能做什么而不是现在能做什么。为了推进全球电子商务的发展,PPI(进步政策研究所)给出了以下一些建议:

- 继续保持目前的国际贸易框架;
- 对电子交易关税的延期偿付保持永久性;
- 把数字交易产品作为无形产品来对待;
- 对低值交易取消关税;
- 为第三方提供解决方法;
- 努力促进客户的教育;
- 起草制定关于网络犯罪活动的全球性公约。

UNIT 4 The Global E-Business Environment

Introduction

The past two years have seen considerable changes in the environment for e-business, in the technologies available and the way in which they are deployed. Some of these changes have slowed the pace of e-business development, and there have been some highly publicized business collapses. Coupled with a major correction in April 2000, and the subsequent global economic downturn, some companies think that e-business is no longer an issue—that it can be ignored, and that business can go on as it always has gone on. Such a belief is ill founded and dangerous.

E-business continues to be one of the major issues facing businesses today. How quickly they adapt, how well they adapt, and how flexibly they respond to changes in technology, in business relationships and in customer behavior will determine their success, and indeed their ability to survive. The adoption of e-business is even more important for businesses in a global economic downturn. Accenture analysis has shown that firms who use e-business effectively are able to generate revenue increases of 10% to 20% and cut costs by 20% to 45%. In an era when firms will be facing an increasingly competitive environment, it is essential that they adopt e-business to cut costs and to drive revenues.

E-Business Revenues

Despite the economic slowdown, worldwide revenues from e-business should continue to grow strongly. eMarketer, an Internet consultancy estimates that worldwide revenues are projected to grow to 3.5 trillion Euros by 2004. E-business growth will be stronger in Europe than in the US, as Europe catches up.

Business-to-business (B2B) rather than business-to-consumer (B2C) revenues account for the most significant element of e-business revenues. While much of the hype surrounding e-business was in the business-to-consumer arena, it is now clear that business-to-business e-business provides the greatest opportunities for the enterprise sector. eMarketer estimated that the relative importance of business-to-business e-business will grow from 69% of total European e-business revenues in 2000 to 77% of total European e-business revenues by 2004. In the US, the relative share of business-to-business revenues will increase from 70% in 2000 to 88% of total e-business revenues by 2004.

Business-to-Business

While most media attention has focused on companies that serve consumers, it is the use of e-business within and between companies that is of real importance. The use of e-business by companies to integrate their supply chains slashes transaction costs and offers companies real tangible business benefits. For example, the use of e-Business in supply chain integration has led to inventory reduction of 25% to 60%, and lowered overall supply chain costs by 25% to 50%. Therefore it remains critical that the enterprise sector continues to develop and implement e-business strategies to build on their e-business capabilities, and to seize on the real opportunities that information and communication technologies (ICT) offer to increase revenues and to reduce costs.

Stock Market Corrections and the Global Economic Downturn

The most significant event affecting the development of e-business in the past two years is the stock market correction of April 2000, which set a trend for lower valuations for technology stocks. This caused, directly or indirectly:
- A shift in investment emphasis from dot-coms to dot-corps, and from pure-play Internet companies to software products firms;
- The spectacular collapse of a large number of dot-coms;
- An increase in merger and acquisition activity in the technology and Internet sector; slower developments throughout the sector and among users.

The European technology sector was seriously hit by capital rationing in the Telecommunications sector, due to the inflated prices paid by telecommunications companies for 3G licenses. The slowdown is, in large part, being driven by the proportionally greater exposure of European technology firms to the Telecommunications sector. The terrorist attack on the World Trade Center has accelerated the negative impact of these trends and sharply reduced business and consumer confidence in the US and Europe. The immediate impact has been a delay in investment decisions, particularly foreign investments and this has focused corporate attention on cost reduction. However, while information technology capital investment in Europe is projected to fall by $50 bn, or 20%, in 2001, Accenture research highlights that leading companies are continuing to invest in ICT as a mechanism to increase revenues and reduce costs.

Change in the Rate of Adoption

Fears of a sustained recession in the US, the downturn in the technology sector, and the subsequent shift in investment interest from dot-coms (pure-play Internet companies) to dot-corps (existing companies who are using e-business) have begun to affect the adoption of e-business.

Large enterprises are taking a more considered approach to the implementation of e-Business, since they no longer fear the loss of business to dot-com competitors; Internationally, the highly publicized collapse of many dot-coms has reduced the perceived competitive threat from e-business. Increasingly, e-business is being regarded as a process that can make existing companies and governments more efficient in how they manage suppliers, customers and internal business processes. Given the complexity of integrating e-business into existing business processes, many organizations are incrementally adopting e-business technologies in order to increase revenues and to reduce costs, though activity is not as apparent as in the dot-com era. However, the number of enterprises that are successfully implementing e-business strategies is growing.

Words and Expressions

considerable [kən'sidərəbl]	adj.	相当大(或多)的,值得考虑的,相当可观的
available [ə'veiləbl]	adj.	可用到的,可利用的,有用的,有空的,接受探访的
deploy [di'plɔi]	v.	展开,配置
collapse [kə'læps]	n.	倒塌,崩溃,失败,虚脱
coupled ['kʌpld]	adj.	连结的,联系的
publicize ['pʌblisaiz]	vt.	宣扬
downturn ['dauntə:n]	n.	低迷时期
ignore [ig'nɔ:]	vt.	不理睬,忽视;[律](因证据不足而)驳回诉讼

adapt [ə'dæpt]	vt.	使适应，改编
flexibly ['fleksəbli]	adv.	易曲地，柔软地
respond [ris'pɔnd]	v.	回答，响应，作出反应
survive [sə'vaiv]	v.	幸免于，幸存，生还
adoption [ə'dɔpʃən]	n.	采用，收养
Accenture		埃森哲（国际著名咨询顾问公司）
analysis [ə'nælisis]	n.	分析，分解
revenue ['revinju:]	n.	收入，国家的收入，税收
competitive [kəm'petitiv]	adj.	竞争的
effectively [i'fektivli]	adv.	有效地，有力地
consultancy [kən'sʌltənsi]	n.	顾问（工作）
account for	v.	说明，占，解决，得分
hype [haip]	n.	大肆宣传，大做广告
arena [ə'ri:nə]	n.	竞技场，舞台
	vi.	倒塌，崩溃，瓦解，失败，病倒
slash [slæʃ]	v.	猛砍，大量削减，严厉批评
	n.	猛砍，（大幅度）削减
tangible ['tændʒəbl]	adj.	切实的
capability [,keipə'biliti]	n.	（实际）能力，性能，容量，接受力
stock market	n.	股票市场
acquisition [,ækwi'ziʃən]	n.	获得，获得物
spectacular [spek'tækjulə]	adj.	引人入胜的，壮观的
proportionally [prə'pɔ:ʃənli]	adv.	按比例地，相配合地，适当地
mechanism ['mekənizəm]	n.	机械装置，机构，机制
sustain [səs'tein]	vt.	支撑，撑住，维持，持续
incremental [,inkri'mentəl]	adj.	增加的，增大的，增长的，增额的
complexity [kəm'pleksiti]	n.	复杂性，复合状态，复合物，复杂的事物

Unit 4　The Global E-Business Environment

Notes

(1) The past two years have seen considerable changes in the environment for e-business, in the technologies available and the way in which they are deployed. 在过去的两年中,在可应用的技术和所能利用的方法上,电子商务的环境发生了相当大的变化。

(2) How quickly they adapt, how well they adapt, and how flexibly they respond to changes in technology, in business relationships and in customer behavior will determine their success, and indeed their ability to survive. 在业务关系和客户行为中如何快速地应用,如何应用得更好,如何灵活地应对技术的变化将决定他们的成功,实际上是决定了他们的生存能力。

(3) While much of the hype surrounding e-business was in the business-to-consumer arena, it is now clear that business-to-business e-business provides the greatest opportunities for the enterprise sector in Ireland. 尽管很多天花乱坠的电子商务方面报道都是围绕 B2C 展开的,但现在非常清楚的是:B2B 模式的电子商务却给爱尔兰企业或部门提供更巨大的机会。

Questions

(1) What is the global e-business environment in the past two years?
(2) What are the e-business revenues?
(3) What is e-business's contribution to job creation?

Exercises

1. Translate the following sentences into Chinese:

(1) The downturn in the world economy and the technology markets has significantly dampened the hype surrounding e-business.

(2) International research also highlights that, as the hype has subsided, many organizations are developing long-term e-business strategies, which are moving beyond just developing a web site, to integrating ICTs and e-business into all aspects of their business processes.

(3) Companies and countries that do not respond dynamically to the challenges that e-business brings, may find themselves at a competitive disadvantage relative to e-enabled companies and countries, when the world economy improves.

(4) E-business is bringing about revolutionary changes in the economy, in work practices and organization, and in business models.

(5) E-business will continue to be one of the most significant drivers of enterprise

development over the next three to five years.

2. Translate the following sentences into English：
(1) 股市震荡和全球经济不景气使得一些公司逐渐忽略了电子商务的重要性。
(2) 尽管经济出现衰退，但世界范围内的电子商务总收入却在持续强劲增长。
(3) 电子商务是公司和政府有效管理供应商、客户和国内业务流程的一个有效手段。
(4) 电子商务还可以创造出大量的就业机会。
(5) 企业与企业间电子商务的收入构成了电子商务收入的主要部分。

Further Reading

The text is selected from *E-Business*：*Where Are We and Where Do We Go from Here*？ This is the national policy and advisory board for enterprise, trade, science, technology and innovation, Ireland.

Translation

全球的电子商务环境

引　言

在过去的两年中，在可应用的技术和所能利用的方法上，电子商务的环境发生了相当大的变化，其中一些变化减缓了电子商务的发展步伐，甚至一些知名企业因此倒闭了。加上2000年4月股市的一次大调整以及随后的全球经济的不景气，一些公司开始认为电子商务不再是个值得关注的议题——它可以被忽略，公司业务可以按照原有的模式运作。产生这样的信念是基于错误的根据，也是十分危险的。

电子商务仍然是当今企业面临的主要问题之一。在业务关系和客户行为中如何快速地应用，如何应用得更好，如何灵活地应对技术的变化，将决定他们的成功，实际上也决定了他们的生存能力。在全球经济下滑的情况下，对于企业来说，电子商务的应用就会更加重要。埃森哲公司的分析已经显示有效地使用电子商务的公司能增加10%到20%的收入，同时降低20%到45%的成本。在公司竞争越来越激烈的时代，用电子商务来降低成本和驱动收入是必要的。

电子商务的总收入

尽管经济在衰退，但是全世界电子商务的总收入仍将保持强劲增长。互联网咨询服务公司 eMarketer 估计到 2004 年全世界的总收入计划将达到 3.5 万亿欧元。随着欧洲的不断追赶，其发展将比美国更迅猛。

企业与企业间（B2B）的收入，而不是企业与客户间（B2C）的，占据着电子商务收入的最主要的部分。尽管很多天花乱坠的电子商务方面报道都是围绕 B2C 展开的，但是现在非常清楚的是：B2B 模式的电子商务却给企业或者部门提供了更巨大的机会。据 eMarketer 预测，B2B 电子商务的重要性将继续加强，到 2004 年其收入占欧洲电子商务总收入的比率，将由 2000 年的 69% 上升到 77%，而在美国则由 70% 增加到 88%。

企业与企业间电子商务

尽管大多数媒体已将注意力集中到服务客户的公司，但在公司内部和公司之间应用电子商务才是真正具有重要意义的。公司通过使用电子商务来整合供应链，从而大大削减了交易成本，并获得了真实、有形的商业利润。例如，在整合供应链方面，电子商务已经使得存货削减了 25%～60%，同时降低了 25%～50% 的总供应链成本。因此，企业各部门将继续发展和实施电子商务策略以构建电子商务的能力，并把握信息通信技术（ICT）带来的在增长收入和减少成本中的机会，对于企业各部门是十分关键的。

股市的调整和全球经济的衰退

在过去的两年中，影响电子商务发展最重要的事莫过于是 2000 年 4 月股市的动荡，以及由此引发了技术股贬值的趋势。这直接或间接地引起了：
- 投资重点从 .com 公司（单纯依靠互联网运营的公司）到 .corp 公司（应用电子商务的实体公司）、从纯粹靠网络运营的公司到软件产品公司的转变；
- 相当数量的 .com 公司大量地倒闭；
- 技术和互联网行业兼并和收购活动的增加；贯穿整个部门和跨越用户的发展趋于缓慢。

由于欧洲电信公司为获得 3G 运营许可证所支付的虚高价格，使欧洲的技术部门正受到电信部门资金配给制度的重创。这种衰退在很大程度上正由欧洲技术公司成比例地剧烈显露出来，并扩展至电信部门。对世贸中心的恐怖袭击加剧了这种趋势的负面影响，在美国和欧洲，这明显地降低了企业和消费者的信心。其直接影响就是投资决策的犹疑，尤其是外国的投资，它开始把重心放在降低成本上。然而，在 2001 年，当信息技术资本在欧洲的主要投资计划减少 500 亿美元，即 20% 时，埃森哲公司研究强调，领导型的公司仍将在信息通信技术继续投资，以形成增加收入和减少成本的机制。

采用比例的变化

对美国经济持续的衰退、技术部门的下滑及随后的投资兴趣从 .com 公司到 .corp 公司转变的恐惧，已经开始影响了对电子商务的采用。

因为不再害怕.com竞争者所带来的商业损失,所以大型企业正在考虑更为周密的实施电子商务的方法;在国际上,许多.com轰轰烈烈地倒闭,已经减少了可觉察到的来自电子商务的竞争威胁。电子商务正越来越被看作实体公司和政府如何在管理供应商、客户和内部业务流程中更具效率的一个过程。考虑到把电子商务集成到现存的业务流程中具有复杂性,一些组织正逐步采用电子商务技术以增加收益和减少成本,尽管活动的开展没有像.com时代那么明显,然而,成功实施电子商务战略的企业数量正在上升。

CHAPTER 2
E-MARKETING AND E-FINANCE

电子化营销与电子金融

- What is E-Marketing Planning
- A New Marketing Strategy for E-Commerce
- Customer Differentiation and Lifecycle Management of E-Marketing
- Payment Applications Make E-Commerce Mobile
- E-Business Strategy in an Online Banking Services: A Case Study of Citibank

UNIT 5 What is E-Marketing Planning

Let's begin by defining a marketing plan and then move onto defining its "new economy cousin": the e-marketing plan. A marketing plan is a written document that details the current marketing situation, threats and opportunities, marketing objectives, and the strategies for achieving those objectives. A marketing plan can be written for each product, service, brand, or for the company as a whole. An e-marketing plan is a bit more focused than the traditional marketing plan. Although it often includes some of the same topics as a traditional marketing plan, it is more centered on the marketing opportunities, threats, objectives and strategies of the Internet.

The e-marketing plan defines your business model, builds commitment from all people who will be involved in its implementation, and establishes performance criteria and benchmarks for success. Development of your e-marketing plan begins with a complete review of your e-business model. What is a business model? In sections that follow, this white paper offers descriptions of e-business models. Review those descriptions and think about which one most closely describes your model. Before you begin an e-marketing plan, think about how to define your e-business model and how it influences your e-marketing plan.

E-Marketing Plan and Your E-Business Model

The e-marketing plan gives you a road map or a blue print to e-business success. The prerequisite to write a good e-marketing plan is a complete understanding of your e-business model. As you prepare your e-marketing plan, you may go through a learning process; you will analyze your e-business model in detail in an attempt to learn what drives your online sales and revenue streams.

What is your e-business model? Can you define it in a paragraph or two? A business model describes your architecture for product, service, and information delivery and a description of sources of revenues (revenue streams). A business model identifies the value chain elements of the business such as inbound logistics, operations (or production), outbound logistics, marketing, service; and support activities.

You must define your business model by writing your own description of it. From that description, can you identify each significant revenue stream and each potential revenue stream? Can you identify expenses that will be incurred in generating those revenue streams? Do you see the critical things that must be measured (metrics) and tracked to help assuring success? Can you see how your business model will use e-marketing to price, promote, sell, and distribute your product?

As you develop your e-marketing plan you must think about how your e-marketing effort "fits" your business model. At a minimum, your business model will influence the way you forecast sales and predict e-marketing expenses. However, beyond basic sales forecasting and budgeting, there are aspects of your e-marketing plan that address the specific way you will do business, generate revenue, and consume resources. Your e-marketing plan should discuss how you will use information technologies to manage the marketing mix (product, price, place, and promotion), how you will plan to optimize your content, and how you will allocate resources to attract new customers, create loyalty with existing ones, and create revenue streams.

Be sure you define your business model before you write your plan. Can you identify your e-business model in the descriptive sections that follow?

Merchant Model

The Merchant model is web marketing of wholesalers or retailers of goods and services. The goods and services might be unique to the web or an extension of a traditional "brick and mortar store front". This model includes catalogers who have decided to complement their catalog operation with a web site or have decided to migrate completely to an online model. Benefits of this model include increased demand for goods and services via an entry into the global market, potential lower costs of promotion and sales, 24/7 ordering and customer service, and one-to-one custom marketing.

Auction Model

The auction model is web implementation of bidding mechanisms through multimedia presentation of goods and services. Revenue streams are derived from licensing of the auction technology platform, transaction fees, and advertising.

Manufacturer Model

The manufacturer model uses the web to compress the distribution channel so that rather than use intermediaries to get your products and services to market, you go direct to the customer via the web. For example, Dell Computer Corporation, maker of personal computer systems, uses this model by selling direct to consumers via their web site. About 50 percent of Dell's sales are Web-enabled (www.dell.com).

Affiliate Model

The affiliate model is a "pay for performance model". Revenue streams are created when customers click through links or banner ads to purchase goods and services. Affiliate marketing is when one web site (the affiliate) promotes another web site's products or services (the merchant) in exchange for a commission. The affiliate earns a commission (i.e., 10% of the purchase) while the merchant derives a sale from an affiliate (partner web site). Through affiliate marketing, merchants can place their advertising banners and links on content sites worldwide and only pay a commission when those links generate a sale or a qualified lead. Affiliated content sites can convert their online content into e-commerce by populating it with these revenue-generating links.

Advertising Model

Like a traditional broadcaster or news media business models, the web advertising model provides content and services (i.e., e-mail, chat, forums, auctions, etc.) supported by banner ads and other forms of online advertising (perhaps e-mail newsletter ads). Some advertising models are called portals (like AOL, Yahoo, and AltaVista) while others are called "Free Models"; like Blue Mountain Arts (www.bluemountain.com) where giveaways (like free electronic greeting cards and invitations) help creating high volume.

Infomediary Model

This is a web model whereby the infomediary collects data from users and sells the information to other businesses. Traffic is driven to the infomediary's site by free offers (such as free Internet access or free hardware).

Subscription Model

In a subscription model, users pay for access to the site and the high value content that they view. Some models offer free content with premium content available only to paid subscribers. Advertising revenues may also be part of the revenue stream.

Brokerage Model

A brokerage model is a web market maker that brings buyers and sellers together.

The model ranges from virtual malls to online stock and bond traders and can include business-to-business (B2B), business-to-consumer (B2C), and consumer-to-consumer (C2C). Transaction fees or commissions generate the revenue under this model.

Virtual Communities Model

The virtual communities' model facilitates the online interaction of a community of users (members, customers, partners, students, etc.). The model makes it easy for the community members to add their own content to the online community web site. Revenue streams are generated from membership fees and advertising revenue.

Logistics Model

A business that utilizes the Internet to help other businesses manage logistical functions such as electronic payments, ordering systems, and shipping services in operating under the logistics model. Fees are the basis for the revenue scheme.

E-Business Models and E-Marketing Planning

What is the relationship between e-business models and e-marketing? Central problems to all the models identified in the previous section are three issues:

- For these models to work, e-marketing planning is critical.
- These models generate tremendous amounts of information; strategic information from web site activity, that can be used to better meet the needs of e-customers and to sell more products.
- Metrics are needed to provide accountability and to analyze the information for strategic advantage.

Preparing the E-Marketing Plan

Writing an e-marketing plan is not an easy task. There are obstacles. However, the intent of this white paper is not to provide a guide for developing an e-marketing plan rather, we will identify some of the hurdles that must be overcome to develop a good plan.

What are some of the obstacles of writing a good e-marketing plan? For starters, procrastination is a problem; busy executives put off writing a plan. Yet, with businesses moving at such a rapid pace (Internet time), there is a big opportunity cost to e-procrastination. Putting off the development of an e-marketing plan can cost you market opportunities and profits.

Another obstacle is time. The process of developing an e-marketing plan is time consuming. Think about ways to streamline the process. Examples and templates could be the answer. Seeing an example plan to emulate and following a proven template can save you a great deal of time. A template suggests an effective outline, headings, and in some cases, texts.

Other issues related to the writing process such as writer's block and the labor-intensive circuitous nature of writing are also major barriers. Other difficulties include the challenge of identifying the right analysis, the tricky nature of developing revenue stream forecasts, and question of which expense budgets to develop.

Words and Expressions

cousin [kʌzn]	n.	堂兄弟姊妹,表兄弟姊妹
commitment [səˈfistikeitid]	n.	委托事项;许诺;承担义务
benchmark [ˈbentʃmɑːk]	n.	基准
prerequisite [priːˈrekwizit]	n.	先决条件
	adj.	首要必备的
inbound [ˈinbaund]	adj.	内地的,归航的
	n.	入站
incur [inˈkəː]	v.	招致
minimum [ˈminiməm]	adj.	最小的,最低的
	n.	最小值,最小化
forecast [ˈfɔːkɑːst]	vt.	预想,预测,预报,预兆
budget [ˈbʌdʒit]	n.	预算
	vi.	做预算,编入预算
address [əˈdres]	vt.	向……致辞,演说;写姓名地址;从事;忙于
marketing mix		营销组合
allocate [ˈæləukeit]	vt.	分派,分配
loyalty [ˈlɔiəlti]	n.	忠诚,忠心
wholesaler [ˈhəulseilə]	n.	批发商
retailer [riːˈteilə]	n.	零售商人,传播的人
catalog [ˈkætəlɔg]	n.	目录,目录册

	v.	编目录
migrate [maiˈgreit, maiɡreit]	*vi.*	移动,移往,移植,随季节而移居
	vt.	使移居,使移植
auction [ˈɔːkʃən]	*n.*	拍卖
	vt.	拍卖
bid [bid]	*vt.*	出价,投标,祝愿,命令,吩咐
	n.	出价,投标
	v.	支付
mechanism [ˈmekənizəm]	*n.*	机械装置,机构,机制
compress [kəmˈpres]	*vt.*	压缩,摘要叙述
	n.	(外科)敷布
intermediary [ˌintəˈmiːdiəri]	*n.*	仲裁者,调解者,中间物
	adj.	中间的,媒介的
affiliate [əˈfilieit]	*v.*	(使……)加入,接受为会员
banner [ˈbænə]	*n.*	旗帜,横幅,标语
commission [kəˈmiʃən]	*n.*	委任,委托,代办(权),代理(权),犯(罪),佣金
	vt.	委任,任命,委托,委托制作,使服役
populate [ˈpɔpjuleit]	*v.*	板上组装,使人民居住,移民
portal [ˈpɔːtl]	*n.*	入口
subscription [sʌbˈskripʃən]	*n.*	捐献,订金,订阅,签署,同意
brokerage [ˈbrəukəridʒ]	*n.*	经纪人之业务,回扣
premium [ˈpriːmjəm]	*n.*	额外费用,奖金,奖赏,保险费,(货币兑现的)贴水
metrics [ˈmetriks]	*n.*	韵律学,作诗法,度量
obstacle [ˈɔbstəkl]	*n.*	障碍,妨害物
hurdle [ˈhəːdl]	*n.*	篱笆,栏,障碍,跨栏,活动篱笆
procrastination [prəuˌkræstiˈneiʃn]	*n.*	延迟,拖延
template(=templet) [ˈtemplit]	*n.*	样板,模板

emulate ['emjuleit]	n.	仿效
circuitous [sə(:)'kju(:)itəs]	adj.	迂回线路的,间接的,迂远的
tricky ['triki]	adj.	狡猾的,机警的

Notes

(1) Your e-marketing plan should discuss how you will use information technologies to manage the marketing mix (product, price, place, and promotion), how you plan to optimize your content, and how you will allocate resources to attract new customers, create loyalty with existing ones, and create revenue streams. 你的电子市场营销计划应该讨论你将如何使用信息技术管理营销组合(产品、价格、渠道和促销)、你怎样计划来优化你的内容,以及你将怎样分配资源来吸引新的客户,利用现有的条件创造忠诚性,并创造收入流。

(2) Benefits of this model include increased demand for goods and services via an entry into the global market, potential lower costs of promotion and sales, 24/7 ordering and customer service, and one-to-one custom marketing. 这种模式的好处在于通过登录全球市场来增加产品和服务的需求、潜在的低成本销售和促销、每天24小时/每周7天的全天候订购和客户服务,以及一对一的客户营销。

(3) Other difficulties include the challenge of identifying the right analysis, the tricky nature of developing revenue stream forecasts, and question of which expense budgets to develop. 其他困难包括识别正确分析的挑战、收入流预测的慎重性,以及制订哪一项费用预算的问题。

Questions

(1) Why is e-business model so important?
(2) What are the business models mentioned in the text?
(3) Give your comment on each of the models.
(4) What are the obstacles of planning an e-marketing plan?
(5) According to the author, how to define an e-marketing plan?

Exercises

1. Translate the following sentences into Chinese:
(1) Any time you need to prepare a multi-page report, like an e-marketing plan,

writer's block can be a problem.

(2) Products like e-marketing Suite by Embellix can help you overcome writer's block by providing you with an effective template and writing outline to follow.

(3) Writing an e-marketing plan is partly an exercise in answering a series of critical questions.

(4) Not only e-marketing experts but also professionals who know how to apply professional styles and formatting to create great looking reports have designed products like e-marketing Suite by Embellix.

(5) Your e-marketing plan content is critical but almost as critical is the look and "feel" of your reports. Management may interpret poor looking e-marketing plans as less credible. Be sure to polish your e-marketing plan document.

2. Translate the following sentences into English:

(1) 电子营销计划记录了当前的销售形势、挑战和机会、营销目标,以及完成这一目标的战略。

(2) 电子商务模式通常包括商人模式、拍卖模式、制造商模式、会员模式、广告模式、信息媒介模式、订购模式、经纪人模式、虚拟社区模式和物流模式等。

(3) 制订电子市场营销计划必须考虑到是否适合自己的电子商务模式。

(4) 虚拟社区为社区用户提供了一个在线互动的平台,有利于在线交易。

(5) 撰写电子市场营销计划是一个复杂的工作,要克服诸多障碍。

Further Reading

You can see the full text in *E-Marketing Planning*: *Accountability and E-Metrics*, the White Paper sponsored by Embellix Software.

Translation

什么是电子营销计划

让我们从定义营销计划开始,然后再确定它的"新经济伙伴"——电子营销计划。市场营销计划是详细记录当今销售形势、威胁和机会、营销目标和达到目标战略的一个书面文件。我们既可以给单个的产品、服务、品牌制订市场营销计划,也可以针对公司整体制订一个相应的计划。与传统的市场营销计划相比,电子市场营销计划更加专注。虽然它经常包含一些与传统市场营销计划相同的主题,但它更侧重于在互联网上的营销机会、营销威胁、营销目标和营销策略。

电子市场营销计划要定义你的商业模式,从参与执行计划的所有人的角度建立起承诺,并制定业绩标准和成功度量。电子市场营销计划的发展开始于对电子商务模式的完整评价。什么是商业模式呢?本文在接下来的部分里对电子商务模式做了描述。读完本文后,你可以回顾那些描述并思考一下哪一个模式最接近你的企业模式。在你开始制订一个电子市场营销计划之前,要考虑怎样来定义你的电子商务模式以及它是怎样影响你的电子市场营销计划的。

电子市场营销计划和你的电子商务模式

电子市场营销计划为你电子商务的成功提供了一张路线图或蓝图。写好电子市场营销计划的先决条件是你要对自己的电子商务模式有一个全面彻底的理解。当你准备做电子市场营销计划时,你可能要经历一个学习的过程;你将详细分析你的电子商务模式以了解是什么在驱动着你的在线销售和收入流。

你的电子商务模式是什么?你能否用一两段文字来描述它?商业模式描述了关于产品、服务以及信息传递和收入(收入流)来源的体系结构。它识别了企业价值链的基本单元,比如入境物流、操作(或生产)、出境物流、营销、服务以及支持行为。

你必须通过你所描述的书面表达方式来定义你的业务模式。从描述中,你是否能识别出每条有效的收入流和潜在的收入流?你能判断出产生这些收入流所需的费用吗?你知道哪些东西极为重要,必须测量并追踪调查以确保成功吗?你能了解你的商业模式将怎样使用电子营销来定价、促销、销售和分销你的产品吗?

当你发展你的电子市场营销计划时,你必须考虑你该怎样努力使你的电子营销"适合"你的商业模式。至少你的商业模式将影响你对销售额以及电子营销费用的预算方式。但是,在基本的销售预测和预算外,你的电子营销计划还应包括你开展业务、产生收入和消耗资源的具体方式等方面的内容。你的电子市场营销计划应该讨论你将如何使用信息技术管理营销组合(产品、价格、渠道和促销),你要怎样来优化你的内容,和你将怎样分配资源来吸引新的客户,打造已有的客户忠诚度,并创造收入流。

在写计划之前你要确信你确定了你的商业模式。你能在接下来的描述部分里确定你的电子商务模式吗?

商人模式

商人模式是商品和服务的批发商或零售商的网络销售。网络上的商品和服务可能具有独特性,或者它们可以被看作传统的有形店铺的拓展。这种模式包括决定用一个网站配合他们的目录操作或者决定完全采用在线模式的编目者。这种模式的好处在于通过登录全球市场来增加产品和服务的需求、降低潜在的销售成本和促销成本、每天24小时/每周7天的全天候订购和客户服务,以及一对一的客户营销。

拍卖模式

拍卖模式是通过商品和服务的多媒体展示将投标机制引入网络而实现的。收入流来自于拍卖技术平台的授权许可、交易费和广告。

制造商模式

制造商模式使用网络来压缩分销渠道,这样,你就不必通过中间人把产品和服务送达市场,而是通过网络使其直接到达消费者。例如,个人电脑系统制造商戴尔计算机公司,就是采用这种通过它们的网站直接向消费者销售的模式。戴尔的销售额大约50%是通过网站(www.dell.com)实现的。

会员模式

会员模式是一个为业绩支付报酬模型。当客户点击链接或者旗帜广告来购买商品和服务时,就创造了收入流。会员销售是一个网站(会员)以代理的方式来宣传另一个网站的商品或服务(销售商)。当销售商从一个会员(合作网站)获得一次销售时,会员提取佣金(即销售的10%)。通过会员销售,销售商可以将他们的广告标语和链接放在世界范围内合适的网站上,并且只有在那些链接产生了销售或有效的引导时才支付代理费。通过那些产生收入的链接,被接纳为会员的内容网站可以实现从在线内容向电子商务的转变。

广告模式

像传统的广播公司或新闻媒介商业模式一样,网络广告模式提供由旗帜广告和其他在线广告形式(特别是电子邮件新闻组广告)支持的内容和服务(如电子邮件、聊天、论坛、拍卖等)。一些广告模式被称为门户(像美国在线、雅虎和AltaVista);其他的被称为"免费模式",像蓝色山峰艺术团(www.bluemountain.com)的赠品(免费的电子贺卡和请柬)已经创造出了很高的价值。

信息媒介模式

这种网络模式依靠从用户那里收集信息,并把这些信息销售给企业来获利。交易主要靠信息媒介网站提供免费服务来驱动,比如免费的互联网接入或者免费硬件。

订购模式

在订购模式内,用户要为他们接入站点和浏览高价值的内容付费。对那些付费的订购者,一些模式把高价值内容作为免费内容提供。广告收入同样是收入流的一部分。

经纪人模式

经纪人模式是把买方与卖方集合在一起的一个网络市场制造者。这种模式的范围从虚拟商业区到在线股票和债券商,它包括商业和商业之间(B2B)、企业对消费者(B2C),以及消费者对消费者(C2C)三种形式。在这个模式下收入来自于交易费或者佣金。

虚拟社区模式

虚拟社区模式促进了一个社区的用户(会员、客户、伙伴、学生等)之间的在线互动。

这种模式方便了社区成员在网上社区网站上添加他们自己的内容。收入流产生于会员费和广告费。

物流模式

在物流模式里,一个企业利用互联网帮助其他企业管理物流功能,例如电子支付、订购系统和装运服务。相关费用是收入流的主要来源。

电子商务模式和电子营销计划

电子商务模式和电子销售之间的关系是什么？前面确定的所有模式的核心问题有三个：

- 对这些模式的运行来说,电子市场营销计划至关重要。
- 这些模式产生大量的信息；来自网站活动的战略信息,可以用来更好地满足电子客户的需要和出售更多的商品。
- 需要通过度量来提供可操作性,并来分析战略优势的信息。

电子营销计划准备

编写电子营销计划不是一项容易的任务,其中有不少障碍。本白皮书的目的不是为制订电子市场营销计划提供指南,而是我们将确认要制订一个好计划所必须克服的困难。

编写一个好的电子营销计划的障碍是什么？对初始者来说,拖延是一个障碍；公务繁忙的经理人会推迟编写计划。然而,随着商业的快速发展（互联网时代）,电子延迟有很高的机会成本。推迟制订一个电子营销计划的代价是市场机会和利润的损失。

另一个障碍是时间。发展一个电子市场营销计划的过程是很费时的。我们应考虑使流程流畅。通过例子和模板我们可以得到解答。通过仿效和学习一个经过验证的模板能节省大量的时间。模板可以给出有效的大纲、标题,在有些情况下还可以给出文本。

其他障碍是与编写过程有关的,例如作者的阻滞和写作的劳动密集的迂回性也是主要的障碍。其他困难包括识别正确分析的挑战、收入流预测的慎重性,以及制订哪一项费用预算的问题。

UNIT 6 A New Marketing Strategy for E-Commerce

Exploring the ideas of product, place, price and promotion, and applying them to e-commerce problems is the main focal point of this article. It is believed that the four concepts of the marketing mix equally play a critical part in the success of e-commerce. Therefore, concentrating on these concepts will prove to be of the utmost importance as an e-commerce provider.

Applying the Marketing Mix

Product

One of the main issues of concern is the intangibility of purchasing online. The intangibility is caused by not being able to focus on tangible aspects when purchasing online. The customer can't actually touch or feel a product, which increases the risk of the purchase. The key to reducing intangibility is creating tangible cues that the customer recognizes. Creating a positive brand image will reduce the risk. For example, buying a product that has a quality image will reduce the risk for customers. Companies need to focus on creating a positive and reliable brand name.

Stressing the actual or perceived benefits received from the product can also reduce intangibility. Relaying to the customer that they will be very satisfied with the benefits of the product is important. For example, if a company sales golf clubs online, they want to stress concept that they will hit the ball farther and straighter, which will allow the person to increase their enjoyment when playing golf. Also, focusing on the actual components of the product is important. Explaining the benefits of the clubs grip and shaft in the product will also redirect the attention away from the intangible aspects.

Focusing on advantages of buying on line is also important for companies to achieve increased sales. On the web site it is important to convey the convenience of buying your product online. Conveying the message that your product is conveniently accessible, lets the customer understand that they don't need to stand in lines or deal with other customers. Long lines and other customers can keep customers from buying or decrease the amount they are willing to purchase. Explaining the convenience of buying on line is a good way to reduce the problem of intangibility.

There are some instances where the convenience of online buying can be diminished. When the customer finally decides to purchase a good it's important for this transaction to be quick and concise. The quicker this action can be done accurately the better. If it takes a long time for this action, customers may defect and buy the product through a local retail outlet. Companies need to be aware of this and implement the proper technology to assure that this barrier is minimized.

Since products can't be seen in person, it creates a barrier between the company and the buyer. A possible way to overcome this factor is through technology. By providing actual pictures of the product, it will allow the customer to get a better understanding of the products. If the web site has high quality pictures, it will reduce the perceive risk, which can increase the sales for a company.

Products that are produced in different sizes, such as clothing, create a problem for companies. Customers that want to buy the product may not because they are not sure how the product will fit. To solve the problem, it is important for the company to have a lenient return policy, but even more importantly, they should purchase software that helps in sizing. This software will allow customers to input their measurements and the web site will recommend which size is best for them. This type of technology will reduce the risk involved, which will increase the number of products sold.

The service involved is also a barrier that must be understood and managed correctly. Having a lenient or fair return system will lower the perceived risk involved. The customer is more likely to purchase the product if they know that returning the product will be of minimal hassle and at no expense. Providing the high service is directly related to increasing sales. Companies should also pay the postage to have the product returned. Paying the postage will again, lower the perceived risk, will most likely help in stimulating sales. Of course, this can only prove to be beneficial if the product doesn't have a high defective rate.

Place

Some of the distribution problems are uncontrollable at this point in the life cycle of the Internet. In some instances the problem of delivering the product to the customers isn't the fault of the online company. Nearly every online company does choose to outsource the delivery function, which at this point is the most efficient. Online companies are having a difficult time satisfying their customers, because of something that isn't their fault. The company that they select to ship their product isn't handling the demand. For high volume companies this can be easier to solve.

There is a definite need for companies to manage the relationship with the shipping companies. The bigger the company the more power it posses in the supply chain. They have the ability to hurt the shipping company by choosing to change shippers. Even though there are few shipping companies, the online company can claim they will switch, if their quality of service doesn't increase. By threatening a switch, it will hopefully create better service for a large company.

One of the biggest problems with online buying is the lack of automated inventory and warehousing systems. The lack of automation really hinders in the efficiency and speed of meeting the customer needs. For small companies, it is a good idea to outsource the warehouse and distribution functions, because they aren't efficient enough to meet customers' needs. Outsourcing will reduce the actual profit, because it is expensive. Over time it will prove to be beneficial, because it will help in building loyalty. The most important thing to understand is choosing the correct outsourcer. Companies want to pick an outsourcer that isn't overbooked with clients so they can efficiently handle demand requirements.

Large online companies really need to consider automating the inventory and warehousing functions. This may be the best way to stay competitive in the future. The use of logistics consultants is a good strategy to assist in choosing an automated system that matches company needs.

Large companies that use outsourcers should look into instituting their own logistics system. Even though it is working for the company, it may be reducing profit. Each part of the supply chain makes a small profit in the online commerce. The actual sale of the product makes a small profit, the warehousing makes a small profit, and the packager makes a small profit. Add up these areas and that means there is a larger profit to be made by taking over these functions. If a company can do these functions themselves they will increase their profits, because they can do it cheaper than an outsourcer.

Managing warehouse systems can be improved through the use of software. Warehouse-management software systems are now available for online companies to purchase. These software packages can increase the efficiency by handling orders and tracking the delivery function. These are possible solutions that a company can do to implement automation in the company.

Price

Price is very important when dealing with e-commerce problems. Price can be a key issue when trying to increase demand or when decreasing demand. Price is definitely a weapon of choice by many companies. The two typical pricing methods are skimming and penetration. Skimming pricing is charging a high price when the product is relatively new, in hope of making more profit. Penetration pricing is deployed to capture a large market share. The theory is based on creating a large market share, by being lower than competitors.

To increase demand, e-commerce companies need to focus on penetrating the market. This will work best for products that are in the introduction and growth stage. If the product is near the maturity stage, lowering the price won't increase profits very much. For relatively new products, offering the product below competitors will increase demand.

Pricing of a product can reduce demand without reducing profit. If an online company is doing very well, but isn't able to keep up with the current demand, it may be smart to actually raise the price of the product. This will do two things; it will keep profits at the same level, but allows the logistics department to handle the orders more efficiently. If companies can't keep up with demand, it will reduce the satisfaction of the customer, which will reduce the loyalty of the customer. A solution to keep customers happy is by reducing the demand through increasing the price, which will lower the number of purchases. Reducing the purchases will allow the company to match demand; in return it will be easier to keep current customers. It is believed that keeping current customers is five times cheaper than finding new ones. When raising the price, it must be by a marginal amount, enough not to cause switching of loyal customers. Doing this will allow a company to keep the same profit and manage demand more efficiently. This solution may want to be done until the company can acquire an automated system.

Price bundling, which is packaging products together for one price. Using this tactic can be beneficial when doing business online. This can increase sales for a company, because customers feel they are getting more value for their money. Increasing the value will reduce the risk for customers. Reducing the price by say 10%, it can allow a company to increase sales. Sometimes this can be done with a product that is trying to be liquidated. This is a chance for the company to accomplish two things: increase sales and reduce unwanted inventory.

Promotion

Promotion is an important part when selling the product; it is a necessary function for e-commerce companies. This is one of the key facets in acquiring and keeping customers. Keeping and acquiring customers is important, but more attention and money needs to be spent on the place factors, such as warehousing and distribution functions. Some of the budget promotion money should be spent on developing better relations with distributors. Creating a strong bond with the delivery carriers will enhance the value of the company. This can be done through personal dealings with vendors. Doing such things as taking their representatives to events or to dinner can build a loyal relationship. These activities are inexpensive means that can really give an advantage to an e-commerce company.

Some troubles for e-commerce companies are the inability of customers to find the web page. If they can't find the web page, it creates a barrier in achieving increased sales. The current technology of search engines, such as Yahoo and Excite, are very broad in nature. When looking for a specific company it will bring up a vast variety of topics. It takes a while to narrow down the possible entries to find the intended company. Reducing the time spent looking for a web site can increase the satisfaction of the customers. If they must spend twenty minutes looking for a particular site, they may stop before they find it. A company can use promotion to combat these problems.

The best way to combat the problem is using promotions that give the web site address. If the product is high involvement, using advertising that is in magazines and newspapers should be efficient. For high involvement goods, people actively search for possible solutions to their problem. If the product is low involvement, people will not be actively searching for the product, so promotional activities must be intense. This can be accomplished by getting a large number of advertisements into television and radio vehicles.

Another possible promotional vehicle is using hyperlinks. Hyperlinks allow a direct passage from another web site. This makes it very easy to find a particular web site. Hyperlinks are usually most efficient when implemented on a web site of similar material. In addition, there is no need to alienate customers or potential customers through promotional tactics. False or unethical marketing as become an issue in recent years, it isn't uncommon to find many of these web sites. This can be just puffery or it can be full blown bait-and-switch tactics.

Buy.com has built a reputation in participating in false advertising on their web site. This is definitely something e-commerce companies need to get away from. With growing popularity of e-commerce, the more this is done the more it will create havoc in the future. With increase volume in online buying, there will be more restrictions and patrolling of false and unethical promotions. With increase in online buyers, it will increase the importance of word-of-mouth communications, which can cause problems. Doing this type of promotion will decrease the confidence and loyalty of customers, which will reduce sales in the future. A company's profit is directly related to customer loyalty, and these types of promotions will decrease loyalty. The question is clear, do they want to make a profit in the short run or be able to make a profit in the long run?

Words and Expressions

intangibility [ˌintænˈdʒəbiliti]	n.	无形;不能把握;不可解
tangible [ˈtændʒəbl]	adj.	有形的;可以触摸的
cue [kjuː]	n.	暗示,提示
relay [ˈriːlei]	n.	驿马;接替;继电器
	vt.	(消息、货物等)分程传递;使接替;转播
	vi.	得到接替;转播
grip [grip]	vt.	紧握,紧夹
	n.	掌握,控制;把手
	v.	抓住
shaft [ʃɑːft]	n.	轴;杆状物
diminish [diˈminiʃ]	v.	(使)减少;(使)变小
concise [kənˈsais]	adj.	简明的,简练的
defect [diˈfekt]	n.	过失,缺点
outlet [ˈautlet, -lit]	n.	出口,出路
lenient [ˈliːnjənt]	adj.	宽大的,仁慈的,慈悲为怀的
hassle [ˈhæsl]	n.	激战
	vi.	争论
	vt.	与……争辩
outsourcing [ˈautˌsɔːsiŋ]	n.	外部采办,外购,(将……业务、工程等)外包
conveniently [kənˈviːnjəntli]	adv.	便利地
accessible [əkˈsesəbl]	adj.	易接近的;可到达的;易受影响的;可理解的
automat [ˈɔːtəmæt]	n.	自动售货(或售票)机;用自动售货机供应食品的餐馆
inventory [ˈinvəntri]	n.	详细目录,存货,财产清册,(财产等)总量清单,报表;(商品的)目录盘存,存货
warehouse [ˈwɛəhaus]	n.	仓库;货栈;大商店
	vt.	贮入仓库;以他人名义购进(股票)

hinder ['hində]	adj.	后面的
	v.	阻碍;打扰
logistic [ləu'dʒistik]	adj.	后勤学的;后勤的;物流的
integration [ˌinti'greiʃən]	n.	综合;整合;(产业的)集中
skim [skim]	v.	撇去
maturity [mə'tjuəriti]	n.	成熟;完备;(票据)到期
bundling ['bʌndliŋ]	v.	打小包;集束,成束
liquidate ['likwiˌdeit]	v.	清算,清算(破产的公司等);了结;清偿(债务等)
bond [bɔnd]	n.	结合(物),粘结(剂),联结;公债,债券,合同
	v.	结合
narrow down		减少,限制,缩小,变窄
intense [in'tens]	adj.	强烈的,剧烈的;热切的,热情的,激烈的
vehicle ['vi:ikl]	n.	交通工具,车辆;媒介物,传达手段
hyperlink	n.	超链接
alienate ['eiliəneit]	v.	疏远,把(资金等)移作他用
puffery ['pʌfəri]	n.	吹捧,鼓吹,吹捧的广告
bait [beit]	n.	饵,诱惑物
	vt.	以饵引诱(动物),把饵装上,欺负,折磨
	vi.	中途休息
tactic ['tæktik]	n.	策略,战略
	adj.	按顺序的,排列的
havoc ['hævək]	n.	大破坏,浩劫
	vt.	严重破坏
patrol [pə'trəul]	v.	出巡,巡逻
	n.	巡逻

Notes

(1) Conveying the message that your product is conveniently accessible, lets the

customer understand that they don't need to stand in lines or deal with other customers. 传递出你的产品可以很方便地得到的信息,让用户明白他们不需要站队或者与其他用户打交道。

(2) If an online company is doing very well, but isn't able to keep up with the current demand, it may be smart to actually raise the price of the product. 如果一家在线公司经营得很好,但不能满足当前的需求量,那么就应该明智地提高这种产品的价格。

(3) With increase volume in online buying, there will be more restrictions and patrolling of false and unethical promotions. 随着在线购买数量的增加,将有更多的对虚假及不道德促销的限制和追查。

Questions

(1) How to solve the problem of intangibility of purchasing online?
(2) What is the benefit of outsourcing the delivery function?
(3) What is the importance of automation in a company's logistic system?
(4) According to the author, how to use the price strategy?
(5) What is the problem with promotion?

Exercises

1. Translate the following sentences into Chinese:
(1) E-commerce has many advantages for most organizations that choose to use this means of operation.
(2) E-commerce is independent of size, for the most part; any organization can operate over the Internet.
(3) The Internet also reduces the advantage of large companies over small companies, because it somewhat levels the playing field.
(4) E-commerce is self-selective, meaning people who are on your site are interested; they want to learn about your organization or product.
(5) E-commerce also allows organizations to gather information on its customers or potential customers.

2. Translate the following sentences into English:
(1) 产品、渠道、价格和促销4个概念的恰当组合是电子商务公司成功的关键因素。
(2) 在线购买可能带来一定的不确定性,因此商家要尽量降低这种无形性,给消费者以积极的暗示。
(3) 缺乏自动化的存货清单和仓储系统是在线购买的一大问题。
(4) 一旦厂家提高价格,将会降低消费者的需求,从而在供求间实现一种平衡。

（5）促销是电子商务公司的一个重要功能，也是获得新客户，保持老客户的一个重要手段。

Further Reading

This text is selected from *A New Marketing Strategy for E-Commerce*, written by Chong Y. Lee Pittsburg State University, Pittsburg, KS 66762, USA.

Translation

一个针对电子商务的新营销策略

本文关注的焦点在于探求产品、渠道、价格和促销等基本营销概念并运用这些概念来解决电子商务过程中遇到的问题。可以确信的是，营销组合的四个概念在电子商务的成功中起着同样至关重要的作用。因此，作为一个电子商务提供者，专注于这些概念无疑是极为重要的。

应用营销组合

产品

在线购买的无形性是我们所要关注的主要问题之一，这种无形性是由在线购买时人们无法集中于商品的有形方面而引起的。消费者不能实际接触或感受到相关的产品，因而购买的风险就会增加，所以，降低无形性风险的关键就是要创造出消费者能明确识别的有形暗示物。一个积极的商标形象将极大地降低风险。例如，购买一具有质量标记的产品将为客户减少风险。据此，公司都应致力于塑造一个积极可靠的商标形象。

其次，强调消费者可从产品中实际获得的利益或可体验的利益同样可以降低无形性风险。向客户传播他们会非常满意的有关商品效用的信息是很重要的，例如，如果一个公司在线销售高尔夫球棒，他们就应强调这样一种观念，即这种球棒能给人们带来倍增的乐趣，使用它能将球打得更远更直。此外，关注于这种产品的实际组件也是重要的。如向顾客传达诸如球棒把手和长柄的优点，也将使他们注意力不再停留在对无形的困惑上。

另外，集中宣传在线购买的诸多优点对公司实现超额销售也是至关重要的。在网站上很重要的一点就是向消费者传达在线购买的便利性，向客户传递你的产品可以方便地获得的信息，让他们明白不再需要站队或者与其他用户打交道，因为长长的队伍或其他顾客都可能使顾客放弃购买或减少他们愿意购买的数量，所以，宣传在线购买的便利性是降低无形性问题的一种好方法。

然而,这里仍有一些人为减少在线购买的便利性的因素。当消费者最后决定购买一件商品后,很重要的一点就是希望这次交易能够迅速和简洁地完成,且越准确、越快速越好。如果这一次交易过程要花费很长的时间,顾客就有可能离去,转而通过一个本地零售点购买这种产品。公司必须意识到这点,并且运用适当的技术,以确保这样的障碍最小化。

由于消费者在线购买时不能亲眼见到实物产品,在公司和购买者之间就会产生一个障碍,克服这个障碍的可行性方法就是利用先进技术,提供产品的实物照片,帮助用户更好地了解此产品。如果在网站上展示产品的高质量的图片,就会有利于降低客户感官上的风险,增加公司的销售额。

像衣服这样的产品能被生产成不同的规格尺寸,这就给公司带来一个问题;那些有购买产品欲望的顾客可能会因担心产品是否合适而放弃购买。为解决这一问题,公司判定一个相对宽松的退货政策是很重要的,但更重要的是购买一套有助于确定规格的相关软件。这种软件将允许用户自由地输入他们所需的尺寸,同时网站将推荐哪个尺寸是最适合他们的。使用这类技术不仅降低了有关风险,而且还能增加产品销售数量。

网上销售的相关服务也是横亘在公司和消费者之间的一个障碍,必须得到正确理解和管理。提供一种宽松的或公正的退货系统将极大地降低相关的感知风险。显然,当消费者知道退回这种产品引起的争议很小且不需任何花费时,他们很可能会购买这种产品。提供高效的服务与销售额增加有直接关系。此外,公司也应该为商品退货承担邮资。支付邮资也能再次降低感知的风险,且很有可能刺激销售。当然,只有在这种产品的缺陷率不高时,利用这种方式才有利可图。

渠道

在互联网生命活动循环点上有一些分销渠道问题是很难控制的。在有的情况下,把产品传递到客户手中的问题并不是在线公司的过错。几乎每家在线公司都选择把配送功能外包,从在这点上来看,也许是最有效率的。因为一些并不属于它们过错的原因,在线公司正普遍处在不能很好地满足其客户需求的困难时期。而与他们合作的货运公司仅负责装运货物,不处理客户需求。对高流通量的公司来说,这一问题比较容易解决。

在线公司有一个明确的、管理装运公司关系的需求。公司越大,它在供应链中的作用就越强,它们就更有能力通过变更托运人来打压运输公司。即使在运输公司数量很少的情况下,如果这些公司的服务质量没有上升,在线公司仍然会宣称变更托运人。由于受到更换的威胁,运输公司只好为一些大公司抱有希望地创造更好的服务。

缺乏自动化的存货清单和仓储系统是在线购买存在的最大问题之一。缺乏自动化的确阻碍了满足用户需求的效率和速度。对小公司来说,把仓储和分销功能外包无疑是个好的思路,因为它们没有足够的能力有效地满足用户需求。然而,外包将降低实际利润,因为它是昂贵的。但随着时间的推移,它将被证明是有收益的,因为它有助于建立顾客忠诚度。正确理解这种模式最重要的一点就是挑选合适的外包商。公司应该挑选那些没被客户超额预定的外包商,只有这样他们才能更有效地处理需求方面的要求。

大的在线公司真的有必要考虑实现存货清单和仓储功能自动化,这可能是未来保持竞争力的最好方法。使用物流顾问是帮助选择适合公司需要的自动化系统的一个好策略。

同时,使用外包商的大的公司也应该考虑建立它们自己的物流系统。尽管外包能为公司有效服务,但仍减少了公司利润。在线商业活动供应链的每个环节都能创造一小部分利润,产品的实际销售创造一小部分利润、仓储创造一小部分利润、包装创造一小部分利润。如果把这些环节的利润加起来,就意味着接管这些功能将会产生更大的利润。如果一家公司能自行实现这些功能,无疑将增加它们的利润,因为它们能比外包商的成本更低。

仓库系统的管理也可以通过使用软件来得到改进。现在仓库管理软件系统已被设计开发出来,在线公司可以花钱去购买。这些软件包通过处理订单以及跟踪交货功能来提高效率,这些是一家公司能在公司里实现自动化交易的可能的解决办法。

价格

在处理电子商务问题时,价格是一个非常重要的手段。尤其是在决定是努力增加需求还是减少需求的时候,价格会成为一个关键因素。价格无疑成了很多公司首选的一种武器。撇脂定价法和渗透定价法是两种典型的定价方法。撇脂定价法是在产品刚上市时就定一个较高的价格,以期赚取更多的利润。而渗透定价法用来追求较大的市场份额,它的理论基础是通过制订比竞争者更低的价格,来获取一份大的市场份额。

为了增加需求,电子商务公司需要注重深入市场。这对于处在推荐和成长阶段的产品来说,是最为有效的。如果这种产品已接近成熟阶段,那么降价将不会增加太多利润。对于相对较新的商品,提供低于竞争者的价格将会增加需求。

产品定价应做到在不减少利润的前提下降低客户的需求。如果一家在线公司经营得很好,但不能满足当前的需求量,那么就应该明智地提高这种产品的价格。因为这将达到两种效果:不仅使利润保持在同一水平上,还允许物流部门更有效地处理订单。如果公司服务不能紧跟需求变化,那么用户的满意度就会降低,其忠诚度也会下降。保持客户愉快的一个解决办法是通过提高价格来降低需求,从而降低购买的数量,以满足不变需求,这样就能更容易地保持当前的客户。事实上,保持一个当前用户比发展一个新用户可节约5倍的成本。提高价格,可能会改变边际数量,但不足以引起忠诚客户的离去。这样做可以让公司保持同等利润的同时,更有效地管理需求。这一解决方案要等到公司能采用一个自动化的系统后才能生效。

价格捆绑,就是将产品打包在一起而只以一种价格出售,使用这种战术在做在线生意时是很有利的。它能为一家公司增加销售,因为这种方法会让客户感到他们所购买的东西物超所值,而且增加价值将为用户降低购买风险。比方说降价10%,它能使公司增加销售。有时若要清仓处理某种产品就可以用价格捆绑的方式。由此公司达到两种效果:增加销售和减少多余库存。

促销

促销是出售商品时的一个重要环节,是电子商务公司必备的一项业务功能,也是在获得和保持客户过程中的关键方面之一。虽然保持和获得用户是如此重要,但是更多的注意力和资金仍需要用在渠道因素上,例如仓储和分销功能。一些预算促销经费应该被用在与分销商发展更好的关系上。创建与配送服务商强有力的关系将会提高公司的价值,这可以通过和卖主的个人交易来实现,这样做可以建立一种忠诚的关系,如邀请他们的代表参加会议或者宴会。这些活动是真正能给一家电子商务公司带来利益的廉价的方法。

对电子商务公司来说,一些头疼的事就是客户不能顺利地找到公司的网页。如果客户不能找到网页,就给增加销售制造了障碍。当今的搜索引擎技术,例如雅虎和Excite,实际上已经十分广泛。当搜索一家具体的公司时,它将额外显示出大量其他相关的主题。客户需要花费不少功夫来缩小他们要寻找的公司的入口范围。缩短查找网站的时间将增加顾客的满意度。如果他们必须花费20分钟才能找到一个专门的站点,那么他们在找到之前很可能已放弃了。公司可以使用促销手段来应对这些问题。

应对这一问题最好的方法是通过宣传来给出网站地址。如果那些待销产品的需求强度比较高,那么在杂志和报纸上刊登广告就应该是有效的。对需求强度比较高的商品来说,人们会积极寻找有关他们问题的可能的解决方案。如果待销产品的需求强度比较低,人们就不会积极地去搜寻,因此促销活动一定要密集有力,这可以选择大量的电视或广播媒体的广告来完成。

另一种可能的促销手段是使用超链接。超链接允许从另一个网站直接链接到另一个网站上去,这使得搜索一个专门的网站变得非常容易,尤其是在一个相似素材的网站上实现超链接时,是非常有效率的。另外,应该注意避免采用不必要的促销手段致使现有客户和潜在客户的离开。近年来,虚假营销或不道德营销问题日益突出,此类网站数量日益增多,屡见不鲜。这可能只是自吹自擂或者是完全神话的诱骗销售法的伎俩。

例如,Buy.com公司因为在网站上做虚假广告而声誉日下,这绝对是需要电子商务公司引以为戒的。随着电子商务的增长普及,这种做法越多,对将来的破坏也越大。随着在线购买量的增加,将有更多的针对虚假和不道德促销的限制和追查。随着在线购买者数量的上升,口头交流的重要性势必也会增加,这有可能引起一些问题。做这类促销会减少用户的信任度和忠诚度,并将减少在未来的销售。一个公司的利润直接与顾客忠诚度有关,但这类促销将减少忠诚度。这里的疑问是很清楚的,他们是想只顾眼前利益还是着眼于长久的赢利呢?

UNIT 7 Customer Differentiation and Lifecycle Management of E-Marketing

 Text

In the world of e-marketing, success is defined by your ability to build long-term customer relationships that bring value to your customer and sustained profitability to your organization.

Technology alone cannot provide a magic solution that will immediately resolve all your marketing challenges. Worldwide, companies are finding e-marketing success by investing in a combination of innovative implementations of technology, business process enhancements, and organizational changes that are part of an overall e-marketing strategy.

Customer Differentiation

The first step toward building successful customer relationships begins by adopting a corporate culture that recognizes that every customer is different. Your customers have different interests, different levels of disposable income, different perceptions of value and perhaps most important, different historical experiences with your company.

The world of one-size-fits-all mass marketing fails to recognize these differences and use them for competitive advantage. The more you can evangelize a customer-centric corporate culture, revising technology, business processes and organizational structure around recognition of customer differences, the more effective your relationship building strategies will be.

This does not mean that you need to develop a separate plan for each individual customer; rather it challenges you to identify the relative value of customers and create a strategy that effectively targets collective customer needs—starting with your most profitable customers.

Using customer differentiation for e-marketing purposes require that you not only identify who your customers are, but more importantly that you recognize who are or are likely to become your best customers. You need to develop profiles based on the characteristics of your best customers and use them as the basis for understanding the profile of customers that you want to acquire. Additionally, it is important to recognize differences in profiles based on where the customer is within the customer lifecycle. This will provide you with insight into customer behavior and allow you to address customer needs most effectively.

The metrics you use to define customer value will vary considerably based on the types of customers you have and your goals. A few key value indicators you may want to consider include:
- Transaction history
- Profitability
- Length of the customer relationship
- Cost to service

To ensure that your value indicators continue to provide valid measurement over time, you'll need to regularly reassess the components that define customer value.

Customer Lifecycle Management

Customer lifecycle is another key e-marketing factor you must address to successfully build customer relationships. While marketers have traditionally used a variety of terms to define the stages of the customer lifecycle, for the purposes of this document we'll use acquire, engage, extend, and retain.

As we focus on strategies for building relationships across phases of the customer lifecycle, our emphasis will be on the business benefits of these strategies. Fundamental to the assumption of business benefit is that the strategy also delivers value to the customer. Like personal relationships, business relationships are best when built on mutual respect, trust, and value to all parties involved.

Acquire

Recent studies show a decrease in the cost to acquire new online customers. However, this doesn't mean your acquisition efforts don't need a well thought out plan and approach. Some of the basic elements that make your site appealing to new customers are detailed below.

Registration Incentives: Contests, promotions, white papers product samples, and demos are all examples of incentives you can provide to get new customers to register or purchase products or services. Customers need to have a clear value proposition in order to be willing to disclose information and begin a relationship with you. Develop a plan to entice customers to come to your site, and track the effectiveness of the promotions and other incentives. Prominently display incentives on your site—so much the better if these incentives are tightly bound to relevant services.

Referral Incentives: Giving incentive to current customers to refer new customers can be a cost-effective way to generate new business. Existing customers are happy to refer others, provided they are happy with the products or services they are receiving and see value in the incentive provided.

Easy Navigation and Robust Search Capability: To get customers to your site, make sure your basic design is planned with your customers in mind. Some of the basic requirements to consider include:

- A visually appealing user interface with a clear message.
- Straightforward navigation on the site; users should never get stranded or lost on your site.
- Robust, easy-to-use search capabilities.

Brand Establishment and Messaging: New brands need development of messages and advertisements to convey their identity to customers. Make sure that the online experience for existing brands with well-known messages is consistent and leverages the same message as their offline advertising and messaging.

Engage

Use content or services to ensure a positive initial experience with your company. Engage visitors in an interactive dialog that goes beyond the initial interest or sale. Demonstrate your knowledge of the product offering as a way to distinguish yourself from your competitors. Welcome visitors to the community. Make it easy for them to do business with you. Provide engaging features that will keep them coming back, as follows:

Content: The most fundamentally engaging feature is simply a Web resource that always has something new to offer when the visitor returns. Ever-changing content, like window-dressing in a storefront, provides a compelling reason for customers to return to your site. This may seem basic, but too few enterprises accurately forecast the staffing and organization needed to sustain lively content over time.

Community Features: Community features such as discussion boards, feedback mechanisms, webcasts, and live chats are proven methods for bringing visitors back to your site. These features actually involve visitors in creating much of your ever-changing content!

Pre-populate Data: To simplify the ordering process, eliminate redundant data collection by pre-populating information. Pre-populating data based on past visits or information entered during the session can expedite the ordering process and make it easier for your customers to use your site. Customers appreciate ease of use and will be more inclined to return to order again.

Notifications, Recommendations, and Alerts Based on Preferences: Provide the ability to customize communications to your customers. Provide notice of promotions and news alerts based on user-indicated preferences.

Online Product Configuration: Provide your customers with the ability to configure your products and services online. Give your customers the information they need to be able to configure products based on their specific requirements.

Extend

When you have truly engaged your customers and established the foundation of a relationship, it is time to look at ways to extend that relationship. Uncovering opportunities to provide additional value-added products and services when built on a solid relationship will not only benefit the customer, but will also enhance the lifetime value of the customer.

Auto Replenishment: Develop a plan to auto-replenish products ordered by your top customers.

Personalized Recommendations: Use data mining and analysis of purchase and transaction history to identify personalized recommendations including potential cross-sell and up-sell opportunities. Intelligently suggesting related products or product upgrades is not only a valuable service to customers, but also a successful method of extending your customer share both vertically and horizontally. Develop targeted campaigns to promote cross-sell and up-sell products and services.

Lifetime Event Selling: Based on the information you have from customers, anticipate lifetime events and develop promotions to make customers aware of products and services you provide based on the event. Examples include promoting PC's when customer's children reach school age, or promoting travel packages for active retirees.

Partner to Complement Your Offering: Develop partnerships and affiliations with other organizations that allow you to provide a complete and compelling package for your customers.

Retain

Retaining customers requires an ongoing commitment to provide increasing levels of value to the customer. Enhancing retention requires customers to continue to provide information about themselves, through their responses and their behavior, so that you are better able to target products and services. Additionally, if your established services make it significantly easier for customers to do businesses with your organization compared to your competition, these services provide barriers to attrition.

Customer-defined Experience: Provide the ability for your customers to customize the content they receive and when and how they receive it when visiting your site. Letting the customer define the experience as much as possible lets the customer know you are in business to serve them. By defining their experience with the information they want, the customer is providing you with valuable information about their needs. Additionally, they are indicating a willingness to do business with you and provide more information about themselves and their interests.

Differentiate Service Programs: Provide higher levels of service for customers that you have designated as your best customers.

Loyalty and Reward Programs: Develop specific programs that reward your customers for making purchases and that encourage them to continue to purchase from your site. Loyalty programs can vary from simple to complex depending upon the products and services you offer.

Words and Expressions

differentiation [ˌdifərenʃi'eiʃən]	n.	区别,差异化
sustain [səs'tein]	v.	支撑,撑住;维持,持续
magic ['mædʒik]	adj.	有魔力的;不可思议的
enhancement [in'hɑːnsmənt]	n.	增进,增加
adopt [ə'dɔpt]	v.	采用;收养
perception [pə'sepʃən]	n.	理解;感知;感觉
evangelize [i'vændʒilaiz]	vt.	传福音;使信基督教
profile ['prəufail]	n.	剖面;侧面;外形,轮廓
metrics ['metriks]	n.	韵律学;作诗法;度量
fundamental [ˌfʌndə'mentl]	adj.	基础的,基本的
	n.	基本原则,基本原理
assumption [ə'sʌmpʃən]	n.	假定,设想;担任
entice [in'tais]	v.	诱惑,诱使
track [træk]	v.	追踪,循路而行;监察

Unit 7 Customer Differentiation and Lifecycle Management of E-Marketing

prominently ['prɔminəntli]	adv.	显著地
referral [ri'fə:rəl]	n.	提名,推举
navigation [,nævi'geiʃən]	n.	导航,航行
robust [rə'bʌst]	adj.	精力充沛的
visually ['vizjuəli]	adv.	在视觉上地;真实地
straightforward [streit'fɔ:wəd]	adj.	正直的,坦率的;简单的,易懂的;直截了当的
	adv.	坦率地
stranded [strændid]	adj.	束手无策的;进退两难的
consistent [kən'sistənt]	adj.	一致的;调和的
leverage ['li:vəridʒ]	v.	影响
initial [i'niʃəl]	adj.	最初的,初始的
engaging [in'geidʒiŋ]	adj.	动人的,有魅力的,迷人的
ever-changing	adj.	经常变化的
compelling [kəm'peliŋ]	adj.	强制的,强迫的;引人注目的
redundant [ri'dʌndənt]	adj.	多余的
expedite ['ekspi,dait]	v.	加速,派出
	adj.	畅通的,迅速的
inclined [in'klaind]	adj.	倾向……的
notification [,nəutifi'keiʃən]	n.	通知,布告,告示
configuration [kən,figju'reiʃən]	n.	构造,结构;配置;外形
uncover [ʌn'kʌvə]	vt.	揭开,揭示
replenishment [ri'pleniʃmənt]	n.	补给,补充
personalize ['pə:sənəlaiz]	v.	使成私人的;人格化
retiree [ri,taiə'ri:]	n.	退休人员,退休者,歇业者
affiliation [ə,fili'eiʃən]	n.	联系;从属关系
attrition [ə'triʃən]	n.	摩擦;磨损

Notes

(1) The text is taken from *The BEA E-Marketing Fieldbook*, Section I.
(2) mass marketing：大规模销售
(3) competitive advantage：竞争优势
(4) well thought out：经过周密考虑的
(5) appeal to：对……有吸引力
(6) be bound to：与……相关，与……有联系
(7) distinguish oneself from：使杰出
(8) do business with：与……做生意
(9) user-indicated preference：客户偏好
(10) top customer：高端客户

Questions

(1) What role does the Customer Differentiation play in building successful customer relationship?
(2) How can a company define customer value?
(3) What are the stages of the customer life cycle?
(4) Can you describe the characteristics of the each stage of customer life cycle?
(5) You think which stage of the customer life cycle is most important in establishing a successful customer relationship. Why?

Exercises

1. Translate the following sentences into Chinese：
(1) The power of e-marketing is its ability to be able to turn mass amounts of data into individualized and personalized communications and treatments for large numbers of customers than ever before.
(2) First and foremost, recognize that e-marketing is an iterative process.
(3) With e-marketing you can generate a wealth of information about your customers, your promotions and your site.
(4) There is tremendous pressure on marketing to produce results and to demonstrate immediate return on investment in marketing programs.
(5) Remember that e-marketing is part of an overall marketing and Customer Relationship Management (CRM) plan and process.

2. Translate the following sentences into English：
(1) 在电子市场中，能否与客户构建长期的客户关系是企业成功的关键。

(2) 客户的不同兴趣爱好、不同可支配收入、不同价值观以及可能是购物经历对网站经营成功与否至关重要。
(3) 电子市场上的客户差异化要求你不仅能够确定谁是你的客户,更重要的是要知道谁是或者谁更可能成为你最好的客户。
(4) 能够提供优质的内容或服务是公司为客户留下良好的第一印象的关键所在。
(5) 简单的服务流程和及时的客户信息更新是吸引并保留客户的重要因素。

Further Reading

You can read the full text of *The BEA E-Marketing Fieldbook* for more information.

Translation

电子化营销的客户差异化与生命周期管理

在电子营销世界中,企业的成功与否取决于其与客户构建长期的客户关系的能力,这种长期的客户关系在给客户带来价值的同时,也能够让你的组织拥有持续的获利能力。

仅仅依靠技术无法给企业提供一把万能钥匙即刻解决面临的各种挑战问题;在世界范围内,许多企业正在把技术创新应用的组合投资、业务流程优化以及作为整个电子营销策略的重要组成部分的组织结构变革,由此来探索电子营销的成功之道。

客户差异化

建立成功客户关系的第一步便是要构建起一种以"每一位客户都各不相同"为理念的企业文化。你的客户不但具有不同的兴趣爱好、不同的可支配收入、不同的价值观,而且可能是最重要的一点,也就是他们过去与你的企业打交道的感受各有差异。

那些一直以一种模式满足所有客户需求进行大规模营销的企业显然是没能够认识到这些差异,更没能利用这些差异形成独特的竞争优势。你越是坚持以客户为中心的企业文化,越是根据客户的不同需求来改进技术、业务流程以及组织结构,你所建立的客户关系策略就越有效。

但这并不意味着你需要为每一位客户量身定做出不同的计划,而需要面对的挑战是:你必须能识别出客户的相对价值,并从最具利润价值的客户入手,制订出一个有效的、以满足群体客户需求为目标的战略。

把客户差异化应用于电子营销,不仅要求你能识别出谁是你的客户,更重要的是让你能确知谁已经是你的最佳客户或谁极可能成为你的最佳客户;你应该分析并总结出现有的最佳客户具备的共同特征的外在表现形式,对照这些,再来明确你希望争取的客户的外在行为特征。此外,识别出处在不同的消费生命周期阶段的客户特征也是非常重要的,这样做可以帮助你更好地洞察客户行为,并最有效地处理客户的需求。

客户的类型各异,企业目标不同,定义客户价值的标准也会有很大的变化。你应该考虑的一些关键价值指标包括:

- 交易历史
- 获利能力
- 客户关系维持时间的长短
- 服务成本

为了确保你所使用的价值指标能够长时间提供准确而有效的评估,你需要定期地对这些定义客户价值的要素进行重新审核。

客户生命周期管理

客户生命周期是你在成功构建客户关系时必须处理好的另一个关键性的电子营销要素。从传统上来看,市场研究人员曾使用各种各样的术语来定义客户生命周期,但出于本文的目的,我们将其划分为获取客户信息、吸引客户注意、扩展客户和留住客户四个阶段。

当我们将发展战略集中到在客户生命周期的不同阶段创建有效的客户关系时,我们的重点将是这些战略所能带来的商业价值。商业价值假设的基础是这一发展战略能给客户带来价值。如同人际关系一样,商业关系也是建立在相互尊重、信任以及对每一个参与者都有利的基础上的。

获取客户信息

最近的研究表明,获得新的在线客户的成本正在不断降低,但这并不意味着"获取客户"阶段不需要一个详细而完整的计划和方法。以下是一些使网站吸引新客户的基本做法。

注册激励:竞赛、促销活动、白皮书产品样品以及试销产品都是吸引新客户注册或购买产品或服务的有效手段。客户只有在一个明确的价值取向的引导下,才愿意公开自己的信息并与你建立客户关系。因此,企业需要制订一个计划来吸引客户访问自己的网站,并跟踪其促销和其他激励的实施效果。将激励元素放在网站显著的位置——如果这些激励元素与相关的服务紧密联系起来,效果将会更好。

介绍性动机:激励现有客户介绍新的客户可能是一个节约成本的吸引新客户的方法。如果现有客户对公司所提供的产品或者服务感到满意,而且可以从所提供的激励因素中获得利益,那么他们将很愿意把别人介绍进来。

易于浏览和强大的搜索功能:为了吸引更多的客户登录,必须牢记站点设计的基本出发点是为客户着想的。一些需要考虑的基本要求包括:

- 一个提供清晰信息、可视化的富有吸引力的客户界面。
- 直接浏览；使用者不应该感到束手无策或迷失方向。
- 强大的、易于使用的搜索功能。

品牌建立与广告宣传：新的品牌需要开发相应的广告词并做广告宣传，才能使其在客户中留下印象。要确保那些有很高知名度的品牌的在线感受与离线的广告及信息具有一致性和相同的影响力。

吸引客户注意

要利用相应的内容或服务以确保客户对你的公司留下积极的初步印象；促进网站访问者与企业的双向交互对话可以超越最初的利润或销售；还要向你的客户展示你所提供的产品知识，以使你的产品与其他竞争者的产品更好地区分开来；欢迎访问者进入讨论社区；可以让客户与公司更加轻松地做生意；另外还应在网站上提供如下特色服务来吸引客户的回访。

内容：最基本的吸引客户的手段就是在网站资源上做文章，当客户回访时，能够看到新的内容。不断变化的内容，就像沿街店面的橱窗布置一样，总能给人耳目一新的感觉，这就为客户提供了一个回访网站的充足理由。这看起来是基本要求，但很少有企业能够准确预测为达到长期持续的内容生动的要求所需要的人员配置和组织设置的情况。

社区特色：社区特色，如讨论区、反馈机制、网络广播和在线聊天被证明是有效吸引客户回访的方法。这些特色实际上包括让访问者为你更新网站提供材料。

直接载入数据：为了简化订购流程，可以使用直接数据载入的功能来减少冗余信息的收集。直接载入的数据来源于客户先前的访问以及在交易期间客户提供的数据。此项功能可以加快订购流程并使得网站更容易使用。客户将因为网站易于使用而再次访问你的网站并订购商品。

基于客户爱好的提示、建议以及提示：向客户提供能够实现个性化沟通的能力。根据客户的偏好提供促销信息和新闻告示。

在线产品配置：拥有为客户提供公司在线产品或服务组合的能力，并向客户提供相关的信息，以使他们可以依据自己的特殊需要自由配置各类产品或服务。

扩展客户

在你已真正地同你的客户建立起了客户关系之后，接下来要做的是扩展这种客户关系；你需要寻找机会为客户提供额外的增值产品或者服务，这不仅仅会使客户受益，而且可以大大延长客户生命周期。

自动补货：当建立起稳固的关系后，制订一个针对高端客户的产品订购自动补货计划。

个性化推荐：使用数据挖掘的方法对以往客户采购和交易历史数据进行深度分析，以确认个性化推荐，如潜在的交叉销售和向上逆向销售的机会。明智地向客户推荐相关产品或者是升级产品，不但为客户提供了有价值的服务，而且还实现了你的客户份额的横向和纵向的扩展。有目的地开展商业活动以促进产品和服务的交叉营销或者向上销售。

客户人生事件营销：依据你获得的客户信息，预测客户的人生事件，制订促销计划让客户意识到你的产品和服务是依据他们的需要提供的，如当客户的小孩到了上学年龄时，你可以向你的客户推销个人电脑，或向活跃的退休人员推销旅游包。

补充产品不足的合作伙伴关系：同其他企业发展伙伴和附属关系，让你为你的客户提供完整和不可或缺的商品。

留住客户

为了留住客户，企业需要能够长期持续不断地向客户提供日益提高的价值水平。提高这种保持客户的力度需要客户能不断地通过他们的反应和举止行为，向企业提供他们自己的信息，只有这样，你才能更好地向他们定位产品或服务。此外，如果你在为客户提供服务的过程中，能够让客户深切地感受到，与你的竞争对手相比，开展业务的程序明显更简单，那么这些服务将会减少摩擦的产生。

客户自定义的体验：当客户访问你的网站时，应为他们提供这样的能力，即能够让他们自主确定自己所需要的内容，并由他们自己确定什么时候以及如何获得。尽量让客户自己来定义体验，让客户察觉到你正在为他们提供服务。如果让客户按他们需要的信息来定义自己的体验，那么客户就会向你提供更多有价值的有关他们自己以及他们需求的信息。此外，客户也会暗示性地流露出一些愿意与你开展业务的愿望，并能提供更多的关于他们自己及其兴趣的信息给你。

差异化服务计划：为那些已经被你认定为最佳客户的客户提供更高水平的服务。

忠诚以及奖励计划：制订特定的计划以奖励已经购买产品的客户，并鼓励他们继续通过你的网站来购买产品或者服务。繁简不一的客户忠诚计划可以依据你所提供的产品或服务的差异而具体制订。

UNIT 8
Payment Applications Make E-Commerce Mobile

Because vendors see a profitable opportunity in applications that let users pay for goods and services via mobile devices, they are releasing easier-to-use mobile-payment applications. Using mobile devices to pay for goods, services, bills, or money transfers offers numerous advantages, including convenience and ease of use for consumers, increased impulse and other sales for merchants, and more income for wireless-service providers, noted Ed Moyle, principal analyst for market research company Security Curve.

However, filling out the forms and typing in the credit-card numbers that have been necessary to make payments on smartphones, most of which have small physical or virtual keyboards, can be tedious and challenging. This is one reason that adoption of mobile payments, particularly in developed countries, has not widened significantly, although the approach has been used for years in some areas of Asia and Europe, said Moyle. Other limiting factors include security challenges and a lack of participation by merchants.

However, vendors are now releasing applications that work directly from mobile phones without additional equipment and that enable payments via several keystrokes.

Why Mobile Payment?

Mobile-payment services began in 1997, when Nokia enabled users to pay for soft drinks in Finnish vending machines via short-message-service transmissions from cellular phones. That year, Finland-based Merita Bank launched the first mobile-phone-based banking service, also using SMS.

However, early mobile-payment systems experienced only modest success because using wireless devices' keyboards and screens for complex transaction procedures was too much trouble and earlier devices weren't able to run sophisticated mobile-transaction applications.

Benefits

Mobile payments can be linked to users' credit or debit cards, phone bills, or prepaid deposits. They offer convenience for buyers by letting them make purchases from wireless devices, which lets them pay for goods or services wherever they are. Enabling easier purchases, including those made on the spur of the moment, yields more income for merchants. Meanwhile, mobile-service providers get revenue from transactions carried on their networks.

Enabling Technologies

The proliferation of smartphones with broadband connectivity, users' growing adoption of mobile data services, and the significant dissatisfaction that merchants today have with credit-card payments and associated fees are increasing mobile-payment adoption, noted Nick Holland, an analyst with the Yankee Group, a market research firm.

Today's highly functional smartphones—such as Apple's iPhone, RIM's BlackBerry, and Google's Android—let users efficiently run mobile-payment applications. "Phones can now download and run payment apps directly, without carrier intervention," said Security Curve's Moyle.

For example, noted Zong vice president of product and marketing Hill Ferguson, "Android permits third-party payment services for developers to use in their apps. We recently launched an Android SDK for apps that let users make purchases without entering credit-card information, usernames, or passwords." This type of approach, which multiple vendors have implemented, addresses users' concern about having to repeatedly enter identification, account, and payment details on devices with difficult-to-use keyboards. Instead, users have purchases either added to their phone bills, deducted from a prepaid account, or sent for payment by a credit-card account to which they have automatically linked their phone-based purchases.

Other Factors Driving Demand

The increased popularity of virtual goods and social networking is driving demand for mobile-payment technology, noted BOKU co-founder and senior vice president for product and marketing Ron Hirson. For example, many users play online games from multiple locations, making the ability to utilize mobile phones to buy virtual currency and other items used in the social games attractive, he explained.

The increasing use of prepaid mobile-phone accounts lets some customers who don't have credit make purchases via mobile-payment technology, said Hirson.

Mobile-Payment Applications

Users are currently employing their smartphones primarily to make small purchases, mainly for digital content such as music and videos, although almost any type of purchase is feasible. Vendors recognize this. For example, mobile-platform vendor Bling Nation focuses on businesses that have a high number of small transactions, such as restaurants and convenience stores. Phone-based purchases are also being used for charitable donations. For instance, users rushed to make text-based donations after a massive earthquake struck Haiti in January. Contributors included their cell phone number or user alias and the amount they wanted to give in a text message, and the carrier added the payment to their phone bill.

BOKU

The company launched in 2009 and grew by acquiring mobile-payment vendors Mobillcash and Paymo. BOKU works with local cell phone carriers worldwide. Merchants and publishers in 65 countries use its principal service, called Paymo.

The company focuses on purchases and transactions, primarily for social gaming and virtual goods, not money transfers. When users are ready to purchase a product from a vendor, BOKU sends a text message asking them to authorize the transaction with a texted response. The system makes payments by having purchase amounts added to users' wireless phone bill.

Obopay

"The services we offer can be used for transferring money between people, paying for goods and services, making donations, topping off phone minutes, or paying bills," noted David Schwartz, Obopay's vice president for product and corporate marketing. "We offer this service and technology to partners, which could include financial-services companies, mobile carriers, merchant, or nonprofits," he said. Obopay lets users issue payments via a command or keyword sent to the company by SMS. Users can spend money from a credit or debit card, a bank account, or a prepaid deposit. After entering information about the desired payment, users go to their personal checkout page and enter the source from which they want to make the payment.

Schwartz said the company's technology uses multifactor authentication—such as the use of an authorized phone and a PIN—to secure the payment process.

Obstacles

Mobile-payment services must work on many types of phones and via the networks and billing services of many cellular-service providers, which adds complexity to the transaction process, said Tom Starnes, principal of market research firm Objective Analysis.

Many services address this issue by making their transactions browser based, noted William Stofega, program director for mobile device and technology trends at market research firm IDC.

Mobile-payment application vendors must convince merchants to work with their technologies. Until they can do so, potential customers might not use the services because they wouldn't have many merchants to work with.

And there isn't high interest among all age groups in making mobile payments.

Security

Some technologies used for mobile payments have inherently weak security. For example, SMS is vulnerable to snooping, spoofing, message interception, and social-engineering based bypasses of security measures.

If consumers whose mobile payments are charged to their phone bill lose their handset and someone uses it to make purchases, carriers may force them to pay for the unauthorized charges.

"Laws and regulations governing phone-bill charges may not cover noncommunications-related charges," explained Suzanne Martindale, associate policy analyst with Consumers Union, a consumer-advocacy organization. "You're protected if you find a bogus long-distance calling charge but may not be if you find a bogus charge for a ringtone download." The greatest challenge will be educating users that their mobile device is more than just a phone and can be attacked by fraudsters while not scaring them into never performing mobile transactions, the Yankee Group's Holland said.

Trust and Familiarity

Mobile-payment technology is relatively new and thus unfamiliar to many users accustomed to buying goods and services with cash, checks, or credit cards, Holland noted.

"Credit-card payment systems are widely deployed," said Rob Enderle, principal analyst with the Enderle Group, a market research firm. "The same has not been done for phones, and neither the phones nor the systems that use them are consistent or widely deployed. And people really don't trust their (wireless) carrier that much because of past unplanned charges and fees. Putting more of their money in the hands of that carrier may not be palatable to them."

Other Challenges

Another challenge for mobile-payment providers is convincing major wireless carriers to lower the fees—sometimes 30 to 60 percent—that they charge vendors for each transaction, noted IDC's Stofega.

By making the process more profitable for vendors and merchants, lower fees would enable more of them to participate in the mobile-payment marketplace and increase the revenue for all players, said BOKU's Hirson.

For mobile-payment vendors, creating the right ecosystem of financial, wireless carrier, and merchant partners that can create widely useful, convenient, and lucrative services is another challenge, according to Obopay's Schwartz.

Conclusion

Some investors have poured a significant amount of money into mobile-payment services. For example, Nokia invested $35 million in Obopay. Some top venture capitalists—including Andreessen Horowitz, Benchmark Capital, DAG Ventures, Index Ventures, and Khosla Ventures—have invested a total of about $40 million in BOKU. "Interest and investment by major market innovators like Apple and Google are already creating excitement and buzz in the industry," said Todd Ablowitz, president of Double Diamond Group, a global electronic payments consultancy. "Starbucks recently expanded its mobile payments trial to 300 more stores. This could drive greater innovation and prompt some traditional payments industry players to step off the sidelines." In South Korea, 10 percent of e-commerce transactions are already handled via mobile payments. However, predicted Security Curve's Moyle, there won't be enough consumer or merchant support for widespread adoption in the US for another three to five years.

According to the Consumer Union's Martindale, mobile-payment systems still come with risks that could undercut their convenience and hamper industry growth. Therefore, he explained, any company offering such applications should provide full consumer protections that mirror those in US debit-and credit-card laws, as well as provide assurances that users won't be held liable for purchases fraudulently made by others.

Bling Nation co-CEO Wences Casares said it took years for consumers to adopt credit and debit cards, and now we can't imagine not using them for purchases. He added, "Mobile payments might just be adopted more quickly and in less time."

Words and Expressions

merchant [ˈmɜːtʃənt]	n.	商人；零售商
cellular [ˈseljələ]	adj.	蜂窝式无线通信系统的
sophisticated [səˈfistikeitid]	adj.	老练的；精密的；精通的
spur [spəː]	n.	激励因素，刺激
proliferation [prəuˌlifəˈreiʃən]	n.	增殖；扩散，繁殖
broadband [ˈbrɔːdbænd]	n.	宽带
intervention [ˌintəˈvenʃən]	n.	介入；干涉，干预
automatically [ˌɔːtəˈmætikəli]	adv.	自动地
authenticate [ɔːˈθentiˌkeit]	adj.	证明是真实的或有效的
inherently [inˈhiərəntli]	adv.	天性地，固有地
bypass [ˈbaipɑːs]	vt.	绕过，避开；不顾
problematic [ˌprɔbləˈmætik]	adj.	成问题的；有疑问的；不确定的
buzz [bʌz]	vt. & vi.	发出嗡嗡声；充满兴奋的谈话声（闲话，谣言）
sideline [ˈsaidˌlain]	n.	副业；兼职
hamper [ˈhæmpə]	vt.	妨碍，束缚，限制

Notes

(1) This type of approach, which multiple vendors have implemented, addresses users' concern about having to repeatedly enter identification, account, and payment details on devices with difficult-to-use keyboards. 这种类型的购买途径已经被很多商家采用，它解决了用户对反复使用难以操作的键盘输入进行识别、账户和付款明细的抱怨。

(2) If consumers whose mobile payments are charged to their phone bill lose their handset and someone uses it to make purchases, carriers may force them to pay for the unauthorized charges. 对于那些把移动支付绑定到移动手机账单上的消费者来说，如果丢失了他们的手机，并且有人利用他们的手机进行支付，运营商会让他们支付并非本人所产生的消费。

(3) The greatest challenge will be educating users that their mobile device is more than just a phone and can be attacked by fraudsters while not scaring them into

never performing mobile transactions, the Yankee Group's Holland said. Yankee集团的Holland指出,最大的挑战将会是如何使用户了解他们的移动设备不仅仅是一个电话,并且可能被行骗者攻击,同时还要确保他们不会因为过多的担忧而不敢进行交易。

(4) Therefore, he explained, any company offering such applications should provide full consumer protections that mirror those in US debit-and credit-card laws, as well as provide assurances that users won't be held liable for purchases fraudulently made by others. 因此,他解释说,任何一家提供此类应用的公司都应该提供完整的消费者保障,能够折射出美国借记卡和信用卡的相关法律。此外,当用户因他人欺骗性的操作免于担责也应提供保障。

Questions

(1) What are the problems of early payment?
(2) What are the benefits of mobile payment applications?
(3) Why should we develop mobile payment?
(4) In the development of mobile payment, what challenge the mobile-payment vendor will face?

Exercises

1. Translate the following sentences into Chinese:
(1) M-payments are payments made using mobile handsets and other devices, either to directly purchase or to authorize payment for goods and services.
(2) Mobile payments are a natural evolution e-payment schemes that will facilitate mobile commerce.
(3) Ericsson said mobile payments and person-to-person money transfers are likely to become some of the most-used mobile applications in many countries in the next two or three years.
(4) The m-payment application must be user friendly with little or no learning curve to the customer.
(5) If security concerns can be eradicated, the m-commerce market may finally reach its long-anticipated exponential growth.

2. Translate the following sentences into English:
(1) 移动支付已成为主流技术,电子商务逐渐转向移动商务。
(2) 根据数据调查和分析可以确定,38%的智能手机用户至少使用过一次他们的设备做过网上消费。

（3）Google Wallet 是一个开放的服务平台，它的形成是产业链上下游各厂商合作的结果。

（4）通过 NFC（近场通信）技术，用户就可以通过手机完成支付过程。

（5）尽管移动支付行业未如预期那样迅速发展，但这一行业仍在继续向前推进。

Further Reading

For more information, you can read *Payment Applications Make E-Commerce Mobile*, written by Neal Leavitt, principal of Leavitt Communications, also a contributing editor to a number of technology and interactive marketing publications.

Translation

支付应用使电子商务移动化

因为供应商在用户通过移动设备进行商品或服务的支付应用中看到了一个盈利的机会，所以他们推出了更容易使用的移动支付应用。市场分析公司 Security Curve 首席分析师 Ed Moyle 指出，使用移动设备支付商品、服务、票据或汇款具有许多优势，包括便利性和消费者的易用性，增加了消费者的消费冲动和商家的其他产品或服务的销售，同时给无线服务提供商带来了更高的收入。

然而，以往使用智能手机支付时需要填写表格，并输入信用卡账号，其中大部分使用小的物理性或虚拟键盘，这可能会比较乏味和富有挑战性。Moyle 说，虽然在亚洲和欧洲的一些地区，这种支付途径已经使用多年，但开展移动支付，特别是在发达国家，并没有明显的增长，上面提到的因素便是造成这种情况的原因之一。其他限制因素包括安全方面的挑战和商家参与的缺乏。

不过，现在供应商已开发出可以直接在移动手机上使用，而不需要额外的设备，并且只通过几个按键就可以完成支付的应用程序。

为什么要发展移动支付

移动支付服务开始于 1997 年，诺基亚使得用户能够通过手机短信息服务来进行芬兰自动售货机中的软饮料支付。同年，芬兰 Merita 银行推出首个基于手机的银行服务，同样可以使用 SMS。

然而，由于使用无线设备键盘和屏幕进行复杂的交易程序非常麻烦，加上早期的设备无法进行先进的移动交易应用，早期的移动支付系统只取得了少许的成功。

益处

移动支付可以与用户的信用卡或借记卡、电话账单或预付存款绑定,通过给买家提供无线设备来进行购买活动,可以让他们无论在哪都能进行商品或服务的支付,这给买家提供了极大的方便。更为简单的购买程序,包括当时的购买激励因素,这些都能给商家带来更多的收入。与此同时,移动服务提供商可从买卖双方的网络交易中获得收入。

使能技术

市场研究公司 Yankee 集团的分析师 Nick Holland 指出,智能手机宽带连接的扩散、越来越多的用户采用移动数据服务,以及用户对购买时使用信用卡支付产生的相关费用产生的强烈不满,这些问题都促进了移动支付的应用。

今天的高性能智能手机如苹果的 iPhone、RIM 的黑莓、谷歌的 Android,都能够让用户高效地运行移动支付应用。市场分析公司 Security Curve 的 Moyle 说:"手机现在可以不需要载体的支撑,而直接下载并运行支付应用程序。"

例如,移动支付公司 Zong 的产品和营销副总裁 Hill Ferguson 指出:"Android 系统允许第三方支付程序在它们的应用程序界面上使用。最近推出的 Android SDK 的应用程序,让用户无须输入信用卡信息、用户名或密码就可以进行购买。"这种类型的购买途径已经被很多商家采用,它解决了用户对反复使用难以操作的键盘输入进行识别、账户和付款明细的抱怨。相反地,用户或者可以把购买费用添加到电话费中,从预付账户中扣除;或者使用信用卡账户付款,这账户会自动连接到基于电话的购买中。

推动需求的其他因素

BOKU 的创始人兼产品和营销高级副总裁 Ron Hirson 指出,虚拟商品和社交网络的日益普及推动了移动支付技术的要求。他解释说,比如许多用户在各个地点玩在线游戏,就可以利用手机随时购买虚拟货币以及社交游戏中用到的其他道具。

Hirson 指出,预付手机账户越来越多的使用让一些没有信用卡的客户也通过移动支付技术来进行交易。

移动支付应用

目前,支付应用几乎可以实现所有类型的商品或服务的购买,但用户通常只使用个人智能手机来进行小额的支付,主要是一些数字内容,比如音乐和视频。供应商认识到了这点,例如,移动平台运营商 Bling Nation 把重点放在大量的小额交易业务上,如餐厅和便利店。基于电话的应用也可以被用于慈善机构,例如,海地发生大地震之后,用户纷纷通过电话文本信息进行捐款,一条文本信息的内容包括自己的手机号或用户别名以及他们想捐的数额,承办人则从他们的电话账单中扣除所捐款项。

BOKU

该公司成立于2009年,并通过收购移动支付厂商 Mobillcash 和 Paymo 逐渐壮大。BOKU 同当地的手机运营商合作,有65个国家的厂商和出版商使用其主要服务——Paymo。

该公司专注于采购和交易的支付服务,主要用于社交游戏和虚拟物品,不支持汇款。当用户准备从供应商处购买某种产品,BOKU 发送文字信息,要求他们以短信的形式响应此次交易的授权,这个系统通过将购买金额加到用户的无线手机话费中来进行支付。

Obopay

Obopay 产品和市场营销副总裁 David Schwartz 说:"我们提供的服务可用于人们之间的转账、支付商品或服务、捐款、电话充值或者支付账单。"他说:"提供这项服务和技术的合作伙伴可能包括金融服务公司、移动运营商、商家或者非营利组织。"Obopay 使得用户可以通过移动浏览器发送指令或通过给公司发送短信来发出支付申请,从信用卡或者借记卡、银行账户或预付款项中进行扣除,输入所需的付款信息后,用户页面转到他们个人的结账页面,进入他们想要支付的账单中。

David Schwartz 指出,该公司的支付技术使用了多种因素验证,比如授权手机的使用和个人身份号码(PIN)的验证,以确保支付过程的安全。

障 碍

市场研究公司 Objective Analysis 的负责人 Tom Starnes 表示,移动支付服务必须依赖于多种类型的手机以及通过网络和许多蜂窝服务提供商的计费服务,这就增加了交易过程的复杂性。

市场研究公司 IDC 移动设备和技术发展趋势项目总监 William Stofega 指出,许多服务通过使他们的交易在浏览器上完成,以解决这个问题。

移动支付应用供应商必须说服商家使用他们的技术。直到他们这样去做了,他们的潜在客户也未必会使用这些服务,因为他们不一定能争取到较多数量的商家进行合作。

此外,并不是所有年龄组都对使用移动支付有很大的兴趣。

安全性

移动支付所使用的一些技术本身都存在一些安全性问题。例如,SMS 在窥探、欺骗、消息拦截和基于社会工程的安全措施方面比较欠缺。

对于那些把移动支付绑定到移动手机账单上的消费者来说,如果丢失了他们的手机,并且有人利用他们的手机进行支付,运营商会让他们支付并非本人所产生的费用。

"电话账单收费的法律和法规可能不包括与通信无关的相关费用。"消费者联盟的副政策分析师 Suzanne Martindale 解释说,"如果您发现一个虚假的长途话费,您的利益会受到保护;但如果您账单中产生了一个铃声下载的虚假收费,将不会受到法律法规的保护。"Yankee 集团的 Holland 指出,最大的挑战将会是如何使用户了解他们的移动设备不仅仅是一个电话,并且可能被行骗者攻击,同时还要确保他们不会因为过多的担忧而不敢进行交易。

信任和普及

Holland 指出,移动支付技术是相对较新的技术,对于许多习惯于使用现金、支票或信用卡购买商品或服务的用户来说相对陌生。

"信用卡支付系统正在被广泛部署。"市场研究公司 Enderle 集团的首席分析师 Rob Enderle 说,"同样的部署并没有在手机上体现,无论是手机还是系统都没有得到一致的或广泛的部署。由于过去遇到过计划外的收费和费用等问题,导致人们确实不是如此地信任他们的(无线)载体,所以让他们将更多的钱放在运行商的手中可能是他们无法认同的。"

其他的挑战

IDC 的 Stofega 指出,移动支付的另一个挑战是说服主要的无线运营商降低收费——有时他们甚至从供应商的每笔交易收益中收取 30%至 60%的费用。

BOKU 的 Hirson 指出,通过制定让更多的厂商和商家盈利的过程,降低费用标准,能够使他们更多地参与移动支付市场,并增加所有参与者的收益。

据 Obopay 的 Schwartz 分析,对于移动支付厂商,构建一个包括金融机构、无线运营商、商家合作伙伴在内的合适的生态体系,以提供广泛有用的、便捷的和利润丰厚的服务,是另一个巨大的挑战。

总 结

一些投资者把大量资金投入到移动支付服务中。例如,诺基亚在 Obapay 上投资了 3500 万美元。一些顶级的风险投资商,包括安德森霍格维茨基金、基准资本、DAG 风险投资公司、Index 风险投资公司、Khosla 风险投资公司,在 BOKU 的投资总额约 4000 万美元。"由像苹果和谷歌这样的主要市场创新者所提供的盈利和投资机会已经在行业中引起了兴奋和躁动。"全球电子支付顾问 Double Diamond 集团总裁 Todd Ablowitz 说,"星巴克最近将移动支付门店扩大到 300 多家,这可以促进更大的创新,促使一些传统的支付行业参与者涉足移动支付这一产业中。"在韩国,10%的电子商务交易已经通过移动支付来处理。然而,据 Security Curve 的 Moyle 预测,在美国,再过三至五年,移动支付也不会在足够多的消费者或厂商中普遍使用。

根据消费者协会的 Martindale 分析,移动支付系统仍然面临便利性被削弱和产业增长被阻碍的风险。因此,他解释说,任何一家提供此类应用的公司都应该提供完整的消费者保障,能够折射出美国借记卡和信用卡的相关法律。此外,对用户因他人欺骗性的操作免于担责也应提供保障。

Bling Nation 的联合首席执行官 Wences Casares 说,让消费者习惯采用信用卡和借记卡进行消费花了很多年的时间,现在我们无法想象不使用信息卡和借记卡怎样进行购物。他补充道:"移动支付的普遍使用可能会更迅速并且只须花更短的时间。"

UNIT 9
E-Business Strategy in an Online Banking Services: A Case Study of Citibank

Introduction

Banks today are aware of both the threat and the opportunity that the Web represents. No traditional bank would dare face investment analysts without an Internet strategy. But even a detailed and thoughtful approach to the Web does not guarantee business success. The main purpose behind the launching of online banking services is to provide the customers with an alternative, more responsive and with less expensive options. With options just a click away, customers have more control than ever. They expect real-time answers and superior usability. They also want personal attention and highly customized products and services. The focus of e-business must always be on the customer. On the other hand, the technology and the business structure follow on form of the value you intend to provide to the customer.

This paper evaluates the success of the e-business model and e-business strategy implemented by Citibank in the United Arab Emirates in offering its retail Internet Banking Service; Citibank Online.

Background Information

E-business relies on the development of new business strategies based on networks. The world has become increasingly inter-connected via telecommunication networks and computers. These offer fast, flexible, and cost-effective ways of doing business.

The Internet is driving the new economy by creating unprecedented opportunities for countries, companies and individuals around the world. CEOs worldwide recognize the strategic role that the Internet plays in their company's ability to survive and compete in the future. To be competitive in the Internet economy, companies need to harness the power of the Internet successfully.

Citibank is a subsidiary of Citigroup, a strong financial brand with more than 100 million customers, 5.9 million online relationships and a global reach spanning 100 countries.

Citibank UAE started its retail business in 1987 in a very highly competitive environment offering a comprehensive line of high quality financial services targeted to the affluent and middle income segments. Citibank has been perceived, as at the edge of innovation leveraging its global expertise, it was the first bank in the UAE to introduce innovative e-business solutions like:

(1) CitiPhone—24 hour Phone Banking Service;

(2) ATMs—Automated Teller Machines;

(3) CitiAlert—GSM Notifications Service;

(4) E-Card—Internet Shopping Card;

(5) CitiDirect—Corporate Internet Banking Service;

(6) Citibank Online—Retail Internet Banking Service.

In the year 2000, Citibank had 160,000 retail customers serviced mainly through five branches, six ATMs and CitiPhone. Given the Central Bank restrictions on opening additional branches, being a foreign bank, the banks' e-business strategy was to focus on remote channels of distribution, mainly Internet Banking solutions.

Ms. Sarah Hussain, Web Administrator at Citibank says, "Given the kind of Internet explosion which the market is going through, Internet is the channel of the future, it is critical for Citibank to leverage this channel aggressively and gain an early and dominant leadership."

What encouraged Citibank to proceed with its investment in this direction is the tremendous growth of Internet usage since its introduction in 1996. In an industry that has become increasingly serviced through remote channels, Citibank UAE wanted to leverage on the advanced technology available within Citigroup to stand out, hence Citibank Online was launched in 2000 offering a comprehensive list of services/functionalities.

E-business Strategy

Based on Porter (1980) generic strategies, Citibank opted for a differentiation strategy for its home banking service by offering a superior web banking option with powerful and relevant functionalities wherein customers can access/operate their banking accounts on the net with full confidence and ease.

In the year 2000, there were only four local banks offering simple home banking solutions, Citibank wanted to be the first multinational bank to launch a multifunctional home banking service and own the category before competition becomes fierce in the field.

Unit 9 E-Business Strategy in an Online Banking Services: A Case Study of Citibank

Citibank's mission was to be a leading e-financial services company in the UAE by becoming trusted, premier e-business enabler for its customers.

The objectives of launching Citibank Online were:

(1) Extend its network and overcome the limited branch situation.

(2) Achieve savings in CitiPhone/Branches' operating costs by diverting customers to the Internet. Citibank Online has one of the lowest "costs per interaction" as compared to the ATM, phone banking or branch banking. It contributes immensely as part of the Strategic Cost Management initiatives the bank is implementing without compromising on the quality of service.

According to an online banking report published by Ernst & Young, the transaction costs of the various banking channels are as follows (Table 9-1):

Table 9-1 The Transaction Costs

Branch	$1.07
Call Centre (human)	$0.85
Automated Response System (AVR)	$0.44
Automated Teller Machine	$0.27
Dialup PC banking	1.5 Cent
Internet Banking	1 Cent

(3) Meet the increased consumer demand for quick and secure banking solutions, anywhere, any time on any device; this is important in staying ahead of competition.

(4) Enhance the brand imagery and values in the mind of the customers and the prospects by owning this channel especially that Citibank are seen to be innovative and ahead of most other banks in terms of technology and product development.

(5) Create another arm for deepening customer relationships through cross sell and acquisitions of new customers.

Updated, Table 9-2 shows the list of Citibank Online functionalities covering all Citibanks' products in the UAE.

Table 9-2 Citibank Online Functionalities

Account Information	Balance Summary
	Account details and Activity
	Download Account Activity
Transfers & Payment	Funds transfers within the UAE
	Funds transfers outside the UAE
	Payments
	Payee list
	Standing Instructions
	Demand draft and managers checks

Investments Services	Open a mutual fund account
	Complete a personal Investment worksheet
	Buy mutual funds
	Sell mutual funds
	Switch mutual funds
	View current mutual funds portfolio
	Mutual funds information
Customer Service	Account servicing
	Rate information
	Apply now
Contact Center	Send messages
	Read messages
	Read saved messages
Information Center	Link to the portal

In order to encourage trial and conversion, Citibank reduced the charges for many services if used on Citibank Online as part of its pricing strategy. Citibank addressed the security issues by using the industry level of encryption of 128 bit Secure Socket Layer (SSL) encryption. The bank also uses firewalls to prevent unauthorized access and an automatic "timeout" feature if no activity was detected for a specific time period. The online session is launched by using a password selected by the customer.

E-Business Model

Citibank Online is considered as a standard Business to Consumer approach, the e-business model Citibank is using can be classified as "Merchant". See Table 9-3.

Table 9-3 E-Business Models

Brokerage	Market makers bringing together buyers and sellers and facilitating transactions.
Advertising	A web-advertising model and extension of the traditional media broadcasting model where websites provide content and services and advertising messages.
Merchant	Retailers selling goods directly to buyers (Citibank Online)
Infomediary	Collecting and disseminating information
Manufacturer	Manufacturers using the web to reach buyers directly, eliminating wholesalers and retailers
Subscription	Payment of fees to access information or services.

Without the intervention of the AVR, ATM or CitiPhone Officers, a Citibank customer can access and operate all his relationships with Citibank at a click of mouse in complete privacy. In doing so, Citibank is balancing between security and accessibility of information leveraging on a robust e-banking service available within Citigroup.

The three elements of the business model: value stream, revenue stream and logistics stream are complementing each other in this specific case. Citibank was certainly focusing on adding value to its customers by offering unmatched level of service and security. Its internal logistics were aligned towards a single objective: launching a powerful service to its customers to complement its e-business strategy overall. Revenues after a period of time started flowing too, making the investment worthwhile.

Evaluation of E-Business Strategy and Model

There are many ways of evaluating the success of the e-business strategies and e-business model of Citibank, one of which is looking at the financials for the performance of the service for the past four years. Ms. Sarah Hussain, Web Administrator at Citibank says, "The results of the service represented in the information management system reports covering the performance of Citibank Online of 4 years are very satisfactory and have met the management's expectations."

Citibank Online is proving to be a successful acquisition and revenue-generating channel, despite the fact that the management did not expect any revenues to be generated for the first three years of the launch.

The deployment of the program to Citibank UAE, played a very important role in gaining those revenues, as Citibank UAE did not fund the development work, there were only a couple of adjustments made to the service to suit the UAE requirements.

According to Timmers (1999), there are two dimensions of analyzing the e-business model:

1. The degree of innovation

Citibank is excelling in building and maintaining the competitive advantage in the Internet era, all functionalities offered were well studied and executed in a way where matching them is indeed a difficult task. Flexibility is built in the system for further enhancements and additions.

2. The extent to which the new functions are integrated within the business model

The functionalities added fit perfectly with the e-business strategy and business model opted. They contribute directly towards meeting the objectives.

Conclusion

This paper examined the e-business strategy and e-business model that have been used by Citibank in the UAE in offering its Retail Online Banking Service to its customers. Based on the evaluation, it is very clear that the e-business strategy is complementing the e-business model used.

According to Timmers (1998), a business model in itself does not yet provide understanding of how it will contribute to realize the business mission of the companies. Therefore, it is important to supplement it with the e-business, marketing and sales strategies.

Through Internet solutions, Citibank has maintained its agility and competitive advantage, gaining substantial benefits from them. It is important to note that customers in the Internet economy are well informed and their expectations continue to increase, therefore the ability to respond rapidly to customer demands and deliver value is imperative. At the end, it will continue to be that—"The bet is on the NET!" Ms. Hussain said.

Words and Expressions

harness ['hɑːnis]	vt.	治理,利用,控制
comprehensive [ˌkɔmpri'hensiv]	adj.	广泛的,全面的,综合的
expertise [ˌekspəːˈtiːz]	n.	专业知识或技术;专长
restriction [ri'strikʃən]	n.	限制,约束,规定,局限
aggressively [ə'gresivli]	adv.	侵略地,攻击地
dominant ['dɔminənt]	adj.	占优势的,主导的;占首位的
tremendous [tri'mendəs]	adj.	巨大的,极大的
fairly ['fɛəli]	adv.	完全地;相当,简直
superior [sju(ː)'piəriə]	adj.	优秀的,卓越的
multinational [ˌmʌlti'næʃənl]	adj.	多国的,跨国公司的
category ['kætigəri]	n.	部门;种类,类型
fierce [fiəs]	adj.	激烈的,凶猛的,残酷的
initiative [i'niʃətiv]	adj.	开始的,初步的,创始的
innovative ['inəuveitiv]	adj.	创新的,革新(主义)的
trial ['traiəl]	n.	试验,试用
conversion [kən'vəːʃən]	n.	改变,转变,改变信仰
element ['elimənt]	n.	元素,要素

Unit 9 E-Business Strategy in an Online Banking Services: A Case Study of Citibank

subscription [səbˈskripʃən]	n.	认购,认股;同意
flexibility [ˌfleksəˈbiliti]	n.	适应性,灵活性
complement [ˈkɔmplimənt]	n.	补充,互补
evaluation [iˌvæljuˈeiʃən]	n.	估价,评价,评定
imperative [imˈperətiv]	adj.	必要的,重要的

Notes

(1) "Given the kind of Internet explosion which the market is going through, Internet is the channel of the future, it is critical for Citibank to leverage this channel aggressively and gain an early and dominant leadership". 由于互联网信息爆炸,传统市场正在经历一次变革,互联网是花旗银行未来发展的主要领域,是花旗银行及早获得并且在金融领域占据主导地位的关键所在。

(2) Without the intervention of the AVR, ATM or CitiPhone Officers, a Citibank customer can access and operate all his relationships with Citibank at a click of mouse in complete privacy. In doing so, Citibank is balancing between security and accessibility of information leveraging on a robust e-banking service available within Citigroup. 如果没有花旗银行自动应答系统、自动柜员机和电话客服的干预,银行客户可以访问并且在完全保密的情况下,利用鼠标点击所有他与花旗银行的合作关系。要实现这个目标,花旗银行凭借花旗集团提供的强大的电子银行服务来平衡系统的安全性和信息的可访问性。

(3) Citibank is excelling in building and maintaining the competitive advantage in the Internet era, all functionalities offered were well studied and executed in a way where matching them is indeed a difficult task. 花旗银行善于建立和维护在互联网时代的竞争优势,它所提供的所有的功能都是经过研究然后执行的,要使它们相互匹配是一项非常艰巨的任务。

(4) It is important to note that customers in the Internet economy are well informed and their expectations continue to increase, therefore the ability to respond rapidly to customer demands and deliver value is imperative. 值得注意的是,在互联网经济中客户的消息是很灵通的,他们的期望值持续提升,因此企业需要快速响应客户的需求并提供有价值的服务。

Questions

(1) How many banking channels do the CitiBank have according to this article?

Which banking channel of CitiBank has the lowest transaction costs?

(2) What are the three elements of business model?

(3) How many types do e-business models have?

(4) Which dimensions are generally used to analysis the e-business model according to Timmers?

Exercises

1. Translate the following sentences into Chinese:

(1) Online banking (or Internet banking) allows customers to conduct financial transactions on a secure website operated by their retail or virtual bank, credit union or building society.

(2) Citibank's free online bill payment service lets you pay virtually any business or individual within the United States anytime, at no charge. You can quickly set up one time or recurring payments.

(3) The advent of the Internet and the popularity of personal computers presented both an opportunity and a challenge for the banking industry.

(4) Banks view online banking as a powerful "value added" tool to attract and retain new customers while helping to eliminate costly paper handling and teller interactions in an increasingly competitive banking environment.

(5) Unlike your corner bank, online banking sites never close; they're available 24 hours a day, seven days a week, and they're only a mouse click away.

2. Translate the following sentences into English:

(1) 电子交易过程中必须确认用户、商家及所进行的交易本身是否合法可靠。

(2) 目前各国都将网上银行作为一个新的经济增长点,各银行纷纷开始筹备或已开展网上银行服务。

(3) 电子银行的出现改变了传统银行服务的传递方式、产品推销方式和交易处理方式等一系列银行营销方式。

(4) 网上银行又被称为"3A 银行",因为它不受时间、空间限制,能够在任何时间(Anytime)、任何地点(Anywhere)以任何方式(Anyway)为客户提供金融服务。

(5) 网上银行服务作为一种为客户所提供的差别服务,是树立银行形象、吸引客户、留住客户的一种手段。

Further Reading

This text is selected from *E-Business Strategy in an Online Banking Services: A Case Study*, written by Abdullah S. Al-Mudimigh, Department of Information Systems, College of Computer & Information Sciences, King Saud University, Saudi Arabia.

Translation

在线银行服务电子商务战略：花旗银行的案例研究

简　　介

　　网络资料显示,现在银行面临着电子商务带来的威胁和机遇。假如传统银行没有互联网战略,或者不愿意面对投资分析师的分析结论,那么即使用细致周到的方法连接至网络,也不能保证银行在当今市场成功地生存下来。很多传统银行都推出了网上银行服务,其背后的主要目的是提供给客户一种替代服务,网上银行对客户需求作出的反应更迅速并且其维护价格更低廉。现在客户只要按按鼠标就可选择相应选项,这样客户可以比以前更好地控制交易过程。客户希望网上银行具有实时解答能力及卓越的可用性,他们还希望网上银行能够吸引他们的关注并且为其提供高度个性化的产品和服务。因此,传统银行必须始终把电子商务建设的焦点集中到客户关系管理上。另外,技术和业务结构必须遵循提供给客户的价值形式。

　　本文评估了花旗银行在阿拉伯联合酋长国实施的较为成功的电子商业模式和网上银行服务的电子商务战略,该银行提供了它的零售互联网银行服务以及"在线花旗银行"服务。

背 景 资 料

　　电子商务依赖于以网络为基础的新业务战略的发展。电信网络和计算机之间的连接使得世界联系越来越紧密,这为开展商业活动提供了快速、灵活和低成本高效益的方法。

　　互联网通过创造前所未有的机遇推动全世界的国家、企业和个人发展新经济,全球的首席执行官们已经认识到互联网在提升他们公司的生存能力和未来竞争中所发挥的战略作用。要在网络经济时代获得竞争力,企业必须成功地利用互联网的力量。

　　花旗银行是花旗集团的分支机构,花旗集团是一个拥有1亿多客户,590万在线关系,业务遍及100多个国家的具有全球影响力的强势金融品牌。

　　阿联酋花旗银行于1987年开始在阿联酋这样一个竞争非常激烈的市场开展业务,有针对性地向富裕和中等收入阶层提供高品质的金融服务以及综合性的个人业务。花旗银行一直被视为充分利用其全球性的专业知识推崇创新,该行是在阿联酋第一家引入创新电子商务解决方案的银行,如：

　　(1) CitiPhone——24小时电话银行服务；

　　(2) ATMs——自动取款机；

　　(3) CitiAlert——GSM通知服务；

　　(4) E-Card——网上购物卡；

(5) CitiDirect——企业网上银行服务；

(6) Citibank Online——个人网上银行服务。

在 2000 年，花旗银行有 16 万客户，这些客户主要是通过五个分公司、六部自动柜员机和花旗电话服务零售获得的。鉴于银行总部对增设分支机构的限制，网上银行的解决方案是把电子商务战略的重点放在远程分销的渠道上。

花旗银行网络管理员萨拉·侯赛因女士说："由于互联网信息爆炸，传统市场正在经历一次变革，互联网是花旗银行未来发展的主要领域，是花旗银行及早获得并且在金融领域占据主导地位的关键所在。"

自从 1996 年推出网上银行以来，花旗银行的网络客户大幅度增长，这促使花旗银行继续在这方面进行投资。在这个越来越多地使用远程渠道开展服务的行业中，阿联酋花旗银行希望利用花旗集团的先进技术脱颖而出，因此花旗银行在线于 2000 推出，提供全面的服务或功能列表。

电子商务战略

根据波特(1980)的通用策略，花旗银行的网上银行服务选择了差异化战略，提供卓越的具有强大关联功能的网上银行选项，客户可以充分信任银行，放心地访问或者操作其银行账户。

在 2000 年，只有四家当地银行提供简单的家庭银行解决方案，花旗银行希望成为第一个推出多功能家庭银行服务的跨国银行，在该市场金融服务竞争激烈之前占领属于自己的市场。

花旗银行的使命是通过成为客户值得信赖的、首屈一指的电子商务推动者，打造成阿联酋占据领先地位的电子金融服务公司。

推出在线花旗银行的目标是：

(1) 扩展其网络，并克服分支机构有限的瓶颈。

(2) 通过将客户转移到互联网，节约花旗银行电话客服/分支机构的运行成本。网上银行与自动取款机、电话银行、分行相比，单位互动成本最低，这非常有助于银行在不损害服务质量的前提下实施战略成本管理。

据安永会计师事务所公布的网上银行报告，银行各种渠道的交易成本如下（表9-1）：

表 9-1 交易成本

分支机构	1.07 美元
呼叫中心（人工）	0.85 美元
自动应答系统（AVR）	0.44 美元
自动柜员机（ATM）	0.27 美元
拨号电脑银行	1.5 美分
网上银行	1 美分

(3) 满足消费者对网上银行在任何时间、任何地方和任何设备上，都能快速、安全的要求，这对保持竞争优势非常重要。
(4) 以客户为中心，增强品牌形象和品牌价值，并且拥有这个渠道的前景，特别是花旗银行在创新及产品和技术等渠道都领先于其他大部分银行。
(5) 通过交叉销售和收购客户深化客户关系。

表9-2 显示了在阿联酋网上银行所包含的所有花旗银行的功能。

表9-2 花旗银行网上银行功能

账户信息	余额汇总
	账户的详细信息和活动
	下载账户活动
转移与支付	在阿联酋境内的资金转账
	阿联酋以外的资金转账
	付款
	收款人列表
	常设指示
	即期汇票和管理人员的检查
投资服务	开设一个互惠基金账户
	完成个人投资工作表
	购买互惠基金
	销售互惠基金
	转换互惠基金
	查看当前互惠基金的投资组合
	互惠基金的信息
客户服务	账户服务
	利率信息
	现在申请
联络中心	发送消息
	读取邮件
	读取保存的邮件
信息中心	链接到门户网站

为了鼓励试验和转换，如果将使用网上银行作为定价策略的一部分，花旗银行减少了很多服务的费用。花旗银行运用产业化级别的128位安全套接层（SSL）加密技术进行加密，以解决安全问题。此外，该银行还使用防火墙，以防止未经授权的访问；如果某一特定时间内没有活动，自动"超时"功能会检测到。在线会话的发起使用的是客户选择的密码。

电子商务模式

花旗银行网上银行被看作是一个标准的B2C方式，花旗银行使用的电子商务模式可以被划分为"商人"模式，参见表9-3。

表 9-3　电子商务模式

经纪	市场制造商汇集买方和卖方,促进交易
广告	网络广告模式和传统媒体广播模式的扩展,网站提供内容、服务、广告信息
商人	零售商直接向买家销售商品(在线花旗银行)
信息中介	收集和传播信息
制造商	制造商利用网络直接到达买家,省去了批发商和零售商
认购	支付费用,以获取信息服务

如果没有花旗银行自动应答系统、自动柜员机和电话客服的干预,银行客户可以访问并且在完全保密的情况下,利用鼠标点击所有他与花旗银行的合作关系。要实现这个目标,花旗银行凭借花旗集团提供的强大的电子银行服务来平衡系统的安全性和信息的可访问性。

商业模式的三个要素：价值流、收入流、物流,三者在特定的情形下是相辅相成的。花旗银行侧重于为客户提供增值服务,主要通过提供无与伦比的服务和安全水平。整合企业内部物流以实现一个目标：面向客户推出强大的服务,以配合其整体的电子商务战略。经过一段时间之后,收入开始出现并流转,使得投资物有所值。

电子商务战略和模式评价

有很多用来评价花旗银行电子商务战略和电子商务模式是否成功的方法,检测战略和模式成功与否的一个方法就是查看过去四年的财务状况。花旗银行的网络管理员萨拉·侯赛因女士说："信息管理系统所展现的花旗银行网上银行四年的服务表现是非常令人满意的,符合管理层的期望。"

尽管事实上,花旗银行管理层并没有期望在网上银行推出的前三年获得收益,但是网上银行的确是一个成功的收获和创收的渠道。

阿联酋花旗银行该方案的部署,在取得这些收入上起到了非常重要的作用,因为阿联酋花旗银行没有为开发工作进行投资,所以只有一些经过调整的服务去适应阿联酋用户的需求。

蒂默尔斯(1999)提出电子商务分析有两个维度：

(1)创新程度。

花旗银行善于建立和维护在互联网时代的竞争优势,它所提供的所有的功能都是经过研究然后执行的,要使它们相互匹配是一项非常艰巨的任务。为了进一步增强和补充功能,系统具有很强的灵活性。

(2)商业模式中新功能的集成程度。

新增加的功能非常适合花旗银行所选择的电子商务战略和商业模式,它们有助于直接实现目标。

结　论

　　本文研究了阿联酋花旗银行向客户提供零售在线银行服务所使用的电子商务战略和电子商务模式。根据评估,很显然电子商务战略和电子商务模式是相辅相成的。

　　蒂默尔斯(1998)认为,商业模式本身并不能指导企业实现目标,因此将商业模式与电子商务和市场营销策略结合起来对企业而言至关重要。

　　通过互联网解决方案,花旗银行一直保持其灵活性和竞争优势,并且从中获得了实实在在的收益。值得注意的是,在互联网经济中客户的消息是很灵通的,他们的期望值持续提升,因此企业需要快速响应客户的需求并提供有价值的服务。到最后会演变成"竞争就在网上展开",侯赛因女士如是说。

CHAPTER 3
E-BUSINESS ABOUT ENTERPRISES

企业电子商务

- How SMBs Can Profit from the Internet
- E-Business Strategy Review Report for Tesco.com
- Could My Business be an E-Business
- Integrating E-Business into Your Small Business

UNIT 10 How SMBs Can Profit from the Internet

 Text

    Businesses of every shape and size have moved to the Internet at an unprecedented rate. The majority of small businesses and medium-sized firms moved from Internet-interested to Internet-active in just three years. Almost all medium-sized firms have access to the Internet, as do about three-quarters of PC-owning small businesses. The share increases to more than 80% once a firm grows to 10 employees or more.

    Once on the Internet, small businesses appear ready to take the next step and add a Web presence; in fact, two out of five have already done so. When it comes to e-commerce, however, adoption has not been as fast, with only about one-third of small businesses with their own URL actually selling online (i. e. , taking the order over the Internet or executing over the phone or by mail after the decision to buy was made while online).

    Online SMBs without a Web presence are very interested in taking the next step of promoting themselves actively on the Internet. About one-fifth of online firms expect to develop their own home page in the next 12 months. About one in eight plans to implement an e-commerce solution. Clearly, small businesses have taken the first steps toward e-business by obtaining Internet access.

    Although most SMBs recognize the opportunity in doing more through the Internet, relatively few have made the investment, either financially or philosophically, to incorporate e-business fully. For even the most "hands-on" small business owner, the commitment necessary to make effective use of new technologies may initially seem overwhelming. They may well ask, "Will the investment pay dividends?"

    Sales growth is even more dramatically tied to technology investment. While 29.8% of small businesses indicate that their revenue grew by 10% or more in the past 12 months, 37.9% of small firms with a Web presence report this level of revenue growth. Not surprisingly, more and more small and medium-sized firms are asking the question: What's the best way to capitalize on the opportunities represented by the Internet?

IDC recommends that SMBs stepping up to e-business should think of a four-stage process, with inward or employee-facing components and outward or customer/partner-facing ones that provide escalating benefits with each new stage.

Stage 1: Foundation strategy. The process begins with establishing broadband Internet access. Connecting to the Internet with a permanent, broadband link requires a modest investment in equipment and services, or you can easily outsource to an Internet service provider (ISP). What are the benefits? Employees can more readily gather information on customers, partners, and competitors, and communicate with customers via e-mail. The connection also serves as the foundation for future e-business steps.

Stages 2 and 3: Customer-facing strategy. For the customer-facing process, the second stage involves creating a basic Web presence. The third stage calls for providing new, interactive and personalized services, such as online customer service, order tracking, reservations, product enhancements and promotions, and commerce for customers and partners.

Building a basic Web site with company and product information requires an additional modest investment in Web server, catalog software, and content creation and design services. The payback comes from being able to reach customers beyond the local area and providing customers with easy access to such information as products offered. The Web site also creates the foundation for Stage 3, the delivery of customer services.

Delivering interactive and personalized services via the Web requires investment in database, customer relationship management (CRM), and e-commerce software, as well as in network and server solutions to ensure reliability and redundancy. Benefits include reduced cost of sales and customer service, the ability to handle customer requests on a 7×24 basis, and the forging of closer bonds with customers and partners.

Stages 2 and 3: Employee-facing strategy. For the employee-facing process, the second stage involves creating a corporate intranet, while the third stage calls for developing and deploying enhanced Web-based tools for specific organizations, such as sales, customer service, procurement, and finance.

With a corporate intranet, SMBs can deliver benefits and product and business information to employees through an internal Web portal, eliminating the need for printing and ensuring timely and consistent dissemination of company information at reduced cost. The intranet also provides a more cost-effective way to communicate with remote and mobile employees.

Developing and deploying internal transactional applications encourages greater cross-company collaboration. It also reduces the design, deployment, and training costs for new applications and allows the company to bring new products to market faster and more effectively. Employees feel empowered because they have better tools and more information to handle customer requests.

Stage 4: Full e-business implementation. The fourth and final stage closes the loop on the customer-and employee-facing processes by interconnecting the SMB and partners' Web sites to enable the delivery of a broad array of services, including one-stop shopping, financing, and design services. SMBs benefit by leveraging their partners' sites as new channels for delivering products and services, while customers benefit from the additional value-added services that become available. In addition, leveraging partners' sites allows SMBs to concentrate their investments in core areas of business.

Matching E-Business with Your Goals

Efficiently selling, buying, and accessing resources are critical processes that lie at the heart of small and medium-sized companies' daily business efforts and remain fundamental to long-term success. E-business can serve as an integral and powerful engine to drive these ongoing efforts. However, like all core business improvements, this integration cannot always be achieved instantly. The process needs to be orderly, with incremental changes that are followed through to completion.

The good news? For most SMBs, undertaking limited, clearly defined e-business initiatives, tied to specific business drivers and highest-benefit opportunities, will be more successful and will provide quicker, more tangible results. Stepping up to e-Business generally doesn't require comprehensive reengineering that may take a while to deliver a bottom-line payoff.

As with most business investments, SMBs' goals for technology investment begin with the most basic: meeting fundamental financial objectives. SMBs, regardless of exact size or industry, are remarkably consistent in identifying the most important challenges they must overcome in order to succeed.

IDC asked firms what major issues or concerns they view as the most important—in effect, what were the things they worried most about, or *what kept them up at night*. Customer and staff concerns were consistently cited most frequently by firms in every size category.

Not surprisingly, reaching new customers and working more effectively with current ones are considered crucial issues, as are internal issues, such as attracting and retaining qualified staff.

E-business can deliver more effective operations, both externally and internally, by putting simple but powerful technology and tools behind your core business processes. Externally, e-business solutions help SMBs to meet and exceed customer needs more readily and cost-effectively; internally, e-business solutions help to build staff satisfaction and improve employee skills and productivity.

Significantly, the benefits of technology, rather than the technology itself, are of interest to small and medium-sized firms. That's why e-business holds such potential for SMB competitive advantage in helping improve customer reach and service while enhancing staff effectiveness and satisfaction.

Words and Expressions

unprecedented [ʌn'presiˌdəntid]	adj.	空前的
initially [i'niʃəli]	adv.	最初，开头
overwhelming [ˌəuvə'welmiŋ]	adj.	压倒性的；无法抵抗的
dividend ['dividend]	n.	股息，红利；额外津贴；奖金；年息
indicate ['indikeit]	v.	指出；显示；象征；预示；需要；简要地说明
revenue ['revənjuː]	n.	收入，税收
inward ['inwəd]	adj.	向内的，内在的
outward ['autwəd]	adj.	外面的，外表的，公开的
permanent ['pəːmənənt]	adj.	永久的，持久的
outsource ['autˌsɔːsiŋ]	v.	外购
payback ['peiˌbæk]	v.	回收，偿还
redundancy [ri'dʌndənsi]	n.	冗余
intranet [intrə'net]	n.	企业内部互联网
portal ['pɔːtəl]	n.	入口
timely ['taimli]	adj.	及时的，适时的
dissemination [diˌsemi'neiʃən]	n.	分发
loop [luːp]	n.	环；线（绳）圈；弯曲部分；回路；回线
	vi.	打环；翻筋斗
	vt.	使成环；以圈结；以环连结
tangible ['tændʒəbl]	adj.	切实的
significantly [sigˈnifikəntli]	adv.	意味深长地；值得注目地

Unit 10 How SMBs Can Profit from the Internet

Notes

(1) The text is taken from *Stepping Up to E-Business—How Small/Medium Businesses Can Profit from the Internet*, which is an IDC White Paper. IDC is a division of International Data Group, the world's leading IT media, research, and exposition company. IDC delivers accurate, relevant, and high-impact data and insight on information technology to help organizations make sound business and technology decisions. 本文节选自《一步一步开展电子商务——中小企业怎样才能从互联网获益》一文,这是由国际数据公司(IDC)提供的白皮书。IDC是国际领先的IT媒体、研究和展示公司,它专门提供有关信息技术的精确的、相应的、具有高冲击力的数据和分析报告,以帮助各类组织做出周密的业务和技术决策。

(2) SMBs:Small/Medium Businesses 中小型企业

(3) PC:the abbr. of personal computer 个人计算机

(4) be tied to:依靠,依赖

(5) a broad array of:一系列的

(6) IDC:International Digital Corporation 国际数据公司

Questions

(1) What is the relationship between Internet and e-business in terms of SMBs?

(2) What role does the Stage 1 play in the whole process?

(3) What factors are necessary in delivering interactive and personalized services via the Web?

(4) What does the third stage call for?

(5) Can partners' Web sites help SMBs? And how to help?

Exercises

1. Translate the following sentences into Chinese:

(1) E-business is here to stay because it can accelerate your business success by enabling you to do the things that you've always done, but better, faster, and often at lower cost.

(2) Strengthen the ties between you and your customers by letting you connect with them 24 hours a day.

(3) When it comes to job creation and wealth creation, these are the firms that make it happen.

(4) Relationships are the most important assets of virtually all small and medium-

105

sized companies.

(5) Identifying what information your customers truly want and delivering it quickly, with minimal flash, is a practical, focused response to an e-business requirement, and one that can transform business obstacle into business opportunity.

2. Translate the following sentences into English:
(1) 大多数的中小企业都能够访问互联网。
(2) 电子商务的应用并没有想象的那么迅速,只有约 1/3 的企业真正实现在线销售。
(3) 访问互联网是中小企业迈向电子商务的第一步。
(4) 通过电子商务,员工能够更容易地与客户沟通并收集关于客户、合作伙伴和竞争对手的信息。
(5) 有效地实现销售、采购和获取资源是中小企业日常业务的核心。

Further Reading

You can read the full text of *Stepping Up to E-Business* or you can visit www.IDC.com for more information.

Translation

中小企业如何从互联网中获利

各种规模和形态的企业已经开始以一种前所未有的速度移师互联网。在仅仅三年的时间里,大部分中小企业已从对互联网感兴趣转变为积极参与。几乎所有的中型企业都接入了互联网,3/4 拥有 PC 机的小型企业也能够访问互联网。一旦企业拥有 10 个或者更多员工,这一比率就将超过 80%。

小型企业一旦接入互联网就准备采用下一步措施并且增加网络发布;实际上,2/5 的企业已经这样做了。但是,当应用于电子商务时,其应用并没有如此迅速,只有约 1/3 拥有自己网址(URL)的小型企业才能真正地做到在线销售(即在网上订购或在网上做出购买决定后,通过电话或电子邮件实现交易)。

没有网络发布的在线中小企业对在互联网上采取下一步措施积极地宣传自己非常感兴趣。约 1/5 的在线企业期望能够在未来的 12 个月中开发他们自己的主页。约 1/8 的企业计划实施电子商务解决方案。很显然,小型企业已经通过接入互联网向电子商务迈出了第一步。

虽然绝大多数的中小企业意识到通过互联网可以有机会做很多事情,但很少有企业在资金上或理念上作出部署以全面发展电子商务。甚至对大多数即使已经亲身实践的小企业主而言，在最初的时候对有效利用新技术的必要的承诺也是十分关注的。他们可能会适当地问："投资有分红吗？"

与技术投资联系起来，销售增长更明显。在有 29.8%的小企业表明在过去的 12 个月中他们的收入增长了 10%或更多的同时，37.9%的拥有网络发布的小企业报道了同样的收入增长水平。不足为奇的是，越来越多的中小企业在问这样一个问题：利用互联网所带来的机会的最好的获利方法是什么？

国际数据公司(IDC)建议正在发展电子商务的中小企业应该考虑一个由内部面向员工的和外部面向客户/合作伙伴组成的四阶段过程，其中每一个新的阶段都将带来逐步增长的利润。

阶段 1：基础战略

该过程始于建立宽带互联网的接入。通过宽带接入与互联网建立永久性联系需要对设备和服务进行最适度的投资，或者你能够很轻松地将其外包给网络服务供应商(ISP)。好处是什么？员工能够更容易地收集关于客户、合作伙伴和竞争对手的信息并通过 E-mail 与客户沟通。这种连接也是未来电子商务实施的基础。

阶段 2 和阶段 3：面向客户战略

对于面向客户的过程而言，第 2 阶段涉及建立一个基本的网络发布。第 3 阶段要求提供新的、交互的、个性化的服务，如在线客户服务、订单跟踪、接受预订、产品升级和促销，以及与客户和合作伙伴的商务往来。

建立一个拥有公司和产品信息的基础网站需要对网络服务器、产品目录软件、内容创新和设计服务进行额外的适度投资。其回报来自于能够接触到外地客户，并且客户能够很容易地了解诸如有关所提供产品的信息。网站也是为第 3 阶段传递客户服务打好基础。

通过网络传递交互的和个性化的服务需要对数据库、客户关系管理(CRM)、电子商务软件以及网络和服务器解决方案进行投资，以确保可靠性和冗余度。其好处包括降低销售成本和客户服务成本、有能力在每周 7 天每天 24 小时的基础上处理客户需求以及与客户和合作伙伴建立更紧密的关系。

阶段 2 和阶段 3：面向员工的战略

就面向员工的流程而言，第 2 阶段包括建立一个公司内部网，同时第 3 阶段需要为专门的机构(如销售、客户服务、采购和财务等方面)开发和配置更强的网络工具。

中小企业在拥有公司内部网后能够通过内部的网络门户向员工传递利益、产品和商务信息，减少印刷文件并能够确保以更低的成本及时、始终一致地发布公司信息。内部网也为与远程和移动员工的沟通提供了一个更具成本效率优势的方法。

开发和配置内部交易应用促进了更广泛的跨公司内部的合作，同时也减少了新应用技术的设计、配置和培训费用，并且使得企业能够更加快速和有效地将新产品投放市场。员工们会觉得自己更有能力了,因为他们拥有更好的工具和更多的信息来处理客户需求。

阶段 4:全面的电子商务实施

第 4 即最后阶段通过能够提供包括一站式购物、财务和设计服务等的一系列服务,相互连接中小企业和合作伙伴的网站,最终将其连接成一个面向顾客和员工的流程环。中小企业得益于利用合作伙伴的网站作为传递其产品和服务的新渠道,而客户则从可实现的额外的增值服务中获利。此外,借助合作伙伴的网站可以使中小企业将其投资集中在其核心业务上。

让电子商务配合你实现目标

有效地销售、采购和获取资源是关键的流程,占据了中小企业日常经营活动的核心地位,也是企业取得长期成功的根基所在。电子商务可以作为必不可少的强有力的发动机来推进这些持续进行的努力。但是,与所有核心业务的改进一样,这样的集成不可能立竿见影,它需要一个有序的、由潜移默化的变化而逐步走向完善的过程。

这是一个好消息吗?对大多数中小企业而言,承担有限的、清晰定义的电子商务计划,并与特定的商业动机和最高利益机会结合起来,将会更加成功,而且将产生更快、更可行的结果。一般情况下,开展电子商务不需要花很长时间进行注重实际回报的广泛的重组。

与大多数商业投资一样,中小企业的技术投资目标的最基本的着眼点是:满足根本的财务目的。不管是什么规模或行业的中小企业,都应该清晰地、始终如一地认识到为了获得成功所必须应对的最重要的挑战。

IDC 询问过许多中小企业主,什么是他们认为最重要的问题或关注点——实际上就是他们最担心的事情或者是那些让他们夜不能寐的问题。客户和员工所关注的问题经常被各种类型和规模的企业所提及。

毫不奇怪,获取新的客户并且为现有的客户更有效地工作,与诸如吸引并保留称职员工等内部问题同等重要。

电子商务通过在核心业务流程中利用简单却强有力的技术和工具在其内部与外部实现高效运行。就外部而言,电子商务解决方案帮助中小企业以更敏捷的反应和更低的成本满足和超越客户的需求;就内部而言,它能够帮助建立员工满意度、提高雇员的技能和生产率。

意义深远的是,技术的价值比技术本身更能引起中小企业的兴趣。这就是为什么电子商务在帮助中小企业提升客户接触面和服务以及提高员工效率和满意度等方面保持潜在的竞争优势的原因所在。

UNIT 11

E-Business Strategy Review Report for Tesco.com

Tesco is currently the UK's largest supermarket chain and the market leading food retailer in the country with the core purpose to create value for customers and thus earn their loyalty. It is the largest British retailer by both global sales and domestic market share, with profits exceeding £3 billion, and the third largest global retailer based on revenue, behind Wal-Mart and Carrefour.

Tesco have branded themselves as selling to everyone and therefore offer a range of products and services from Value to Finest prices thus appealing to all segments of the market.

Technological factors which have perhaps had the most impact on Tesco has been the growth in the use of the internet. They have capitalized on the use of online shopping and provide a delivery service through their website at www.tesco.com.

Tesco focused on the individuals. To gain loyal customers, customers must be at the center of your CRM strategy (as well as the focus of the business itself). It's not the technology, not customer profitability, not loyalty programs or cards; it's the customers themselves—as individuals—that should truly be at the center of all that you do.

Tesco.com considers that customers are at the very heart of their business and they believe that they should come first with the Competition Commission too. Customers value any time savings of not having to drive to the store, do the manual labor of picking out the groceries, stand in line to pay for them, drive home and unload the car. Customers do, however, usually enjoy the opportunity to touch and feel the fresh produce and to make "impulse buys". Here's how Tesco's team worked to streamline the customer's shopping scenario while maintaining the attributes that customer's value: getting the quality, the assortment, and the prices they want.

In a rapidly changing business environment with a high competitors' pressure Tesco have to adopt new expansion strategies or diversified the existing in order to sustain its leading market position in an already established retailing market. The company must constantly adapt to the fast changing circumstances. Strategy formulation should therefore be regarded as a process of continuous learning, which includes learning about the goals, the effect of possible actions towards these goals and how to implement and execute these actions. The quality of a formulated strategy and the speed of its implementation will therefore directly depend on the quality of Tesco's cognitive and behavioral learning processes.

The figures in the table below (Table 11-1) include 52 weeks/12 months of turnover for both sides of the business as this provides the best comparative.

Table 11-1 Financial Performance

Year	Turnover (£m)	Profit before tax (£m)	Profit for year (£m)	Basic earnings per share (p)
2010	62,500	3,200	—	29.02
2009	54,300	3,128	3,090	28.92
2008	47,298	2,803	2,130	26.95
2007	46,600	2,653	1,899	22.36
2006	38,300	2,210	1,576	19.70
2005	33,974	1,962	1,366	17.44

As of its 2006 year end Tesco was the fourth largest retailer in the world behind Wal-Mart, Carrefour and Home Depot. Tesco moved ahead of Home Depot during 2007, following the sale of Home Depot's professional supply division and a decline in the value of the U.S. dollar against the British Pound. Metro was only just behind and might move ahead again if the euro strengthens against the pound, but Metro's sales include many billions of wholesale turnover, and its retail turnover is much less than Tesco's.

Tesco Products and Services Offered

Things you can buy from Tesco's online shop include the following:

- Tesco Extra—Books, Videos, DVDs to rent, CDs, Gas and Electricity.
- Tesco Finance—Credit cards, Mortgages, Loans, Savings.
- Tesco Groceries—Healthcare, Cooking Ingredients, Fresh Fruit, Garden, Toiletries.
- Tesco Insurance—Breakdown insurance, Pet insurance, Home insurance, Life insurance, Car insurance.
- Tesco Telecoms—Dial up internet access, Broadband, Tesco mobile value SIM, Tesco mobile network, Mobile phones.

Situational Analysis

Tesco is the giant of all supermarkets due to its UK dominance. Three main rea-

sons have been identified for this:
(1) Tesco's are everywhere;
(2) sell to everyone;
(3) sell everything.

Due to the nature of the Tesco organization with particular reference to how it has branded and marketed itself, and the current economic climate, the assessment of external factors by a PESTLE analysis has been crucial in Tesco's success. This is because Tesco has taken into account the implications for consumers, employees, stakeholders, associated organizations and the company's mission statement. Each external factor would have been and continues to be examined and categorized in terms of whether its implication is negative or positive, large or minor significance, intermittent or continuous impact and so on.

PESTLE Analysis Factors Examined

Politically, the credit crunch may lead to higher numbers of unemployment. As one of the largest and fastest growing retailers more jobs will be available with Tesco therefore helping to reduce the levels of unemployment. A PESTLE analysis is therefore useful in keeping Tesco up to date with their environmental surroundings, for example, realizing in advance that we were heading for a recession would have helped them to plan ahead.

Whilst one of Tesco's competitive advantages at present relates to their overwhelming physical presence, there are issues about Tesco driving out the competition from other retailers. There are policies as well as laws and regulations governing monopolies and competition which would be identified though a PESTLE analysis. This is potentially one of the main issues that Tesco's are faced with. Protecting consumers and ensuring that entrepreneurs have the opportunity to compete in the market economy are important within consumer law. Due to the current state of the economy, many small businesses are failing and many unable to enter the market. A PESTLE analysis helps to assess where location wise there is a demand for expansion. The situation is in no way being assisted by the ever expanding Tesco's chains of store. Under EU law, there is presumption that an organization with a large market share is dominant. The concerns with this are that quality of products and services will slip and there is a risk of paying higher prices. Tesco to date has not been assessed as posing a risk of exploitation but should bear this in mind. This is the reason why regular or continuous scans making use of the PESTLE analysis will lead to continuous assessments which can ensure that Tesco's dominance is not in any way exploitative.

In addition, planning permission is an issue that Tesco seriously need to be aware of due to their continued expansion. Planning permission is heavily regulated in the UK. A thorough PESTLE analysis would help to identify the relevant laws on planning permission and whether any resistance to planning was on lawful grounds or merely local people's dissent. The PESTLE analysis would therefore initially assess the potential success of a store in a new area.

With the economy being as it is at present, Tesco are fortunate that they have not been as badly affected as some retailers by the recession. Tesco have branded themselves as selling to everyone and therefore offer a range of products and services from Value to Finest prices thus appealing to all segments of the market.

The Sociological aspect of the PESTLE analysis involves considerations such as the increase in immigration of Eastern Europeans or increase in young professionals. Naturally there is therefore a demand for new goods, for example, the career minded professional who is a single person. This has seen a rise in the meals for one or quick microwaveable meals to make cooking quick and easy for those always on the go.

Technological factors which have perhaps had the most impact on Tesco has been the growth in the use of the internet. They have capitalized on the use of online shopping and provide a delivery service through their website at www.tesco.com.

Tesco's are also instrumental as a retailer in supporting carbon reductions and have created a £100 million Sustainable Technology Fund for this purpose. They also encourage their customers to make low carbon choices. Yet if Tesco's did not take their corporate responsibilities seriously in relation to environmental issues it could have dire consequences for Tesco's reputation.

A PESTLE analysis is therefore vital to the development and the success of Tesco's in addition to the day to day management of each store in line with strategic decisions. Without knowing what external factors affect the organization, it is difficult to manage the business in an efficient manner.

Industry Analysis: Porter's Five Forces

Threat of New Entrants

The UK grocery market is primary dominated by few competitors, including four major brands of Tesco, Asda, Sainsbury's and Safeway that possess a market share of 70% and small chains of Somerfield, Waitrose and Budgens with a further 10%. Over the last 30 years, according to Ritz (2005), the grocery market has been transformed into the supermarket-dominated business. Majority of large chains have built their power due to operating efficiency, one-stop shopping and major marketing-mix expenditure. This powerful force had a great impact on the small traditional shops, such as butchers, bakers and etc. Hence, nowadays it possesses a strong barrier for new companies who desire to enter the grocery market. For instance, it becomes rather difficult for new entrants to raise sufficient capital because of large fixed costs and highly developed supply chains. This is also evident in huge investments done by large chains, such as Tesco, in advanced technology for checkouts and stock control systems that impact new entrants and the existing ones. Other barriers include economies of scale and differentiation (in the provision of products or services with a higher perceived value than the competition) achieved by Tesco and Asda seen in their aggressive operational tactics in product development, promotional activity and better distribution.

Bargaining Power of Suppliers

This force represents the power of suppliers that can be influenced by major grocery chains and that fear of losing their business to the large supermarkets. Therefore, this consolidates further leading positions of stores like Tesco and Asda in negotiating better promotional prices from suppliers that small individual chains are unable to match. UK based suppliers are also threatened by the growing ability of large retailers to source their products from abroad at cheaper deals. The relationship with sellers can have similar effects in constraining the strategic freedom of the company and in influencing its margins. The forces of competitive rivalry have reduced the profit margins for supermarket chains and suppliers.

Bargaining Power of Customers

Porter theorized that the more products that become standardized or undifferentiated, the lower the switching cost, and hence, more power is yielded to buyers. Tesco's famous loyalty card-Club card remains the most successful customer retention strategy that significantly increases the profitability of Tesco's business. In meeting customer needs, customizing service ensure low prices, better choices, constant flow of in-store promotions enables brands like Tesco to control and retain their customer base. In recent years a crucial change in food retailing has occurred due to a large demand of consumers doing the majority of their shopping in supermarkets that shows a greater need for supermarkets to sell non-food items. It has also provided supermarkets with a new strategic expansion into new markets of banking, pharmacies, etc. Consumers also have become more aware of the issues surrounding fairer trade and the influence of western consumers on the expectations and aspirations of Third World producers. Ecologically benign and ethically sound production of consumer produce such as tea, coffee and cocoa is viable, and such products are now widely available at the majority of large chains.

Threat of Substitutes

General substitution is able to reduce demand for a particular product, as there is a threat of consumers switching to the alternatives Porter M. In the grocery industry this can be seen in the form of product-for-product or the substitute of need and is further weakened by new trends, such as the way small chains of convenience stores are emerging in the industry. In this case Tesco, Asda and Sainsbury's are trying to acquire existing small-scale operations and opening Metro and Express stores in local towns and city centers.

Bargaining Power of Competitors

The grocery environment has seen a very significant growth in the size and market dominance of the larger players, with greater store size, increased retailer concentration, and the utilization of a range of formats, which are now prominent characteristics of the sector. As it was mentioned above, the purchasing power of the food-retailing industry is concentrated in the hands of a relatively small number of retail buyers. Operating in a mature, flat market where growth is difficult (a driver of the diversification into non-food areas), and consumers are increasingly demanding and sophisticated, large chains as Tesco are accruing large amounts of consumer information that can be used to communicate with the consumer. This highly competitive market has fostered an accelerated level of development, resulting in a situation in which UK grocery retailers have had to be innovative to maintain and build market share. Such innovation can be seen in the development of a range of trading formats, in response to changes in consumer behavior. The dominant market leaders have responded by refocusing on price and value, whilst reinforcing the added value elements of their service.

E-Business Strategy

Tesco-Internet Operations

Tesco has operated on the internet in the UK since 1994 and was the first retailer in the world to offer a robust home shopping service in 1996. Tesco also has Internet operations in the Republic of Ireland and South Korea. Grocery sales are available within delivery range of selected stores, goods being hand-picked within each store. This model, in contrast to the warehouse model initially followed by UK competitor Sainsbury, and still followed by UK internet only supermarket Ocado, allowed rapid expansion with limited investment, but has been criticized by some customers for a high level of substitutions arising from variable stock levels in stores. Nevertheless, it has been popular and is the largest online grocery service in the world.

In 2001 Tesco invested in GroceryWorks, a joint venture with Safeway in the United States, operating in the United States and Canada. GroceryWorks has stepped into the void left by the collapse of Webvan, but has not expanded as fast as initially expected.

Concerned with poor web response times (at the time of its launch in 1996, broadband was virtually unknown in the UK), Tesco offered a CDROM-based offline ordering program which would connect only to download stock lists and send orders. This was in addition to, rather than instead of, ordering via web forms, but was withdrawn in 2000.

Tesco.com currently has 850,000 customers worldwide. More than 250,000 online orders are completed each week, with up to 5,000 orders placed per hour during peak business periods.

The Tesco.com site is also used as a general portal to most of Tesco's products, including various non-food ranges (under the "Extra" banner), Tesco Personal Finance and the telecoms businesses, as well as extra services which it offers in partnership with specialist companies, such as flights and holidays, music downloads, gas, electricity and DVD rentals. It does not currently sell clothing online. In May 2005 it introduced a clothing website, but initially at least this serves solely as a showcase for Tesco's clothing brands, and customers still have to visit a store to buy.

Tesco & CRM (*Customer Relationship Management*)

Tesco focused on the individuals. To gain loyal customers, customers must be at the center of your CRM strategy (as well as the focus of the business itself). It's not the technology, not customer profitability, not loyalty programs or cards; it's the customers themselves—as individuals—that should truly be at the center of all that you do.

The fact is that CRM is difficult to define. It's somewhat misunderstood, largely misused, and in some cases abused... often by the very people who strive to define it.

The one thing we can all agree on is that the focus is on the customer. Unfortunately, people often put too much emphasis on the components (such as the technology) of CRM instead of the basis (the customer). Once this customer-centric vision has truly been established, the individual customer can truly begin to be understood and valued, and loyalty can be earned.

Usually U.S. based businesses focus their CRM programs too heavily on the communication; the "how and what do I communicate" portion of their CRM strategy. Instead, Tesco proposed that more time be spent using CRM towards strategic business decisions. While the communication or "who-what-how-when" strategy is undoubtedly a very important component, Tesco made sure they spend as much time thinking about the business decisions that should come out of CRM as they do about the communication and messages themselves.

Once a loyalty program is established, a company can move from old performance reporting to building a basic customer language to using the language to gain a detailed customer understanding.

If CRM is approached correctly and applied effectively, marketing spend can often be reduced—an outcome the entire organization can benefit from and appreciate. For Tesco, the media effectiveness of the Club Card Program has allowed them to save money on promotions and increase sales at the same time.

Tesco's ensured that:
- Becomes a part of the company's culture
- Solves real problems, not just those associated with your marketing strategy
- Is not there "just for data's sake"

The secret of Tesco's CRM is taking insights to change the way you think about your customers and your business; to move away from averages and towards customers as individuals.

CRM to Support to Its E-business Strategies

With Tesco's focus on technology, and the launching of company's highly successful loyalty card in 1995, it enabled Tesco to develop extensive knowledge of its customer base and to segment customers according to purchases, location, and life stage.

Armed with this information, Tesco has carefully tailored its offerings to customers: vegetarians are never sent special offers on meat products and children's products are not sent to childfree shoppers. Moreover, Tesco's money-off coupon program encourages customers to try related, higher-priced products, not just receive discounts on goods they routinely purchase.

Tesco further adapted its business processes and added technology for a second innovation-online shopping. By thinking through the customer experience every step of the way, Tesco established the gold standard for UK online supermarket shopping with its repeat order functions and lists of favorites and previous purchases. A delivery time slot is selected before orders are made to limit the inconvenience of waiting around for orders, and customers can give Tesco staff discretion to replace list items with alternatives should their first choice be out of stock. Tesco is now the world's largest online grocer.

Tesco.com Customer Value Delivery

Excellent service, which satisfies the customers and meets the strategic intentions of the organization—is usually the result of careful design and delivery of a whole set of interrelated processes. Tesco.com considers that customers are at the very heart of their business and they believe that they should come first with the Competition Commission too.

Early customers of Tesco can find the products via Internet they couldn't find in their local store. This would save the searching time and efforts for them. For the people who are familiar with the home shopping over the Internet and the single professional, a £5 delivery fee is well worth the time savings if not shopping themselves. In the same way, the people with small children will purchase the products from Tesco.com as well because it set their hearts at rest instead which is more worth than £5 delivery fee.

Legal & Ethical Issues

Like a number of leading companies, Tesco attracts criticism from those who are suspicious of big business. Tesco is a target for people in the UK who disapprove of large retailers and the effects they can have on farmers, suppliers and smaller competitors.

The group has also been criticized for its tactics, including allegedly misleading consumers with a "phoney" price war.

Tesco's 2004 Adminstore acquisition led to local and national protests. Tesco's other store openings and expansions are sometimes contested by campaign groups. These campaigns have not hindered Tesco's expansion programme very much.

Another point of controversy is the recent expansion of Tesco into the convenience store market. When a company controls more than 25% of a business sector in the UK, it is usually blocked from buying other companies in that sector (but not from increasing its market share through organic growth). The Office of Fair Trading currently treats supermarkets and convenience stores as two distinct sectors—although this definition has been challenged by smaller retailers, including the Association of Convenience Stores.

Tesco is also criticized by those who think that it infringes upon the interests of farmers and smaller suppliers. The company responds by claiming that it follows industry—best practice and sources locally where it can to meet customer demand. In March 2005 the Office of Fair Trading published an audit of the workings of its code of practice on relationships between supermarkets and their suppliers. It reported that no official complaints had been received against Tesco or any of the other major supermarkets, but the supermarkets' critics, including Friends of the Earth, contested that suppliers were prevented from complaining by fear of losing business, and called for more rigorous supervision of the supermarkets. A further report by the Office of Fair Trading in August 2005 concluded that the aims of the Code of Practice were being met.

In May 2004, Tesco announced it was reducing sick pay in an attempt to reduce levels of unplanned absence, which however implies that workers may be forced to work whilst setting their personal health to risk for fear of a decrease in their income. In December 2005, a committee of UK MPs produced a report accusing Tesco of "riding roughshod over planning rules". The accusation stemmed from the company's building of a store in Stockport that was 20% larger than the company actually had permission to build.

Conclusion

The success of the Tesco shows how far the branding and effective service delivery can come in moving beyond splashing one's logo on a billboard. It had fostered powerful identities by making their retiling concept into a virus and spending it out into the culture via a variety of channels: cultural sponsorship, political controversy, consumer experience and brand extensions.

In large organizations as Tesco strategy should be analyzed and implemented at various levels within the hierarchy. These different levels of strategy should be related and mutually supporting. Tesco's strategy at a corporate level defines the businesses in which Tesco will compete, in a way that focuses resources to convert distinctive competence into competitive advantage.

Words and Expressions

currently [ˈkʌrəntli]	adv.	目前,现在
domestic [dəˈmestik]	adj.	国内的
individual [ˌindiˈvidjuəl]	adj.	个人的,个体的
rapidly [ˈræpidli]	adv.	很快地,迅速地
implement [ˈimplimənt]	vt.	履行,实施,执行
behavioral [biˈheivjərəl]	adj.	行为的;行为方面的
positive [ˈpɔzitiv]	adj.	确定的,确信的
surroundings [səˈraundiŋz]	n.	环境,周围的事物
competitive [kəmˈpetitiv]	adj.	竞争激励的;具有竞争力的
overwhelming [ˌəuvəˈhwelmiŋ]	adj.	压倒的,势不可挡的
concern [kənˈsə:n]	vt.	关于;涉及,影响到
consequence [ˈkɔnsikwəns]	n.	结果,后果
efficient [iˈfiʃənt]	adj.	效率高的,高效的
aggressive [əˈgresiv]	adj.	侵略的,有进取精神的

expectation [ˌekspekˈteiʃən]	n.	期待,预期
established [isˈtæbliʃt]	adj.	已建立的,已确立的
adapted [əˈdæptid]	adj.	适应的,适合的
criticize [ˈkritisaiz]	vt./vi.	批评,批判;评论,评价

Notes

(1) In a rapidly changing business environment with a high competitors' pressure Tesco have to adopt new expansion strategies or diversified the existing in order to sustain its leading market position in an already established retailing market. 在瞬息万变的商业环境中和竞争对手的压力下,特易购不得不采取新的扩张战略或者使现有的服务更加多元化,以维持其已经在零售市场确立的领先地位。

(2) Due to the nature of the Tesco organization with particular reference to how it has branded and marketed itself, and the current economic climate, the assessment of external factors by a PESTLE analysis has been crucial in Tesco's success. 由于特易购组织推广自身的品牌和产品的特征,以及当前的经济环境和 PESTLE 分析法对其外部因素进行的详尽评估,促使了特易购的成功。

(3) Porter theorized that the more products that become standardized or undifferentiated, the lower the switching cost, and hence, more power is yielded to buyers. 波特理论说明,产品越是标准化、无差别,其转化成本越低,因此,买家越易获取主动权。

(4) Concerned with poor web response times (at the time of its launch in 1996, broadband was virtually unknown in the UK), Tesco offered a CDROM-based offline ordering program which would connect only to download stock lists and send orders. This was in addition to, rather than instead of, ordering via web forms, but was withdrawn in 2000. 考虑到网页反应时间太久(1996 年推出网上超市的时候,宽带在英国几乎还不为人所知),特易购推出了以 CDROM 为基础的离线订购计划,它只连接到已下载的货物清单和发货订单。这是网页订购的附加功能,而不是替代功能,但是这种服务已在 2000 年撤销。

(5) Here's how Tesco's team worked to streamline the customer's shopping scenario while maintaining the attributes that customers value: getting the quality, the assortment, and the prices they want. 这里阐释了特易购团队是如何运作的,以简化顾客购物场景,同时保持客户价值属性,包括获得质量、品种和他们期望的价格。

Questions

(1) What is PESTLE Analysis?

(2) Which aspect will Porter Model force on?

(3) What is Tesco's customer relationship management purpose?

Exercises

1. Translate the following sentences into Chinese:

(1) Technology allows the identification and tracking of individual consumers, both within an online store and across different websites.

(2) Customization can be based on a set of preferences specified directly by consumer, or more subtly, the features of the customized product might be deduced automatically.

(3) As a starting point, online retailers can increase the number of product offerings and the information provided about each product, because they are not constrained by physical shelf space.

(4) They may also vary across time: In the short run, benefits may be captured by the sellers who are early movers on retail e-commerce, but after a time, those benefits will likely be eroded by competition.

(5) The integration of CRM and B2B will benefit all related parties in business processes, including sales, marketing, customer service, and information support.

2. Translate the following sentences into English:

(1) 零售业电子商务又称网上零售是指个人通过 Internet 购买商品或享受服务。

(2) 沃尔玛网络零售业务发展的经历,对其他企业网络零售很有借鉴价值。

(3) 特易购是较早采用在线销售模式的连锁商店之一。

(4) 企业必须将实施电子商务看做是客户关系管理整体战略的首要部分。

(5) 在电子商务发展时代,有效实施客户关系管理是企业保持旺盛生命力的强劲动力。

Further Reading

For further information, you can read *E-Business Strategy Review Report for Tesco.com*, prepared by Hussain Sajjad.

特易购^①网电子商务战略评估报告

　　特易购是英国目前最大的连锁超市和在国内市场领先的食品零售商,以为客户创造价值为核心目的,从而赢得了客户的忠诚度。无论从全国销售还是国内市场占有率来看,特易购都是英国最大的零售商,每年创造超过 30 亿英镑的利润;从营业额来看,它是全球第三大零售商,仅次于沃尔玛和家乐福。

　　特易购有自己的品牌,并以合理的价格、精致的品质提供一系列产品和服务,从而吸引各个细分市场的客户。

　　特易购最具影响力的技术因素,已经通过互联网的使用取得了增长。他们对利用 www.tesco.com 网站实现网上购物服务和提供送货服务进行了相应的投资。

　　特易购十分关注客户,为了获得忠诚的客户,特易购将客户作为客户关系管理战略的中心(这也是企业本身的重点)。它关注的不是技术,不是客户盈利能力,也不是客户忠诚度计划或发的卡,而是客户本身——客户应该真正成为你所做的一切的中心。

　　特易购网将客户看做是其业务的核心,他们相信应将客户与竞争管理委员会一起放到首要的位置。网站对客户的价值在于可以节省很多时间,不用开车去商场或者花费体力挑选,也不用排队付款或者取车、开车回家。但是,客户通常在享有机会接触和感受鲜活的农产品时,便会"冲动购买"。这里阐释了特易购团队是如何运作的,以简化顾客购物场景,同时保持客户价值属性,包括获得顾客期望的质量、品种和价格。

　　在瞬息万变的商业环境中和竞争对手的压力下,特易购不得不采取新的扩张战略或者使现有的服务更加多元化,以维持其已经在零售市场确立的领先地位。企业必须不断适应瞬息万变的情况,因此战略的制定被看做是一个不断学习的过程,其中包括目标的学习,了解这些目标可能带来的影响,学习如何落实并执行这些行动。因此,制定战略的质量和实施战略的速度直接取决于特易购认知和行为的学习过程。

　　下表(表 11-1)是 52 周/12 个月的营业额数据,对业务的发展情况作了很好的比较。

表 11-1　财务状况

年份	营业额 (百万英镑)	税前利润 (百万英镑)	年利润 (百万英镑)	每股基本收益 (英镑)
2010	62,500	3,200	—	29.02
2009	54,300	3,128	3,090	28.92
2008	47,298	2,803	2,130	26.95
2007	46,600	2,653	1,899	22.36
2006	38,300	2,210	1,576	19.70
2005	33,974	1,962	1,366	17.44

---

① "特易购"系"Tesco"的音译,常译为"乐购",例如 Tesco 在中国所开的超级市场名为"乐购"。

到2006年年底，特易购成为全球第四大零售商，仅次于沃尔玛、家乐福、家得宝。由于家得宝专业销售部门的销售额下降以及美国对英镑的汇率下降，在2007年特易购超过了家得宝。麦德龙紧随其后，如果欧元对英镑汇率增长，麦德龙的排名可能会更加靠前。但事实上，麦德龙的销售总额（其中包括批发营业额）比特易购的销售额要少得多。

特易购提供的产品和服务

你可以从特易购在线商店购买到的东西包括：
- 特易购附属店——书籍，录像带，租用DVD光盘，光盘，天然气和电力。
- 特易购金融——信用卡，抵押，贷款，储蓄。
- 特易购食品杂货——医疗保健，烹饪原料，新鲜水果，花园，洗漱用品。
- 特易购保险——意外事故保险，宠物保险，住房保险，人寿保险，汽车保险。
- 特易购电信——拨号上网，宽带服务，特易购移动储值SIM卡，特易购移动网络，移动电话。

形势分析

特易购在英国超市行业具有统治地位，它的统治地位可以从三个方面看出：
(1) 特易购随处可见；
(2) 向所有人销售商品；
(3) 销售所有商品。

由于特易购组织推广自身的品牌和产品的特征，以及当前的经济环境和PESTLE分析法[①]对其外部因素进行的详尽评估，促使了特易购的成功。这是因为特易购充分考虑到了消费者、员工、利益相关者、相关组织和公司的使命的关系。每一个外部因素对公司的影响是积极的还是消极的，影响很大还是基本无影响，是间歇性的还是持续性的，特易购都将对其进行长期的审查和分类。

PESTLE分析因素的审查

在政治上，信贷紧缩可能会导致高失业率。作为一个最大的、增长最快的零售商之一，特易购可以提供更多的就业机会，因此有利于降低失业率。PESTLE分析可以帮助特易购适应外部环境，与时俱进。例如，在衰退时期到来之前提前做好规划。

诚然，特易购当前的竞争优势之一是其压倒一切的实体店铺，但是在与其他竞争对手竞争的过程中，特易购存在一些问题。PESTLE分析，由于政策以及法律法规的约束，存在政府的垄断和竞争是必然的。这是特易购存在的潜在竞争问题之一。消费者保护法在保护消费者权益的同时保护企业能够在市场经济环境中竞争是非常重要的。由于当前的经济状况，很多小企业面临失败，无法进入市场。PESTLE分析有助于评估哪

---

① PESTLE是一种分析工具，它用来帮助企业分析其现在所处的或将来可能出现的外部环境情况。其中"P"代表"Political"（政治）；"E"代表"Economic"（经济）；"S"代表"Social"（社会）；"T"代表"Technological"（技术）；"L"代表"Legal"（法律）；"E"代表"Environmental"（环境）。

里是有扩张的需求,如何定位才是正确的。曾经不断扩展的特易购连锁商店是不存在这个问题的。根据欧盟的法律,有这样一个假设,拥有较大市场份额的组织是垄断者,与此相关的是产品和服务的质量将下滑,并将担负较高的价格风险。特易购迄今为止还没有被认定为垄断者,但应该顾及这一点。这就是为什么要利用PESTLE分析法进行定期检查和持续性观察的原因,这种持续性评估可以确保特易购的霸主地位并不是一种剥削。

此外,特易购如果要继续扩张必须严肃对待规划许可问题。规划许可在英国受到严格的监管,一个彻底的PESTLE分析有助于确定规划许可是否在相关法律范围内,以及是否有合法理由或者是否会引起当地人民的异议。PESTLE分析评估可以促使商店在一个新的区域获得成功。

就目前经济的发展情况来看,特易购很幸运没有像其他一些零售商那样受到经济衰退的影响。特易购有自己的品牌,它将产品和增值服务以合理的价格提供给客户,以吸引社会各阶层的顾客。

PESTLE分析涉及社会学方面的思考,如东欧移民人数的增加或年轻专业人员的增多,很显然在那将会有新的产品需求,例如,出现很多单身的职业人士,这样对微波炉加热食品的需求就会上升。

互联网技术也许是对特易购最具影响力的技术因素,它们通过网站 www.tesco.com 提供网上购物和送货上门服务。

特易购是一家支持减少碳排放的零售商,它设立了一个总额达1亿英镑用于此目的的可持续发展技术基金会,它还鼓励其客户作出低碳选择。如果特易购没有担负起关于环境问题的企业责任,那么将对它的声誉造成严重的后果。

PESTLE分析法对特易购门店的每日管理以及战略决策非常重要,如果特易购不知道什么外部因素会影响组织,那么领导者将很难以有效的方式管理业务。

行业分析:波特五力模型

新进入者的威胁

英国的食品杂货超市主要的几个竞争对手,其中四大品牌特易购(Tesco)、阿斯达(Asda)、塞恩斯伯里(Sainsbury's)和西夫韦(Safeway)拥有70%的市场份额,另外塞姆非(Somerfield)、维特罗斯(Waitrose)、布京斯(Budgens)这样小的连锁店占了10%的市场分额。根据丽思(2005)的统计,在过去的30年中,副食品市场已经被改造成以超市为主的市场,大多数大型的连锁超市建立了一站式购物和多种营销模式组合,提高了经营效率并获得了市场地位。这种强大的力量对于传统的店铺,如肉铺和面包店等产生了很大影响。因此,现在对于想进入该行业的新公司形成了强大的进入壁垒。例如,新进入者难以筹措到足够的资金,缺少高效稳定且低成本的供应链。大型连锁超市的巨大投资对新进入者的影响也很明显,如特易购,其对现有的结算和库存控制系统等先进技术的投资影响着新进入者和已经进入者。其他的进入障碍有规模经济和市场细分(提供的产品或者服务比竞争对手更有价值),这些优势都是特易购和阿斯达这样的企业通过产品开发、开展促销活动和更好的配货等经营手法获得的。

供应商的议价能力

供应商的议价能力代表了供应商的权利大小,这种能力可能会被大型连锁超市影响,因为供应商担心失去与大型超市的合作关系。因此,这进一步巩固了像特易购和阿斯达这样的大型超市在与供应商议价方面的主动权,这是一些小型连锁店无法比拟的。英国的供应商也受到大型零售商的威胁,因为他们可以从国外以更低的价格进货。这种买卖关系会制约供应商的决策自由并且影响其利润。这种竞争对抗的压力减少了连锁超市和供应商之间的利润空间。

客户的议价能力

波特理论说明,产品越是标准化、无差别,其转化成本越低,因此,买家越易获取主动权。特易购著名的忠诚卡(会员卡)仍然是最成功的客户保留策略,大大增加了特易购业务的盈利能力。在满足客户需要方面,定制服务以保证低廉的价格,提供更好的选择,保证店内促销不断,这使像特易购这样的品牌能够保留自己的客户群体。近年来,食品零售业发生了巨大的变化,消费者更多地选择在超市购物,这为超市销售非食品商品提供了很大的需求。这对超市扩展到银行、药店等新市场提供了新的战略机遇。消费者越来越关注贸易公平问题和西方消费者对第三世界生产者期望及意愿的影响。生态良性且道德健全的消费品的生产,例如茶、咖啡、可可是行得通的,而且这类产品在大多数大型连锁超市广泛出售。

替代品的威胁

一般的替代产品能够减少对某一特定产品的需求,根据波特模型,消费者的需求有转移到替代品的可能。在食品行业,可以看到以产品替代产品、需要的替代、被新的趋势削弱等形式,如小型的连锁便利店正在行业中兴起。在这种情况下,特易购、阿斯达、塞恩斯伯里正试图收购现有的小型店铺,在当地的城镇和城市中心开设特大店和快捷店。

竞争对手的议价能力

食品杂货店已经取得了较大的市场规模并占据了市场的主导地位。现在食品杂货店突出的特点是:更大的存储仓库,不断增加的商铺密度,规范统一的模式。正如上文所述,食品零售业的购买力集中在少数零售商买家手中。在一个成熟、平坦的市场,要获得市场增长是非常困难的(这驱使零售商进入多元化的非食品领域),消费者的要求越来越复杂多变,像特易购这样的大型连锁超市积累了大量的消费者信息,这些信息可以用来与消费者进行沟通。这个竞争激烈的市场已经达到了一个加速发展的水平,这使得英国的零售商们不得不进行创新,以保持原有的市场份额并开拓新的市场。这种创新可以看作是一系列交易模式的发展,是针对消费者行为变化作出的回应。占据市场主导地位的领导者,已经通过重新聚焦价格和价值而重新定位,同时加强了服务等元素的附加值。

电子商务战略

特易购——互联网业务

特易购自 1994 年以来就已经在互联网上经营了,在 1996 年成为世界上第一家提供全面的家庭购物服务的零售商。特易购在爱尔兰共和国和韩国也有网上商店。商店销售的产品从送货范围内的商店选择,每家店的产品都经过精心挑选。这种模式与其竞争对手塞恩斯伯里发起的、英国唯一一家网上超市也在使用的仓库模式不同,它利用有限的投资迅速扩张,但是这种模式却遭到了顾客的反对,因为这样商店必须保持大量的库存以满足不同的需要。不管怎么样,这种模式已经非常流行,并成为世界上最大的在线超市服务方式。

在 2001 年,特易购和西夫韦合资在美国推出 GroceryWorks,在美国和加拿大经营。GroceryWorks 已经填补了 Webvan 解体留下的空白,但是发展速度没有像预期的那么快。

考虑到网页反应时间太久(1996 推出网上超市的时候,宽带在英国几乎还不为人所知),特易购推出了以 CDROM 为基础的离线订购计划,它只连接到已下载的货物清单和发货订单。这是网页订购的附加功能,而不是替代功能,但是这种服务已在 2000 年撤销。

Tesco.com 目前在全球有 85 万用户,网上订单每周超过 25 万笔,在业务高峰期每小时可达 5000 笔订单。

Tesco.com 也被用作特易购大部分产品的一般门户,包括各种非食品的范围("特定店"旗下)、特易购个人理财和电信业务以及一些合作伙伴。这些合作伙伴包括航空、度假、音乐下载、天然气、电力、DVD 出租等方面的专业公司。目前它还不在线销售服装,在 2005 年 5 月,推出了一个服装网站,但这仅仅作为展示特易购服装品牌的平台,顾客还是要去实体店进行购买。

特易购与 CRM(客户关系管理)

特易购的成功在于关注每个客户的需求。在企业 CRM 战略规划中,只有把客户的需求放在战略的核心位置(当然,我们同时也不能忽略了对企业本身的关注),才能最终获得客户忠诚度。所谓的把客户放在核心位置,并非指某种技术或某个旨在提高客户忠诚度的方案,而是指关注客户本身,关注每一个客户的需求,这也才是客户关系管理的核心所在。

事实上 CRM 是一个很难界定的概念。正因为如此,那些努力想把它界定清楚的人经常会误解、误用甚至于滥用这个概念。

但有一点是大家都认可的,就是我们应该更多地关注客户管理系统中的核心——客户本身。可惜,我们时常过多强调这一系统中其他围绕客户本身的构成部件(比如技术),而忽略了最核心的基础——客户本身。但同时,一旦我们正确地认识到这一点并付诸实践,很快我们就能极大地提高客户忠诚度。

一般来说,在秉承美国商业文化的公司里,会特别注重与客户沟通这个环节,认为这是客户管理系统中尤为重要的一环。但与之不同的是,尽管特易购认为"5W"的沟通法则毫无疑问是客户管理系统的重要部分,但特易购建议企业在通过良好的沟通来提升忠诚度的同时,也应该多多考虑制定以顾客满意度为导向的公司战略。

特易购之所以强调这一点是因为一旦我们制定出了有效的以顾客满意度为导向的公司战略及方案,就能在很短的时间内通过方案的实施获得客户需求与公司价值的共鸣,并由此引发客户忠诚度的提升,进而提高公司的业绩。

如果我们公司的客户管理系统能够高效的运转,通常情况下我们将会收获经济和社会双重效益。特易购就是一个很好的例子:特易购开展的"Club Card Program"计划在其精心策划下,不但替特易购节省了很多促销费用,而且其销售业绩也呈上升趋势。

特易购确信:

- 让顾客融入企业文化,成为我们的一员;
- 为顾客解决现实问题,而不仅仅局限于那些和我们销售业绩挂钩的事情;
- 切实地关注并尽力满足顾客的多样化的需求。

特易购 CRM 方面做得出色的秘诀在于采取改变对客户和业务的思维方式,把他们从大众消费者中分离出来,作为独立的个体来看待。

CRM 支持其电子商务策略

随着特易购将工作重点放在技术上,公司于 1995 年推出忠诚卡并且取得了巨大的成功。这样特易购可以根据客户的年龄、购买的物品、住址等分析出用户的特点,将客户群细分。

通过这些信息,特易购可以筛选产品推荐给用户:素食主义者不会对肉类产品的促销活动感兴趣;儿童产品不会推荐给没有孩子的客户。特易购的省钱优惠券计划,鼓励客户试用相关的高价格商品,而不只是购买他们经常光顾的打折商品。

为了进一步适应其业务流程,特易购增加了第二个在线购物的创新。通过从客户的角度思考客户购物的每一个步骤,特易购为英国网上超市的重复排序功能、收藏列表、购买历史等建立了一个黄金标准。在订单确立之前,选择一个交货时间间隙以减少等待订单所带来的不便;客户给予特易购的员工酌情处理权,在顾客的第一选择商品脱销时,员工可以为他们选择替代品列表中的产品。特易购现在是全球最大的网上超市。

Tesco.com 客户价值传递

满足客户需求和符合组织战略意图的出色服务通常是精心设计的一整套相互关联策略的结果。特易购网认为,客户是其业务的核心,应该和竞争管理委员会共同放在第一位。

早期的用户可以通过互联网找到他们在当地商店找不到的产品,这可以节省搜索时间,并省很多事。对于经常在家进行网上购物的人或者一个单身的职业人士,花费 5 英镑而省去自己购物所花的时间是非常值得的。同样地,有小孩的客户从网上选购商品,也是因为这样可以使他们身心放松,这种放松比 5 英镑更值得。

法律和道德问题

像其他一些龙头企业一样,特易购受到了对大企业质疑人士的批评和反对。在英国有很多人反对零售商,特易购是目标之一,他们认为大型零售商会危害农民、供应商和竞争力小的企业。

零售商们也因为他们的商业策略而受到民众的批评,其中包括涉嫌利用虚假的价格战误导消费者。

特易购在2004年收购了Adminstore,这一行为遭到了当地人民和全国性的反对。特易购开设新店或者扩建店铺有时候也会遭到一些运动团体的反对。但是这些反对活动并没有影响到特易购的发展。

另一个受到非议的事情是特易购开始向便利店市场扩张。在英国,当一个企业占有该市场25%的市场份额之后,便会通过兼并该行业里其他小公司来增加市场份额(而不是通过企业自身的有机增长)。公平贸易办公室将超市和便利店定义为两个不同的行业,尽管小型零售商和便利店协会已经打破了这个定义。

人们指责特易购侵犯了农民和小型零售商的利益。特易购公司声明遵循行业最佳做法经营其超市,并且他们的产品均产自当地,符合当地居民的意愿,并没有侵犯农民或者小型零售商的权益。公平贸易办公室在2005年3月发表了一份关于超级市场和与供应商之间合作关系处理守则的审核报告,该报告表明特易购以及其他主要超级市场并没有收到正式的投诉,但是有一些批评指责,比如"地球之友"指出超级市场因为担心客户流失而禁止供应商提出抱怨,另外指出必须更加严格地对超级市场进行监管。此外,2005年8月,公平贸易办公室进一步报告:现在的情况是符合行业守则的。

2004年5月,特易购宣布正在尝试减少病假工资,希望以此减少计划外的员工缺席,这意味着员工可能会因为担心工资减少而将健康问题置之不顾,被迫选择带病工作。2005年12月,英国国会议员委员会提出了一份报告,指责特易购"无视法规、为所欲为"。这条指控源于特易购在斯托克波特建立的公司的面积比其有权建设的面积大了20%。

结 论

特易购的成功表明:品牌和有效的送货服务远比将Logo喷印在广告牌上更有效。它树立了病毒式销售的概念,并且通过文化赞助、政治争议、消费者体验和品牌延伸等多种渠道从当地文化中脱颖而出。

像特易购这样的大型组织,战略必须从每个层面得到分析和实施,并且这些不同的战略层次应该是相互关联、相互支持的。特易购从企业层面定义了参与竞争的业务战略,在某种程度上,特易购集中资源,将独特的竞争力转化成了竞争优势。

UNIT 12 Could My Business be an E-Business

Text

Definition

There is a sharp line between companies that are capable of using Internet technologies and the web to spur innovation and those that are not. Do you have the desire, motivation and resources available to make e-business a reality?

Overview

Becoming an e-business requires considerable research, analysis and planning. Starting the process now could reap enormous benefits for you in the future. This factsheet will help you realize the steps that need to be taken in becoming an e-business:
- Identify the e-business opportunity
- Plan your e-business
- Build a business case for change
- Manage the change

Topic Areas

Identify the e-business opportunity.
When considering e-business, examine your customer and supplier relationships to see where you could add the greatest value to your business:
- What parts of your customer model are the weakest?
- Where could the greatest cost savings be made (for yourself and your customers)?

- How can you offer a better service than your competitors?

The more opportunities you can identify across your customer and supplier business models, the greater the justification for introducing e-business activities. Split your business operations into individual functions, and examine their e-business potential:

- Customer: Market Research; Promotions; Sales; Operations; and After Sales Service.
- Sourcing: Tenders; Managing Contracts; Logistics; and Payment & Monitoring.

Plan Your E-Business

Know where your company is going and have a clear understanding of what is possible, what your business framework is and what your customers require.

Your company must define its e-business vision, state its objectives to achieve that vision, and plan the activities it will undertake to meet the stated objectives.

Identify the key objectives you will work towards. You need to consider what can be done quickly and what will bring the biggest net benefit:

- What are your priorities?
- Where are you currently losing money?
- What is the weakest link in your business?
- Are there any 'quick wins'?

Deliver proof of benefits quickly, choosing the lowest risk and easiest option to implement.

Take incremental steps. E-business is about changing how you do business inside and outside the company. This involves change with customers, suppliers and business partners. It will mean opening up your systems to your staff, as well as to customers and suppliers.

Build a Business Case for Change

Consider the business case for proceeding.

Your justification for adopting e-business will be measured by the tangible and intangible benefits:

Tangible: increasing revenues; increasing margins; reducing purchasing costs; reducing transaction costs.

Intangible: enhancing customer service; improving business relationships; improving decision-making.

Tangible benefits, like the cost-saving benefits of e-business, are often the only justification that companies will address in deciding to implement new technologies or business services.

Do not, however, ignore some of the softer, more intangible benefits of adopting e-business. Providing direct customer order entry may save you money in transaction costs, but also offers a real benefit to customers who prefer the flexibility.

Manage the Change

Becoming an e-business is about management and leadership not technology. Managing technology is easy; changing people's attitudes and actions is harder.

Providing the right cultural environment for e-business to flourish is critical and a challenge for most companies. Assess your e-business environment based on the following questions:

- Is time made available for company-wide improvements?
- Are people informed of issues or changes?
- Are the appropriate stakeholders consulted in decision-making?
- Is there a clear understanding of customer requirements?
- Is there an organizational perspective on individual actions?

Your company's ability to change, adapt and respond to dynamic market conditions will depend on the desire, motivation and innovation of your staff.

Be realistic. It may take longer than you anticipate to adopt e-business practices and fully exploit the opportunities that exist.

At the end of the day, what will make the difference in transforming your company will be the strength of your e-business vision and everyone's commitment to its principles.

Case Study

***Nexfor** (www.nexfor.com).*

Nexfor was part of an initial programme of work, sponsored by Scottish Enterprise, to look at e-business within the Forestry Industry.

Nexfor first developed a vision "to implement and use technology to achieve profitable and sustainable growth…" and from this came their strategy and action plan for e-business. This was shared with their key suppliers and customers.

Initial efforts concentrated on developing web-based solutions for their customers to place and track orders; performance was closely related to ROI (Return On Investment) and customer service improvements.

E-business is now key for Nexfor, and from the early wins in terms of reducing paper costs, it had planned further initiatives, including XML-based (Extensible Mark-up Language) supplier invoicing.

Nexfor is now at the forefront of e-business adoption within the Forestry Industry in Scotland.

Actions and Next Steps

- Identify the e-business opportunity: e-business will succeed where: you differentiate your business proposition; you make it difficult for your competitors to imitate; your business is capable of exploiting the opportunities; and you make your business transparent to partners.
- Plan your e-business: assess where your priorities are, where you are losing money, where quick wins are to be made. Focus on one functional area e.g. procurement or after sales service, before tackling the rest of the organisation.
- Build a business case: assess the tangible and intangible benefits of your e-business projects. Measure your e-business initiatives against your reasons for implementation.
- Manage the change: create an environment to motivate and innovate your e-business. Inform staff of changes, take time for company-wide improvements, understand your customers' needs and focus on the organisation rather than the individual.

Words and Expressions

spur [spə:]	v.	鞭策;刺激;疾驰;驱策
reap [ri:p]	v.	收割,收获
justification [ˌdʒʌstifiˈkeiʃ(ə)n]	n.	认为有理,认为正当;理由;辩护;释罪
tender [ˈtendə]	v.	招标
logistics [ləˈdʒistiks]	n.	后勤学,后勤;物流
incremental [ˌinkriˈmentəl]	adj.	增加的
tangible [ˈtændʒəbl]	adj.	有形的,切实的
stakeholder [ˈsteikhəuldə(r)]	n.	股东;利益相关者
sustainable [səˈsteinəbl]	adj.	可以忍受的;足可支撑的;养得起的
initiative [iˈniʃiətiv]	n.	提议;倡议;主动
invoicing [ˈinvɔisiŋ]	n.	货品计价
availability [əˌveiləˈbiliti]	n.	可用性;有效性;实用性

Notes

(1) When considering e-business, examine your customer and supplier relationships to see where you could add the greatest value to your business. 在考虑发展电子商务时,应调查公司与顾客以及公司与供应商之间的关系,找到最适合发展电子商务的地方。

(2) Your company must define its e-business vision, state its objectives to achieve that vision, and plan the activities it will undertake to meet the stated objectives. 公司必须首先确立发展电子商务的长期目标;继而确立短期目标,以最终实现这一长期目标;进而规划行动,以实现这些短期目标。

(3) Consider the business case for proceeding. Your justification for adopting e-business will be measured by the tangible and intangible benefits. 在工作开展之前应审查商务案例。公司是否适合发展电子商务取决于电子商务能带来多少有形和无形的利益。

Questions

(1) What are the steps to be taken to become an e-business?
(2) How to justify your adoption of e-business?
(3) What do you have to consider in assessing your e-business environment?

Exercises

1. Translate the following sentences into Chinese:

(1) When considering e-business, examine your customer and supplier relationships to see where you could add the greatest value to your business.
(2) Your company must define its e-business vision, state its objectives to achieve that vision, and plan the activities it will undertake to meet the stated objectives.
(3) Deliver proof of benefits quickly, choosing the lowest risk and easiest option to implement.
(4) It may take longer than you anticipate to adopt e-business practices and fully exploit the opportunities that exist.

2. Translation the following sentences into English:

(1) 在顾客-供应商这一商业模式中,若能发现越多的机会,就越适合发展电子商务。
(2) 建立电子商务重在管理和领导而不是科技本身。
(3) 初步工作重点是为顾客解决各种网络问题,方便客户订购及追踪订单。
(4) 如果你的企业有能力挖掘机遇,并且完全向合作伙伴公开,你的电子商务就会成功。

Unit 12　Could My Business be an E-Business

Further Reading

This e-business factsheet is part of a series developed by Scottish Enterprise. You can download the rest of the factsheet series by visiting www.hie.co.uk/ebusiness.

Translation

我的业务能发展成电子商务吗？

定　义

那些可以利用互联网技术及网络来激发创新的企业和没有这一能力的企业有明显的差别。你是否有发展电子商务的期望、动力和可用资源呢？

概　述

实现电子商务需要大量的研究、分析及计划。现在开始实施，你将可以在未来收获丰厚。这一情况简报将帮助你实现发展电子商务必须经历的几个步骤：
- 识别发展电子商务的机遇
- 制订电子商务计划
- 创造适宜变化的情形
- 管理变化

讨论领域

识别发展电子商务的机遇

在考虑发展电子商务时，应调查公司与顾客以及公司与供应商之间的关系，找到最适合发展电子商务的地方：
- 顾客模式中哪些方面最薄弱？
- 哪些方面可以最大程度地降低成本（为公司及顾客）？
- 怎样提供优于竞争对手的服务？

在顾客—供应商这一商业模式中，若能发现越多的机会，就越适合发展电子商务。把整个业务流程按不同的职能划分开来，研究各自发展电子商务的潜能：
- 从顾客角度划分：市场研究；促销；销售；运行；售后服务。
- 从资源角度划分：投标；合同管理；物流；付款及监测。

制订你的电子商务计划

首先要了解公司的发展方向,清楚地知道哪些方面可以发展电子商务、公司的商业框架怎样以及顾客的需求是什么。

公司必须确立发展电子商务的长期愿景;继而确立短期目标,以最终实现这一长期愿景;进而规划行动,以实现这些短期目标。

确立要实现的主要短期目标。必须考虑哪些短期目标可以很快实现,哪些短期目标可以带来最大的纯收益:

- 公司的优势何在?
- 公司哪些方面正处于亏本状态?
- 业务环节中哪个环节最薄弱?
- 有没有实现"快赢"的可能?

选择风险最小最简便的途径,快速实现盈利。

采取"增值"措施。电子商务意味着改变公司内外的商业运作模式,这一改变涉及公司与顾客、公司与供应商以及公司与商业伙伴关系的变化。电子商务同时意味着将公司公开,不仅向公司职员公开,而且向顾客以及供应商公开。

创造适宜变化的情形,改变公司经营模式

在工作开展之前应审查先前的业务情形。

你对是否发展电子商务的判断取决于电子商务能带来多少有形或无形的收益。

- 有形收益:增加收入;增加利润;减少购买成本;减少交易成本。
- 无形收益:提高客户服务质量;改善商务关系;改进决策进程。

企业在决定使用新技术或提供新服务时,通常只会考虑电子商务可以节约成本等有形收益。

但在采用电子商务时,不能忽略一些相对比较模糊的无形利益。提供顾客直接订购登录不但可以降低交易成本,而且可以为偏爱灵活性的顾客带来真正的便利。

管理变化

建立电子商务重在管理和领导而不是科技本身。运用技术容易,难的是改变人们的态度和行为。

为电子商务的快速发展提供一个恰当的文化环境至关重要,大多数公司都面临这样的挑战。要以下面的几个问题为基础,评价公司发展电子商务的环境:

- 若要改进整个公司的运作,时间安排上是否充裕?
- 人们了解这些新情况和变化吗?
- 在决策过程中是否与适当的股东商议过?
- 对顾客的需求是否有清晰的了解?
- 对单个的活动是否有组织性的考虑?

公司职员的愿望、动力及创新意识决定一个公司改变商业运作模式、适应市场变化及对动态的市场环境作出反应的能力。

要面对现实。要想实现电子商务模式并充分发掘存在的机遇可能会比预期的时间要长。

最后，公司改变以往经营模式、发展电子商务的成效取决于公司发展电子商务长期愿景的力量以及大家对这一变化原则的遵循。

案 例 分 析

Nexfor（www.nexfor.com）
由苏格兰企业发起的 Nexfor 是在林业领域发展电子商务计划的启动项目。

Nexfor 首先建立起"实施和利用科技实现利润持续增长"这样的愿景，并由此制定出发展电子商务的策略和行动计划。他们主要的供应商和客户也对此达成共识。

初步工作重点是为顾客解决各种网络问题，方便客户订购及追踪订单。工作绩效与 ROI（投资回报）及顾客服务质量的改善密切相关。

现在，电子商务已经成为 Nexfor 发展的至关重要的因素。从早期开始，Nexfor 由于降低了纸张成本而实现盈利。从那时开始，Nexfor 计划采取进一步的行动，包括基于 XML（可扩展标志性语言）的供应商货品计价。

Nexfor 现在已经成了苏格兰林业采用电子商务的"领头羊"。

行动及进一步举措

- 识别发展电子商务的机遇：如果你的商业理念与众不同，使竞争者难以模仿；如果你的企业有能力挖掘机遇，并且完全向合作伙伴公开，你的电子商务就会成功。
- 制订电子商务计划：分析企业的优势所在，估计哪些方面会亏本，哪些领域可以实现"快赢"。只有先聚焦整个业务流程的某个职能部门，比如采购部或售后服务部，整个业务流程才能顺利地展开。
- 创造适宜变化的情形：分析电子商务工程的有形、无形收益。列出发展电子商务的理由，检验电子商务动议的可行性。
- 管理变化：创造一个适合的环境，促进电子商务的发展，革新电子商务。让职员了解到这种变化，花时间改善整个公司的运作，了解顾客的需求，着眼于整个组织体系而不是单一的个体。

UNIT 13 Integrating E-Business into Your Small Business

Text

E-Business is an Important Part of Your Business

E-business can be defined as the use of the Internet to conduct business. For the most part, e-business is about your company's website and how you use the site (and your e-mail) to help operate and grow your business. In today's marketplace e-business is a very important tool that can help you increase sales and reduce costs.

Why Does E-Business Matter

E-business is very important because the number of your customers that are online and looking for information about products and services is always increasing. Consumers expect to be able to communicate with your company through your website and via e-mail. They expect your company to deliver the information they need immediately. According to Statistics Canada, in 2003 about 64 percent of Canadian households used the Internet regularly. The number of businesses using the Internet is even higher. The important point to note here is that the majority of Canadians are now Internet users, and this percent will only increase with national broadband initiatives. If you haven't embraced the Internet yet, you are among a dwindling minority.

Key E-Business Issues to Consider

You should always think about your goals and objectives and plan how e-business is going to work for your business. Hire a professional to help you determine your needs.

It is also important to consider the return on investment. Any e-business initiative should pay for itself, either by increasing your sales or reducing the costs of operating your business. When integrating e-business into your small business, there are several key issues to consider, including:

- Proper planning—Hire a professional to help you;
- Return on investment—The e-business initiative should pay for itself;
- Sales and marketing—How does e-business fit with your sales cycle?
- Customer relationship management—Provide a superior customer experience;
- Business productivity—Increased efficiency translates to profit;
- Managing and updating your website—Stay connected with your audience.

How E-Business Works with Your Sales and Marketing

Sales and marketing is all about communicating with your target audience, and e-business is a great communications tool. E-business can help you reach your target market and convince customers to purchase a product or service. E-business can also help you manage your sales and marketing process more efficiently which, in turn, increases your profit margin.

Sell More Stuff

E-business isn't always about your customers buying directly online with a credit card. Many business models just don't fit well with direct online sales. It all depends on how your customers buy from your company. Your website might work best as an information resource that tells visitors why your company is great and why your products offer value. Or your website might be a product catalog with deep information that helps people begin to configure their orders. After the sale, your website can act as a support tool, answering common questions your customers have about your new products, or it can provide technical support information.

Reach More Customers

E-business can help you get a lot more out of your marketing budget. A website (and e-mail communication) can reach new markets at much lower costs than traditional marketing. For example, your website can offer an online product catalog, allowing you to spend less money on printing paper catalogs. Instead you might spend that money on a teaser brochure that you can send to a wider target audience or on a targeted e-mail marketing campaign. These marketing tools can direct people to the full online catalog. The result is that you reach far more people for the same amount of money.

Keep It Professional

Now that you'll be reaching so many more possible customers with your website, it's important to have a good website that mirrors the quality and reputation of your brick-and-mortar company. Hire a professional consultant to help you sort out the issues of how your e-business strategy will work best with your business. A poor website will spread a negative impression of your company, and you certainly want to avoid that.

Build Stronger Relationships with Your Customers

E-business can help you improve your customer relationships which, in turn, should lead to increased sales and good word-of-mouth about your business. Customers expect your business to have a good website that delivers useful information, and they expect to be able to communicate with you quickly and easily through e-mail. Don't disappoint them.

Know Your Customers

Every business should have a good CRM (Customer Relationship Management) software package (whether it's on the office computer or web-based). This software allows you to build a database of all your customers, and enter all sorts of details about each customer. Good CRM software will help you see purchasing trends, track customer requests or complaints, and much more.

Communicate with Customers Regularly

Through your website and e-mail communications, you can stay in contact with your customers at a very low cost. As you interact with customers you should build up a permission-based mailing list, so that you can start sending out a regular e-mail newsletter. It's important to get permission from your customers before putting them on the e-mail list. Customers appreciate useful information, but they will have a very poor impression of your company if you spam them with useless information they didn't request.

What Kind of Information Should You Send to Customers?

The simple answer is this—information that is useful and meaningful to your customers. Here are a few examples of information you might send to customers:
- New product announcements and details of new product features;
- Product information tailored to a customer's specific request and preferences;
- Relevant news items about your company;
- Price changes or special offers such as website-only deals;
- General industry news and helpful tips.

Managing and Updating Your Website

Updating your website with timely and useful information is a key strategy for success. Your customers expect you to keep your site current, with new pricing or product information, news articles, company information, and more.

Pay Your Developer to Update Your Website

Unless your business is building and managing websites, you should consider outsourcing the job of updating your site to a professional. There is a huge time and opportunity cost in doing it yourself. Having someone inside your business update your website costs you not only the money you pay that person for that amount of time, but it also costs you the time that person could have spent working on your business. A good website will pay for itself many times over, including the cost of updating, so it's a poor use of time and resources to try a do-it-yourself solution. There are some content management solutions that can make it easier and more cost effective to update your own website.

Make a Plan and Stick to a Schedule for Updates

While you may not be updating your own website, you do need to be actively involved in providing your technical partner with the content to add to your site. Talk to your web developer about how you will deliver information (such as in a Word document) and set up a schedule for regular updates (once per week, once per month, quarterly). Your website developer should be able to guide you.

Appoint an Editor

You should decide who in your business is going to be responsible for organizing the content for updating the site. This person is essentially an editor, and it is his or her job to gather up content for updates and make sure it gets to the website developer on time and in the correct format. It's still important to keep an eye on the opportunity cost. Make sure people in your business aren't spending too much time creating content for the website. Look for efficient ways to source content for your website and identify which content is most valuable to your customers. Often you can get permission to add industry newsletter or magazine articles to your site, or even content from other websites.

Words and Expressions

integrate ['intigreit]	vt.	使成整体;使一体化;求……的积分
	v.	结合
household ['haushəuld]	n.	一家人;家庭;家族;王室
	adj.	家庭的;家族的;家属的;普通的;平常的
dwindle ['dwindl]	v.	缩小
productivity [ˌprɔdʌk'tiviti]	n.	生产力

catalog ['kætəlɔg]	n.	目录,目录册
	v.	编目录
configure [kən'figə]	vi.	配置;设定
	vt.	使成形;使具一定形式
brochure [brəu'ʃuə]	n.	小册子
mortar ['mɔ:tə]	n.	臼;研钵;灰泥;迫击炮
spam		兜售信息(邮件、广告、新闻、文章)、非索要信息。与垃圾邮件(junk mail)同义
newsletter ['nju:z,letə(r)]	n.	时事通信

Notes

(1) Your website might work best as an information resource. 如果你的站点能作为一个信息源,这或许就已经起到了网站的最大功用。

(2) Teaser brochure: a marketing tool, usually a one to two-page brochure summarizing the attractive features of the product. The purpose is to generate further interest from the customer. 用作预告、宣传的小册子。

(3) brick-and-mortar company: 有固定经营场所的传统公司

(4) Having someone inside your business update your website costs you not only the money you pay that person for that amount of time, but it also costs you the time that person could have spent working on your business. 若让企业内部的人来更新站点,你不仅要向他支付更新工作应得报酬,而且还损失了他本可以花在本企业工作上的时间。

(5) A good website will pay for itself many times over, including the cost of updating. 一个成功的站点足以补偿它本身所需费用,包括站点更新的费用,并且是绰绰有余。

Questions

(1) What else benefits can e-business bring to a business, besides direct online sales?

(2) What's the advantage of adopting e-business for marketing, comparing to traditional marketing?

(3) How does a good CRM software package work?

(4) Can you give me more examples of information you might send to customers?

(5) Which is the better way of updating your website, having someone inside your business do it or outsourcing the job? Why?

Exercises

1. Translate the following sentences into Chinese:
(1) E-business is very important because the number of your customers that are online and looking for information about products and services is always increasing.
(2) Any e-business initiative should pay for itself, either by increasing your sales or reducing the costs of operating your business.
(3) Sales and marketing is all about communicating with your target audience, and e-business is a great communications tool.
(4) Your website might work best as an information resource that tells visitors why your company is great and why your products offer value.
(5) For example, your website can offer an online product catalog, allowing you to spend less money on printing paper catalogs.

2. Translation the following sentences into English:
(1) 当今市场上,电子商务是一个非常重要的手段,可以帮助你增加销售,降低成本。
(2) 任何电子商务活动都应补偿它自己所需的费用,无论是通过增加销售还是通过减少运行成本的方法。
(3) 重要的是在把客户放到清单上之前要先征得他们的同意。
(4) 用适时、有用的信息来更新站点是通向成功的关键战略。

Further Reading

There are lots of resources and information available for anyone who wants to explore the subject of integrating e-business into your small business. *Your Local Busiess Service Center* is a great place to start. This guide was prepared by the Saskatchewan E-Future Centre, www. e-future. ca/sask.

Translation

将电子商务集成到你的小企业中去

电子商务是企业的一个重要组成部分

电子商务可被定义为利用互联网来管理业务。大多数情况下,电子商务涉及你的公司站点,以及如何利用该站点(包括电子邮件)来帮助实现业务的运营及增长。当今市场上,电子商务是一个非常重要的手段,可以帮助你增加销售、降低成本。

为什么说电子商务重要?

电子商务非常重要,因为在线搜索产品及服务信息的客户数量一直在增加,而且消费者也希望能够通过你的站点及电子邮件与你的公司进行交流,他们希望能够立刻从公司获得所需要的信息。据加拿大统计,2003年,约64%的加拿大家庭经常使用互联网,使用互联网的企业的比例就更高了。在此需要注意的一点是,绝大多数加拿大人现都为互联网用户,且随着国家宽带的发展,该数字只会上升不会下降。如果你尚未使用互联网,那你就属于不断缩减的少数异类了。

电子商务须考虑的主要问题

你应时刻考虑你的目标并计划好如何让电子商务为你的企业服务。雇用专业人员来帮你决定你的需求。同样重要的是要考虑到投资回报率。任何电子商务活动都应补偿它自己所需的费用,无论是通过增加销售还是通过减少运行成本的方法。当把电子商务集成到你的小企业中时,须考虑一些主要问题,包括:

- 恰当的计划——雇用专业人员帮助你完成;
- 投资回报率——电子商务项目应该有相应的回报;
- 销售与营销——怎样让电子商务适应你的销售循环?
- 客户关系管理——提供一种高级客户体验;
- 企业生产力——提升效率并转化为利润;
- 管理并更新你的站点——与你的受众保持联系。

如何协调电子商务与销售和营销的合作

销售及营销都是关于如何与目标受众交流的,而电子商务正是一个绝佳的交流工具。电子商务可以帮助你接触到目标市场并说服顾客购买商品或服务。电子商务还可以帮助你更有效地管理销售及营销过程,从而提高利润率。

销售出更多产品

电子商务并非总是意味着顾客用信用卡直接在线购买,因为很多业务模式并非很适合直接在线销售,这完全取决于顾客如何从你的公司购买。如果你的站点能作为一个信息源,告诉访问者为什么你的公司是出众的,以及为什么你的产品很有价值,这或许就已经起到了网站的最大功用。或者,你的站点可作为一个产品目录册,提供详尽的信息,以帮助人们来下订单。实现销售后,你的站点可起到支持工具的作用,来回答客户有关新产品的普遍问题,或者可提供技术上的支持信息。

获得更多的顾客

电子商务可帮助你从营销预算中获益更多。站点(及电子邮件沟通)能够以比传统营销低得多的成本开拓新市场。例如,你的站点可提供在线的产品目录,这样就能少花些钱去印制纸张目录,而省下的钱可用来制作宣传小册子,发给更广泛的目标受众,或用在锁定的电子邮件营销商业活动中。这些营销手段可以把人们引导到详尽的网上目录上去。结果是,你用相同数目的钱却接触到更多的对象。

专业的运作

既然你已利用站点争取到多得多的潜在顾客,现在重要的是,有一个好站点,能反映你的公司的品质与声誉。雇用专业顾问,帮你就如何使电子商务战略与企业达到最佳结合挑出需注意的问题。一个糟糕的站点会传递一种消极的公司形象,你当然不希望那样。

与客户建立更牢固的关系

电子商务能帮你改进客户关系,反过来,这又可以带来销售增加以及良好的口碑。顾客希望企业拥有好的站点,能发布有用信息,并希望能够通过电子邮件与你进行快速简便的交流,这一点,不要让他们失望。

了解客户

每个企业都应有良好的 CRM(客户关系管理)软件程序包(不管它是存于公司电脑里还是基于网络的)。该软件使你能建立一个包含了所有客户的数据库,并能得到有关每个客户的所有信息。良好的 CRM 软件可帮助你看出购买趋势,并能追踪客户要求或埋怨,还有更多用处。

与客户保持定期交流

通过站点及电子邮件,你可以以相当低的成本与客户保持联系。由于要与客户互动,你应建立基于客户许可的邮件发送清单,这样你就可以开始定期发送电子邮件时事通信了。重要的是在把客户放到清单上之前要先征得他们的同意。顾客乐于收到有用的信息,但如果净收到强加的无用信息、垃圾邮件,他们就会对公司产生非常糟糕的印象。

应向顾客发送什么样的信息

答案很简单——向顾客发送有用、有意义的信息。这里举出几例信息,可供向顾客发送:

- 新产品发布以及有关新产品特征的详细资料;
- 符合客户特定要求及偏好的产品信息;
- 公司的相关新闻;
- 价格变动或特价供应,例如仅限于网络的交易;
- 行业大体新闻及有用的小贴士。

管理以及更新站点

用适时、有用的信息来更新站点是通向成功的关键战略。顾客希望你的站点持有最新动态,包括新的定价或产品信息、新闻、公司资讯,以及其他相关信息。

雇用开发人员来更新站点

除非企业自行建设并管理站点,否则就得考虑请外界的专业人员来做更新站点的工作。公司自己做的话需耗费大量时间及机会成本。若让企业内部的人来更新站点,你不仅要向他支付更新工作应得报酬,而且还损失了他本可以花在本企业工作上的时间。一个成功的站点足以补偿它本身所需费用,包括站点更新的费用,并且是绰绰有余,所以想要尝试亲自动手的方法真是对时间和财力的不明智利用。有一些令人满意的管理方案,使你在更新自己的站点时更加简易,对于成本的利用也更加有效。

制定更新计划,并严格执行进度表

尽管你没有在更新自己的站点,但你也需要积极地参与,向你的技术伙伴提供需要添加到站点上的内容。告诉你的网络开发者,你想怎样发布信息(比如是以 Word 文档格式),并且设立一个定期更新计划表(1周1次,1个月1次,1季度1次)。站点开发者应有指导你的能力。

任命一个编辑

你应决定企业里由谁负责收集用作更新站点的内容。从根本上说,这个人就是一个编辑,他或她的职责就是收集好用来更新的内容,并且确保及时把内容以正确格式传达给站点开发者。还有重要的一点是要密切关注机会成本,确保企业内部人员没有花费过多的时间用在制作内容上。寻找高效的途径来获得用于站点的内容,并且识别出对于客户最有价值的内容。通常情况下,你都会获得许可,将行业时事通信或者杂志文章,甚至是其他站点上的内容添加到你的站点上。

CHAPTER 4
E-BUSINESS ABOUT INDUSTRIES

行业电子商务

- Retail "E-Procurement": Minimizing Costs and Improving Productivity
- Using the Internet to Market Agricultural Exports
- Selling Products on Facebook: The Emergence of Social Commerce
- Scan of E-Business in Higher Education

UNIT 14 Retail "E-Procurement" : Minimizing Costs and Improving Productivity

Text

Introduction

The inflation and subsequent deflation of the dot-com era and a tougher economic climate are forcing retailers to focus on "back to basics" execution of their business strategies. While many companies are wary, industry leaders are looking to build e-Business capabilities that drive real and lasting value.

While e-commerce euphoria was largely driven by the fear of lost market share, the e-business strategies of today are seeking sustainable competitive advantage. Electronic procurement ("e-procurement") can be a primary source of competitive advantage for retailers in:

- **Reducing and/or avoiding costs and improving productivity** by eliminating manual, paper-based processes and empowering employee procurement within a controlled set of parameters.
- **Enforcing on-contract buying** by providing an easy-to-use tool that automatically puts procurement standards and business rules into effect.
- **Developing reporting capabilities** that provide a consolidated record of spending, supplier performance and transaction costs, which can then be used for strategic sourcing, contract negotiation and supplier relationship management.
- **Reducing purchasing cycle times and effort** by streamlining procurement processes.

Enter E-Procurement

Electronic procurement is a prudent advancement in the quest to create a highly efficient virtual value chain, where complex transactions become a fluid, collaborative process between buyers and sellers. "E-procurement" continues the trend toward process automation and replacement of manual labor through information technology. By automating processes, like requisitioning approval and payment, e-procurement essentially eliminates the need for human intervention.

"E-Procurement" Models

The expensive and frequently complex world of one-to-one EDI exchanges and supplier enablement is unlikely to survive long in the "cheaper, faster" online world. While electronic procurement can at first seem complex and confusing, lower-cost benefits and continuous availability will ultimately win the day. Already, "e-procurement" has developed into several major public and private models for buyers and suppliers looking for better ways to handle their basic procurement processes:

Private Models
- **Supply-side**—A company creates its own online catalog that allows a number of buyers to browse and purchase products online with realtime, contract-specific buying tools.
- **Buy-side**—In this example, the buyer maintains the online catalogs and databases of multiple suppliers' goods and services, and is responsible for tying all transactions into those companies' purchasing and financial systems.

Public Models
- **Independent trading exchanges**—In this model, an independent Web site provides the entry point for multiple buyers and sellers to transact business for a fee or on a subscription basis.
- **Vertical trading exchanges**—This model typically focuses on the needs of one industry, with sponsorship provided by one or more industry leaders.
- **Horizontal trading exchanges**—This model cuts across industry boundaries and focuses on broad categories of goods and services that are common to many companies.
- **Auctions**—Electronic auctions, which are a subset of online trading exchanges, provide online, realtime exchange of goods through a forum in which buyers and/or sellers log on and make offers against a request. Can be private or public in form.

Third-Party Procurement Service Models
Third-party procurement services typically offer a hosted, buy-side solution—a pri-

vate procurement model for enhancing supply chain efficiency and maximizing savings without incurring significant costs.

In the third-party procurement service model, the service provider builds and manages the online catalogs, often providing leveraged pricing by aggregating its subscribers' buying power.

Expected Results

What you can expect from "e-procurement"?

Online procurement can completely transform the way retailers purchase goods, making process efficiencies and permanently lower costs not only possible, but affordable to achieve.

Today, most company purchasing of indirect materials is done by telephone (85 percent), fax (65 percent) and face-to-face discussions with suppliers (50 percent).

To understand the scale of what automating purchasing process can do, consider data offered by those who have initiated strong "e-Procurement" programs:

- Average transaction costs dropped from USD 107 to USD 30.8.
- Cycle times dipped from 7.3 days to 2 days.
- Average costs of generating an order fell from USD 35 to less than a single dollar.
- Direct purchasing costs dropped from USD 60 to USD 5.11.
- The number of full-time purchasing employees plummeted from 29 to 2.

Clearly, "e-procurement" can have a dramatic effect on a retailer's bottom line.

Words and Expressions

procurement [prə'kjuəmənt]	n.	获得,取得;采购
inflation [in'fleiʃən]	n.	胀大,夸张;通货膨胀;(物价)暴涨
subsequent ['sʌbsikwənt]	adj.	后来的;并发的
tough [tʌf]	n.	恶棍
	adj.	强硬的;艰苦的;坚强的,坚韧的;强壮的
execution [ˌeksi'kju:ʃən]	n.	实行;完成;执行
wary ['wɛəri]	adj.	机警的
euphoria [ju:'fɔ:riə]	n.	精神欢快;欣快

manual ['mænjuəl]	n.	手册;指南
parameter [pə'ræmitə]	n.	参数;参量;起限定作用的因素
empower [im'pauə]	v.	授权与;使能够
consolidated [kən'sɔlideitid]	adj.	加固的;整理过的;统一的
transaction [træn'zækʃən]	n.	办理;处理;会报;学报;交易;事务;处理事务
cycle time		周转时间
requisition [ˌrekwi'ziʃən]	n.	正式请求,申请;需要;命令;征用;通知单
eliminate [i'limineit]	vt.	排除,消除
	v.	除去
availability [əˌveilə'biliti]	n.	可用性;有效性;实用性
	vt.	征用;要求
multiple ['mʌltipl]	adj.	多样的;多重的
	n.	倍数;若干
	v.	成倍增加
win the day		得胜,成功;获胜;战胜
ultimately ['ʌltimətli]	adv.	最后;终于;根本;基本上
catalog ['kætəlɔg]	n.	目录,目录册
	v.	编目录
responsible [ris'pɔnsəbl]	adj.	有责任的;可靠的;可依赖的;负责的
independent [ˌindi'pendənt]	n.	中立派;无党派者
	adj.	独立自主的;不受约束的
vertical ['və:tikəl]	adj.	垂直的;直立的;顶点的;头顶的
	n.	垂直线;垂直面;竖向
sponsorship ['spɔnsəʃip]	n.	赞助者的地位、任务等
horizontal [ˌhɔri'zɔntl]	adj.	地平线的,水平的
host [həust]	n.	主人;主机
	vt.	主办;主持
maximize ['mæksəmaiz]	vt.	取……最大值;最佳化

aggregate [ˈægrigit]	n.	合计,总计;集合体
	adj.	合计的;集合的;聚合的
	v.	聚集,集合;合计
subscriber [sʌbsˈkraibə]	n.	订户;签署者;捐献者
transform [trænsˈfɔːm]	vt.	转换;改变;改造;使……变形
	vi.	改变;转化;变换
	n.	变换(式);转换
permanently [ˈpəːmənəntli]	adv.	永存地;不变地
plummet [ˈplʌmit]	n.	铅锤;重荷
	vi.	垂直落下

Notes

(1) The inflation and subsequent deflation of the dot-com era and a tougher economic climate are forcing retailers to focus on "back to basics" execution of their business strategies. .com 时代的膨胀以及随之而来的萧条,加上日益严峻的经济气候,迫使零售商不得不把目光又集中在了执行"回归基本"的商务战略上来。

(2) While e-commerce euphoria was largely driven by the fear of lost market share, the e-business strategies of today are seeking sustainable competitive advantage. 如果说对电子贸易的热衷是由对失去市场份额的担心而大力驱动的话,那么今天的电子商务战略正在寻找可持续的竞争优势。

(3) The expensive and frequently complex world of one-to-one EDI exchanges and supplier enablement is unlikely to survive long in the "cheaper, faster" online world. 在"更便宜、更快捷"的在线世界中,昂贵且常常是复杂的一对一的 EDI 交易和供应商驱动的模式是无法长期生存下去的。

Questions

(1) According to the author, why should we focus on e-procurement in retail?
(2) What are direct procurement and indirect procurement?
(3) What are the five processes of indirect procurement?
(4) What are the e-procurement models introduced in this article?

(5) What can we expected from e-procurement?

Exercises

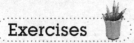

1. Translate the following sentences into Chinese:
(1) Participating in a public system is also a fairly low-risk alternative; however, functionality has been slow to develop, and in many cases participants have had to manually update their internal systems.
(2) "E-procurement" capabilities privately or publicly is to determine whether your current procurement processes are better than those of the public exchanges.
(3) One of the key advantages of the private system is that many Enterprise Resource Planning (ERP) vendors are already adding this capability to their systems, which may greatly reduce the difficulty and expense of integrating those functions.
(4) We believe retailers will eventually participate in an amalgamation of these models.
(5) Smaller retailers may learn to rely on public models and third-party procurement services.

2. Translate the following sentences into English:
(1) 网络时代的泡沫经济以及相对萧条的经济氛围,迫使零售商不得不调整其经营战略。
(2) 制造商可以通过对购买程序实施流线化改进以缩短购买周期。
(3) 在线采购能够完全改变零售商的采购方式,从而降低成本,提高效率。
(4) 电子拍卖作为在线交易的组成部分,主要是通过论坛形式提供在线、实时的商品交易。
(5) 对所有商品的有效采购是所有零售业的基石。

Further Reading

For the full text, you can see *Retail "E-Procurement" 2002: Minimizing Costs and Improving Productivity*, issued by IBM.

零售业电子采购分析：成本最小化，提高生产力

前　言

.com 时代的泡沫经济以及随之而来的经济萧条，加上日益严峻的经济形势，迫使零售商不得不把目光又集中在"回归基本"的商务执行战略上来。当很多公司非常谨慎小心不敢越雷池半步的时候，产业领头羊正努力构建电子商务体系，这一体系能够带来真实和持久的利润。

如果说对电子贸易过热的最大驱动力源于对失去市场份额的担心，那么今天的电子商务战略正在寻找可持续的竞争优势。对零售业来说，电子化采购表现在以下方面作为竞争优势的主要来源：

- 通过减少手工的、基于纸面的流程，并授权员工通过一整套参数进行采购，可以达到降低成本、避免浪费、提高生产力的目的。
- 通过提供简单易用的工具，实现采购标准与商业规则的自动化处理，以增强按合同购买的能力。
- 建立一个可以扩展的数据库，这一系统可提供一个关于购买、供应商信息和交易成本的安全记录，这个记录进而可以用于企业战略的资源、降低价格的谈判以及供应商关系的管理等。
- 通过精简采购流程，可以减少采购周期和难度。

加入电子采购

在寻求建立高效的虚拟价值链方面，电子采购是一个显而易见的进展。它使得复杂的交易变成买卖者之间一个流畅的协作过程。"电子采购"继续朝向程序自动化和通过信息技术代替手工劳动这样一个趋势迈进。通过自动化程序，如申请和支付，电子采购从根本上消除了人为的干预。

电子采购模型

在"更便宜、更快捷"的网络世界中，成本高昂且常常是程序复杂的、一对一的 EDI 交易和供应商驱动模式是很难长期生存下去的。尽管电子采购乍看起来似乎复杂并令人迷惑，但更低成本的收益和持续的有效性将最终赢得未来。目前，一些厂商已经为那些寻求更好方法来处理基本采购流程的采购商和供应商开发出了一些主要的公共和私营的电子采购模式：

私营模型

- 卖方——一个公司建立起它自己的在线目录，允许一系列买家在线浏览和通过实时、分类合同等购买工具在线购买他们的产品。
- 买方——在这个模型中,购买者维护各供货商货物、服务信息的在线目录和数据库,并负责把所有的交易与公司的购买与财务系统联系起来。

公共模型
- 独立贸易交易平台——在此模型中,一个独立的网站为多个买主和卖主开展交易业务提供一个入口,以便他们在此实现现金交易或者为他们提供订购业务。
- 垂直贸易平台——这一模型主要集中一个行业的需要,并且由一个或多个行业领导者发起。
- 水平贸易平台——这一模型打破了行业间的界限,并集中于更宽泛的货物和服务分类,这些分类普遍适用于许多公司。
- 拍卖——电子拍卖,是在线贸易交易的一个组成部分,通过论坛的形式提供在线、实时的商品交易,在这一论坛中,采购商和/或销售商注册登录,并且针对需求请求讨价还价。其在形式上可分为公共或私营两种模式。

第三方采购服务模型

第三方采购服务,主要提供一个独立主办的,以买方为中心的解决方案——这是一个私营的采购模型,它在不增加高额成本的前提下提高供应链效率并且使节约成本最大化。

在第三方采购服务模型中,服务提供商建立和管理在线目录,经常通过聚集客户购买力来提供有影响的定价。

期望的结果

你能从电子采购中期望什么?

在线采购能够完全颠覆零售商采购商品的方式,这使得流程高效化和永久性地降低成本不但在理论上成为可能而且能够在实践中可行。

现在,大多数公司是通过电话(85%)、传真(65%)和面对面与供应商讨论(50%)的方式购买间接材料。

为了理解采购流程自动化可以在多广的范围内起作用,我们可以参考以下数据,这些数据由已经发起强大电子采购计划的厂商提供:
- 平均交易成本从107美元降低至30.8美元;
- 周转时间从7.5天降到2天;
- 形成一份订单的平均成本从35美元降低到不超过1美元;
- 直接交易成本从60美元下降至5.11美元;
- 专职采购的雇员数量从29人下降至2人。

显然,电子采购对零售商的底线产生了戏剧性的影响。

UNIT 15 Using the Internet to Market Agricultural Exports

Text

The possible use of the Internet in the marketing of agricultural exports of developing countries can be considered along similar lines as the use of the Internet in the rest of the economy. While there are various types of online marketing models, the more commonly used ones are e-markets and online auctions. Online marketing can lead to reduced transaction costs, disintermediation or the emergence of new types of Internet-based intermediaries, price transparency, and the possible re-distribution of earnings along the supply chain.

Like many other areas of economic activity, the marketing of agricultural commodities has witnessed widespread adoption of the Internet. There are many business-to-business (B2B) e-markets dealing with agricultural and related commodities. Many of them engage in domestic trade in the United States, but there are also a number in international exchanges. The available information shows that the Internet is used widely by farmers to sell and advertise farm products, exchange information and buy farming inputs. According to Forrester, by 2004 the food and agricultural industry in the United States will conduct $211 billion in online B2B trade in the US food and agricultural industry, which will represent 12 percent of total B2B online trade for all industrial sectors.

1. E-markets

A general examination of B2B e-markets is contained in UNCTAD (2001), with an overview of their main characteristics and an assessment of their overall potential for developing countries. The report gives a few examples of e-markets for commodities of interest to developing countries, but no detailed investigation was made, and at the time of publication such markets were in very early stages of their development.

E-markets have been used as marketing channels for agricultural commodities in such countries as Australia, Canada and the United States, where markets have been established for a wide range of commodities such as cotton, grain, soybeans, wood products, cattle, dairy products and a variety of other food products. In the various forms of online markets, transactions can be conducted in different ways, including the following:

- Offer/Request e-market models where many sellers trade with many buyers: the buyers request quotes and the sellers provide price information;
- One seller deals with multiple buyers and pricing is dynamic through a bidding process;
- Sellers compete for the market of one buyer with dynamic pricing through bidding;
- Single buyers negotiate with single sellers, usually involving long-term contractual sales;
- Many-to-many transactions where prices are determined instantaneously through auction type bidding.

While e-markets largely focus on online trading or intermediating transactions, some tend to concentrate their functions on offering information and other value-added services.

E-markets in general have undergone ups and downs over the last few years, and there is no reliable assessment of the performance of those involved in trading agricultural commodities. Overall, the critical determinants of the success of e-markets include the following:

If an industry is fragmented in the sense that there are many buyers and sellers, the e-market has better prospects of success, since the market creates value by aggregating the volume of trade in one trading platform, allowing buyers and sellers to discover each other more readily and to facilitate decisions on selling and buying. The agricultural industry, especially in developing countries, is highly fragmented, particularly on the sellers' side, and thus well suited to e-markets.

Where a product is fairly standard, as many agricultural commodities are, online marketing is feasible since such products do not require customization for particular buyers' needs. However, where producers sell a commodity that has unique characteristics or is highly differentiated as regards quality or other attributes, sellers may use e-markets but may prefer seller-driven marketplaces to open markets.

The volume of the commodity traded on the marketplace should be large enough to ensure that the marketplace is viable. This means that there must be a minimum number of buyers and sellers participating in order to provide a critical mass that can sustain the viability and operations of the marketplace.

2. Online auctions

Online auctions differ from e-markets in that they are one-off events and the participants do not retain an ongoing membership, as in e-markets. However, e-markets can use online auctions as one of the methods for organizing transactions between members. Quite a number of agricultural commodities, including many exported by developing countries, have traditionally been sold through floor-based offline auctions. Online auctions follow the same basic procedures as floor-based offline ones, although they provide benefits over traditional auctions.

During an online auction, lot numbers are displayed on a website and buyers present bids that are shown to all participants. Buyers can see their bids on the screen or can check later via e-mail how their bids compare with those of other bidders. After the winning bid is determined, the auction manager facilitates the arrangements for payment and delivery. However, in some auctions such arrangements are left entirely to the buyers and sellers, after the auction site has collected its fees from the participants. Some online auctions maintain strict confidentiality so that bidding, sales, payment and delivery are effected without revealing the identity of the seller or the buyer. Online auctions may last from several hours to several days, depending on the volume of goods being auctioned.

Like e-markets, online auctions take different forms such as independent auctions, where buyers and sellers use third-party auction sites, and private auctions, where sellers auction their own goods to invited buyers on their own auction sites. Some auction sites aggregate databases of a large number of other auction sites, thus enabling buyers to obtain information from many auctions through a single source.

3. The benefits of e-markets and online auctions

■ Reduced costs

Use of the Internet for marketing can reduce transaction costs in a number of ways. The first is the reduction of search costs. Agricultural marketing chains are characterized by multiple intermediaries, and buyers spend much time searching for information about suppliers, products and prices. The Internet may reduce search costs in terms of effort, time and money, because information can be exchanged more efficiently via the Internet than through traditional channels.

In e-markets, for example, a large number of agricultural commodity producers and buyers are brought together into a single trading community, which reduces search costs even further. In this connection, the Internet can play a vital role in the development and marketing of what are popularly known as specialty agricultural products. There is a growing demand for differentiated food products in major food-importing countries in

Europe and North America. On the demand side, specialty products cover a given consumer population whose size is growing but is not fully established. On the supply side, there are a variety of producers and traders who may be widely distributed in several countries. Because buyers and producers lack information about each other, it is difficult to match supply and demand. Use of the Internet can allow producers to match their products or planned production to the relevant "specialty" characteristics of the demand. It also allows prospective buyers to seek and exchange information with producers. Buyers can inform producers about the product characteristics that are most attractive to consumers, thus providing the producers with an indication of the demand.

■ Reduced or transformed use of intermediaries

The Internet can reduce the use of intermediaries in the traditional supply chain by enabling producers to interact and transact directly with buyers. This is largely because producers and buyers can obtain trade information from each other and can carry out transactions at a much lower cost than in an offline supply chain with multiple intermediaries.

Use of the Internet can also increase the efficiency of existing intermediaries to the extent that they adopt the new information technologies. Also, e-markets can be viewed as new intermediaries that can replace traditional offline intermediaries. Independently, third-party agricultural e-market places are themselves intermediaries by definition, as they are situated between producers and buyers. On the other hand, many large farmers and producers tend to establish their own private exchanges to link up directly with the food traders and processor, with whom they have long established trading relationships, thus effectively reducing the role of intermediaries.

■ Price transparency and formation

By bringing together large numbers of producers and buyers, e-markets reveal market prices and other transaction information to all parties. By contrast, accessing information in offline markets is costly, and channeling it though various intermediaries may distort information on prices and other trade data. Increased price transparency reduces price differences prevailing in the marketplace. It also allows buyers to compare prices and make more informed purchasing decisions.

Online auctions provide bidders the convenience of bidding from their home or office without necessarily being on an auction floor. Also, while offline auctions oblige all bidders to participate at the same time and require them to be present for the duration of the auction, online auctions are more flexible as they allow bidders to submit bids at different times. This flexibility increases the market for the auctioned goods. Furthermore, online auctions can be organized at short notice and yet reach a large number of buyers. Also, buyers can readily search databases containing large numbers of goods being auctioned instead of going through the printed listings of traditional auctions. Finally, online auctions are much cheaper to run than traditional ones, thus making it feasible for more goods, including very low-value goods, to be auctioned.

The main disadvantage of online auctions is the difficulty faced by bidders in inspecting goods they want to buy. While this problem is being partly solved by sellers making available electronic images of the goods being auctioned, for some agricultural commodities, such as coffee and tea, tasting is an essential factor in the buyer's decision. However, in some instances samples can be shipped in advance and tasting conducted offline. The results are then made available to prospective bidders in the auction.

Words and Expressions

auction ['ɔːkʃən]	n.	拍卖
witness ['witnis]	n.	目击者;证据,证词
	v.	作证;成为证据
contain [kən'tein]	vt.	包含,容纳;容忍
	vi.	自制
overview ['əuvəvjuː]	n.	一般观察;总的看法
dynamic [dai'næmik]	adj.	动力的;动力学的;动态的
instantaneously [ˌinstən'teniəsli]	adv.	即刻地;瞬时地
fragment ['frægmənt]	vt.	使……成碎片;使……成片断
aggregate ['ægrigeit]	v.	聚集,集合;合计
readily ['redili]	adv.	乐意地,欣然地;容易地
facilitate [fə'siliteit]	v.	使容易;使便利;推动,促进
viable ['vaiəbl]	adj.	可行的;能养活的
confidentiality [ˌkɔnfiˌdenʃi'æləti]	n.	机密性
indication [ˌindi'keiʃən]	n.	指出,指示;迹象;暗示
processor ['prəusesə]	n.	处理器;加工者
distort [dis'tɔːt]	v.	弄歪(嘴脸等);扭曲;歪曲(真理、事实等);误报
informed [in'fɔːmd]	adj.	见多识广的

Notes

(1) The text is adapted from *E-Commerce and Development Report* 2003 *Chapter* 6 *Section D*, prepared by the United Nations Conference on Trade and Development secretariat, complete version. 本文根据《电子商务与发展报告 2003》第 6 章 D 部分改编,这是由联合国贸易发展会议秘书处提供的完整版本。

(2) engage in:使从事于,参加

(3) request quotes:询价

(4) negotiate with:与……磋商,讨论

(5) in the sense:就某种意义(或某方面)来说,多少有点

(6) critical mass:临界值

(7) lot number:批号

(8) prospective buyer:可能的买方

(9) go through:经历,经受,用完,参加,搜查,履行

Questions

(1) What ways can transactions be conducted in the online markets?

(2) E-market is more suitable for which kind of industry?

(3) What are the benefits of e-markets compared with the traditional markets?

(4) Please summarize the benefits of online auction compared with the offline auction in your own words.

(5) What is the main disadvantage of online auction? How to solve this kind of problem?

Exercises

1. Translate the following sentences into Chinese:

(1) Developing-country agricultural exports, particularly coffee and tea, have tended to represent an important development because of their overall economic impact on the exporting countries.

(2) For example, practically all of the world's coffee is grown in developing countries, while 80 percent is sold to Western Europe, the United States and Japan.

(3) During the early 1980s, agricultural commodity chains were largely producer-driven in terms of price setting and quality maintenance.

(4) The processed tea is sold to brokers or auctioned directly for international sale.

(5) Further processing or value addition takes place in importing countries by tea blenders and packers who purchase the tea either from the auctions in the pro-

ducing countries or from international traders.

2. Translate the following sentences into English:

(1) 互联网在农业产品销售中所起的作用变得日趋重要。
(2) 电子营销和在线拍卖是两种应用最普遍的在线销售模式。
(3) 电子交易市场涉及国内贸易和国际贸易。
(4) 联合国的报告表明电子交易市场仍处于发展的初级阶段。
(5) 在线拍卖不同于电子交易市场,在于它是一次性的而且参与者无须保持会员资格。

Further Reading

You can see the complete version of *E-Commerce and Development Report* 2003 for more detailed information.

Translation

利用互联网推销农业出口产品

在发展中国家的农产品出口营销中,互联网可能的使用方式被认为与其在经济的其他方面的使用相类似。尽管有很多在线营销模型,但是使用最普遍的是电子营销和在线拍卖。在线营销能够降低交易成本、非中介式的交易或者基于互联网的中介新模式的出现、价格透明度的提高,实现供应链收益的可能性的再分配。

与经济活动的其他领域一样,农产品营销已被证明广泛使用了互联网。现在有很多从事农业和相关产品销售的企业与企业间(B2B)的电子交易市场。在美国,大多数的电子交易市场从事国内贸易,但也有一些电子市场从事国际贸易。已有的信息表明农民广泛使用互联网销售和推广其农产品、交换信息和采购农业原材料。根据Forrester统计,到2004年美国食品和农业产业界通过在线的B2B的交易,食品和农产品的交易额将达到2110亿美元,这将占据所有产业部门B2B在线交易12%的份额。

1. 电子交易市场

2001年联合国贸易和发展会议的部分报告,对B2B电子交易市场做了全面考察,充分阐述了它的主要特征,并评估了在发展中国家的潜力。该报告给出了一些对发展中国家有益的某些商品的电子交易市场例子,但是没有做更详细的调查。在该报告发表时,这样的市场仍处在发展的起步阶段。

电子交易市场已经在澳大利亚、加拿大和美国等国家用作农产品的营销渠道,包括棉花、谷物、大豆、木制品、家畜、奶制品以及一系列其他食品在内的电子市场已经建立。

在多种形式的在线市场中,可以用不同的方式来实施交易,包括以下几方面:
- 在多个销售商与多个客户交易时,提供/请求电子交易市场模型是,客户要求报价,销售商提供价格信息;
- 一个销售商与多位买家进行交易,价格的形成是动态变化的;
- 通过出价,销售商通过动态的定价来完成单一客户的市场竞争;
- 单个客户与单个销售商磋商,通常涉及长期合同买卖;
- 基于拍卖出价形式的多对多的交易,价格是通过拍卖实时确定的。

当电子交易市场把重点放在在线交易或中介性交易时,有某种倾向却希望其把焦点集中在提供信息和其他增值服务上。

在过去几年中,电子交易市场经历了大起大落,也没有对包括销售农业产品在内的交易进行可靠的绩效评价。总的来说,电子交易市场成功的关键因素包括以下一些方面:

如果一个产业有很多买主和卖主处在某种程度的分离状态,那么电子交易市场就更容易取得成功,这是因为市场通过将贸易量聚集到一个交易平台而创造了价值,允许买方和卖方更容易彼此发现,也更有利于促使双方做出买卖决定。特别在发展中国家,农业是高度分散的,尤其是销售这一方,因此非常适合应用电子交易。

正如很多农产品一样,当一种产品相当标准化时,由于不需要根据特定客户的需要进行定制,因此在线交易是可行的。然而,当制造商销售的产品具有独特的特征或者在品质和其他属性是差异化的时候,销售商可能会使用电子交易市场,但是更可能倾向于以销售商驱动的市场以打开销路。

在市场上,产品的交易量应该足够大以确保这个市场是可行的。这意味着必须有最低数量的买方和卖方来参与,以提供维持这个市场生存和运行的最低规模。

2. 在线拍卖

在线拍卖不同于电子交易市场,在于它是一次性的并且参与者不需要像电子交易市场那样参与者必须是会员。然而,电子交易市场可以使用在线拍卖作为组织会员交易的一种方法。相当多的农业产品,包括很多发展中国家出口的产品,都通过交易厅现场(离线)拍卖的传统方式来销售。在线拍卖遵循传统的交易厅现场拍卖程序,尽管所带来的效益远高于传统的拍卖。

在在线拍卖过程中,拍卖品的批号被显示在网络上,并且买方出示的报价面向所有参与者公开。购买者可以在屏幕上看到他们的出价,或者随后通过电子邮件检查他们的出价与其他出价的比较情况。当获胜的投标确定以后,拍卖管理者就要安排付款和送货了。然而,在一些拍卖中,拍卖网站在向参与者收取费用后,这样的事项就全部留给销售商和客户自己解决了。一些在线拍卖需要高度保密,以致投标、销售、付款和递送等都是在不透露卖方或买方身份的情况下进行的。在线拍卖可以持续几个小时到几天不等,这取决于拍卖的货物数量。

像电子交易市场一样,在线拍卖有不同的形式,如买卖双方使用第三方拍卖网站的独立拍卖,销售商在自己的拍卖网站上向受邀客户拍卖自己产品的私人拍卖。一些拍卖网站聚集大量其他拍卖网站的数据库,这样使客户通过单个消息来源就可以得到很多拍卖的信息。

3. 电子交易市场和在线拍卖的优点

■ 降低成本

使用互联网来完成销售可以在很多方面降低交易成本。第一是降低搜索成本。农业的营销链具有多个中间商的特征,购买者需花费大量的时间来寻找供应商、产品和价格的信息。互联网可以减少精力、时间和金钱等方面的搜索成本,因为与传统的交易渠道相比,通过互联网交换信息更加高效。

例如,在电子交易市场中,大量的农业产品生产者和客户被带到一个单一的交易社区,这将进一步降低搜索成本。在这种联系中,互联网在开发和营销广为熟知的特色农产品中起到很重要的作用。在欧洲和北美洲,主要的食品进口国对食物的差异性需求持续增长。就需求而言,特色产品覆盖一个特定的持续增长的但尚未完全形成的客户群。就供给而言,有许多广泛分布在几个不同国家的制造商和销售商。由于买方和制造商彼此缺乏信息,所以把供应和需求联系起来是比较困难的。互联网的使用使得制造商将其商品或计划的生产与相应的特色需求结合起来。互联网也使可能的买主寻找信息并与制造商交流信息。购买者可以告知制造商最吸引消费者的产品特征,这样就可把需求的指示提供给制造商。

■ 减少或转变中间商的使用

互联网可以通过使制造商直接与客户交流和交易来减少传统供应链中中间商的使用。这在很大程度上是因为制造商和客户之间能够得到对方的交易信息,由于不像传统供应链中具有多个中间商,所以能以一个更低的成本实现交易。

互联网的使用也可以使已经存在的中间商采用新的信息技术在某种程度上提高效率。当然,电子交易市场也可以被看作用来替代传统中间商的新的中间商。由于独立的、第三方农业电子交易市场居于制造商和客户之间,根据定义,其本身也是中间商。另外,很多大的农场主和制造商倾向于建立与食品销售商和加工商的直接联系,并与他们维持长期的贸易关系,从而有效地减少中间商的作用。

■ 价格的透明度及其形成

通过把大量的制造商和客户联系在一起,电子交易市场向各方揭示了市场价格和其他交易信息。与此形成对照的是,在离线的情况下获取信息的成本是高昂的,并且在通过中间商传递信息的过程中可能会扭曲价格和其他贸易数据信息。提升价格的透明度可以减少在市场上盛行的价格差异。它也可以使客户比较价格,并做出更明智的购买决策。

在线拍卖提供给投标者不用去拍卖交易厅而可以在家或办公室出价的便利。离线拍卖迫使所有的投标者在同一时间参加拍卖并且要求他们在整个拍卖过程中都要在场,而在线拍卖更加灵活,它允许投标人可以在不同的时间投标。这种灵活性拓展了所拍卖货物的市场。此外,在线拍卖通过一个简短的通知就能组织大量的买家。买家也能够很容易地查找包含大量正在拍卖货物信息的数据库而不是浏览传统拍卖中的印刷清单。最后,在线拍卖费用比传统拍卖的运营费用要低很多,这样就使得对包括低值货物在内的更多货物进行拍卖成为可能。

在线拍卖的主要缺点在于投标者检查想购买的货物十分困难。尽管这个问题已经由销售商为拍卖货物拍摄电子图片得到了一定程度的解决,但是对于某些农产品,如咖啡和茶叶,口味才是客户做出购买决策的主要因素。然而,在某些情况下,样品可以被提前在网下运送来品尝。这些举措对于拍卖中的潜在中标者是有用的。

UNIT 16 Selling Products on Facebook: The Emergence of Social Commerce

Text

The Importance of Facebook Commerce for E-commerce Businesses

It is no secret that Facebook dominates the social networking field. Facebook controls more than half of the US traffic to social media sites and has more than 500 million active users who together spend over 700 billion minutes per month on the site. Facebook is now taking on E-commerce, and changing the way that people shop online and interact on social media sites.

Facebook commerce (F-commerce), the ability for merchants to sell products directly from their Facebook Fan page via the creation of a "shop" tab, is one of the fastest growing subsets of social commerce. The Facebook shopping experience gives users the ability to view a product catalog, read reviews, make a purchase, and interact with their friends, all from a company's Facebook fan page.

An October 2010 Vertical Rail study found that 87 of Internet Retailer's top 100 retailers had a Facebook fan page with a combined 36 million fans. However, of these 100 companies, only four offer a "shop" tab on their Facebook. This illustrates that merchants have done the legwork to develop their social networks and build their fan base, but only a few have taken social commerce to the next step, using F-commerce to turn fans into customers.

The Benefits of Selling Products on Facebook for E-commerce Businesses

Facebook commerce gives merchants the opportunity to succeed by using this viral selling platform to maximize the results of their social media efforts. Here are just some of the ways that selling products on Facebook can benefit E-commerce merchants:

Increase Online Sales

According to a report by eMarketer, frequent Facebook users spend an average of $67 online, compared to the average of $50 spent by occasional Facebook visitors and $27 spent by non-Facebook users. This means that by allowing consumers to shop directly from Facebook, merchants are targeting a highly profitable segment of active online shoppers.

Demonstrable ROI

According to an August 2009 survey by Mzinga and Babson Executive Education, 84% of business social media programs don't measure return on investment. Many of the Facebook shopping applications provide detailed analytics to give merchants deeper insight into the strengths, weakness, and overall health of their social media marketing program.

Build Brand Awareness

Many of the businesses currently selling products on Facebook require users to "like" the brand before they can begin shopping. Once someone "likes" the business, their entire network is notified, prompting more Facebook users to check out the site and repeat the process. The result is that Facebook users are constantly seeing your company and products in their news feed, increasing brand awareness and recognition.

The Benefits of Selling Products on Facebook for Consumers

Facebook commerce provides a unique experience for online shoppers, giving fans access to Facebook-only sales, exclusive coupons, and sneak peeks at unreleased products. Here are just a few ways that consumers can benefit from shopping on Facebook.

Convenience

By combining shopping and social media, consumers no longer have to jump from site to site trying to research a product, make a purchase, and connect with their friends. When consumers shop on Facebook, they are able to ask the opinions of their friends and can share purchases or wish lists with the rest of their social network. Facebook commerce allows shoppers to research, shop, and share without leaving the Facebook site.

Special Discounts and Coupons

According to a June 2010 study from Compete, more than half of consumers who used a coupon during their last online purchase would not have bought the item without it. The study also found that consumers who use coupons or purchase items on sale actually spend more money and are more satisfied with the shopping experience. By providing coupons and specials for Facebook fans, merchants are providing something interesting, exclusive, and valuable to their customers.

Read Reviews and Comments

An August 2010 survey from ChannelAdvisor found that 83% of shoppers are influenced by customer reviews. Online shoppers rely heavily on ratings and reviews to guide their purchasing decisions, so it is essential that merchants have this information readily accessible. Shoppers using Facebook are able to read product ratings and reviews directly from the company's fan page, without having to visit a third party rating and review site.

Facebook Commerce Applications

In order for merchants to sell products on Facebook, they must first install an application that creates a "shop" tab on their fan page. Currently, only a handful of companies provide F-commerce applications. Some companies offer flat-fee services, while others operate on a revenue-share pricing model. A few of the applications allow consumers to complete the entire checkout process on Facebook, while others transfer the shopper back to the company website to finish the transaction.

The following five companies are leaders in this new industry. Each offers a unique Facebook application that benefits both businesses and consumers. These companies offer a variety of pricing and structural options, ensuring that there is a solution for every size and type of company.

Milyoni (Million-eye)

Milyoni helps integrate E-commerce business with social media in a "conversational commerce" site that operates on a performance driven pricing model. Milyoni offers a managed solution instead of a software download, and they provide the necessary technology, hosting, and customer service to ensure a successful Facebook store integration. The goal of Milyoni is not only to increase online sales through a Facebook store, but also to connect fans in a social context to promote customer engagement and loyalty.

Dean Alms, VP of Strategy and Marketing at Milyoni believes that what makes Milyoni unique is their "very innovative set of social merchandising tools including the ability to do image posts, audio posts, and video posts. Each of these posts allows you to engage with your customers first in topics of interest and follow up with a commerce opportunity." Milyoni has recently added a new feature to their social merchandising arsenal, called Instant Showcase, which allows a fan to purchase a product directly from their news feed with as few as three or four clicks.

Payvment

Currently in its beta stage, Payvment offers a free shopping application for merchants who want to sell products directly from Facebook. Merchants using Payvment will benefit from the easy installation process, integrated marketing features, and built-in sales tracking. Payvment allows merchants to sell an unlimited number of products and offers domestic and international shipping options. Their promotional features include Facebook fan discounts, the ability to "share" store and item information with Facebook friends, and built in review and commenting capabilities.

According to Christian Taylor, CEO of Payvment, the most important feature they offer merchants and consumers is their Facebook-wide shopping network. He explained, "When you launch a store on Facebook using Payvment, your products are available to be discovered across the entire network of Facebook stores. Over 30,000 strong with over 200 new store launching daily. Plus, if a Facebook user leaves your Facebook store without purchasing the items in their cart, they can complete their purchase across the entire network. Only Payvment provides the Facebook-wide shopping solution."

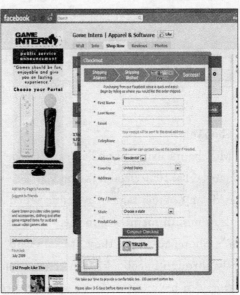

ShopFans

ShopFans is a social commerce application created by Adgregate Markets. Their pricing is based on revenue share and is unique to each client. The ShopFans application allows merchants to sell products directly on their Facebook Fan page, and consumers can complete the entire secure transaction without leaving the Facebook site. This application allows businesses to market to their social networks and gives shoppers the ability to post products on their wall, sign up for registries, and participate in exclusive sales. Their goal is to turn "conversations into conversions" by fully integrating social commerce with E-commerce to create a unique shopping experience.

When it comes to shopping on Facebook, one of the primary concerns for consumers is privacy and security. Henry Wong, CEO of Adgregate explained that, "Adgregate's ShopFans is the only social commerce solution secured by McAfee, the exclusive provider of consumer security software to Facebook, and TRUSTe. This solution enables e-retailers to have a custom Facebook store, secured by McAfee and TRUSTe that utilizes all of Facebook's social plumbing."

ShopTab

Merchants using ShopTab can choose from three different pricing options ($10/500 products, $15/1000 products, or $20/5000 products) with no long term contract, no set up fee or any percentage of revenue when setting up their Facebook application—only a month to month membership fee. When shoppers are ready to check out from the merchant's ShopTab page, they are taken to the actual business website instead of paying directly through Facebook. This transition from Facebook to merchant website removes any worry of payment delay or security breach and has proven to be an amazing website traffic generator from the over 500 million Facebook fans. With a low monthly cost and easy self-management tools, ShopTab is a great way to get involved in Facebook commerce with almost no risk. ShopTab also integrates Facebook social sharing for each product to help merchants gain awareness among other Facebook users.

ShopTab prides itself of being simple for both merchants and customers. ShopTab's co-founder, Jay Feitlinger cited the low cost, customer focus, data feed upload based off Google Base platform, and automatic scheduled updates for merchants who require daily pricing and inventory changes completed automatically as the benefits that set ShopTab apart. He explained, "We took the time to understand how customers want to engage with a shopping tab on Facebook and made sure that the usability provided the best experience possible. ShopTab was also the first Facebook commerce application that allowed merchants to upload a data feed that immediately published product information such as price and description, as well as pulled in product images so merchants don't have to take the time to upload each individual product image." In addition, with ShopTab retailers don't have to worry that other competitors products will show on their ShopTab because only their products will show on their Facebook ShopTab.

SocialShop

SocialShop operates on the belief that combining social media and E-commerce leads to more customers and more sales. SocialShop, created by Big Commerce, offers five programs that range from $24.95/month to $299.95/month with a $49.95 startup fee. SocialShop is easy to use and connects merchants and customers in a social context by allowing Facebook users to browse products through a "shop" tap on the business fan page, view product photos, and quickly share products with friends.

Mitchell Harper, co-founder and co-CEO of Big Commerce believes that the ease of use makes SocialShop stand out from other F-commerce applications. He explained, "Merchants can add the application to Facebook and have it completely configured to show their products in less than two minutes. Their fans can not only browse products directly on Facebook, but they can also share the products on their wall. This is an excellent, form of viral marketing."

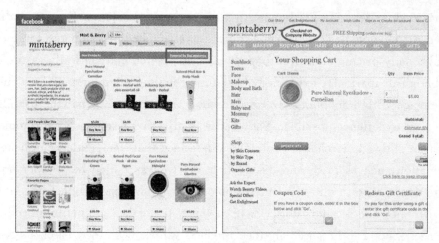

Facebook Commerce Strategy for E-commerce Businesses

The secret to a successful Facebook commerce strategy is to come up with interesting ways to involve your audience and add value to their shopping experience. Like most marketing and sales channels, one size does not fit all, so each company needs a unique F-commerce strategy to maximize the success of their "shop" tab. The following five strategies can help you effectively engage your fans and get involved with F-commerce the right way.

Identify Your Fan Base Demographics

Each F-commerce strategy should by customized so that it appeals to the interests and preferences of your specific Facebook fan base. Erica Terrell, Sr. Marketing Manager at Adgregate Markets believes that the key for merchants selling products on Facebook is to, "Identify their fan base demographics and try to engage them according to their interests." By understanding exactly who you are communicating with, you will be able to truly connect with your fans and create a successful F-commerce marketing campaign.

Focus on the News Feed

People are on Facebook to socialize, see what their friends are doing, look at pictures—they are not on Facebook to shop. Dean Alms, VP of Strategy and Marketing at Milyoni explained that, "The vast majority of time is spent on the news feed. Facebook users are not going to find your store and ultimately buy products from you unless you engage them on the news feed. "Engaging your fans on their news feed can include anything that adds to the conversation, whether that is posting interesting status updates, uploading new pictures, or commenting on other people's pages.

Turn Fans into Evangelists

Selling products on Facebook provides merchants with an interesting sales channel that combines marketing, sales, and interaction. According to Jay Feitlinger, CEO of ShopTab, when a company actively engages customers through a Facebook store, "The fans become evangelists, using Facebook to help in spreading the word about the products you sell. When you can start the shopping process right where people talk about it, the time and energy to get a consumer from awareness to an actual purchase is shortened."

Incentivize

According to Christian Taylor, CEO of Payvment, "Exclusive deals and sales from your Facebook page can be huge for driving interest and building fans." Merchants can incentivize product sales on Facebook by providing access to new product launches, Facebook specific coupons and specials, or distressed inventory sales. These exclusive events add to the viral component of Facebook commerce that is unparalleled by any other form of advertising.

Be Transparent

Retailers have worked hard to develop their Facebook base and gain the trust of their fans. Now that social media is becoming commercial, it is essential that merchants maintain that trust by respecting their Fans. Mitchell Harper, Co-Founder and Co-CEO of Big Commerce reminds merchants, "The key is transparency. Don't look at Facebook as another way to 'sell' your customers. Instead, look at Facebook as a way to build transparent relationships with both customers and prospects."

The Future of F-commerce

No matter how successful Facebook commerce becomes, it is essential to remember that Facebook is a social networking site, not a shopping site. Dean Alms compared Facebook commerce to going to a baseball game. "You are there to enjoy a ballgame, but during the game you are likely to buy some food, beverage and maybe even a ball cap or T-shirt. You never went there to 'shop'. Those that appreciate this role of Facebook will do better in the future than those that see Facebook as just another E-commerce channel."

In this early stage, it is unclear how this new sales channel will evolve and grow in the future. Both Jay Feitlinger and Mitchell Harper believe that Facebook Credits (Facebook's virtual currency) will play a significant role in future of F-commerce, while

Erica Terrell predicts big changes in brand marketing strategies. All agree that Facebook commerce is about to revolutionize the way we shop, making it a truly social experience. The question is—how will your business take advantage of this exciting new opportunity?

Words and Expressions

illustrate ['iləstreit]	vt.	说明,阐明;表明;(用示例、图画等)说明,解释
legwork ['legwə:k]	n.	〈口〉外出搜集情况的工作(如新闻采访、案件调查等)
viral ['vaiərəl]	adj.	病毒的,病毒引起的
demonstrable [ˈdemənstrəbl]	adj.	可论证的;显而易见的
notify ['nəutifai]	vt.	通知,告知,报告
exclusive [iks'klu:siv]	adj.	排外的;除外的;全部的;唯一的;(新闻等)独家的;(商品等)独家经营的;(式样等)独一无二的
coupon ['ku:pɔn]	n.	配给券;(购物)票证;(购物)优惠券
sneak peeks		先睹为快,偷窥
merchandising [ˈmə:tʃəndaiziŋ]	n.	商品的广告推销,销售规划
arsenal ['ɑ:sənəl]	n.	兵工厂,军火库;任何事物的集成
launch [lɔ:ntʃ]	vt.	开始从事,发起,发动(尤指有组织的活动);(首次)上市,发行;开展(活动、计划等);开始出版;首创,首映
inventory ['invəntri]	n.	详细目录,存货清单,(商店的)存货,库存;细账;细目表;详细目录
startup ['stɑ:t.ʌp]	n.	启动;新兴公司(尤指新兴网络公司)
configure [kən'figə]	vt.	配置,设定,使成形,使具一定形式
demographics [diməˈgrɑ:fiks]	n.	人口统计资料(如年龄、性别、收入等等)
customize [ˈkʌstəmaiz]	vt.	订制,定做,改制(以满足顾主的需要)
evangelist [iˈvændʒilist]	n.	圣经新约福音书的作者,福音传道者
incentivize [in'sentivaiz]	vt.	以物质刺激鼓励

Unit 16 Selling Products on Facebook: The Emergence of Social Commerce

Notes

(1) Facebook commerce (F-commerce), the ability for merchants to sell products directly from their Facebook Fan page via the creation of a "shop" tab, is one of the fastest growing subsets of social commerce. Facebook 商务（F-commerce），即商家通过在 Facebook 粉丝网页上创建的一个"购买"选项卡来直接销售他们的产品，这是社交商务中增长最快的子集之一。

(2) This illustrates that merchants have done the legwork to develop their social networks and build their fan base, but only a few have taken social commerce to the next step, using F-commerce to turn fans into customers. 这表明了商家已经为开发社交网络并建立粉丝基础铺好了路，但只有少数公司已将社交商务作为下一步，使用 F-commerce 将粉丝转变成顾客。

(3) Many of the Facebook shopping applications provide detailed analytics to give merchants deeper insight into the strengths, weakness, and overall health of their social media marketing program. 很多 Facebook 购物应用给商家提供了详细的分析，使商家能够更深入地了解社会媒体营销计划的优势、劣势以及总体健康状况。

(4) Once someone "likes" the business, their entire network is notified, prompting more Facebook users to check out the site and repeat the process. 一旦有人"赞"了某个业务，他们整个网络就会被互相通知，这会促使更多的 Facebook 用户登录站点并重复这个过程。

(5) Online shoppers rely heavily on ratings and reviews to guide their purchasing decisions, so it is essential that merchants have this information readily accessible. 在线购物者很大程度是依赖于等级和评论来指导他们的购买决策。因此，对商家来说，立即得到这些信息是至关重要的。

Questions

(1) What benefits will F-commerce bring to merchants and consumers respectively?
(2) What is Instant Showcase?
(3) Which company is the only one that provides the Facebook-wide shopping solution?
(4) Do consumers pay directly through Facebook when shoppers are ready to check out?
(5) According to Mitchell Harper, what makes SocialShop stand out from other F-commerce applications?

Exercises

1. Translate the following sentences into Chinese:

(1) Web sites like MySpace, Facebook attract millions of users a year, and people ranging from teens to elders are signing up to use the online social networking services around the world.

(2) "F-Commerce," as the Facebook marketplace is sometimes known, has grown 9 percent in the past four months, according to British online research firm eDigitalResearch.

(3) Then there's Wrapp, a Swedish site that's expanding to the U.S. early next year, which encourages users to buy virtual gift cards from selected retailers for Facebook friends on their birthdays or for other life events.

(4) Every time a user adds an application, the user is required to grant the application access to your profile information.

(5) By allowing commercial and freelance software developers, Facebook has opened up its coveted user communities to various advertisers and businesses.

2. Translate the following sentences into English:

(1) 社交通讯将给商品营销方式带来一场巨大的变革。

(2) 对于零售商而言,Facebook 已经成为一个标准的广告和营销渠道。

(3) News Feed 这项专利更侧重于向用户提供好友的消息,而非仅仅进行状态更新。

(4) 目前为止,Facebook 上规模最大的电子商务应用是通过广告吸引流量,或者在 Facebook 上发布折扣或新品信息。

(5) 社会化购物的本质,是让优质商品的信息供应链更有效率,从而让信息供应链下游的消费者更快做出购买决策。

Further Reading

This text is from Vertical Rail, an e-commerce marketing agency that specializes in data feed optimization and comparison shopping enginemanagement. Vertical Rail helps e-commerce merchants develop smart strategies for social media and comparison shopping inclusion. For more information about this topic, you can visit verticalrail.com.

在 Facebook 上销售产品：社交商务的出现

Facebook 商务对电子商务业务的重要性

毋庸置疑，Facebook 统治着社交网络领域。Facebook 控制了一半以上的美国社交媒体网站流量、拥有 5 亿多的活跃用户，这些用户平均每月在网站上共花费了 7000 亿分钟。目前 Facebook 正在采用电子商务，并正改变着人们网上购物以及在社交媒体网站上互动的方式。

Facebook 商务（F-commerce），即商家通过在 Facebook 粉丝网页上创建的一个"购买"选项卡来直接销售他们的产品，这是社交商务中增长最快的子集之一。Facebook 的购物体验了用户查看产品目录、阅读评价、购物以及跟朋友交互的能力，这些功能都来自公司的 Facebook 粉丝网页。

在一项 2010 年 10 月份的 Vertical Rail 研究中发现网络零售商的前 100 强企业中有 87 家都各自拥有 Facebook 粉丝网页，共涉及了 3600 万名粉丝。然而，在这 100 家公司中，仅仅只有 4 家在他们的 Facebook 上提供"购买"这个选项。这表明了商家已经为开发社交网络并建立粉丝基础铺好了路，但只有少数公司已将社交商务作为下一步，使用 F-commerce 将粉丝转变成顾客。

在 Facebook 上销售产品对电子商务业务的益处

Facebook 商务通过使用病毒性销售平台，最大化地利用他们社会媒体的努力成果，给商家提供了成功的机会。以下是在 Facebook 上销售产品能使电子商务商家受益的一些方面。

增加网上销售

根据一份 eMarketer 的研究报告，相比较 Facebook 的偶尔使用者平均消费 50 美元，不使用 Facebook 的用户消费 27 美元来说，Facebook 的频繁使用者平均在线花费 67 美元。这意味着通过允许消费者直接在 Facebook 上购物，商家们正在把目标瞄向活跃的在线购物人群中这个非常有利可图的这部分对象。

显而易见的投资回报率（ROI）

根据 Mzinga 和 Babson 高层经理培训项目中 2009 年 8 月份的一项调查，84% 的商务社交媒体项目都不衡量投资回报率。很多 Facebook 购物应用给商家提供了详细的分析，使商家能够更深入地了解社会媒体营销计划的优势、劣势以及总体健康状况。

建立品牌知名度

目前许多在 Facebook 上销售产品的企业要求用户在开始购物之前就要"赞"某个品

牌。一旦有人"赞"了某个企业,他们整个网络就会被互相通知,这会促使更多的Facebook用户登录站点并重复这个过程。结果就是Facebook上的用户不断地在动态消息汇总中看到公司和产品信息,这就增加了品牌的知名度和认可度。

在Facebook上销售产品对消费者的益处

Facebook商务为网上购物者提供了一个独特的体验,让粉丝可以获得Facebook的唯一销售、独家优惠券以及事先目睹还未发布的产品。以下是在Facebook上销售产品能使消费者受益的一些方面。

便利性

通过将购物和社交媒体相结合,消费者再也不用从一个网站跳到另一个网站去试图研究产品和购物,并与他们的朋友联系。当消费者在Facebook上购物时,他们能够询问自己朋友的意见,并可以与社交网络的其他成员分享购物体验或心愿清单。Facebook商务允许购物者无须离开Facebook网站就可以研究、购物以及分享体验。

特别折扣和优惠券

根据Compete的2010年6月的研究,超过一半的消费者在他们上一次网上购物时使用优惠券,如果没有优惠券则不会购买该产品。研究还发现,消费者使用优惠券或购买打折的产品实际上花费更多的钱,但购物体验更满意。通过为Facebook的粉丝提供优惠券和特别商品,商家为客户提供了一些有趣的、独有的以及有价值的商品。

阅读评论和意见

来自Chann elAdvisor 2010年8月的调查发现,83%的购物者会受到顾客评论的影响。在线购物者很大程度上依赖等级和评论来指导他们的购买决策。因此,对商家来说,立即得到这些信息是至关重要的。使用Facebook能够使购物者可以直接从公司的粉丝页面上阅读产品的等级和评论,而无须访问第三方等级和评论网站。

Facebook商务应用

商家为了在Facebook上推销他们的产品,首先必须安装一个应用以便在他们粉丝的网页上添加一个"购买"按钮。目前,只有少数公司提供F-commerce应用。一些公司提供统一收费服务,而其他公司则使用收入一份额定价模型。一部分应用允许消费者在Facebook上完成整个校验过程,然而其他的则将顾客转移到公司网站完成交易。

以下五家公司是这个新产业中的领头羊。每家公司都提供了一个有利于企业和消费者的独特的Facebook应用。这些公司提供各式各样的定价和结构选择,确保公司每一个型号和类型的产品都有一个解决方案。

Milyoni（Million-eye）

Milyoni帮助在"对话式商业"网站上整合电子商务企业与社交媒体，采用以绩效为驱动的定价模型进行运作。Milyoni提供了一个取代软件下载的可管理的解决方案，并且他们还提供必要的技术、主机托管、客户服务以确保成功的Facebook商店的整合。Milyoni的目标不但要通过Facebook商店增加网上销售，而且要在社交背景下连接粉丝以提升顾客的参与度和忠诚度。

Milyoni的战略和营销副总裁Dean Alms认为，Milyoni的独特之处是他们的"非常富有创新精神的社会推销工具集，包括对图像帖子、音频帖子和视频帖子进行处理的能力。每一个这样的帖子都能让你第一时间参与到顾客感兴趣的话题并跟踪一个商业机遇。"Milyoni最近在它们的社会化的商务集成中增加了一项新的功能，叫做"即时展示"，这使得粉丝只要按三四下鼠标就可以直接从动态消息汇总中购买产品。

Payvment

目前在测试阶段，Payvment向那些想直接在Facebook上销售商品的商家们提供了一个免费的面向其客户的购物应用。使用Payvment的商家将从容易安装的过程、整合营销的功能与内置的销售跟踪受益。Payvment允许商家出售数量不受限制的商品，以及提供国内外发货选项。他们的促销功能包括Facebook粉丝折扣，跟Facebook朋友"分享"商店和产品信息的能力，建立审查和评论的能力。

根据Payvment的CEO Christian Taylor的介绍，他们提供给商家和消费者最重要的特色就是他们的"泛Facebook"的购物网络。他解释说："当你使用Payvment在Facebook上开一家商店，你的产品在Facebook商店的整个网络上都是可以被见到的。已经拥有超过30,000家的商家，并且每天会有200家以上的新店成立。此外，如果一个Facebook用户离开了你的Facebook商店但并没有在他们的购物车里购买商品，他们能在整个网络上完成购买。只有Payvment提供了"泛Facebook"的购物解决方案。"

ShopFans

ShopFans是由Adgregate Markets创造的一种社交商务应用。他们的定价基于收益份额并且对每一位客户来说都是独特的。ShopFans应用允许商家在Facebook粉丝网页上直接销售他们的商品，并且消费者在不离开Facebook网站的条件下可以完成整个安全的交易。这个应用允许商家向他们的社交网络进行营销，并给予消费者在网页上张贴他们的商品、报名登记和参与独家销售的能力。他们的目标就是通过社交商务与电子商务的全面整合，将"对话变成转换"，从而创造一种独特的购物体验。

当谈论到在Facebook上购物时，消费者主要关心的问题之一就是隐私和安全。Adgregate的CEO Henry Wong解释道："Adgregate的ShopFans是唯一依托McAfee保证安全的社交商务解决方案，McAfee是Facebook消费者安全软件的独家供应商，TRUSTe也是。这个方案允许电子零售商有一个自定义的Facebook商店，由利用所有Facebook社会探测手段的McAfee和TRUSTe保障安全。"

ShopTab

当设立自己的 Facebook 应用程序时,商家可以使用 ShopTab 从三个不同的定价选项(每 500 件商品 10 美元,每 1000 件商品 15 美元或者每 5000 件商品 20 美元)中选择,除了一个月的会员费,并不需要签署长期合同,也没有开设费用或任何收入的百分比。当购物者准备从商家的 ShopTab 页面付款时,实际上他们链接的是实际的商业网站,而不是直接通过 Facebook 支付。从 Facebook 过渡到商家网站的做法消除了顾客对任何延迟付款或违反安全的担忧。Facebook 已经被证明是一个粉丝点击量超过 500 万的惊人的网站。ShopTab 凭借每月低成本和简单的自我管理工具,以一个几乎没有风险的伟大的方式参与着 Facebook 商务的运行。ShopTab 还为每一个产品集成了 Facebook 的社交共享功能,以帮助商家获得其他 Facebook 用户之间的想法。

让 ShopTab 引以为傲的是同时方便了商家和顾客。ShopTab 的联合创始人——Jay Feitlinger 引用了一系列战略:低成本、顾客导向、通过谷歌平台上传产品数据源、为需要日常定价和库存变化的商家自动完成定时更新,这些优势使 ShopTab 成为行业的佼佼者。他解释说:"我们花时间去了解客户想要怎样链接 Facebook 上的购物标签,并确保提供可用性最好的体验。ShopTab 是第一个允许商家上传动态更新的数据,立即公布产品价格和产品描述信息以及产品图片的 Facebook 电子商务应用程序,以至于让商家不需要花时间去上传每个产品图案。"此外,ShopTab 零售商也不用担心其他竞争对手的产品将显示在他们的 ShopTab 标签上,因为只有自己才能将自己的产品显示在他们的 Facebook ShopTab 上。

SocialShop

SocialShop 经营的理念是将社交媒体和电子商务结合起来将会吸引更多的客户,增加更多的销售。由 Big Commerce 创建的 SocialShop 提供了范围从 24.95 美元/月到 299.95 美元/月再加上 49.95 美元开户费用的五个程序。SocialShop 易于使用,在社交背景下将商家与客户联系起来,它允许 Facebook 用户通过公司粉丝页上的"购买"选项浏览产品,查看产品的照片,与朋友快速分享产品。

Big Commerce 联合创始人兼 CEO Mitchell Harper 认为,易用性使得 SocialShop 从其他的 Facebook 商务应用中脱颖而出。他解释说:"客户可以在不到两分钟的时间内将应用程序添加到 Facebook,然后完全配置,以显示自己的产品。他们的粉丝不仅可以直接在 Facebook 上浏览产品,也可以在他们的个人网页上分享他们的产品。这是一个很好的病毒性营销形式。"

电子商务企业的 Facebook 商务战略

一个成功的 Facebook 商务战略的秘密是想出有趣的方式,吸引观众并且使他们的购物体验环节增值。就像大部分的营销和销售渠道一样,一种方式并不适合所有公司。因此,每个公司都需要一个独特的 Facebook 商务战略,从而最大限度地使他们的"购买"选项成功。以下五个策略可以帮助你通过正确的 Facebook 商务方式有效地吸引粉丝。

确定你的粉丝群体的人口特征

每个 Facebook 商务策略的定制应该迎合你具体的 Facebook 粉丝群的利益和偏好。Adgregate Markets 的高级营销经理 Erica Terrell 认为,对商家而言,在 Facebook 上销售产品的关键是,"确定粉丝群的人口特征,并尝试根据他们的兴趣吸引他们"。通过正确地了解你是在和谁沟通,你将能够真正地连接你的粉丝,创造一个成功的 Facebook 商务营销活动。

关注动态消息汇总

人们上 Facebook 是为了社交,看他们的朋友在做什么,看看图片,而不是在 Facebook 购物。Milyoni 战略和市场营销部的副总经理 Dean Alms 解释说:"绝大多数的时间都花在新闻提要上。Facebook 用户并不打算查找你的商店并最终购买你的产品,除非你通过动态消息汇总吸引他们。"通过动态消息汇总吸引粉丝可以包括增加话题的任何方式,诸如发布有趣的状态更新、上传新照片或评论别人的页面等。

将粉丝变成福音传播者

在 Facebook 上销售产品为商家提供了一个有趣的营销渠道,它将营销、销售和互动结合起来。ShopTab 的 CEO Jay Feitlinger 认为,当一个公司通过 Facebook 的商店积极吸引客户时,"粉丝们成为福音传播者,使用 Facebook 帮助传播有关你销售的产品的口碑。当你可以在人们谈论和传播你的商品时正确地开始他们的购物流程,那么让消费者从认知到实际购买的时间和精力会缩短"。

物质激励

Payvment 的 CEO Christian Taylor 认为:"从你的 Facebook 页面完成的独家交易和销售,可以带来巨大的吸引力和粉丝群体。"商家可以通过提供新产品、Facebook 的优惠券和特殊产品,以及贱卖库存销售来刺激产品在 Facebook 上的销售。这些独有的推广方式是 Facebook 商务病毒性营销的组成部分,是任何其他形式的广告无法比拟的。

变得透明

零售商们努力发展自己的 Facebook 基地,并获得他们的粉丝的信任。现在社交媒体正在变得商业化,对商家而言,通过尊重他们的粉丝来维持粉丝们的信任是必要的。Big Commerce 的联合创始人兼 CEO Mitchell Harper 提醒商家:"关键是透明度,不要把 Facebook 看作另一种"推销"你的客户的方式。相反,要把 Facebook 看作建立所有客户与发展前景透明关系的一种方式。"

Facebook 商务的未来

无论 Facebook 商务如何成功,最重要的是要记住,Facebook 是一个社交网站,而不是一个购物网站。Dean Alms 把 Facebook 商务比作棒球比赛。"你在享受球赛,但在比赛过程中,你很可能会购买一些食品、饮料,也可能甚至是一顶球帽或一件 T 恤。但你本来不会去那里'购买'。那些正确地认识 Facebook 角色的企业比那些仅仅把 Facebook 当成是一个电子商务渠道的企业会在未来做得更好。"

　　在这个早期阶段,目前还不清楚这种新的销售渠道在未来将如何演变和成长。Jay Feitlinger 和 Mitchell Harper 都认为,Facebook 的积分(Facebook 的虚拟货币)在未来的 Facebook 商务中将扮演一个重要的角色,而 Erica Terrell 预测,品牌营销策略将会有巨大变化。大家都同意,Facebook 商务正在变革我们的购物方式,使其具有真正的社会意义。问题是——你的企业将如何利用这一激动人心的新机遇?

UNIT 17

Scan of E-Business in Higher Education

Text

Summary

The following scan of e-business across higher education in Australia discusses issues, trends, activities, incentives and benefits. The scan highlights the rising popularity of e-procurement in universities' current planning for e-business; identifies systemic influences on the development of e-business in the sector; and provides a number of international examples of e-business in higher education.

The development of e-business is in its early stages in this sector, with implementation moving from student administrative systems to online financial transactions such as procurement, smart cards and online student payments.

The main gaps are at the start of the strategic planning sequence and the lack of a holistic business approach across the sector could give rise to incompatible standards of technology. Impediments to the further uptake of e-business are identified and case studies provide examples of how particular issues have been successfully addressed.

Current Usage and Plans for the Future

In the higher education part of the education sector, a major focus of IT developments in the 1990s was on student administrative systems, which are one component of e-business. Suppliers of student administrative systems such as Callista, PeopleSoft and StudentOne are each moving towards providing a facility for conducting financial transactions online.

Various universities such as Deakin University are actively implementing online procurement systems and other e-business components such as smart cards and online student payments at the Bookshop. At the University of Western Australia, student fees can be paid online and Flinders University has plans for online student enrolment and fee payment.

A university conference held by Higher Education Systems (HES) in May 2001 showed that e-procurement is still uncommon in universities although some universities such as Monash and Edith Cowan are actively planning for the implementation of e-procurement systems. The Securities Institute of Australia is an exception in installing a full-scale Customer Relationship Management System.

A comprehensive implementation of e-business across the front office, back office and supply chain of a university is not yet the norm in higher education.

Impact on Principal Industry Processes and Supply Chains

E-Business has the potential to impact on three principal industry processes:
- *Material flows*. Physical product flowing from suppliers to customers through the supply chain, as well as reverse material flows, such as production returns, servicing, recycling and disposal.
- *Information flows*. Demand forecasts, order transmissions and delivery status reports.
- *Financial flows*. Credit card information, credit terms, payment schedules, and consignment and title ownership arrangements.

E-Business also has potential to improve efficiencies in three different parts of the supply chain:
- *Upstream activities* involving accessing material and service inputs from suppliers.
- *Internal activities* involving the manufacturing and packaging of goods.
- *Downstream activities* involving the distribution and sale of products to distributors and customers.

For example,
- *Upstream*, organizations such as Edith Cowan University and Monash University are exploring ways in which e-procurement can improve efficiencies in accessing goods and services from their suppliers.
- *Internally*, a range of Australian universities are seeking to reduce the costs of issuing printed materials to external students by exploring ways to prepare and provide materials online.
- *Downstream*, organizations such as the University of Western Australia are implementing online payment of student fees.

Interviews for this study suggest that most Australian universities are just beginning to realize the full potential of e-business for improving efficiencies in the supply chain. To stimulate the adoption of e-business in the higher education sector, Higher Education Systems (HES) convened the "E-Commerce in Higher Education Conference 2001". The conference focused particularly on e-procurement and related supply chain issues. The new priorities of the HES Working Group on e-procurement that emerged from the HES conference are:

- Focus on the critical functions and processes;
- Rank e-procurement projects to optimize benefits & return on investment (ROI);
- Recommend pilot program options;
- Provide for an incremental implementation path linked to ROI;
- Incorporate economies of scale in infrastructure;
- Recommend an e-procurement management structure;
- Be compatible with university culture and environment;
- Incorporate future-proofing against technology changes;
- Provide a clear e-procurement road map and business case.

The conference reinforced the value of a collaborative approach to e-business across the higher education sector and the potential for HES to play a leadership role in facilitating this collaboration.

Gaps in the Take-up of E-business

The case studies on the Queensland University of Technology and the Securities Institute of Australia indicate that some Australian higher education organizations are advanced in their planning and implementation of e-business and are world-class in their approach. There are also gaps in the take-up of e-business in higher education by many other organizations. The main gaps occur near the start of the strategic planning sequence, where the challenges of undertaking wholesale changes are identified.

1. Comprehensiveness

Australian universities could rightly claim that they have been involved in some aspects of e-business for some time, as they embraced with vigor in the 1990s one of the building blocks of e-business: computerized administrative systems. For instance, the Callista student administration system, developed at Deakin University and used in a number of universities, was licensed by Oracle worldwide in 1998.

Despite such achievements, e-business—as a set of business principles for integrating organization-wide information and communication systems, business processes and electronic customer services—is not yet prominent in many Australian universities. Realizing the full potential gains from e-business requires comprehensive planning for and integration of the business processes and technology in the back office, front office and supply chain. This study shows that e-business is currently not being embraced in a holistic manner across many individual higher education organizations. Some of the reasons for this reluctance are:

- The newness of much of the technology available for e-business;
- The risks involved in adopting new e-business processes;
- The difficulties and costs of changing systems and processes in large organizations.

Interviews for this study also suggest that a cautious approach to e-business by the higher education sector is possibly a result of disappointments experienced by some universities with the costly and protracted development of computerized administrative systems in the 1990s.

2. Interoperability

The transition to an e-business approach is more effective when undertaken in a way that ensures interoperability between systems, both internally and externally.

There is potential for the development of islands of technology and incompatible standards of technology, particularly in the e-procurement domain, unless data and systems are compatible. Collaborative arrangements between the different owners of data sets and systems greatly enhance operational efficiency. For example, Australian universities tend to use one of three different computerized student administration systems, PeopleSoft, Callista and StudentOne. Each of these systems either provides now or will in the near future, an e-business facility for conducting financial transactions online. Individual institutions and the sector as a whole would benefit if these different e-commerce systems conformed to agreed standards, so that suppliers to different universities, for instance, were able to interface with all universities' systems.

The need for standards and software which provides interoperability between different applications on offer to institutions in a competitive market environment is being recognized by vendors, and facilitated by government. The Australian procurement and Construction Council's (APCC) Framework for Cooperation on Electronic Commerce for procurement provides a useful approach to standardization in this area.

3. Strategic Planning

If e-business is to eventually expand in the higher education sector, holistic strategic planning approaches to the development of e-business within each organization and collaborative planning approaches across the sector are desirable. However, such extensive planning requires substantial commitment of time and effort at both the organizational and systemic levels. In the short term, many higher education organizations are adopting some specific components of e-business, mostly the e-procurement component and Customer Relationship Management.

Impediments to the Further Uptake of E-business

The reasons for the hesitation about or slow adoption of e-business in many Australian higher education are complex and numerous. In the response to a fact finding survey as part of this study, Deakin University identified the following impediments to the development of e-business:

- Security concerns
- Authentication concerns
- Cost of development
- Limits on other resources for development and implementation
- Disparate information technologies
- Interactivity of systems
- Difficulties in defining and using international standards
- Future reading, committing to particular platforms and/or technologies
- Attitudes of mistrust or perfectionism
- De-humanizing processes
- Lack of a universal consistent industry-wide standard
- Possible limitations of technology

The response from Deakin University echoes the views expressed by interviewees from other higher education organizations: while different organizations have a number of achievements in e-business, the take-up of e-business in higher education is influenced by a range of impediments which require persistent attention to address.

Final Comment

As in the rest of the world, many Australian higher education institutions are in the early stages of moving into e-business and the challenges as well as the incentives are numerous. Some world-class developments in e-business are evident in the sector in Australia. A key to the introduction of an integrated, whole-of-organization approach to e-business in the sector will be a focus on collaboration between universities, government and suppliers. Sharing of findings about the business benefits of e-business will significantly influence future decisions.

Words and Expressions

incentive [in'sentiv]	n.	动机
	adj.	激励的
administrative [əd'mini‚streitiv]	adj.	管理的；行政的
incompatible [‚inkəm'pætəbl]	adj.	性质相反的；矛盾的；不调和的
holistic [həu'listik]	adj.	整体的；全盘的
impediment [im'pedimənt]	n.	妨碍，阻碍；障碍物
procurement [prə'kjuəmənt]	n.	获得，取得；(政府的)征购，采购
potential [pəten∫(ə)l]	adj.	潜在的，可能的
	n.	潜能，潜力；电压
servicing ['sə:visiŋ]	n.	维修
disposal [dis'pəuzəl]	n.	处理，处置；布置，安排；配置，支配
credit terms		赊销付款条件 信用证条款，贷款(信用)条件
consignment [kən'sainmənt]	n.	(货物的)交托，交货；发货；运送；托付物，寄存物
external students		走读生，校外生
convene [kən'vi:n]	v.	召集，集合
incremental [inkri'mentəl]	adj.	增加的
economies of scale		因经营规模扩大而得到的经济节约；规模经济
infrastructure ['infrə'strʌkt∫ə]	n.	下部构造；基础下部组织
undertaking [‚ʌndə'teikiŋ]	n.	事业，企业；承诺，保证
wholesale ['həulseil]	n.	批发，趸售
	adj.	批发的；[喻]大规模的
prominent ['prɔminənt]	adj.	卓越的，显著的，突出的
cautious ['kɔ:∫əs]	adj.	谨慎的，小心的
protract ['prɔtrækt]	v.	延长
interoperability ['intərɔpərə'biləti]	n.	互用性；协同工作的能力

interface ['intə(:),feis]	n.	分界面,接触面,界面
vendor ['vendə]	n.	卖主
on offer		出售中
facilitate [fə'siliteit]	vt.	使容易,使便利;推动;帮助;使容易;促进
substantial [səb'stænʃəl]	adj.	坚固的,实质的,真实的,充实的
authentication [ɔ:ˌθenti'keiʃən]	n.	证明,鉴定
disparate ['dispərit]	adj.	全异的
echo ['ekəu]	n.	回声,回音
	vi.	发回声,共鸣;随声附和

Notes

(1) The development of e-business is in its early stages in this sector, with implementation moving from student administrative systems to online financial transactions such as procurement, smart cards and online student payments. 高等教育系统中,电子商务发展还处在初级阶段,其应用正在从学生管理系统转向在线金融交易,例如电子化采购、智能卡和学生在线支付。

(2) The case studies on the Queensland University of Technology and the Securities Institute of Australia indicate that some Australian higher education organizations are advanced in their planning and implementation of e-business and are world-class in their approach. 对昆士兰科技大学和澳大利亚证券学院的个案分析,表明了一些澳大利亚高等教育机构在电子商务的规划和实施方面保持领先,并且它们的成就是世界级的。

(3) Australian universities could rightly claim that they have been involved in some aspects of e-business for some time, as they embraced with vigor in the 1990s one of the building blocks of e-business: computerized administrative systems. 澳大利亚大学完全可以声称他们很早就开始对电子商务有所接触了,因为他们在20世纪90年代已积极采用了电子商务的基础——计算机处理的管理系统。

(4) The need for standards and software, which provides interoperability between different applications on offer to institutions in a competitive market environment, is being recognized by vendors, and facilitated by government. 虽然存在市场竞争,但不同的应用软件开发者们已经开始意识到需要标准和软件来实现不同系统之间的互操作性,同时政府也在推动其实现。

(5) The response from Deakin University echoes the views expressed by interview-

ees from other higher education organizations: while different organizations have a number of achievements in e-business, the take-up of e-business in higher education is influenced by a range of impediments which require persistent attention to address. 来自Deakin大学的回应也证实了那些其他高等教育组织的受访者的观点：尽管不同的组织在电子商务方面取得了许多成就，但是高等教育机构中电子商务的兴起还受一系列障碍的影响，这些需要长久的关注。

Questions

(1) What is the current usage of e-business in most Australian universities? Why so?
(2) What is e-business's impact on principal industry process and supply chain?
(3) What is the gap in the take-up of e-business?
(4) What is the impediment to the further uptake of e-business?
(5) According to you, what is the future trend of e-business in higher education?

Exercises

1. **Translate the following sentences into Chinese:**
(1) The university is investigating the payment of parking fines via the web.
(2) Payment data is transferred from the bank to the university via a dial-in facility.
(3) The university plans to implement online payment to major suppliers in 2002 following the implementation of Peoplesoft Financials version.
(4) The university has implemented a smart card system whereby all staff and students have a card that has the facility to hold money in two electronic purses.
(5) Facilities to accept payment are located in the parking office, sports centre, guild shops and tavern, libraries and several other university offices that accept payment for services or resources.

2. **Translate the following sentences into English:**
(1) 在当前各大学的电子商务规划中，电子采购正日益普及。
(2) 高等教育部门的电子商务发展还处在早期阶段，其实施正在从学生管理系统转向在线的金融交易，例如采购、智能卡和学生在线支付。
(3) 许多澳大利亚的大学刚认识到电子商务对提高供应链效率的潜力。
(4) 个案分析表明，一些澳大利亚高等教育机构在电子商务的规划和实施方面保持领先，而且他们的成就是世界级的。
(5) 高等教育机构中，电子商务的兴起还是受到一系列障碍的影响，这些需要长久关注。

Further Reading

This text is selected from *E-business in Education*: *Case Studies on the Effective Use of Electronic business in the Education Sector*. The information in this publication is based on the research and consultations of John Mitchell from John Mitchell & Associates on behalf of the Australian National Office for the Information Economy (NOIE); May 2002.

Translation

高等教育电子商务扫描

概　　述

以下这篇文章扫描了澳大利亚高等教育系统中电子商务的应用情况,谈到了许多问题,包括高等教育系统中电子商务的发展趋势、具体应用、开展的动因与益处。重点读到了在现今大学规划中越来越受到欢迎的电子化采购,电子商务发展对教育部门系统化的影响;同时也提供了一些国际上高等教育电子商务的案例。

高等教育系统中,电子商务发展还处在初级阶段,其应用正在从学生管理系统转向在线金融交易,例如电子化采购、智能卡和学生在线支付。

高等教育电子商务规划是战略性的,何时开始这一规划造成了主要的差距,同时缺乏一个跨部门的从全盘的视角进行考虑的实施方案也会导致互不兼容的技术标准的产生。文章指出进一步推进电子商务存在的障碍,案例的研究为我们提供了如何解决特定问题的范例。

现状与规划

20世纪90年代,教育部门的高等教育这一块对信息技术的关注主要表现是在学生管理系统,这一系统是电子商务的一个组成部分。学生管理系统提供商,诸如Callista、PeopleSoft和StudentOne,都开始提供在线金融交易工具。

比如Deakin大学等许多大学,都在积极地采用在线采购系统和其他的电子商务项目,比如使用智能卡以及在书店实现在线支付。在西澳大利亚大学,学生的学费可以在网上支付,而且Flinders大学已经打算在网上登记注册入学和支付学费。

2001年5月由高等教育系统(HES)主办的大学讨论会表明,虽然在一些大学,例如Monash、Edith Cowan等都在积极准备实施电子采购系统,但电子采购在大学中仍未普及。澳大利亚证券学院是个例外,他们安装了一套全方位的客户关系管理系统。

电子商务在大学的前台办公、后台办公以及供应链中的综合实施仍然不是高等教育的一般标准。

对主要行业流程和供应链的影响

电子商务对主要的三个业务流程有潜在的影响：
- 物流。物质产品通过供应链从供应商流入顾客，也可以进行物资的反向流动，比如产品回收、维修、服务、循环和处置。
- 信息流。需求预报、订单传送以及交货状况报告。
- 资金流。信用卡信息、信用证条款、支付计划表以及委托支付和财产所有权安排。

电子商务还拥有提高供应链中三个不同部分的效率的潜力：
- 上游活动，包括从供应商处获得物资和服务的投入。
- 内部活动，包括产品的制造和包装。
- 下游活动，包括产品向分销商及顾客的分发销售。

举例来说：
- 上游，如 Edith Cowan 大学和 Monash 大学等这些组织正在探索一些途径，通过电子化采购以提高从供应商那里获得商品和服务的效率。
- 内部，许多澳大利亚大学正在探索方法并准备提供在线材料给校内学生，以减少提供纸质印刷品的成本。
- 下游，一些组织（如西澳大利亚大学）正在实施在线支付学费。

为本研究所作的访谈表明大多数澳大利亚大学才刚刚开始意识到电子商务对提高供应链效率的潜力。为了促进电子商务在高等教育部门的使用，高等教育系统（HES）召集举办了一次"高等教育电子商务 2001 年会"。这次会议特别集中讨论了电子采购和相关的供应链问题。这次 HES 会议提出的 HES 电子采购工作小组新的优先工作领域包括：
- 集中于关键性功能和流程；
- 把电子采购列为收益和投资回报率（ROI）最乐观的项目；
- 推荐试点性的项目选择；
- 增加一个链接到 ROI 的实施途径；
- 通过整合使之体现设施方面的规模经济；
- 推荐一种电子采购的管理结构；
- 使之与大学文化氛围及环境相协调；
- 对未来的技术变革有所准备；
- 提供一个清晰的电子交易的发展蓝图与商务案例。

这次会议加强了高等教育部门以合作方式实施电子商务的价值，同时强调了 HES 在促进这种合作方面发挥领导作用的潜力。

在电子商务执行中存在的差距

对昆士兰科技大学和澳大利亚证券学院的个案分析,表明了一些澳大利亚高等教育机构在电子商务的规划和实施方面保持领先,并且它们的成就是世界级的。但在其他高校部门的执行中还存在着不小的差距。主要的差距在进行电子商务这一战略性规划的起始阶段就已存在,在这一阶段要经受全局变革的挑战是确信无疑的。

1. 综合性

澳大利亚大学完全可以声称他们很早就开始对电子商务有所接触了,因为他们在20世纪90年代已积极采用了电子商务的基础——计算机处理的管理系统。比如说,Callista 大学学生管理系统,由 Deakin 大学开发并为许多大学所使用,并已在1998年获得 Oracle 公司的全球认证。

电子商务作为一整套的商业规则,旨在整合机构内的信息和交流系统、业务流程和电子化客户服务,然而这一作用在大部分澳大利亚大学中仍不明显。要认识到来自电子商务的全部潜在收益,就需要全面规划并整合后台办公、前台办公和供应链的业务流程和技术。这项研究表明,目前,高教机构中的许多单位并不是全方位地实施电子商务的部分原因如下:

- 对电子商务带来的新技术不熟悉;
- 采用新的电子商务流程的风险性;
- 在大型组织中改变系统和流程的困难和成本。

这份研究的访问还暗示了高等教育部门采取这种小心谨慎的态度来接触电子商务,可能是因为一些学校在20世纪90年代采用计算机化管理系统时由高额成本和冗长拖沓所带来的失望情绪。

2. 互操作性

如果保证了系统之间的互操作性,那么无论是内联的还是外联的,都将使得向电子商务的转换更为有效。

除非数据和系统是兼容的,否则技术孤岛和技术标准不兼容的情况仍有出现的可能性,特别是在电子采购领域。而在不同的数据集合和系统所有者之间的协同安排将极大地提升操作效率。比如说,澳大利亚的大学选择的三种计算机化学生管理系统,PeopleSoft、Callista 和 StudentOne,在现在或不久的将来都会利用电子商务手段实现在线的金融交易。如果这些不同的电子商务系统可以遵从统一的标准,那么单独的机构以及作为整体的部门都将从中受益。比如,不同大学的供应商都能够与所有大学的系统进行对接。

虽然存在市场竞争,但不则的应用软件开发者们已经开始意识到需要标准的软件来实现不同系统之间的互操作性,同时政府也在推动其实现。澳大利亚采购与建设委员会(APCC)为实现基于电子商务平台的电子化采购合作所制订的框架为这一领域的标准化提供了一条有效的途径。

3. 战略规划

如果电子商务要最终在整个高等教育系统展开，那么每一组织内部必须进行电子商务全盘战略规划和跨部门协作的规划。然而，这样全面的规划需要在组织层面和系统层面上有巨大的时间和精力的投入。短期内，许多高教组织正在采纳一些具体的电子商务项目——主要是电子采购和客户关系管理。

未来电子商务发展的阻碍

许多澳大利亚高等教育部门对是否采纳电子商务踌躇不定或行动迟缓的原因是复杂和多样的。作为这份研究的一部分，在对 Deakin 大学的实际调查中，其指出了以下一些电子商务发展的阻碍：

- 安全顾虑
- 认证顾虑
- 发展的成本
- 所需的其他资源的限制
- 全异信息技术
- 系统的交互性
- 定义和使用国际标准的困难
- 未来趋势，致力于专门的平台和(或)技术
- 不信任或完美主义者的态度
- 非人性化流程
- 缺乏一个通用一致的行业化的标准
- 可能的技术局限性

来自 Deakin 大学的回应也证实了那些其他高等教育组织的受访者的观点：尽管不同的组织在电子商务方面取得了许多成就，但是高等教育机构中电子商务的兴起还受一系列障碍的影响，这些需要长久的关注。

总　　结

正如与世界上的其他地区一样，许多澳大利亚高等教育机构正处在向电子商务转型的早期阶段，挑战与激励都是巨大的。一些世界级水平的电子商务成果在澳大利亚教育部门中已引人注目。在该部门中引入一个综合的、全盘的电子商务解决方法的关键将在于大学、政府和供应商之间的协同。共同分享电子商务商业价值的研究成果将极大地影响未来的决策。

CHAPTER 5
E-BUSINESS CASE STUDIES

电子商务案例

- Case Study of CRM: Securities Institute of Australia
- TDC's Implementation of E-Commerce
- Deutsche Bank's E-Trust
- Viral Marketing of Kettle Foods
- Groupon Case Study
- Hitachi Group Achieves an Integrated Collaboration Environment through E-business

UNIT 18 Case Study of CRM: Securities Institute of Australia

Text

Customer relationship management (CRM) systems are used by membership based organizations, but not by many educational bodies. One Australian provider of higher education programs, the Securities Institute of Australia (SIA), a specialist in financial planning and related education courses, recently took the unusual step of buying and modifying an off-the-shelf CRM system to provide a range of functions including a student management system. Most other higher education providers in Australia purchase a student management system before considering the addition of CRM. The case study explains why the Securities Institute of Australia took this innovative approach.

Background

The not-for-profit Securities Institute of Australia is both an educational body and a membership-based organization in the finance industry. Apart from providing fee-for-service, customized and continuing professional development activities, the SIA offers a range of accredited courses ranging from Associate Diploma level to Masters Level, in programs such as the Diploma of Financial Advising and the Graduate Diploma in Financial Planning.

Over 28,500 subject enrolments were taken in 2000, with 40% of diploma and graduate diploma subjects completed via distance education. The 2,000 enrolments included 1,200 international students from 59 different countries. The institute has a joint venture with a Malaysian fund management organization and regularly delivers courses in Kuala Lumpur. The SIA has also secured a tender to provide an intensive training program in China in credit risk management.

SIA members in 2000 totaled 9,700 and included professionals in fields such as financial planning, superannuation and investment. The SIA has offices and teaching facilities in Sydney, its headquarters, Melbourne, Brisbane, Adelaide and Perth and its revenue in 2000 was $26.6 m.

CRM business Drivers

Prior to the development of the CRM system, customer relationship management capabilities within the Securities Institute were limited due to the lack of centralized information, lack of flexibility in its information systems and inadequate information analysis. CRM now provides an opportunity for the Securities Institute to improve information handling, improve relationships with customers and reduce manual processes.

Another driver for the Securities Institute is the threat from competitors. The threat is a reality for the Securities Institute, as students in most countries of the world can easily enroll with organizations say, in the USA, which offer similar, specialized programs to the Institute and use online technologies extensively. The online revolution means that the Securities Institute needs to match and surpass global competitors in its industry if it is to survive.

The CRM development at the Securities Institute was also stimulated by the need to replace an aging technology infrastructure, the threat from competitors in the use of online communication with students and the desire to improve internal efficiencies. To address these and other issues, the Securities Institute decided to purchase an existing CRM software package, Onyx, and to modify the software to suit the Institute, according to Information Technology Manager David Mitchell.

"We had a dire business need to replace the previous technological infrastructure: it was so bad it was threatening the business. Purchasing the CRM system was an opportunity to sweep away the old technology and to start again with a clean slate," Mr. Mitchell said.

Another driver for the initiative was the desire of the Securities Institute to relate to its many distance education students in a more holistic way, offering them more than just a one-off course. It wanted to provide an enhanced range of one-to-one services to its students and members, rather than offer a restricted range of services for cohorts of students. According to General Manager, business Development and Service, Dennis Macnamara the CRM approach enabled the Securities Institute to relate to students as individuals, not as members of a class.

"The CRM system provides us with intelligence about each student or member and enables us to match each individual with value-added services. For instance, in an increasing number of our courses, a student can enroll at any time of the year, select what mix of distance education, online and face-to-face support is preferred, and communication between the two parties can continue for the rest of their career, not just for a semester," Dennis Macnamara said.

Description of the CRM System

The implementation of the CRM system involves three core parties: the Securities Institute, the supplier of the CRM system Onyx and the website developer XT3. A team of up to eight staff from Onyx worked on the project from late 2000 to mid 2001, assisted by four Institute staff. Implementation of the Onyx Employee Portal (OEP) began as part of the first stage of the project in January 2001 with functionality rolled out progressively during first semester 2001. Onyx Customer Portal (OCP) development—in conjunction with SIA's revamped transactional website began in June 2001, with a launch scheduled for August 2001. Functionality implemented in the first stage includes a central location to:

- access and manage information about students, practitioners, members and prospects;
- capture and maintain multiple addresses against each contact;
- capture and maintain multiple phone numbers against each contact;
- track demographic information (e. g. market sector and geographic region) against each customer;
- maintain one running tally of continuing professional development points against each individual;
- provide systematic address validation and formatting.

A feature of the functioning CRM system is the easy-to-use web interface, which sits above the different databases in the Securities Institute. The second phase of the project, in 2001, involves the implementation of the Customer Portal and the redevelopment of the website and the following functions:

- Customer portal functionality, lead capture and profiling.
- Commerce functionality, online product catalogue; order processing.
- Additional services, product registration; order history; profile management; online product and literature catalogue; web self-help; online service and support.

With the implementation of the second phase of the project completed in late 2001, a student is able to use the site to find out information about the Institute and its products. They can also search for a type of course to suit his/her needs, register interest to be notified about when an event might be available in their area, enroll in a course and a subject and apply for membership. In addition they can find a program to suit his/her needs by answering a number of questions, e-mail an interesting part of the site to a friend, communicate with other students using a moderated web based forum, change their contact details and view their timetable and results.

Besides providing each user with the above services, the CRM system allows the Institute to secure the site; provide restricted and value-add content to designated or targeted Securities Institute customers and promote its products and services and any news or success stories.

Challenges and Responses

The major challenges for the Institute in implementing the CRM system were not only to modify existing CRM software to suit the Institute's hybrid customer mix of students and members, but to understand how the system might impact on the Institute's business processes. It needed to alert staff to the impending changes on their jobs and help them develop new skills required to support the CRM system. Hence, a business process reengineering expert was engaged by the Institute to identify business processes that would be affected and to work with the staff. To ensure the CRM system is used optimally, internal policies also needed addressing.

According to David Mitchell, operational sections of the Institute needed to be alerted to what was going to happen with the implementation of the CRM system.

Dennis Macnamara is conscious of the risks taken and the benefits that are possible.

"It was a brave decision by the Securities Institute Board, as a CRM system normally sits on top of an existing system and doesn't drive it", he said.

"People don't yet realize how good it will be: it has huge potential. It breaks down the division in our business between students doing our accredited courses and our continuing professional development courses and our members. All of them can be serviced equally well, in a customized manner and more quickly with the CRM system. However, it is still early days and we have much more to do; we underestimated the amount of effort to get it right; and we still need to access infrastructure funds to make best use of it."

While the first two stages of the project will cost around $2.5 m, the Securities Institute believes it chose the right path. There is now some potential for the Securities Institute to sell its intellectual property in how it customized an off-the-shelf CRM product to suit its specific context.

Research by the SIA and their supplier suggests that the Securities Institute's initiative, as an educational and membership body, in implementing a powerful CRM system as its main software engine, sitting atop the other software applications in the organization, is a world-class achievement.

Conclusion

The Securities Institute case study shows a small, dynamic organization taking an innovative approach to integrating its back office and front office systems. The case study highlights the benefits of CRM when thoroughly planned and carefully implemented, in moving an organization to change its focus from supplying product to meeting customer demand.

Words and Expressions

securities [si'kjuəritiz]	n.	有价证券
addition [ə'diʃən]	n.	加,加起来;增加物,增加,加法
accredit [ə'kredit]	vt.	信任;授权;归于
associate [ə'səuʃieit]	vt.	使发生联系,使联合
	vi.	交往,结交
	n.	合作人,同事
	adj.	副的
diploma [di'pləumə]	n.	文凭,毕业证书;证明权力、特权、荣誉等的证书,奖状
Malaysian [mə'leiziən]	adj.	马来群岛的
	n.	马来群岛
credit risk	n.	信用风险,信贷风险
superannuation [ˌsjuːpərænju'eiʃən]	n.	领养老金退休,退休金
dire ['daiə]	adj.	可怕的
holistic [həu'listik]	adj.	整体的,全盘的
cohort ['kəuhɔːt]	n.	军队,步兵大队;一群
intelligence [in'telidʒəns]	n.	智力,聪明,智能
revamp ['riː'væmp]	v.	修补
central location		中央位置
demographic [deməˈɡræfik]	adj.	人口统计学的

designate ['dezigneit]	vt.	指明,指出,任命,指派
	v.	指定,指派
hybrid ['haibrid]	n.	杂种,混血儿,混合物
	adj.	混合的,杂种的
impend [im'pend]	vi.	进行威胁;即将发生
optimal ['ɔptiməl]	adj.	最佳的,最理想的

Notes

(1) One Australian provider of higher education programs, the Securities Institute of Australia(SIA), a specialist in financial planning and related education courses, recently took the unusual step of buying and modifying an off-the-shelf CRM system to provide a range of functions including a student management system. 作为一个澳大利亚高等教育项目的提供者,澳大利亚证券学院(SIA)是财经计划及相关课程方面的专家。最近它采取了一个不寻常的举动:购买并优化了一套能提供包括学生管理系统功能在内的一系列功能的现有 CRM 系统。

(2) Apart from providing fee-for-service, customized and continuing professional development activities, the SIA offers a range of accredited courses ranging from Associate Diploma level to Masters level, in programs such as the Diploma of Financial Advising and the Graduate Diploma in Financial Planning. 除了提供付费服务、客户定制的持续的职业发展活动外,SIA 还提供了一系列官方认可的课程计划,范围从大学预科文文凭到硕士层次水平,比如金融广告文凭和金融计划硕士文凭。

(3) The CRM development at the Securities Institute was also stimulated by the need to replace an aging technology infrastructure, the threat from competitors in the use of online communication with students and the desire to improve internal efficiencies. 证券学院的 CRM 发展也来自于取代过时的技术设施的需求的刺激、来自竞争者与学生应用在线交流沟通的威胁以及改善内部效率的愿望。

(4) Another driver for the initiative was the desire of the Securities Institute to relate to its many distance education students in a more holistic way, offering them more than just a one-off course. 这一指施的另一个动力则是来自于证券学院希望以一种更加全面的方式与那些接受远程教育的学生进行联系,而不仅仅向他们提供是一次性的课程。

(5) Besides providing each user with the above services, the CRM system allows the Institute to secure the site; provide restricted and value-add content to designated or targeted Securities Institute customers and promote its products and services and any news or success stories. 除了给每一个使用者提供以上服务外,CRM系统允许学院维护网站安全;提供严格限定的增值内容给指定或者目标客户以促销产品和服务,并提供一些新闻和成功的例子。

Questions

(1) What are the CRM business drivers of SIA?
(2) What are the components of CRM system? And how were it implemented?
(3) How to describe the CRM system?
(4) What is the major challenge for the institute in implementing CRM system?

Exercises

1. Translate the following sentences into Chinese:
(1) Flinders University has plans for on-line student enrolment and fee payment to be implemented by end of 2002. The University is looking at e-procurement but has no real plans to implement yet.
(2) Principal supply chain of interest to the university is in procurement.
(3) Curtin University has participated in an online auction process for studying.
(4) The West Australian government is piloting an e-procurement initiative (the GEM project) and some West Australian universities are waiting to participate.
(5) The University of Melbourne operates procurement and workflow system (electronic in-tray) that uses digital signatures and eliminates internal paper flows associated with orders, staff leaves, etc.

2. Translate the following sentences into English:
(1) 澳大利亚证券学院认为CRM是其生存的基础,证明了风险与投资的恰当性。
(2) 澳大利亚证券学院既是金融行业中的教育实体,也是一个基于会员化管理的组织。
(3) 缺乏集中的信息、信息系统缺乏弹性以及信息分析不充分,都对证券学院的客户关系管理能力构成挑战。
(4) 证券学院希望给学生和会员们提供更大范围的一对一服务,而不是给一大批学生提供一个范围严格限定的服务。
(5) 尽管人们目前还没有认识到CRM有多么地好,但它拥有巨大潜力。

Further Reading

You can see the full text in *E-business in Education*: *Case Studies on the Effective Use of Electronic business in the Education Sector*, issued by the commonwealth of Australia. This publication is also available online from www.noie.gov.au.

Translation

CRM 案例研究：澳大利亚证券学院（SIA）

客户关系管理（CRM）系统被用于基于会员化管理的组织中，却不能为大多数教育机构所使用。作为一个澳大利亚高等教育项目的提供者，澳大利亚证券学院是财经计划及相关课程方面的专家。最近它采取了一个不寻常的举动：购买并优化了一套能提供包括学生管理系统功能在内的一系列功能的商品化的 CRM 系统。澳大利亚大多数其他的高等教育提供者在考虑增加 CRM 之前都只是购买学生管理系统。本案例研究解释了澳大利亚证券学院（SIA）为什么采取这一创新之举。

背　　景

非营利性的澳大利亚证券学院既是金融行业中的一个教育实体，又是一个基于会员化管理的组织。除了提供付费服务、客户定制化的持续的职业发展活动外，SIA 还提供了一系列官方认可的课程计划，范围从大学预科文凭层次到硕士层次水平，比如金融广告文凭以及金融计划硕士文凭。

在 2000 年，注册的课程数超过了 28,500 人，40% 的文凭和研究生文凭的课程完全通过远程教育实现。注册的 2000 名学生中有 1200 名是来自 59 个不同国家的国际学生。该学院与马来西亚基金管理组织合资并且定期在吉隆坡授课。SIA 还正式中标在中国提供关于信用风险管理方面的集训课程。

在 2000 年 SIA 的成员已达 9700 人，包括在一些诸如金融计划、退休金和投资等领域的专业人士。SIA 在总部悉尼以及墨尔本、布里斯班、阿德莱德、珀斯有办事处和教学机构，2000 年它的总收入为 2660 万美元。

CRM 商业动力

在 CRM 系统开发前，由于缺乏集中的信息、信息系统缺乏弹性以及信息分析的不充分，证券学院的客户关系管理能力是有限的，CRM 现在为证券学院提供了用来改进其信息处理能力、改善与客户关系并减少人工流程的机会。

证券学院的另一个动力来自竞争者的威胁。威胁对于证券学院而言是实实在在存在的,因为世界上大多数国家的学生能很容易在一个教育机构注册,比如说在美国,它们与证券学院提供相似的专业程序并广泛使用在线技术。在线革命意味着证券学院要想生存的话,就要与本行业的全球竞争者保持相当,并超越他们。

证券学院的 CRM 发展也来自于取代过时的技术设施的需求的刺激,来自竞争者与学生应用在线交流沟通的威胁以及改善内部效率的愿望。为了解决以上和其他问题,证券学院决定购买现存的 CRM 套装软件包——Onyx,据信息技术主管大卫·米歇尔称他们对该程序进行了修改,使之适合学院的需要。

米歇尔先生说:"我们有一个强烈的商业需求去取代先前的技术设施,它太糟糕了,以至于对业务产生了威胁。购买 CRM 系统是清除陈旧技术并开创一个清晰记录的机会。"

这一动议的另一个动力则是来自于证券学院希望以一种更加全面的方式与那些接受远程教育的学生进行联系,而不仅仅是向他们提供一次性的课程。它想要给学生和会员们提供更大范围的一对一的服务,而不是给一大批学生提供一个范围限定的服务。按照业务发展与服务总经理 Dennis Macnamara 的说法,CRM 使证券学院把学生作为个体进行联系,而不是作为班级的成员。

Dennis Macnamara 说:"CRM 系统提供给我们每一个学生或会员的智力信息,使我们能够根据每一个个体提供增值服务,比如,在数量不断增加的课程中,一个学生可以在一年的任何时候注册上课,选择任意组合的远程教育,在线和面对面的支持成为首选。双方的交流可以持续其整个职业生涯而不仅是一个学期。"

CRM 系统的描述

CRM 系统的实施包含三个主要参与者:证券学院、CRM 系统软件提供者 Onyx 和网站开发商 XT3。来自 Onyx 的八人工作小组在证券学院 4 名工作人员的帮助下从 2000 年后期到 2001 年中期从事此项目的工作。在 2001 年 1 月,Onyx 雇员门户(OEP)作为该项目第一阶段的一个部分开始实施,并在 2001 年第一学期功能性地渐进式铺开。按照一份 2001 年 8 月的启动计划,Onyx 客户门户(OCP)开发——与修改后的证券学院交易网站的对接——在 2001 年 6 月展开,并按计划在 2001 年 8 月试开通。第一阶段功能的实施包含一个核心定位:

- 获得并管理有关学生、从业者、会员和可能的候选人的信息(潜在顾客);
- 针对每一次联络获取和维护多重地址;
- 针对每一次联络获取和维护电话号码;
- 针对每一个顾客,追踪人口统计学信息(例如市场部门和地理区域);
- 针对每一个人,保持一个连续职业发展的动态记录;
- 提供系统化的地址确认和格式编排。

功能性 CRM 系统的其中一个特征是基于证券学院的不同数据库基础之上的易于使用的网络界面。在 2001 年,项目的第二阶段包含顾客门户实施和网站再开发及以下功能:

- 客户门户功能,引导吸引和给出产品介绍;

■ 交易功能,在线产品目录、订购处理;
■ 额外服务,产品登记、订购历史、产品介绍管理、在线产品和文献目录、网页自助及在线服务支持。

随着项目第二阶段在 2001 年后期的完工,学生能够利用站点查找学院及其产品信息。他们还可以查找适合于他们需要的课程类型,登记其兴趣,以便当有其兴趣的事件发生时可以接到通知,注册课程及科目并申请加入会员。除此之外,他们还能通过回答一系列问题找到适合于他们需要的节目并将有趣的部分通过 E-mail 发送给朋友,使用适度的网络论坛与其他学生进行交流,改变他们的联系方式并浏览他们的课表和成绩。

除了给每一个使用者提供以上服务外,CRM 系统允许学院维护网站安全;提供严格限定的增值内容给指定或者目标客户以促销产品和服务,并提供一些新闻和成功的例子。

挑战和回应

在实施 CRM 系统时,学院最主要的挑战不仅仅是需要修改现存的 CRM 软件以适应机构中由学生和会员组成的混合客户群体,而且还需要了解该系统如何影响学院的业务流程,出于使员工关注他们工作上即将到来的变化,以及培养他们使用 CRM 系统新技能的需要,该学院聘请了业务流程重组专家来分析可能受影响的业务流程,并与员工共事。为了确保 CRM 系统得到最佳使用,内部的政策也需要得到调整。

米歇尔先生认为,必须使职能人员留心 CEM 系统实施情况。

Dennis Macnamara 意识到实施 CRM 系统所带来的风险和可能的收益。他说:"证券学院董事会作出了一个勇敢的决定,因为 CRM 系统通常是位于现有系统尖端之上的,而不是对原有系统的改良。"

"人们还没有认识到它会带来什么样的好处:它拥有巨大的潜力。它打破了学习我们的认证课程及继续职业发展课程的学生和会员之间的分隔。借助于 CRM 系统,他们所有人都能以客户定制方式,快捷而平等地享受良好的服务。然而,现在只是处在早期,我们需要做的事情还很多,我们低估了取得成果所要付出的努力,我们还需要去争取基础设施资金,以实现这一系统的最佳利用。"

尽管在项目的头两阶段将耗费 250 万美元时,证券学院相信自己的选择是正确的。证券学院拥有销售知识产权的潜力:那就是如何将现成的 CRM 套装软件定制成适应自己具体环境的应用。

SIA 和它们的供应商所做的研究表明,证券学院作为一个教育机构,一个会员制机构,其实施强大的 CRM 系统,并使之成为位于其他软件应用之上的软件引擎,他们的成就是世界级的。

结　论

证券学院案例研究展示了一个小型的、充满活力的组织采用革新的方法来整合它的前台与后台系统。案例研究强调了详细规划和认真实施时,CRM 系统的收益,即促使一个组织从提供产品转向满足客户需要过程中的收益。

UNIT 19 TDC's Implementation of E-Commerce

 Text

Brief Introduction of TDC

Headquartered in Copenhagen, Tele Danmark Communications (TDC) is one of the most successful companies in Denmark, and indeed in Europe. What started out as a small operation with just 22 subscribers has grown into a tele-communications giant with a customer base of over 15.5 million. The company employs more than 11,000 people across regional subsidiaries in Denmark as well as 12 other countries in Europe and the Middle East. TDC offers its residential and business customers a full range of telecommunication services, including broadband, ISDN, and mobile services, and also supplies the relevant hardware. As well as having a comprehensive product portfolio, TDC is characterized by efficiency and a commitment to core values. A successful combination of profitable growth, cost efficiency, and strict cost management has given the company an enviable bottom line. Not content with simply defining its values, TDC consistently applies them to its business strategy, building an enterprise that is trustworthy, customer-focused, team-oriented, and a respecter of individuality. This, in turn, has made the TDC Group the leading telecommunications player in Scandinavia. Much of this success is due to its visionary outlook.

A Pioneering Vision

TDC achieved its leading position by tirelessly pursuing the vision of becoming the top provide of communications solutions in Europe. Consistently satisfying user requirements, delivering user-focused solutions, and providing excellent customer care are all key to achieving this goal, supported by dedicated employees who drive forward technical development and share in defing the organization's values.

This ambitious vision has translated into impressive growth. In order to retain its strong customer focus and maintain maximum customer satisfaction, the company needed a new webshop based on a performing e-commerce platform. This platform had to be able to maintain the existing high standard of products and services while also offering the ability to achieve further improvements. After evaluating the available e-commerce software, TDC opted for Intershop's packaged product. By highlighting the ability of the platform to leverage TDC's vision, Intershop demonstrated that it had a profound insight into the Danish customer's needs—and was in a position to provide the necessary assistance to pursue the vision further. The two companies duly teamed to produce a new platform that offers unrivaled stability, scalability, performance, and user-friendliness. All products are available online in the new, one-stop TDC Shop at www. tdc. dk(see Figure 1).

Figure 1   one-stop TDC Shop at ww. tdc. dk

Turbo-shopping at TDC's Webshop

With just one click of the mouse, customers enter a whole new world of shopping—this stylish site is easy on the eye and equally easy to navigate. Products are clearly arranged, ensuring customers can quickly locate and order the desired items. The intuitive design makes a virtual visit to TDC a pleasant experience both for the Internet-savvy and for novices.

The unique webshop leverages sophisticated technology to ensure the website fully reflects individual customer needs and preferences. Based on Enfinity Multisite technology from Intershop Communications, the new platform requires access to TDC's internal system to obtain the necessary data. Superficially, these systems run separately alongside each other, but deeper down they are tightly integrated. Although this integration is invisible to customers, they benefit from the fast, stable performance it brings every time they visit the site. It enables the two systems to interact smoothly without errors or communication problem. Similarly, the close working relationship between TDC and Intershop ensures that both systems run quickly and reliably.

Unique Customers, Unique Service

TDC's organizational structure is modeled within the Intershop application as a standardized enterprise organization. All products are prepared for sale in this defined environment. The TDC customer base is extensive and varied, comprising residential customers, business customers, and key accounts. The different customer types are mapped using different channels: sales to residential customers take place in the consumer channel, while the partner channel is used for business customers and key accounts. There is a separate portal in the partner channel where key accounts can make their purchases.

Critically, these channels offer a shopping experience to suit each type of customer and make personalized service a reality. A new pricing module was implemented to manage this complex pricing system and ensure that prices and customers are always correctly matched. This functionality provides TDC with a valuable tool for fine-tuning customer focus even further.

All-Inclusive Bundles

Which agreement applies to which mobile phone? Can agreements and handsets be freely combined on a "pick and mix" basis? Thanks to the use of bundles, these and similar questions are now a thing of the past. On the legacy platform, mobile phones and agreements were offered separately, but the Enfinity platform features new functionality that packages the mobile telephone and agreement as a bundle. Customers no longer need to search for the relevant agreement—the correct one is already shown. This also saves a lot of time because the simplified processes significantly speed up both pricing and ordering. A positive side effect for TDC is that this approach makes it easier to manage the services and products in the system. Also, any handset subsidies can be incorporated into the bundle. Both customers and TDC benefit from this all-inclusive functionality.

Migration—Safe and Sound

Not everything about webshop is new. Although the new platform features slick, much of the data relating to customers, products, and the catalog, also business logic and program code had to be converted and adapted to the new system. To minimize the potential problems associated with this complicated procedure, Intershop's Enfinity software is equipped with a standardize migration module. This development and migration environment contains tools and packages to support migration, making it possible to complete even complex migration processes involving converting n-dimensional data to "n-1"-dimensional data and bundles quickly and reliably—two vital attributes for a successful project.

Come Closer

Benefits of the new platform include streamlining of complex processes, improved performance, and enhanced usability. The result is an outstanding Internet portal. TDC is now well on course for even greater success, with its many satisfied customers testifying to both its vision and the platform—TDC is the Danish telco with the lowest number of customer complaints compared to other global players.

"Intershop Enfinity has given us the opportunity to develop a centralized e-commerce project that exactly matches our needs, while also providing the scalability to cope with future requirements," comments Rlkke Ebel Nielsen, technical manager at TDC. By delivering a solution that met the needs of both TDC and its customers, Intershop effectively achieved customer satisfaction twice over, embracing the customer-focus mindset reflected in TDC's "Come closer" slogan.

Words and Expressions

customer base		客户圈;客户群
subsidiary [səb'sidjəri]	n.	子公司
product portfolio		产品组合
bottom line		底线;净利润
navigate ['nævigeit]	vt.	航行
module ['mɔdju:l]	n.	模块

fine-tuning		优化；微调
code [kəud]	n.	代码；规则
streamline ['stri:mlain]	adj.	流线型；简单化
embrace [im'breis]	vt.	拥抱；包括
slogan ['sləugən]	n.	口号

Notes

(1) In order to retain its strong customer focus and maintain maximum customer satisfaction, the company needed a new webshop based on a performing e-commerce platform. 为了保持其以客户为中心和最大客户满意度的理念，TDC 需要一个基于可行的电子商务平台的网店。

(2) Based on Enfinity Multisite technology from Intershop Communications, the new platform requires access to TDC's internal system to obtain the necessary data. 该平台以 Intershop 通信公司的 Enfinity Multisite 技术为基础，接入 TDC 的内部系统获取数据。

(3) On the legacy platform, mobile phones and agreements were offered separately, but the Enfinity platform features new functionality that packages the mobile telephone and agreement as a bundle. 在传统的平台上，手机与协议是分别提供的，但是 Enfinity 平台具有将手机与协议关联的功能，顾客不再需要搜索相关的协议——正确的协议已经摆在眼前了。

(4) Not everything about webshop is new. Although the new platform features slick, much of the data relating to customers, products, and the catalog, also business logic and program code had to be converted and adapted to the new system. 网店并不是什么都是新的。尽管新的平台，灵活而且与客户和产品数据关联，但仍然需要将商业逻辑和程序规范整合进来。

Exercises

1. Translate the following sentences into Chinese：

(1) TDC offers its residential and business customers a full range of telecommunication services, embracing broadband, ISDN, and mobile services, and also supplies the relevant solution.

(2) Characterized by efficiency and a commitment to core business process, TDC also have a comprehensive product portfolio.

(3) Critically, these channels offer a shopping experience to suit all types of customers and their personalized service demand.

(4) Benefits of the new platform include streamlining of complex processes; improved performance, and enhanced usability.

(5) A positive side effect for TDC is that this approach makes it easier to deal with the services and products in the system.

2. Translate the following sentences into English:

(1) 利润增长、成本效益与严格的成本管理这三者的成功组合,使得 TDC 的净利润令同行们羡慕不已。

(2) 提供客户满意、以客户为中心的解决方案以及卓越的客户服务是 TDC 成功的关键。

(3) 这一平台必须既有高标准的产品及服务,又具有进一步改善的能力。

(4) 这个复杂的定价系统中应用的新的定价模块,保证价格与客户能保持匹配。

(5) 鼠标轻点,顾客便进入了一个全新的消费天地——这个网站即时髦好看又易操作。

丹麦电信电子商务应用

丹麦电信简介

总部位于哥本哈根的 TeleDanmark 通信公司(TDC)是丹麦最成功,实际上也是欧洲最成功的公司之一。TDC 从一个只有 22 位用户的小公司起步成长为拥有 1550 万用户的通信巨人,雇员超过 11,000 人,分布在丹麦、欧洲以及中东的 12 个国家的子公司中。TDC 为其个人用户和商业用户提供全方位的通信服务,包括宽带、ISDN 和移动服务,同时也提供相关的硬件。除了拥有全面的产品组合,TDC 同样以核心价值的高效和专注而形成特色。利润增长、成本效益与严格的成本管理这三者的成功组合,使得 TDC 拥有了令人羡慕的净利润。它没有满足于仅仅简单地定义自身的价值,而是力图将这些价值作为其商业战略,打造一个可信赖的、以客户为中心的、团队合作和尊重个性的企业。正因为此,TDC 集团成为斯堪的纳维亚半岛(瑞典、挪威、丹麦、冰岛的泛称)的最主要电信运营商,它的成功大部分归功于其长远的目光。

开拓性的眼光

本着成为欧洲顶级通信解决方案提供商的愿景,TDC 一直在不懈地努力,并取得了现今的领先地位。持续提供客户满意、以客户为中心的解决方案以及卓越的客户服务是达到这一目标的关键,同时这也离不开具有献身精神的员工的支持,他们开发新的技术,共同定义 TDC 的价值。

　　这一宏伟的愿景已经变成了惊人的发展。为了保持其以客户为中心和最大客户满意度的理念,TDC 需要一个基于可行的电子商务平台的网店。这一平台必须既可以保持现有产品及服务的高标准,又具有进一步改善的能力。经过对现有电子商务软件的评估,TDC 选择了 Intershop 公司的产品包。通过突出其平台对 TDC 宏伟愿景的支持作用,Intershop 公司不仅证明了其对丹麦顾客需求的深刻理解而且能够为实现该愿景提供进一步的协助。两家公司适时地组队研发平台,提供无与伦比的稳定性、可测性、绩效以及用户友好。TDC 所有产品都可以在 TDC 新的一站式网店 www.tdc.dk(见图 1)中找到。

TDC 网店,便捷消费体验

　　鼠标轻点,顾客便进入了一个全新的消费天地——这个网站既时髦好看又操作简单。产品整理得当,保证顾客可以很容易找到并订购所需产品。直观的设计,使得访问 TDC 网店成为一次轻松愉快的体验,对网络高手如是,对"菜鸟"亦如此。

　　独特的网店设计要求尖端的技术来保证网店可以充分反映客户个性化的需求与喜好。该平台以 Intershop 通信公司的 Enfinity Multisite 技术为基础,接入 TDC 的内部系统获取数据。表面上,这些系统独立运行,没有任何联系,但在深层次上,它们是紧密一体的。尽管顾客并看不到这种一体化,但他们在访问网站时,都享受着这种一体化带来的快捷和稳定,它使得两个系统之间可以平稳互动,而没有任何错误或通信问题。同样,紧密协作关系也保证了两个系统自身快速可靠地运行。

独特的客户,独特的服务

　　Intershop 应用软件模仿 TDC 的组织结构,并将之作为标准的企业组织形式。在这个固定的环境中,所有的商品都用于销售。TDC 的客户群广大而多样化,包括个人用户、商业用户和关键客户。不同用户使用不同的频道:个人用户使用顾客频道;商业用户与关键用户使用伙伴频道。在伙伴频道中有一个独立的关键客户入口,关键客户可以在此订购。

　　准确地说,这些频道提供适合顾客特点的消费体验,同时也使个性化服务成为了现实。一个全新的定价模块被应用于这个复杂的定价系统中,保证价格与客户始终能保持匹配。这一功能是 TDC 进一步发展其以客户为中心的理念的有力工具。

全方位关联

　　哪份协议应用于哪个手机?协议和手机可以在"挑选混合"的基础上自由组合吗?

由于关联技术的使用,这些问题和相似问题已经再也不成问题了。在传统的平台上,手机与协议是分别提供的,但是 Enfinity 平台具有将手机与协议关联的功能,顾客不再需要搜索相关的协议——正确的协议已经摆在眼前了。这同样也节省了大量时间,因为简化了流程在很大程度上也加快了出价与订购。这一方法给 TDC 带来的另一好处是在这个系统中,管理服务与产品更加简便。同样也可以关联任何手机补助金,顾客和 TDC 都从这个全方位捆绑功能中得益。

转移——完好无恙

网店并不是什么都是新的。尽管新的平台灵活而且与客户和产品数据关联,但仍然需要将商业逻辑和程序规范整合进来。为了最大限度地减少由于复杂程序带来的潜在问题,Intershop 公司的 Enfinity 软件平台设置了一个标准转移模式。这种发展与转移环境中包含着转移支持工具和软件包,使复杂的转移也可以进行,包括把 n 空间数据转换为 n-1 空间的数据,并进行关联,迅速而可靠——这是成功项目的两大特征。

更贴近一步

新平台的益处包括:简化复杂流程、提高性能和增强可用性,其成果是一个杰出的互联网门户。TDC 正在向着更大的成功迈进,众多满意的顾客验证着 TDC 的宏伟愿景也检验着这个平台——TDC 是丹麦一家通信企业,与全球同类型企业相比,它的客户投诉量最低。

"Intershop Enfinity 平台带给我们发展集中的电子商务计划的机会,这正符合我们的需要,同时也为处理未来的需求提供了可延展性。"TDC 技术主管 Rlkke Ebel Nielsen 说道。通过提供同时满足 TDC 及其顾客双方要求的方案,Intershop 有效地取得了两倍的客户满意,包括 TDC 的口号"更贴近一步"中所蕴含的以客户为中心的理念。

UNIT 20 Deutsche Bank's E-Trust

Introduction

E-business is a driver of change. The new virtual world provides a lot of business opportunities to traditional corporations as well as to dot. com companies. There is a particular need for established businesses with existing processes to actively face the challenge of the new digital and global market.

But this opportunity can also be a threat—transparency of business partners and transaction security are major barriers to e-business, if not addressed properly. Applying trust and security as a fundamental component of e-business is the answer to this threat and Identrus is Deutsche Bank's strategic solution to the problem.

What did the Internet Really Change?

The easiest way to become a millionaire these days is to go to a venture capitalist firm, selling the idea of a dot. com company, working in the field of e-commerce—it is a sure bet to raise as much money as required for retirement. That's the theory and, astonishingly, it has been the reality very often, too. But the times are nearly over. Investors and businesses now ask for revenue, return on investment, solid financing and a real business case with comprehensive numbers. Suddenly the New Economy centred around e-commerce looks more traditional again.

Selling goods over the Internet—this is new. Who is taking the liability for this order? —that is an old question.

Paying online 50,000 Euros for a delivery from Asia to Europe—this is new. But who authorised the payment? —this is certainly the traditional business, too.

In the traditional world the pre-identification of business partners is standard practice. Who would accept a letter of credit without proof that the person who signed it really exists and is authorised to do so? The same requirements for conducting business in the traditional world are valid in the online world as well, certainly in a different dimension, but using the same principles.

These principles are based on security and trust between business partners:
- The security that the retrieved message is the same one which was sent, without modifications.
- The security that pricing information via the Internet has not been visible to competitors.
- The trust that the counterparty of a business transaction is the person he or she claims to be—preferably before the transaction is processed.

Trust Me—I'm a Bank!

Banks are in a traditional trusted relationship with their customers. Clients do disclose their "private" and "corporate" financial situation to banks. Hence, banks have access to corporate accounts and financial information; they are partners for many financial requests. Building up a trusted relationship takes time and costs a lot of effort.

Trust Services need an entity, which can act as a trusted party and—at least as important—which is accepted as trustworthy by a large group, too. Especially in the New Economy of the Internet a national border is non-existent, the reach is truly global.

Therefore global financial institutions are perfectly positioned to provide this trusted role and extend it from the traditional world into the virtual world.

This acceptance has to be taken into account when looking at trusted solutions. Who in the US would rely on a German virtual seal "Trusted Application", if issued by a German private authority?

Identrus as Global "Trusted" Trust Provider

As a global financial institution, Deutsche Bank thinks also globally in terms of e-commerce and the applied trust infrastructure for it. Over the past two years, Deutsche Bank, together with several other financial institutions, has worked to form a corporation which provides global Trust Services for corporate clients on the Internet.

The corporation, known as Identrus, LLC, was set up in April 1999 with eight founding members, including Deutsche Bank and Bankers Trust as well as Bank of America, Citibank, Chase, ABN Amro, Barclays and HypoVereinsbank. Since that time, around 30 new member banks have joined Identrus, with a further 50 financial institutions soon to join. They have created a global customer reach across nearly 100 countries with currently more than 13 million corporate customers. These financial institutions have developed operating practices, a global legal framework and the technology to carry out verification of identity for corporations doing business over the Internet. Identrus offers these Trust Services based on Public Key Infrastructure technology. PKI technology provides unique key pairs. One of the keys (the private key) is used to digitally sign a message, and the other (the public key) to decrypt the digital signature in order to validate the original message.

Basically, the digital signature is the electronic counterpart of a handwritten signature. It can be created only by the owner of the private key.

But the signature alone is just one component of the infrastructure. The public key proves that one particular person has signed a message. But is this public key really trustworthy?

Certificates Enable the "E" of E-Commerce

For this trustworthiness, Deutsche Bank's Certification Authority serves as Trusted Third Party, which issues a Digital Certificate for each customer. Digital Certificates attached to a message can provide verifiable identification of the sender of the information. Checking that certificate can ensure that the party on the Internet is who he says he is. Technically speaking, the certificate can prove that the public key was issued to exactly that person who signed the message initially (using the private key).

Certificates can also provide assurance of integrity of message content and non-repudiation so that parties cannot deny that they sent or received messages.

The Identrus Trust Service is organised in a hierarchy of trust (see chart 1). The Identrus root certifies the identity of banks (Level 1 banks, like Deutsche Bank, Bank of America or National Westminster), which, in turn, issue digital certificates to employees of corporate clients so that they can do business over the Internet. When requested, the contacted bank will check the status of certificates to ensure that messages have been sent by parties who hold valid certificates from their employers.

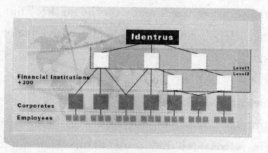

Chart 1　IDENTRUS TRUST HIERARCHY

The "Touch" of Trust

The trust infrastructure presents excellent security features, which will be a mandatory requirement in any future e-commerce engagements. But the virtual world of digital signatures and digital certificates applies a physical medium for an even higher level of security: the smartcard.

The smartcard is a physical entity which holds an embedded microchip. This microchip contains the private and public key, which is used for the generation and the validation of the digital signature. Therefore a small processor is also part of the chip. Hence, the creation of the signature is performed on the chip and only the final signature "leaves" it. All other information is kept secure on the smartcard.

In order to actually sign a message or transaction, the owner has to enter a specific PIN-code (6 or 8 digit number) which is the starting point for the signature generation. Without entering this PIN number, the user will not be able to apply the digital signature.

Furthermore the chip also stores the digital certificate, which can be read from and forwarded to an Internet business partner when required.

This additional hardware-based security medium together with the Identrus framework provides the highest trust and security standard currently available.

1. The next generation

The next generation of personal identification will most probably be based on biometrics. A fingerprint for example has a unique pattern, which can be used for an individual identification. The iris of the human eye has an even more complex pattern.

Some of these "next generation identifiers" will probably substitute the physical smartcard at some time in the future, because of one very simple reason: everywhere a person goes these identifiers are with him or her and cannot be copied (also many fingerprint readers nowadays support blood circulation control as well).

Currently a lot of investigations and experiments are being undertaken to look for these alternatives. Some solutions are already on the market, but for the foreseeable future, a robust, customer friendly and affordable alternative is not expected to be available for a broader market.

2. eTrust within Deutsche Bank

DB-eTrust is a strategic component for Deutsche Bank's e-commerce initiatives. Online risk management is considered as a mandatory element for any application and services emanating from e-commerce. This is covered by the db-eTrust solutions.

For example, the electronic marketplaces initiative provides financial and non-financial products and services to corporate clients and marketplaces. The products, like escrow services or online payment services, need to be trust-enabled to be accepted on the virtual market. Therefore Identrus provides the digital signature component for the client authorisation of the payment. Before such a payment is processed the back office system validates the signee's signature and upon the positive approval the payment is initiated.

The development of the first Identrusbased customer application worldwide by Deutsche Bank demonstrates the strategic importance of Identrus within the bank. The Electronic Bill Presentment and Payment System (db-eBills) for corporate customers requires the trust component in two ways.

Firstly, the system handles financial information and sensitive customer data, which need to be secured against third party access. To provide this security the system contains a secure logon procedure using the Identrus services for identification. The digital certificate is validated in real-time and if the status check is positive the user is gained access to the system. The data shown can be personalised based on the identification and any further activity within the application is secured and trusted.

Secondly, the approval of an outstanding bill and the subsequent payment can be initiated online (see chart 2). The payment initiation message, including payment account data, customer information and secondary payment data, is signed using the Identrus digital signature (applying the user's private key to the payment message) and then forwarded to the payment server together with the attached digital certificate of the signer. Before the payment initiation is processed within the back office systems, the identification is validated and upon its approval the further processing can take place.

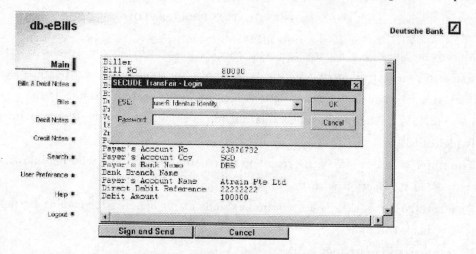

Chart 2 DEUTSCHE BANK'S FIRST IDENTRUS CUSTOMER APPLICATION

The workflow graphic (see chart 3) describes the process in detail: to start the commercial transaction between Payor and Biller (steps 1a and 1b), the Payor attaches his Identrus certificate to an electronic transaction (e. g. the payment initiation). The Biller receives the message and recognises its electronic signature and the attached digital certificate.

The Biller sends the certificate to his own bank (step 2), meaning that he does not have to rely on another bank with which he may have had no previous business contact. His bank, in turn, presents the certificate to the Payor's bank (step 3), which confirms the correctness and validity of the certificate (step 4). At this point, the identity of the Payor is established.

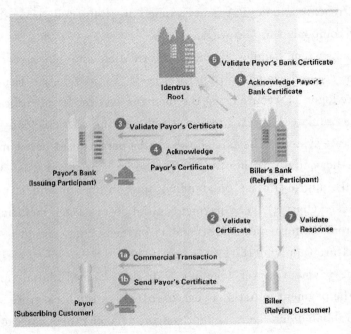

Chart 3 AUTHENTICATION PROCESS FLOW

Moreover, the Biller's bank can now check whether the Payor's bank is actually authorised to check an Identrus certificate. For this purpose, the certificate is sent to Identrus (step 5), which verifies whether such an authorisation exists. If the reply is positive (step 6), a trusting business relationship is established with all parties involved clearly identified.

The Biller's bank reports the result to its customer (step 7), who may now safely settle a trusted transaction with the Payor.

As a result, the workflow automation extends major benefits for trading parties and the biller's bank through

- Minimization of paper work
- online authorisation processes for unique identification
- legally binding signature of the payment initiation in case of claim processing re-

quests.

But using Identrus for this Deutsche Bank application goes one step further.

Any customer who owns an Identrus compliant smartcard (Identrus public and private key and digital certificate) can apply the Identrus signature and certificate for the required authorisation purposes. Due to the global Identrus framework a customer of Deutsche Bank can be legally validated by a Spanish bank, although the bank never had any contact before with this client.

This infrastructure enables a truly e-business framework, an Internet with no geographical boundaries and business processes based on legally binding identities. The virtual world as well as the traditional world requires trust and security as a business enabler.

3. To trust or not to trust—this is the question!

Trust is the enabler, but not a stand-alone feature which solves all problems. To understand the role of trust it is also important to know what trust alone is not able to deliver.

Trust provides identification of business partners, provides non-repudiation services and data integrity. Trust does not encompass the authorisation of capabilities for the identified partners.

Certainly, trust can and will be the entry point for this authorisation (entitlement systems), but the interaction between those two components has to be done first. A trusted entitlement system opens the Internet for a highly secure and trusted infrastructure.

Using Identrus through the db-eTrustCard (see Chart 4) within Deutsche Bank, we can remove the major entry barrier for business-to-business e-commerce: the lack of trust and security.

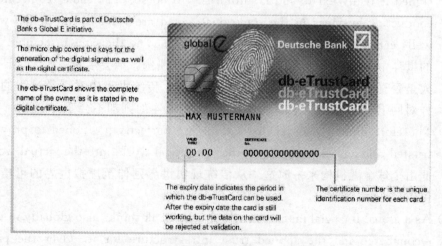

Chart 4   THE db-eTrustCard ENABLES TRUSTED E-COMMERCE

Words and Expressions

transparency [træns'pɛərənsi]	n.	透明;透明度;幻灯片;有图案的玻璃
identification [ai,dentifi'keiʃən]	n.	辨认,鉴定;证明;视为同一
corporate accounts		公司账户
practice ['præktis]	n.	惯例
entity ['entiti]	n.	实际并独立存在的事物
foreseeable [fɔː,siːəbl]	adj.	可预见到的
initiative [i'niʃiətiv]	n.	主动;首创精神,进取心;措施
mandatory ['mændətəri]	adj.	命令的,强制的,托管的
validate ['vælideit]	vt.	使有效,使生效,确认,证实,验证
certificate [sə'tifikit]	n.	证书,证明书
Infrastructure ['infrə'strʌktʃə]	n.	下部构造,基础下部组织;基础设施
business processes		业务流程

Notes

(1) In the traditional world the pre-identification of business partners is standard practice. Who would accept a letter of credit without proof that the person who signed it really exists and is authorised to do so? The same requirements for conducting business in the traditional world are valid in the online world as well, certainly in a different dimension, but using the same principles. 在传统的世界中,对生意伙伴进行事先鉴定是标准惯例。谁会接受一份无法证明签署人是否真实存在以及是否有授权的信用证?传统世界中对交易过程的要求同样对网上世界有效,虽然尺度有所不同,但基本原则却不会变。

(2) Therefore global financial institutions are perfectly positioned to provide this trusted role and extend it from the traditional world into the virtual world. 因此由全球金融机构来扮演这一从传统现实世界延伸至虚拟世界的可信赖的角色,再合适不过。

(3) As a global financial institution, Deutsche Bank thinks also globally in terms of e-commerce and the applied trust infrastructure for it. Over the past two years, Deutsche Bank, together with several other financial institutions, has worked to form a corporation which provides global Trust Services for corpo-

rate clients on the Internet. 作为一家全球金融机构,德意志银行同样也以全球眼光来考虑电子商务及应用于电子商务的信用基础设施。在过去的两年里,德意志银行联同其他七家金融机构致立于建立一家为企业客户提供网上全球信用服务的公司。

(4) For this trustworthiness, Deutsche Bank's Certification Authority serves as Trusted Third Party, which issues a Digital Certificate for each customer. 为了达成这一可信性,德意志银行认证机构作为可信的第三方,向每一位顾客提供一份数字证书。

(5) ETrust within Deutsche Bank db-eTrust is a strategic component for Deutsche Bank's e-commerce initiatives. Online risk management is considered as a mandatory element for any application and services emanating from e-commerce. This is covered by the db-eTrust solutions. 电子信用是德意志银行电子商务措施的战略性组成部分。网上风险管理被认为是任何电子商务的应用与服务的必备部分,这包括在德意志银行的电子信用解决方案之中。

Questions

1. Translate the following sentences into Chinese:

(1) Venture investors and businesses now ask for revenue, economic return, solid financing and a real business case with comprehensive numbers.

(2) It is a standard practice, the pre-identification of business partners, in the traditional world.

(3) With clients disclosing their "private" and "corporate" financial situation to banks, banks have access to corporate accounts and financial information.

(4) Firstly, the financial information and sensitive customer data which the system handles need to be secured against third party access.

(5) An Internet with no geographical boundaries and business processes based on legally binding identities, this infrastructure enables a truly e-business framework.

2. Translate the following sentences into English:

(1) 机会与挑战并存——发展电子商务的主要障碍是商业伙伴透明度及交易安全。

(2) 虽然尺度有所不同,但基本原则却不会变,传统世界中对交易过程的要求同样对网上世界有效。

(3) 数字证书可以保证信息内容的完整及提供反拒认协议服务,以防止某一方否认接受或发送过信息。

(4) 网上风险管理被认为对任何电子商务的应用与服务都是不可或缺的。

(5) 这一体系促成了真正的电子商务框架——一个没有地理边界的因特网与基于法律约束力的身份认证流程。

Further Reading

You can see the full paper with the title: *Identrus: Trusted E-business for Traditional Commerce* which is originally punished in *Treasury Management International*. By Stephan Paxmann. September 2000.

Translation

德意志银行的电子化信任

简 介

电子商务是变化的驱动者。新兴的网络虚拟世界不但为"dot.com"公司提供了大量商机,同样也给传统企业带来了机会。著名企业特别需要运用现有的手段积极应对新兴的数字化和全球化市场的挑战。

但机会同时也是挑战——可以说,商业伙伴透明度及交易安全是发展电子商务的主要障碍。将信任与安全作为电子商务的基本组成部分,则是应对这一挑战的方法,而Identrus则是德意志银行应对这一难题的战略性方案。

因特网到底改变了什么?

现今,成为百万富翁的最简易方法便是向风险投资公司兜售"dot.com"公司这样的构想,拓展电子商务——这一定会获得多得连到退休都够用的钱。这看起来是不太可能的,然而,令人惊讶的是,这样的事常常在发生。但这样的时代已经快结束了。投资者及企业需要盈利、投资的回报、实实在在的资金及大宗现实的买卖。突然之间,以电子商务为中心的新经济似乎突然又回到了传统的模式中。

网上销售——这是新生事物。谁为订购的可靠性负责?——那却是个老问题。

欧洲人向亚洲人购买商品需要在线支付5万欧元——这是新事物。但是谁来认证支付?——这当然又是一项传统的业务。

在传统的世界中,对生意伙伴进行事先鉴定是标准惯例。谁会接受一份无法证明签署人是否真实存在以及是否有授权的信用证?传统世界中对交易过程的要求同样对网上世界有效,虽然尺度有所不同,但基本原则却不会变。

这些原则建立在生意伙伴之间的交易安全与信任的基础上:
- ■ 获取信息的安全,即中间未经改动,与发送的信息一致。
- ■ 报价信息的安全,即通过互联网报价的信息对其竞争对手是不可见的。
- ■ 信任——业务活动的对方身份如他或她所称的那样真实可信,最好在交易进行之前得到确认。

相信我——我是银行！

银行与其客户的关系是传统的信用关系。客户向银行透露"个人"与"公司"的财务状况,从而,银行可以接触到公司账目及其财务信息。银行是满足资金需求的伙伴,与企业建立信任关系需要大量的时间与努力。

信用服务要求存在一个实体,以作为可信任的一方存在——至少与之同样重要——它也要能被相当数量的人认为是可信的。对于基于因特网的新经济尤其如此,因为因特网上国界不复存在,其范围是真正的全球化。

因此由全球金融机构来扮演这一从传统现实世界延伸至虚拟世界的可信赖的角色,再合适不过。

考虑信用解决方案时,接受程度也需要考虑其中。如果由德国一家私人机构发出的带有虚拟德国印章的"可信任的应用",那么美国人会认可吗？

Identrus,全球"可信任的"信用提供者

作为一家全球金融机构,德意志银行同样也以全球眼光来考虑电子商务及应用于电子商务的信用基础设施。在过去的两年里,德意志银行联同其他几家金融机构致立于建立一家为企业客户提供网上全球信用服务的公司。

这一名为"Identrus, LLC"的公司成立于1999年4月,其创始成员为八家银行,包括德意志银行、银行家信托以及美国银行、花旗银行、大通银行、荷兰银行、巴克莱银行和德国联合抵押银行。此后,约有30家银行加入了Identrus,同时约有50家金融机构即将加入。它们的客户遍布全球约100个国家,拥有的企业用户数超过13,000,000户。这些金融机构在为网上经营的公司提供认证方面有着成熟的操作程序、全球的合法框架及技术。Identrus提供基于公共密钥基础设施(PKI)技术的信用服务。PKI技术提供唯一的钥对,其中一把(私钥)用来为信息进行数字签名,而另一把(公钥)则用来解译数字信号验证原文。

基本上,数字签名是手写签名的电子对应,且只能由持有私钥者签署。但是签名仅仅是体系架构的一个组件,公钥可以证明某一特定的人签署了一份信息,可是公钥真可依赖吗？

认证使电子商务真正实现"电子化"

为了达成这一可信性,德意志银行认证机构作为可信的第三方,向每一位顾客提供一份数字证书。数字证书附加于信息之中,可以证明该信息发送者身份。核对数字证书,便可知网上的对方是否就是其本人。从技术上来讲,数字证书可以证明公钥正确地发送给了原信息签发人(使用私钥)。

数字证书同时还可以保证信息内容的完整及提供反拒认协议,以防止一方否认接受或发送过信息。

Identrus信用服务依信用层级(见图1)进行。Identrus根发放银行数字证书(第一级,如德意志银行、美国银行或(英国)国民西敏斯银行),这些银行则向企业客户的雇员发放数字证书,使其可以网上交易。当有请求时,被请求行便会检查数字证书的状态,以确保那些从雇主处获得有效证书发送方发送信息的真实有效。

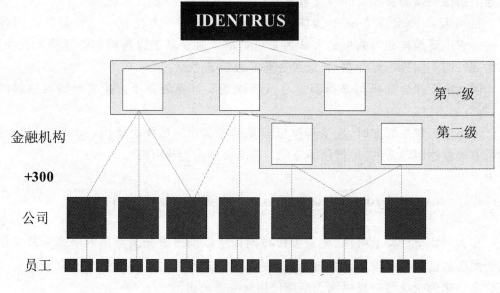

图 1　IDENTRUS 信用层级图

"触摸"信任

信用基础建设表现出许多安全优势,这些正是未来任何电子商务事务的必然要求。但是数字签名与数字证书的虚拟世界采用物理媒介达到了更高层次的安全:智能卡。

智能卡是植入了微芯片的物理实体,这种芯片包含了用以生成及确认数字签名的公钥与私钥,该芯片也包括一个小型处理器,因此数字签名在芯片内计算产生,只有最终结果"分离"出来,其他的信息均安全地保存在智能卡中。

要给信息或交易签名,首先使用者需要正确地输入一串 PIN 码(6 或 8 位数字)以产生签名。如果不输入 PIN 码,则无法完成签名。

而且该芯片中还存贮着数字证书,在需要时,可以被读取并发送给网上交易伙伴。

这一附加的硬件安全媒介加上 Identrus 构架提供了当前可用的最高信用与交易安全标准。

1. 下一代

下一代个人身份鉴别很可能是基于生物测定学的,比如说,有其独特模式的指纹,可以用来鉴别身份。人类的眼球的虹膜甚至有更为复杂的模式。

其中一些"下一代身份鉴别器"可能会在未来某一天取代现在的物理智能卡,理由很简单,一个人无论走到何地,这些鉴别器一直都在身边,而且不可复制(现在许多指纹读取器还支持血液循环控制)。

最近,人们做了大量的调查和实验来寻找这些措施。一些方案已经商用,但是在可预见的将来,还没有可以大规模使用的既可靠、用户友好又经济的措施。

2. 德意志银行电子信用

电子信用是德意志银行电子商务措施的战略性组成部分。网上风险管理被认为是任何电子商务的应用与服务的必备部分,这包括在德意志银行的电子信用解决方案之中。

举例说明,电子市场向企业客户及市场提供金融或非金融产品与服务,比如第三方契约服务或网上支付服务,均需要激活信用以在虚拟市场上完成交易,因此,Identrs 为客户提供了支付确认数字签名。在支付进行之前,银行内部系统首先认证该签名,如果得到确认则进行支付。

德意志银行全球第一项基于 Identrus 的客户应用的发展表明 Identrus 对银行的战略意义。电子账单、电子支付系统(db-eBills)从两个方面对客户信用作出要求。

首先,该系统拥有客户财务信息及一些敏感数据,这些信息和数据不对第三方开放。为达到这一目的,系统包括安全登录程序,利用 Identrus 服务进行身份认证。数字证书实时启用,如果通过检验,则用户可以进入系统。所显示信息因用户不同而有所区别,同时在该系统中的进一步活动也是有安全与信用保障的。

其次,网上便可以进行账单认证及其支付(见图 2)。支付信息(包括账户、用户、次级支付信息)均利用 Identrus 电子签名(使用用户私钥),然后与发送者的数字证书一同发往支付服务器。在进行支付之前,后台系统首先进行身份认证,只有通过身份认证,才进行下一步操作。

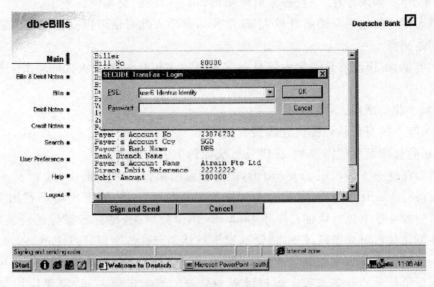

图 2　德意志银行的第一个 Identrus 客户应用

详细的流程(见图3)：付款人附加其数字证书给电子交易(如支付)以开始与开单人之间的交易(步骤1a、1b)。开单人接收到信息并识别其数字签名与所附数字证书。

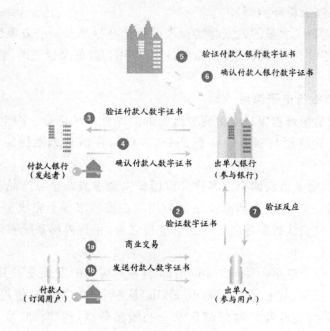

图3　认证流程图

开单人将该数字证书发送给他自己的银行(第2步)，这意味着他没有必要依赖于其他先前没有业务联系的银行。他的银行则将数字证书发送付款人银行(第3步)，由其确认该份数字证书的正确性与有效性(第4步)。由此，便可确认付款人的身份。

此外，现在开单人银行也可以检查付款人银行是否有权验证Identrus数字证书。为达到这一目的，将发送一份数字证书给Identrus系统(第5步)，检查是否有该验证授权存在(第6步)。如果存在，一桩各方身份明晰、相互信任的交易便促成了。

开单人银行将结果反馈给开单人(第7步)，开单人此时便可以安全地与付款人进行该桩可信的交易。

由上可见，工作流的自动化为贸易各方及开单人银行带来了极大的益处，这是因为整个过程中：

■ 最小化的纸面工作；
■ 为唯一的身份认证提供在线授权流程；
■ 遇到处理请求的需要时，提供具有法律约束力的签名。

但因为在这一方面使用了Identrus，使得德意志银行应用又进了一步。

任何持有Identrus智能卡(Identrus公私钥及数字证书)的用户均可利用Identrus数字签名与数字证书进行认证。由于Identrus的全球框架，德意志银行的一名客户，他的合法性可以被西班牙银行接受，尽管这家银行从未与这位客户打过交道。

这一体系促成了真正的电子商务框架——一个没有地理边界的因特网与基于法律约束力的身份认证的业务流程。虚拟世界与传统的真实世界一样，需要信用与交易安全作为商务活动的使能器。

3. 信还是不信——这是一个问题!

信用是关键,但却不能一下子解决所有问题。要理解信用的作用,很重要的一点是要知道仅有信用是不足以完成交易的。

信用服务告知业务伙伴的身份,提供认证服务保证数据完整性。信用却不包括给对经过认证的业务伙伴进行授权的能力。

当然,信用可以而且会成为授权(权利系统)的切入点,但是双方预先必须有一定的相互交流。一个可信任的权利系统使开放的因特网成为高度安全和可信任度的基础设施。

通过德意志银行电子信用卡(见图4)使用Identrus系统,我们可以消除企业与企业之间电子商务活动的最大进入障碍:信用与交易安全的缺乏。

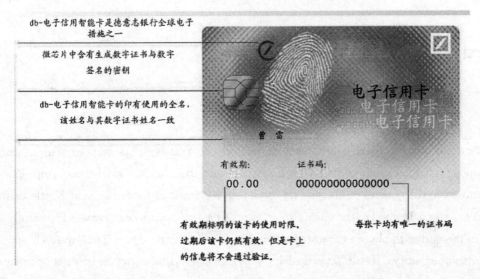

图4 德意志银行电子信用卡使可信任的电子商务成为可能

UNIT 21 Viral Marketing of Kettle Foods

Overview

So, you want to make a difference in the world? You say you want to start a business revolution? That is exactly what Kettle Foods did with their latest e-marketing campaign. The company gave the general public and its loyal fans a chance to name the next Kettle chip flavor. Yes, you actually had the chance to create the flavor *Strawberry Cream*. Thankfully, our faith in the voting public was restored when *Cheddar Beer* and *Spicy Thai* were chosen, but that's another story. Kettle leveraged its super-loyal base of customers to get momentum. The campaign then spread nationally via media outlets, word of mouth, and achieved strong results for Kettle by growing its loyal list of customers and increasing brand awareness. Figure 1 is the homepage of Kettle Foods.

Figure 1   The homepage of kettle

The Kettle Foods "Crave" e-marketing campaign is outlined in the following case study. Overall, the study focuses on the planning stage of a successful campaign through to the results stage. The case study is meant to inform you on what it takes to create a successful e-marketing and viral campaign. It draws in aspects of word of mouth, word of mouse, and pre-existing marketing practices. Figure 2 is the trademark of kettle.

Figure 2　The trademark of Kettle

Step 1: Strategic Planning

All e-mails created for an e-marketing campaign and sent to a list of prospects or customers should be backed by a strategic plan. The Kettle strategic plan was in the form of a project brief written by Kettle's PR agency, Maxwell PR. The plan included a creative online customer interaction piece to be developed by eROI. This case study outlines the business and marketing strategies for the e-marketing campaign, as well as the intended creative approach to meet those objectives. The project briefs included a scope of work and resources required, as well as timeline and budget.

While each company has a different set of objectives and requirements, there are commonalities in both strategy and tactical execution. The objective for Kettle was quite simple: develop a new and exciting chip flavor to add to their current 20 flavor offering. The new flavor needed to be as unique as Kettle itself. Can you say "Spicy Thai"? Kettle capitalized on its strong brand equity and was able to step outside the box on flavor and its approach in naming the new flavor. Have you ever been asked by another company to help choose an aspect of its next product? Figure 3 are some aspects of kettle.

Figure 3　Some aspects of kettle

Step 2: Driving Momentum and List Management

It's necessary to start with a solid foundation to build a larger structure. List procurement for this campaign was just the beginning. Oregon-based Kettle Foods seeded their opt-in list by setting up booths in many trade shows in both Washington and Oregon. Where better than your own backyard to start generating buzz about a new offering? During the tradeshows, Kettle asked attendees of all ages to come up with a new flavor they would like to see Kettle produce as their next chip flavor. The information was passed along to Maxwell PR and then uploaded to Kettle's eROI account. The goal of the e-marketing campaign was to learn as much as possible about the customer or prospect.

The focus of the campaign was to foster the emotional connection with the Kettle brand in a way that customers were co-creating and owning a part of the company by naming a chip flavor. Ultimately, Kettle was able to accomplish this AND grow its potential consumer base and build brand awareness. The important metrics were the Kettle Crave site's Send-to-a-Friend function and the Web Sign-up form. The viral nature of this campaign drove customers to Kettle's site and encouraged them to subscribe to Kettle's e-mail list. Additionally, Kettle set two more measurable goals of a 25% Read Rate and a 5% Click—through rate on its e-newsletter to launch the campaign. Both were very obtainable given the list quality, PR and creative involved with this campaign.

In order to engage and retain the customer's attention, Kettle and Maxwell PR collaborated with eROI to create the "Crave-O-Meter?" (Figure 4). This piece was the most engaging element of the campaign. The Crave-O-Meter enabled the customer to be a part of the Kettle brand, and generated opt-ins for further contact and brand awareness. As the online chip voters moused over the Crave-O-Meter?, they were greeted with "<1> *I'll try anything once, except this*" to middle-of-the-road "<3> *I'm on the fence*" to the ecstatic "<5> *This sounds delicious*! *I could eat an entire bag.*"

Figure 4 Trademark votiof device

One of the primary purposes of this campaign, like most campaigns, was to grow list size and list quality. The secondary purpose was to grow brand awareness over a larger demographic, extending from the Northwest to the rest of the country. The objective and vehicle to achieve these goals was the Crave-O-Meter? to develop a new chip flavor.

Kettle's call to action resonates throughout the campaign; all actions are tied back to the Crave-O-Meter. This is the driving force for customer communication. The goal is to drive the customer from the e-mail back to Kettle's website where they rate their taste buds. It is easily passed on to others, making e-mail growth quite efficient.

The Kettle campaign scored with its list management and list growth capabilities. Imagine the ability to grow your list from 5,000 emails to 15,000 quality emails in less than 10 weeks.

Every person voted on each of the 5 flavors for a cumulative total of 50,000 votes. The original list was generated by direct contact with consumers and potential consumers. The growth of the list happened organically and took off virally through word of mouth and word of mouse. This type of marketing yielded excellent results. The Crave-O-Meter? was the key viral component of the campaign by driving users to the website and then having them add themselves to the e-mail list.

Results:
-4,000 votes in first week
-Taste test on "Good Morning America"
-Interest by "Ellen Degeneres Show"
-Over 50,000 votes cast by the end of a 10-week campaign
Figure 5 is the results of votes.

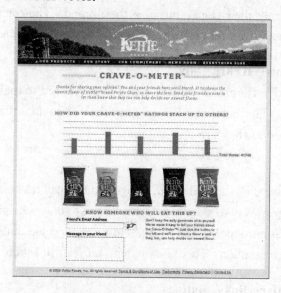

Figure 5　The results of votes

Step 3: Email Creative and Production

In order to create an e-mail that will generate a response, we must first analyze its elements, the most important of which include:

From

This is the sender's name and e-mail. In this case "Kettle Foods" and "thedirt@kettlefoods.com." By using this e-mail address and e-newsletter name "The Dirt", Kettle created a brand within a brand. In effect, the company created a "Trusted Sender". Now, the recipient has a better chance of recognizing the sender and responding to a more engaging e-mail.

Subject

The "subject" line is perhaps one of the most critical components of any e-mail campaign. Kettle took the approach of inviting the potential consumer to be a part of the Kettle family. The company maintained a concise, relevant subject line, "The Dirt—January 2005". It is descriptive, memorable, and true to the Kettle brand.

Personalization

Kettle highlighted personal names of its customers who submitted the 5 initial flavors to be voted on. While a personalized greeting can be an important element in an e-mail, Kettle did not use a salutation in its launch of "The Dirt".

Body Copy

The format chosen by Kettle is one that stretches across its brand. Kettle spent time and space to highlight not only their chips, but also their brand. The company is creating more awareness as the consumer transfers from the e-mail to Kettle's landing page.

Graphical Elements—HTML Only

A picture is worth a thousand words, and Kettle wanted to make sure to convey the correct 1,000 words. The company chose graphical elements that truly focus on its grassroots brand and who they are as a company.

Offer

Things must be placed in a logical order. Having the e-mail lead off with a value proposition or "grabber" is a great way to start out. Consider this: you are helping decide the flavor of the next chip Kettle will introduce to the world. How many people can say they helped choose a product for a major corporation? This leads us into our call to action.

Call to Action—Hyperlinks, Buttons

What do you want your customer to do? In this e-mail campaign, the call to action was to visit www. crave. kettlefoods. com and vote online for the 5 potential chip flavors. At a larger level, the implied call to action was to help be a part of the next big thing. Lastly, once you've gone through this authentic, unique, and fun online experience, you can tell your friends about how you just voted for *"Cheddar Beer"* as the next flavor of chips from Kettle and they should, too.

Step 4: Email Launch and Campaign Management

Carefully timed follow-up emails provide an additional reminder to the respondents and serve to keep the brand in the consumer's mind.

Media outlet measurement is focused and driven to the Kettle Foods landing page (Figure 6). This was charted by a 24% increase in newsletter signups, an increase of 1,000 new names a month.

Campaign management takes many factors into account, such as the day to send your message off, the time the e-mail will go out, how to test multiple messages and designs, and the platform you are going to use to send your emails off. In the world of e-mail, you only have moments to react and when you send a message erroneously, you can't stop it or take it back. If you are sure everything is in the right place and all the pieces fit, send a test off first.

Figure 6　Kettle Foods landing page

Step 5: Distribution and Tracking

The e-mail statistics within eROI's e-mail ROI platform show a 30% read rate and a 5.4% click through rate on the first e-mail campaign (see Figure 7).

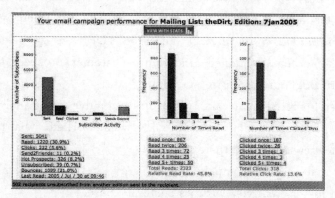

Figure 7　The e-mail statistics result

Not only could Kettle push personalized data to a website from the e-mail ROI platform, but Kettle could also pull it from www.crave.kettlefoods.com through a lead capture form and back into the e-mail tracking platform (see Figure 8). This brings us full circle. The campaign leveraged a strong brand and garnered solid, track-able results.

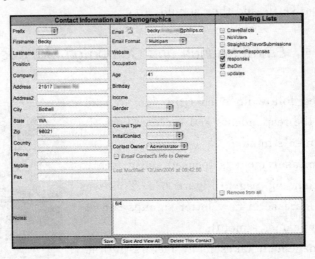

Figure 8 the e-mail tracking platform

Tracking individual customer behavior through the entire site was a much needed aspect of the campaign. Kettle learned more about the customer's perceptions and behavior and how those reflected on its brand. Ultimately, Kettle learned what products worked and which products were missing.

Step 6: Reporting and Analysis

The reporting was the reason Kettle embarked on this strange trip to begin with. What are the results? We did all this work, now show us the money, and that is what Kettle got.

-List growth to the tune of 1,000 new names per week.

-Brand Awareness—50,000 votes and campaign received national media attention in the form of TV (Good Morning America and interest from the Ellen Degeneres Show), newspapers (*Portland business Journal*), and radio (OPB).

-Useful consumer data obtained—individual customer/prospect behavior tracked from e-mail and throughout the entire micro-site.

The next step for Kettle is to take the results and move to the analysis phase to create their next campaign. The company will look at what worked, what people want, and what will drive new customers to their site.

Take a look at the current campaign (www.crave.kettlefoods.com), which continues to evolve and foster creativity with its customer base.

So what are you waiting for? Start working on your new viral campaign today and see what kind of business you can start. With proper planning and a strong message, you too will be successful.

Words and Expressions

viral ['vairəl]	adj.	滤过性毒菌的,滤过性毒菌引起的
leverage ['li:vəridʒ]	n.	杠杆作用
	vt.	举债经营(用信用或贷款增加自己的投机能力并增加投资收益率)
momentum [məu'mentəm]	n.	动力;要素
outline ['əutlain]	n.	大纲;轮廓,略图,外形;要点,概要
	v.	描画轮廓,略述,概述
through to	adv.	直到
PR (public relation)	abbr.	公共关系
equity ['ekwiti]	n.	公平,公正;公平的事物;资产净值
tactical [tæktikəl]	adj.	战术上的
capitalize on	v.	利用
procurement [prə'kjuəmənt]	n.	获得,取得
Oregon ['ɔrigən]	n.	俄勒冈州(美国州名)
subscribe [səb'skraib]	v.	捐款;订阅;签署(文件);赞成;预订
collaborate [kə'læbəreit]	vi.	合作;通敌
demographic [demə'græfik]	adj	人口统计学的
vehicle ['vi:ikl]	n.	(为达到某种目的的)工具;手段
resonate ['rezəneit]	vt.	(使)共鸣,(使)共振
cumulative ['kju:mjulətiv]	adj.	累积的
organically [ɔ:'gænikəli]	adv.	器官上地;有机地
highlight ['hailait]	vi.	加亮;使显著;以强光照射;突出
concise [kən'sais]	adj.	简明的,简练的
descriptive [dis'kriptiv]	adj.	描述的,叙述的
salutation [sælju(:)'teiʃən]	n.	招呼

hyperlink	n.	[计]超链接
embark on	v.	开始从事
look at	v.	考虑；研究某物

Notes

(1) The campaign then spread nationally via media outlets, word of mouth, and achieved strong results for Kettle by growing its loyal list of customers and increasing brand awareness. 这项运动便透过媒体、人们的口头宣传，在全国扩散开来，为克特赢得了更多的忠诚客户名单，并提高品牌知名度，取得了丰硕成果。

(2) Can you say "Spicy Thai"? Kettle capitalized on its strong brand equity and was able to step outside the box on flavor and its approach in naming the new flavor. 你能说"泰国辛辣口味"？克特凭借其强大的品牌资产，有能力通过命名新口味的方式走出传统口味的限制。

(3) Lastly, once you've gone through this authentic, unique, and fun online experience, you can tell your friends about how you just voted for "Cheddar Beer" as the next flavor of chips from Kettle and they should, too. 最后，一旦你经历了这次权威的、独一无二的、有趣的在线经历，你就可以告诉你的朋友你是怎么把切达啤酒口味选为克特的下一种口味的，并告诉他们，他们也应该这样做。

(4) Campaign management takes many factors into account, such as the day to send out your message, the time the e-mail will go out, how to test multiple messages and designs, and the platform you are going to use to send out your emails. 活动管理要考虑多方面的因素，如你发出信息的日期，发出电子邮件的时间，如何测试多种信息、方案，以及你将要用来发送电子邮件的平台。

(5) We did all this work, now show us the money, and that is what Kettle got. 我们做了一切努力，现在我们看到了效益，而这是克特所得到的。

Questions

(1) How did the Kettle use the Internet to grow its list?
(2) How did the Kettle design the e-mail sent to the customer list?
(3) What did the Kettle get from the e-mail campaign?
(4) What can we learn from this case?

Exercises

1. Translate the following sentences into Chinese:
(1) The Kettle food encouraged its super-loyal customer to name for its next flavor

which will be introduced to the world.

(2) Although each company has different goals, there is still something doing in the same way, such as the strategy and tactical execution.

(3) The Crave-O-Meter? was one of the most important components in the campaign, which drove the customers to Kettle's website, voting for the next flavor, and added themselves to the e-mail list.

(4) It is necessary for a company to start with a solid foundation to be a famous one in the future.

(5) The function of "send to a friend" provide more opportunity for the Kettle food to grow its e-mail list, increasing its brand awareness at the same time.

2. Translate the following sentences into English:

(1) 树立良好的口碑是企业提升其知名度的一个十分有效的方法。

(2) 为了能够更好地实现个性化营销、提高客户满意度、加深顾客对企业的感情,企业应像克特食品公司一样,将自己的一部分经营策略交给消费者来决定。

(3) 病毒性营销是利用其"病毒"的特性来提高点击率和阅读率,进而达到更好的宣传效果的。

(4) 跟踪客户、了解客户需求,是企业求得长期有效发展的必要组成部分。

(5) 克特食品为我们提供了一个成功的电子营销方案——电子邮件运动,亦称病毒性营销。

Further Reading

This text is from Viral Marketing Case Study. To learn more about Viral Marketing, you can read *The Six Simple Principles of Viral Marketing*, MAY 10, 2012 on Web Marketing Today.com.

Translation

克特食品的病毒性营销①

概　述

　　嗯,你想要在世上与众不同么?你说你想要进行一次商业变革?这正是克特食品(Kettle Foods)最新的电子营销活动所做的。该公司为公众及其忠实客户提供为下一种克特薯片口味命名的机会。是的,你确实有机会创造草莓乳酪口味。让人欣慰的是,当切达啤酒和泰国辛辣口味被选中的时候,我们对公众投票这一决策又恢复了信心。不过,那是另一个故事。克特以其超级忠诚的客户基础为杠杆,获得了强劲的发展势头。

---

① 未作翻译处理的图表参见英文原文。

这项活动随后透过媒体，人们的口头宣传，迅速在全国扩散开来，为克特赢得更多的忠诚客户名单，并提高品牌知名度，取得了丰硕成果。图1显示的是克特食品主页。

图1　Kettle 主页

克特食品"Crave"电子化营销可概括为以下案例研究。总体而言，本研究着重于一次成功的宣传活动的规划阶段直到成果阶段。案例研究的目的是要告诉你如何去创造一个成功的电子化营销和病毒性活动。本文从口头宣传、网络宣传以及原有的销售惯例等方面加以描绘。图2为克特食品的注册商标。

图2　Kettle 注册商标

第1步：战略规划

为进行电子化营销活动所创造的，并传送到客户的所有电子邮件都应该得到战略规划的支持。克特战略规划以项目的形式由克特的公关机构——马克斯韦尔公关简要写成。这项计划包括一个创造性的网上客户互动板块，并依照电子化投资回报率（eROI）的要求进行开发。这个案例研究概述了此次电子化营销活动的业务及营销策略，并制订创造性的途径来实现这些目标。本项目简介包括工作范围和所需资源，以及时间表和预算。

虽然每家公司有不同的目标和要求，但双方在战略和战术执行上有共同点。克特的目标很简单：发展新的和令人振奋的味道添加到目前已存在的20个风味中，新口味必须像克特本身一样独特。你能说"泰国辛辣口味"？克特凭借其强大的品牌资产，有能力通过命名新口味的方法一步跳出传统风味的限制。你曾经被其他公司要求为其下一个产品选择外表么？图3是克特食品的一些种类。

图3　克特食品的一些种类

第2步：驱动要素和列表管理

　　要建设更大的机构，就要有坚实的基础。采购清单仅仅是这项运动的开始。克特食品以俄勒冈为基地，根据参加人员名单在华盛顿和俄勒冈州的许多商展中设置摊位。还有哪里会比在自己的地盘上发行一种新的产品更合适呢？在商展过程中，克特要求在场的各个年龄段的人群提出他们所希望的克特生产下一种新的产品的口味。信息传递给麦克斯韦公关，然后上传到电子投资回报率的账户。电子化营销战略的目标是尽可能多地了解顾客或潜在顾客。

　　本次活动的重点是要通过对新口味命名，使顾客共同创建和拥有公司的一分子，来培养顾客与克特的感情。最终，克特做到了这一点，并扩展其潜在的消费者基础，并建立起品牌认知度。克特的最重要的手法是在Crave网站的提供了"发送给朋友"的功能与网站登录的入口。这项运动的"病毒"特性驱使顾客浏览克特的网站，并鼓励他们把电子邮件添加到克特的电子邮件列表中。此外，克特设置了两个更可用来测量的目标——电子简讯25％的阅读率和5％的点击率，作为发起这项活动的条件。融合了高质量的名单，公共关系和这项活动的创造性，这两个目标是很容易实现的。

　　为了引起顾客的注意，克特和麦克斯韦公关通过电子投资回报率协同，创立了"Crave-O-Meter™"商标（见图4）。这是从事这项活动最主要的部分。"Crave-O-Meter?"，使顾客成为克特的一部分，并产生选择进一步接触的意识和品牌认知。当在线投票人的鼠标掠过"Crave-O-Meter™"的时候，映入他们眼帘的是："1. 任何东西我都可以尝试一下，除了这迎合大众口味的东西。""3. 我犹豫不决，不知是否该欣喜若狂。""5. 这听起来真好吃！我可以吃一整袋。"

　　这次活动的主要宗旨之一，同大多数的活动一样，就是为了增加名单的规模和质量。其次是要通过从西北扩展到其他国家，以期在更大的地域范围内扩大对品牌的认知度。这一活动的目的和实现这些目标的方法是开发新口味。

　　克特的呼吁行动响彻整个活动；一切行动都与"Crave-O-Meter™"相关。这是顾客沟通的动力,目的是为了推动客户从电子邮件回到他们评定味蕾的克特网页。这很容易传给他人,使电子邮件数量高效增长。

图 4　商标投票器

克特运动的列表管理和名单增长为其能力赢得了高分。可以想象一下这种能力,在不到 10 周的时间里,客户的名单从 5000 个电子邮件增加到 15,000 个高质量的电子邮件。

每个人给这 5 种口味中的投票数累计都达五万多票。原来的名单是由直接接触消费者和潜在的消费者组成。通过口头上的宣传和网上宣传,名单的增长发生质的飞跃。这种营销取得了很好的效果。"Crave-O-Meter™"是这次病毒营销的关键组成部分,它使用户连接到克特网站,并将自己加入到电子邮件列表中。"Crave-O-Meter™"界面见图 4。

结果:

- 第一周共 4000 票
- "早安美国"中的口味测试
- 引发了"艾伦·德杰尼勒斯脱口秀"的讨论
- 第 10 周周末已超过 50,000 票

图 5 为投票结果。

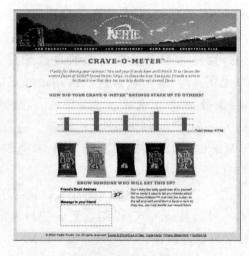

图 5　投票结果图

第 3 步：E-mail 创作与生产

为了创造一个有回应的电子邮件，我们必须先分析其成分，其中最重要的内容如下。

发件人

这是发件人的姓名和电子邮件。在该例中为"克特食品"和"thedirt@kettlefoods.com"。用该邮件地址和取名为"The Dirt"的电子通信，克特创造了品牌中的品牌。实际上，该公司设立了"可信赖寄件人"。现在，收件人有更好的机会赏识寄件人，并回应更生动的电子邮件。

主题

"主题"是任何电子邮件的一个关键的组成部分。克特采取的做法是邀请潜在消费者成为克特大家庭中的一部分。该公司保持着简明扼要的相关主题线，"The Dirt——2005 年 1 月"。它是描述性的、令人难忘并忠实于品牌的。

个性化

克特突出对最初提出的 5 种口味进行表决的顾客的名字。虽然个性化的问候在一封电子邮件中可以发挥重要作用，但克特在其发送的"The Dirt"中不使用问候语。

附件

克特选择的是一个横跨其品牌的格式。克特花费时间和空间不仅突出了食品，而且也强化了其品牌形象。该公司正在创造更多的机会，使消费者从电子邮件转移到克特的登录页。

图表元素——只有网页

一幅画胜过千言万语，而克特要清楚准确地传达这 1000 字。作为一家公司，该公司选择能够将切实的重点放在基层品牌的图形元素。

出价

事情一定要有一个逻辑顺序。在电子邮件中率先实现价值命题或"抓取"是一个重大的开端。试想：你是帮助决定将介绍到世界各地的克特的未来口味。有多少人可以说他们曾帮助大公司选择产品？这种想法将成为我们的动力。

呼吁行动——超链接，按钮

你希望你的客户做什么？在这个电子邮件运动中，呼吁的是访问 www.crave.kettlefoods.com，并在线为 5 种可能的口味进行投票。在更大的层面上，隐含呼吁采取行动，是希望能帮助为未来大做文章。最后，一旦你经历了这次权威的、独一无二的、有趣的在线经历，你就可以告诉你的朋友你是怎么把切达啤酒口味选为克特的下一种口味的，并告诉他们，他们也应该这样做。

第 4 步：电子邮件发送及活动管理

定时向受访者发送后续邮件，提供额外的提醒，有助于消费者将该品牌记在心里。

媒体评价的重点集中在克特的登录页(见图6)。每月增加1000个用户,用图表表示为24%的增长率。

活动管理要考虑多方面的因素,如你发出信息的日期,发出电子邮件的时间,如何测试多种信息、方案,以及你将要用来发送电子邮件的平台。在电子邮件的世界里,你只有瞬间的时间作出反应,而且当你错误地发送信息的时候,你无法阻止它或把它收回。如果你确信每一处都是准确的,那么首先发出一封测试邮件。

图6 克特食品登录页

第5步:分配和跟踪

电子投资回报率的电子邮件平台回报率显示,在首次的电子邮件活动中有30%的阅读率和5.4%的点击率(见图7)。

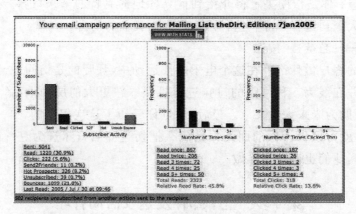

图7 邮件数据结果

克特不仅能从电邮投资回报率的平台推送个性化数据到一个网页,而且也可以通过捕捉表格的形式把它从 www.crave.kettlefoods.com 返回到邮件跟踪平台(见图 8),这带给我们一个完整的循环。该活动以强势品牌为杠杆,赢得了稳固的、有迹可循的结果。

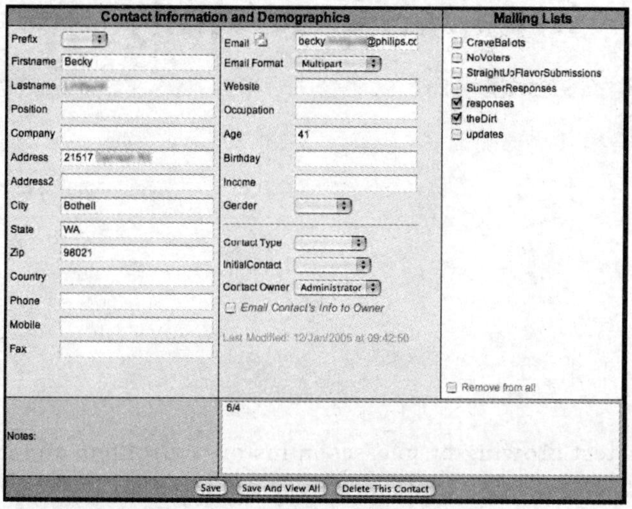

图 8　邮件跟踪平台

在整个网站中追踪个别客户的行为是这项运动的一个非常必要的方面。克特更多地了解了客户的观念和行为,以及如何将这些反映到自己的品牌中。最终,克特了解到什么样的产品能达到预期的效果以及哪些产品将要消失。

第 6 步:报告和分析

这份报告是克特开始这一充满神奇的活动作为开端的原因。结果如何?我们做了一切的努力,现在我们看到了效益,这是克特所得到的:

- 增长速度高达 1000 名/周;
- 品牌认知——5 万票并且该运动得到全国媒体的关注,包括电视(早安美国,艾伦·德杰尼勒斯脱口秀的讨论)、报纸(波特兰商业杂志)以及无线电台(OPB)等形式;
- 消费者的有效资料——从电子邮件到整个微型网站的个别顾客/潜在客户行为跟踪。

克特下一步要采集结果并进入分析阶段,创造它们的未来运动。该公司将考虑怎样能达到预期效果、人们想要什么、什么会促使新客户进入其网页。

注视当前运动(www.crave.kettlefoods.com),继续发展和培养基于客户的创造性。

所以,你还在等什么呢?从今天开始从事你的新病毒性的活动,看看你可以启动什么样的商务活动。凭借适当的规划和作用强大的信息,你也一定能取得成功。

UNIT 22 Groupon Case Study

Text

One of the fastest growing businesses in history, Groupon and its latest daily deals were news the business media could not resist. From the local corner bakery to national retailers such as Gap, sizzling offers were projected to triple Groupon's 50 million subscribers by the end of the year. But while the limelight remained focused on the headline "feature" deals, Groupon was quietly testing new models to expand this core platform. In late 2010, the company introduced Groupon Stores, a self-service model that equipped stores with the tools to build their own promotions. Sales chief and co-founder Eric Lefkofsky mused that when customers could "go on their own and put up a deal, Groupon would become their commerce strategy," alluding to yet another new angle of the business, Merchant Services. That said, Lefkofsky quickly cautioned that such lighter-touch models were still very new and represented just one faction of the many tests Groupon was running.

The Groupon Model

Groupon's initial value proposition was crystal clear: help local merchants introduce people to their businesses. Every day, Groupon subscribers received a daily deal (see Exhibit 1), typically from a local business such as a sushi restaurant or spa, though the offerings had also expanded to include some incentives from national entities such as FTD and Gap. The name "Groupon" was a mix of "group" and "coupon." Users had until midnight on the day the deal was announced to purchase that day's coupon from Groupon, but the discount only became valid once a certain number of people had signed up for the offer. If the volume threshold was not crossed, neither Groupon nor the business made money. If the tipping point was hit, Groupon made money by commanding a revenue share of the total coupons sold, typically 50% of the revenue generated. That said, as the company had achieved critical mass in the marketplace, it became less about collective buying and more about exposure and discounting. Lee Brown, SVP National Sales for Groupon, commented that by early 2011, achieving the requisite tipping point was nearly a "foregone conclusion;" Groupon reported that less than 5% of all deals purchased in North America failed to reach the required quantity threshold.

At the company's onset, Andrew Mason, the 30-year-old CEO of Groupon, sought to help local businesses navigate the Internet in a straightforward and comfortable way: *"We help businesses navigate the new world of social media and Internet marketing in an approachable, creative way. An appearance on Groupon validates these businesses as a cool part of their community."* —Andrew Mason (via New York Times).

Exhibit 1   Sample Groupon Daily E-mail

Groupon delivered value to merchants in several different ways. First, the company provided tremendous exposure to new customers through its daily e-mail alerts; in other words, its power as an online marketing/advertising tool was immense. Second, the company introduced new potential for price discrimination (e.g. Groupon enabled merchants to offer discounts to consumers who valued their products and services less than ordinary/existing customers, whereas typically merchants would normally be working within the confines of their own existing customer base, which was a smaller but substantially more engaged set of consumers). Third, the Groupon platform paved the way for the so-called "buzz" factor in two key ways: Groupon consumers were not only readily sharing their Groupon conquests through social media outlets such as Facebook and Twitter, but they were also likely to spread word about the local merchant—either formally through venues such as Yelp or informally over dinner with friends—after they had used their coupons. The Groupon model was notably pioneering where the social component was concerned: the initial crux of the business, group buying, was instrumental in aiding the company to grow as quickly as it did; word of mouth marketing was no longer a passive phenomenon, but rather an active dialogue that was required in order to gain access to the deal. At the same time, the Groupon model also delivered obvious benefits to the consumer segment: access to deep discounts for venues and services they may not have otherwise tried, or perhaps may never have even come to learn about.

The Fastest-Growing business in History

In 2010 alone, Groupon expanded from 1 to 35 countries, launched almost 500 new markets (from a base of 30 in 2009), grew its subscriber base by 2,500% (from 2 million to over 50 million), partnered with 58,000 local businesses to serve over 100,000 deals, and saved consumers over $1.5 billion. By January 2011, the company was estimated to be growing at 50% per month, with a revenue run rate of over $2 billion per year (at its early year run rate). By comparison, when Google filed for its IPO in 2004, it reported growing from under $200 million in revenue to $1.6 billion in less than three years; Groupon accomplished the same feat in just one single year.

How did Groupon achieve this astonishing growth? Most obviously, by providing small and medium sized businesses (SMBs) with what they wanted most: more customers. Founder Andrew Mason saw the potential to fundamentally change the way that people buy from local businesses in the same way that e-commerce changed the way that people buy products.

But at a more operational level, this tremendous growth was driven by expertise in telesales and access to capital, driven primarily by co-founders and investors Lefkofsky and Brad Keywell. Indeed, this duo was said to be the true operating force of the business; prior to Groupon, they had extensive experience running big companies and had made a science of bringing human-heavy, sales-dependent, call center type companies onto the Internet. That said, some suggested that they had the resources, relationships, and expertise necessary to fuel the intensely rapid growth of the Groupon sales force. The other side of the business ecosystem, namely user acquisition, was fairly straightforward: through a combination of direct advertising, enticing offers, and basic web social mechanics, Groupon was able to attract a monstrous user base very cost-efficiently. That said, the true effort had to live on the sales side; gaining traction from these large call centers needed to be the bread and butter of Groupon's model. As far as funding was concerned (and significant funding was needed on both the B2B and B2C sides), Lefkofsky and Keywell had both previously been backed by New Enterprise Associates—one of the largest technology-focused private equity firms in the US, with $8.5 billion of capital under management—which may have also made access to substantial venture capital investments relatively straightforward.

While its sales operations were at the crux of its success, Groupon had also benefited from inherent features of its business model, particularly negative working capital. A negative working capital metric, measured as the differential between current assets and current liabilities on the balance sheet and more practically understood to be the funds required to keep a company in business, implies that a company is effectively being financed by its customers. In other words, because Groupon charged its users upfront, took a cut of the revenue generated and then paid merchants back later, it quickly recovered its upfront costs surrounding promotion design and distribution. This strategy had proven critical for the Groupon's profitability, especially in light of the robust costs associated with company's sales operations.

That all said, Mason, Lefkofsky, and Keywell faced an important question: what was the right level of touch with B2B customers? While Lefkofsky asserted that the "vast majority of Groupon merchants require some level of hand-holding," Groupon was feverishly testing less intensive models. Should the Groupon model be a mechanism for buzz, or an end-to-end solution for the partner merchants? As the company planned for its continued path ahead, it became evident that they would need to understand not only which models would work best in the long run, but also which models would be most viable where scale was concerned.

Competition

By March 2011, Groupon faced three significant competitors in the daily deals landscape: LivingSocial, Bloomspot, and Buywithme. With the exception of LivingSocial, Groupon was rumored to be ten times the size of other competitors in the space; Exhibit 2 provides more details about market share. Though a host of other "flash sale" models such as Gilt Groupe and RueLaLa had also emerged and could be loosely construed as competitors, most companies in this bucket were more focused on clearing inventory for well-known national brands rather than on helping SMBs to improve their revenues through buzz, so they were not direct competitors, though they were certainly competing for the attention of consumers in their e-mail inboxes.

LivingSocial

From a consumer vantage point, Groupon and its largest competitor, LivingSocial, were fundamentally very similar products; they key difference between the products was that LivingSocial did not have any required tipping points for deals to become active. Indeed, whereas Groupon was about group/social buying, LivingSocial was more about social discovery. From a B2B vantage point, while Groupon leveraged large call centers to reach many of its merchant customers, LivingSocial fielded a local sales force in every city in which it was operating. Clearly this "hyper-local" model was capital intensive, and some wondered if the cost structure really translated into customer dedication. Regardless, the company had proven financially sound and had attracted investments from well-regarded industry figures such as Steve Case (founder of AOL) as well as a $175 million infusion from Amazon.com.

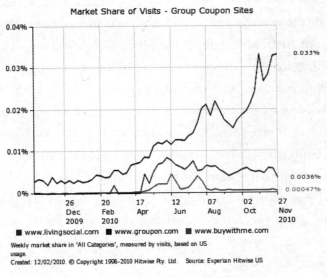

Exhibit 2

Bloomspot

Bloomspot's core model, the daily e-mail and flash sale, was similar to Groupon's, but the company focused on the notion of "attainable luxury," so it had a slightly different target market than Groupon. Moreover, Bloomspot had demonstrated a marked interest in the health of their merchant partners; indeed, the company had launched a host of programs to increase incremental sales to merchants. One such program awarded consumers with reward points for every $1 they spent above and beyond the baseline value of the deal; so if the offer were for $25 for a $50 service, the consumer would earn points for every dollar spent beyond that $50 mark. Emily Smith, a marketing and business development manager for the company, noted that companies like Bloomspot were beginning to think that "Groupon had become so big, that focusing on the implications for the end client, namely the merchants didn't even really matter anymore."

Buywithme

As the name implied, Buywithme leveraged the same concept of group buying that had made Groupon so successful. The key difference between the two models was that Buywithme deals were live/available for a full week rather than for just 24 hours. Because new deals were introduced each day, a consumer had multiple deals to peruse at any one point in time. From the B2B perspective, Buywithme was similar to Living Social in that the personal interaction element of the sales process was immensely important; for instance, BuyWithMe sales representatives personally visited each merchant that ran a deal. The company was well-poised for growth; in July 2010 it closed a $16 million Series B funding round from Bain Capital, and by early 2011 it was continuing to expand its offerings to a host of new geographic markets.

Limitations of the Groupon Model

Traditional marketing frameworks advocate that merchants consider a few key factors when contemplating a sales promotion such as Groupon: awareness, product trial, repeat purchases or visits, and (where appropriate) party size (e. g. at restaurants). Critics pointed out that while Groupon nailed the awareness and trial elements, it was less clear they had built a model that encouraged repeat visits. While Groupon touted that 97% of its merchants indicated they would be interested in being featured on Groupon again, a 2010 Rice University research study implied otherwise. That study surveyed 150 local businesses in 19 American cities and 13 product categories that ran a Groupon promotion between June 2009 and August 2010. Indeed, the results were very different from Groupon's 97% internal figure: 42% of the businesses said they would never use Groupon again. Merchants reported that Groupon redeemers were so extremely price sensitive that they barely spent beyond a discounted product's face value (again, if the offer was $25 for $50 worth of sushi, the table sought to net out as close to $50 worth of sushi as possible). The study also examined the issue of repeat purchases, and suggested that of those Groupon deals that proved profitable to the merchant, less than 31% of consumers returned to the product or service, and for unprofitable deals, that figure was only 13%. Obviously the study and the press surrounding it spurred some degree of merchant concern, as using discounts to attract new customers would surely only boost profits when those customers actually returned on their own and pay full price later down the line.

"I really wanted {Groupon} to work... It didn't drive in new people, and the people that were coming in didn't spend even our average sale. It was just sad."—Jonathan Freiden, Co-CEO of U. S. Toy Co. (via Wall Street Journal)

A January 2011 exposé in The Wall Street Journal showcased some alleged limitations of Groupon when it uncovered the story of U. S. Toy Co., a family-owned toy retailer with eight stores across the US. One of its stores near Kansas City, Kansas drew 2,800 customers from a Groupon promotion offering $20 worth of U. S. Toy merchandise for $10; this 2,800 figure initially seemed impressive given the store typically attracted only a few thousand customers in any given week, but the aftermath was a different tale. Most Groupon shoppers bought only the minimum $20 worth of merchandise at U. S. Toy, and moreover, about 90% of the Groupon takers were existing customers of the store.

Looking beyond the traditional frameworks, Groupon critics began to assert that these promotions were often cannibalizing existing revenues and profits, as many long-time customers were beginning to rely on discounts for products/services for which they had previously paid full price. Moreover, some merchants claimed negative brand implications from using Groupon—as one merchant explained, "places that before signing up with Groupon had good reviews [on yelp] are starting to get 3-star reviews that say things like 'The food wasn't that great but we had a Groupon so we didn't expect much.'" Lee Brown countered, arguing that while using cannibalization tools was a novel idea for acquisition, merchants "have long been cannibalizing in their CRM." In other words, once a consumer signed up for a merchant's mailing list, he was often inundated with special deals and promotions that did not always make sense financially for the merchant. Indeed, business developers like Brown wondered why merchants would not leverage the discounting tactic for user acquisition if such deals really brought in materially higher volumes of customers. These issues surrounding the viability of acquiring a consumer on promotion were further complicated by the fact that local businesses did not always have the resources to fully assess and understand the comprehensive economics of the promotions they offered.

Indeed, the industry debate surrounding the merits and the viability of the Groupon economics reaffirmed an important question: what was the appropriate degree of "hand-holding" with the merchants and what, if anything at all, was Groupon doing to inspire longer-term relationships with its merchants? How could the company effectively work with merchants to optimize Groupon's rapid growth as well as the efficacy of its value proposition where the merchants were concerned?

These questions were important as Groupon prioritized its growth levers for the company. By early 2011, the company was leveraging four key forces to propel its growth: geographic expansion of the existing product, international expansion (mostly through acquisition, but the company had recently launched in China), buzz (in terms of generating even more user signups), and finally, innovative new marketing models. With lower barriers to entry for competitors on three of the four drivers, Groupon sought to make bold and effective decisions where the development of new models was concerned.

What Next

Historically, small businesses created more than 50% of the U. S. gross domestic product and generated more than 75% of net new jobs each year. Over the past decade, there had been two key marketing platforms that added value to the bottom lines of these businesses, the Yellow Pages and Google; the Yellow Pages was a proxy for the rise of the telephone as a lead generation platform, whereas Google emerged as a proxy for the rise of the Internet as a platform for lead generation. Internet experts such as Battelle believed that Groupon had the potential to be a new third proxy, one that subsumed the platforms of both the telephone and the Internet, and added multiple dimensions beyond them both. Local online advertising was a $1.4 billion market in 2010, and there was ample opportunity to grow it even further when one considered that 36% of small businesses in the U.S. still did not even have a website at that time. Moreover, paid local search spending was expected to decline from $3.1 billion in 2010 to $2.8 billion in 2015, whereas spending on e-mail was projected to double during the same period. The market for Groupon's platform was unequivocally ripe.

But projections aside, some wondered if merchants may eventually begin thinking less about unit-based economics and more about macro factors such as cannibalization and customer lifetime value. Groupon's rollouts of Groupon Stores (see Enhibit 3) and Groupon Merchant Services signaled a commitment to the merchants, but analysts wondered what was next. How could Groupon ultimately own the relationship between merchants and customers? Did it even want to own that relationship?

Exhibit 3　Groupon Description of "Groupon Stores"

Words and Expressions

sizzling ['sizliŋ]	adj.	极热的
alluding to		暗指,提到
crystal ['kristl]	adj.	水晶的,水晶制的;水晶般的,清澈的,透明的
incentive [in'sentiv]	n.	刺激;鼓励;动机
	adj.	刺激的;鼓励的,奖励的
coupon ['ku:pɔn]	n.	配给券;(购物)票证;(购物)优惠券
threshold ['θreʃhəuld]	n.	门槛;出发点,开端,起点;

			临界值;阈值
requisite ['rekwizit]		adj.	需要的,必不可少的
		n.	必需品;必要条件
a foregone conclusion			预料中的结局;大势已定;成定局
navigate ['nævi,geit]		vt.	航行于;飞行于;驾驶;操纵;导航
validate ['vælideit]		vt.	使有效;使生效;承认……为正当;确认;证实
immense [i'mens]		adj.	巨大的;广大的;无边无际的;无限的;非常好的,极妙的
confine [kən'fain]		vt.	限制;使局限
		n.	边界,边缘;区域,范围
venue ['venju:]		n.	(事件、行动等的)发生地;集合地
crux [krʌks]		n.	紧要关头;关键;要点;难题
instrumental [,instru'mentl]		adj.	可作为手段的;有帮助的
telesales ['teliseilz]		n.	电话销售,电话售货
enticing [in'taisiŋ]		adj.	引诱的,迷人的
inherent [in'hiərənt]		adj.	内在的,固有的,与生俱来的
robust [rəu'bʌst]		adj.	强健的;健康的;粗野的;粗鲁的
incremental [,inkri'məntl]		adj.	增加的,增值的
merchandise ['mə:tʃəndaiz]		vt.	买卖,经营;推销
cannibalize ['kænibəlaiz]		vt.	食(同类的)肉;拆取(飞机、车辆等的)部件
		vi.	同类相食
inundate ['inʌndeit]		vt.	浸水,泛滥;(洪水般)扑来,压倒
proxy ['prɔksi]		n.	代理人,代理权;取代物
subsume [səb'sju:m]		vt.	把……归入,纳入;把……包括在内,包含
cannibalization [,kænibəlai'zeiʃən]		n.	品牌替换

(1) Users had until midnight on the day the deal was announced to purchase that

day's coupon from Groupon, but the discount only became valid once a certain number of people had signed up for the offer. 用户必须等到当天午夜宣布交易的时候才能在 Groupon 购买当天的优惠券，但这个折扣只有在购买者达到临界点（特定的数量）时才有效。

(2) Groupon enabled merchants to offer discounts to consumers who valued their products and services less than ordinary/existing customers, whereas typically merchants would normally be working within the confines of their own existing customer base, which was a smaller but substantially more engaged set of consumers. Groupon 允许商家给消费者提供折扣，商家会把他们的服务和产品估价到低于普通客户或现有客户接受的水平，不过一般商户会把价格控制在他们现有客户基础的价格范围内，这群现有客户是一群占少数但是稳定的客户。

(3) A negative working capital metric, measured as the differential between current assets and current liabilities on the balance sheet and more practically understood to be the funds required to keep a company in business, implies that a company is effectively being financed by its customers. 负营运资本，是由资产负债表中的流动资产和流动负债的差来衡量的，实际上它就是维持一家公司经营所需要的资金，这就意味着一家公司实际上是靠其客户进行融资的。

(4) But projections aside, some wondered if merchants may eventually begin thinking less about unit-based economics and more about macro factors such as cannibalization and customer lifetime value. 但无法预料的是，有人怀疑，商家最终是否可能会开始较少地考虑以单种商品为基础的经济，而更多地考虑一些宏观因素，如品牌替换和顾客的终身价值。

Questions

(1) How does Groupon create value and for whom is this value created?
(2) What do you think has prompted Groupon's slow transition toward deals with national brands?
(3) Could a less sales-intensive approach like Groupon stores be the next phase of product growth?
(4) Which competitive model should Groupon worry most about? Why?

Exercises

1. Translate the following sentences into Chinese:
(1) Group purchasing is a process that allows several individuals or businesses to come together for the purpose of purchasing various types of goods and services at discounted rates.

(2) But if someone wants a trip to Hawaii or a new car, why can't you have a collective group of people put in the amount they're comfortable spending and collectively purchase that gift for you?

(3) Ecommerce has gone social-collective buying sites are able to integrate tools that allow users to easily share deals, make recommendations and plan activities with friends on social networking sites or e-mail.

(4) Facebook has its virtual collective buying concept: "buying-with-friend", which lets users get discounts on items that their friends buy.

(5) As a comparatively new industry it's essential that we move as quickly as possible to implement measures that make group buying a rewarding and successful experience for consumers, merchants and group buying platforms alike.

2. Translate the following sentences into English:

(1) 价格的优势让团购受到许多人的欢迎，团购网站也如雨后春笋般迅速增加。

(2) 团购网站的获利渠道是从商家在本次交易的交易额中抽取。

(3) Groupon 的成功在于可成交的项目与免费的抓眼球的项目之间达到了一个平衡。

(4) 团购是能够给消费者、销售商及团购参与者带来多赢的一种购买方式。

(5) 团购产品覆盖越来越广，呈现多元化趋势。

Further Reading

You can read the full text of Groupon for more detailed information. This case was written by MBA Research Fellow Cassie Lancellotti-Young T'11 under the direction of Professors M. Eric Johnson and John F. Marshall of the Tuck School of Business at Dartmouth. It was written as a basis for class discussion and not to illustrate effective management practices. Version: June 1, 2011.

Groupon 案例研究

作为历史上发展最迅速的企业之一，Groupon 和它最近的每日一团，已成为各商业媒体无法抵挡的新闻来源。从地方性的街头面包店到全国性的大型零售店（像 Gap），狂热的赞助商预计 Groupon 已有的 5000 万的订阅户数量会在年底增长到三倍。然而，当外界的焦点仍然停留在"特色"交易这个主题的时候，Groupon 正悄悄地测试着新的模式来扩展这一核心平台。在 2010 年末，该公司又推出了 Groupon Stores，这是一种自助的模式，它让商家可以自主进行商品推销。创始人兼销售主管 Eric Lefkofsky 深信当客户可以"自助交易时 Groupon 将会成为他们自己的商业策略"。这是一种新的商业视角，即商家服务。也就是说,Lefkofsky 快速告诫道,这种轻点触摸模式只是一种很新的模式,只代表 Groupon 众多正在进行的测试中的一例。

Groupon 模式

Groupon 的最初价值定位很清晰,即帮助当地商家把他们的业务介绍给老百姓。Groupon 的订阅者每天会收到一封"每日一团"邮件(见图 1),这些交易虽然扩大到了包括一些如 FTD 和 Gap 这样的全国性的实体企业所给的支持,但通常是由当地的企业,如寿司餐厅、水疗场所等提供的。"Groupon"的名称是由"group"和"coupon"合成而来的。用户必须等到当天午夜宣布交易的时候才能在 Groupon 购买当天的优惠券,但这个折扣只有在购买者达到临界点(特定的数量)时才有效。如果没有达到这个临界点,Groupon 和商家都不会获利。一旦达到临界点,Groupon 就会从总销售量的收入分成来获取利益,一般是收益的 50%。也就是说,这个公司在市场中能获取相对较高的利润,但是在团购中,它会获得较少的利润,团购中更多的是产品的曝光和折扣。Groupon 销售副总裁 Lee Brown 评论说,到 2011 年年初,达到这个临界点几乎是必然的事情,根据 Groupon 的报道,在北美只有不到 5% 的交易达不到这个临界点。

图 1

在公司成立之初,Groupon 年仅 30 岁的 CEO,Andrew Mason,致力于帮助当地的商家用简单和适当的方式操控互联网。"我们帮助商户们操控新兴社会媒体和网络市场,使它们更便捷、更有创造力。在 Groupon 上的展示证实了这些企业是社会很出色的一部分。"——Andrew Mason(摘自《纽约时报》)

Groupon 以多种方式给商家提供利益。首先,公司通过它的每日邮件提醒为新客户产生大量的商品曝光;换句话说,它作为一个网络营销或者广告工具,影响力是巨大的。其次,公司为商家产生新的潜在差价(例如 Groupon 允许商家给消费者提供折扣,商家会把他们的服务和产品估价到低于普通客户或现有客户接受的水平,不过一般商户会把价格控制在他们现有客户基础的价格范围内,这群现有客户是一群占少数但是稳定的客户)。最后,Groupon 平台以两种主要的方式为所谓的"造势"因素铺平了道路:Groupon 的消费者使用了他们的折扣券之后,不但会通过像 Facebook 和 Twitter 这样的社交媒体分享,而且还会在像 Yelp 这样的正式场合发表评论,或者随意性地在饭后与朋友们交流分享。Groupon 模式在关注社会构成方面尤为前卫:团购作为最初的核心业务,对企业的增长帮助很大;口碑营销已经不再是一种消极的现象,反而成为达成交易所必需的积极的对话。同时,Groupon 模式也给消费者带来了明显的好处:它使消费者能得到一些场所和服务的更大折扣价,有些场所或服务甚至是消费者从没尝试过的或者从未了解过的。

历史上发展最迅速的业务

仅在 2010 年，Groupon 从 1 个城市扩展到 35 个城市，投放大约 500 个新的市场（在 2009 年 30 个的基础上），订阅者的增长率达到 2500%（从 200 万到超过 5000 万），当地的合作商家有 58,000 家，交易达 100,000 笔，为消费者节省了 15 亿美元。到 2011 年 1 月，这个公司估计以 50% 的月增长率增长着，其年收入运营率将超过 20 亿美元（以其年初的增长率预测）。相比之下，谷歌在 2004 年申请上市时，其对外报告总收入在不到三年的时间内从不足 2 亿美元增长至 16 亿，而 Groupon 仅在一年内就完成了同样的壮举。

Groupon 是如何实现这一惊人的增长的呢？最明显的，是通过为中小企业（SMBs）提供他们最渴望的资源：更多消费者。创始人 Andrew Mason 看到了如同电子商务改变人们购买产品的方式一样能够根本性地改变人们从当地企业购买的方式的潜在可能。

但是在更多的执行层面，这种巨大的增长是由电话销售的专业性和资本的获取驱动的，主要由创始人及投资者 Lefkofsky 和 Brad Keywell 驱动。事实上，这二人组才是这个业务的真正执行力量；在 Groupon 之前，他们已经有很丰富的经验了，他们曾经运营过大公司，曾做过把繁重人力、销售依赖、呼叫中心类型的公司搬到网络上的科学研究。一些观点认为，他们具有推动 Groupon 销售快速发展所必要的资源、关系和专业知识。商业生态系统的另一方面，即用户获取，是相当简单的：只要通过把广告、诱人的优惠和基本的网络社会力学相结合的方式，就能使 Groupon 吸引到一个巨大的用户群，并且这种方法具有非常高的成本效益。也就是说，真正的经营成果必须依赖于销售；而 Groupon 模式必须依附这些大型客服中心。至于资金也得到了充分的考虑（在 B2B 和 B2C 中都需要大量的资金），Lefkofsky 和 Keywell 已预先得到了"新企业协会"（New Enterprise Associates，美国最大的以技术为重点的私人股权投资公司之一）所投入的 85 亿美元的资金的支持，这也可能使获得大量的风险资本投资变得相对简单一些。

虽然销售业务是其成功的关键所在，但 Groupon 的成功还得益于其商业模式的内在特性，尤其是负营运资本。负营运资本，是由资产负债表中的流动资产和流动负债的差来衡量的，实际上它就是维持一家公司经营所需要的资金，这就意味着一家公司实际上是靠其客户进行融资的。换句话说，正是因为 Groupon 向用户预收费，并削减自身收入，然后再偿还商家，便很快恢复了其预付的用于促销活动的设计和分配的费用。这一策略已经证实了 Groupon 盈利能力的关键所在，尤其是与公司的销售业务相关的巨大成本的节省。

整体看来，Mason、Lefkofsky 以及 Keywell 面临着一个重要的问题：如何与 B2B 客户进行恰当的接触？正如 Lefkofsky 所断言的"大多数 Groupon 的商家需要一定水平的接触"，而 Groupon 也热衷于测试这些非密集型的模式。Groupon 的模式应该是一种造势机制，还是给合作商家的一种端对端的方案？很显然，当公司为其继续前进的道路制订计划时，他们需要清楚的不仅是从长远来看哪种模式运作最好，还有当考虑到规模大小时哪种模式最可行。

竞 争

到 2011 年 3 月，Groupon 在每日一团市场中面临三个显著的竞争对手：LivingSocial、Bloomspo 和 Buywithme。除了 LivingSocial，传言 Groupon 在空间上是其他竞争对手的规模的 10 倍，图 2 提供了关于市场份额的更多细节。虽然也出现了一系列其他的"快闪销售"模型，如 Gilt Groupe 和 RueLaLa，可以看作松散的竞争对手，在这里面大多数公司更侧重于帮助知名的民族品牌清理库存，而不是通过造势帮助中小企业提高他们的收入，所以他们并不是直接的竞争对手，虽然他们肯定在他们的电子邮件收件箱中争夺消费者的注意。

LivingSocial

从消费者的角度，Groupon 及其最大的竞争对手 LivingSocial，从根本上来说是非常相似的产品；它们之间的产品的主要区别是，LivingSocial 没有任何交易所需的临界点即能奏效。事实上，尽管 Groupon 是有关团体或社会购买，LivingSocial 更关注社会的发现。从 B2B 的角度，Groupon 利用大型呼叫中心争取到许多商家客户，LivingSocial 在各个开展业务的城市开展本地化的销售。显然，这个"超本地"模式是资本密集的，有些人怀疑成本结构是否真正能转化为客户贡献。无论如何，该公司已被证明财务稳健，并吸引了来自广泛关注的业内人士，如 Steve Case（AOL 创始人），以及亚马逊网站 1.75 亿美元的投资。

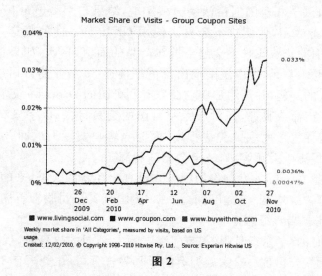

图 2

Bloomspot

Bloomspot 的核心模式是每天的电子邮件和快闪销售，与 Groupon 较为类似，但该公司注重"可得到的奢侈品"的概念，因此它有略不同于 Groupon 的目标市场。此外，Bloomspot 对其商业合作伙伴的健康状况表现出浓厚的兴趣；事实上，该公司已推出一系列计划，以帮助商家增加销路。这一计划对超过消费基准值的每一美元的花费都给予积分奖励，因此如果对 50 美元的服务出价是 25 美元，则消费者对超过 50 美元基准值的每一美元的花费均可挣得积分。公司的营销和业务开发经理 Emily Smith 指出，像 Bloomspot 这样的公司开始认为，"Groupon 已变得如此巨大，其专注于终端客户即商家的影响，几乎可以无所顾忌了"。

Buywithme

正如其名称所暗示的那样，Buywithme 利用了使 Groupon 取得成功的团体购买的相同的概念。两种模式之间的关键区别是,Buywithme 交易是整整一个星期有效的,而不是仅仅 24 小时。由于新的交易每一天都会被推出,消费者在任何一个时间点有多个交易。从 B2B 的角度来看,Buywithme 类似 LivingSocial,因为在销售过程中的个人互动元素是极其重要的。例如,Buywithme 销售代表亲自拜访每一个经营交易的商家。该公司增长较为平稳,在 2010 年 7 月完成了 1600 万美元的 B 系列贝恩资本的新一轮融资;2011 年年初,它在继续扩大其产品的新的地域市场。

Groupon 模式的限制

传统的营销框架主张,当商家在诸如 Groupon 上进行促销时需要考虑几个关键因素:认知度、产品试用、重复购买或访问以及(合适的地点)聚会的规模(例如,在餐馆)。批评者指出,虽然 Groupon 考虑到了认知度和试用元素,但是还不清楚他们已经建立了鼓励重复访问的模型。虽然 Groupon 吹捧,97%的商家表示,他们将对再次出现在 Groupon 上感兴趣,但一份 2010 年莱斯大学的研究暗示则不然。这项研究调查了在 19 个美国城市和 13 个产品类别的 150 家当地企业,这些企业于 2009 年 6 月至 2010 年 8 月在 Groupon 上开展了相应的促销活动。事实上,结果与 Groupon 97%的内部数据截然不同:42%的企业表示,他们决不会再次使用 Groupon。商家报道,Groupon 买主对价格极度敏感,他们的花费几乎不会超出折扣产品的面值(再次,如果报价是价值 50 美元的寿司则售价为 25 美元,表中试图找出价值越接近 50 美元的寿司越好)。这项研究还考察了重复购买的问题,并表明那些对商家有利可图的 Groupon 交易中,低于 31%的消费者再次购买了产品或服务,而对于无利可图的交易,这一数字只有 13%。显然,研究和它周围的报道促进了商家的关注程度,因为当客户实际上返回并随后在线下支付全额时,使用折扣优惠吸引新客户,一定会提高利润。

"我真的很希望 Groupon 发挥作用……它没有驱动新的人群,来的人甚至并没有花费我们的平均销售。这是很令人沮丧的。"——美国玩具公司联合首席执行官 Jonathan Freiden。(摘自《华尔街日报》)

当 2011 年 1 月的《华尔街日报》揭露了美国玩具公司的故事时,展示了 Groupon 所谓的限制。美国玩具公司是一家家族拥有的玩具零售公司,在美国有 8 家商店。其中一家商店在堪萨斯城附近,堪萨斯店在 Groupon 的促销活动中吸引了 2800 名顾客,该活动提供的价值 20 美元的产品而售价只有 10 美元;2800 这个数字最初令人印象深刻是因为商店通常在任何一周最多只能吸引几千名客户,但最终的结果是一个不同的故事。大多数 Groupon 购物者在美国玩具公司购买的仅仅是价值 20 美元的商品。更值得关注的是,约 90%的 Groupon 购买者是商店的现有客户。

放眼传统的框架,Groupon 批评家开始断言,这些促销活动往往正在蚕食现有的收入和利润,许多长期客户已开始依赖折扣,先前这些产品或服务需要支付全价。此外,一些商家声称自己的品牌因使用 Groupon 所遭遇的负面影响——一个商家解释说:"在与 Groupon 签约前在 Yelp 上所得到的好评现在开始变成了 3 星级的评论,诸如'食物并没有那么好,但我们有 Groupon,所以我们没有期望太多'。"Lee Brown 反驳,认为使用品牌替换工具是获得客户的一个新的想法,商家的"CRM 正在被逐步蚕食"。换句话说,一旦消费者签署了商家的邮件列表,他就经常被特殊的交易和促销活动所淹没,而这对商家来说并不总是有经济意义的。事实上，像 Brown 这样的业务开发人员想知道为什么商家不会利用折扣的方式来争取用户的战术，如果这样的交易真正能带来更多的客户数量的话。本地企业并不总是有足够的资源去充分评估和了解他们提供优惠的全面经济合理性，这一事实使得这些围绕通过促销获得客户可行性的问题进一步复杂化。

事实上，业界争议的 Groupon 经济的优点和可行性重申了一个重要的问题：什么是商家"手挽手"的合适的程度？如果有可能的话，Groupon 应怎样做以保持与商家较长期的关系？公司如何能有效地与商家合作优化 Groupon 的快速增长以及商家关注的其价值取向的有效性？

这些问题极其重要，因为 Groupon 优先考虑公司的增长杠杆。2011年年初，该公司利用四个关键的力量来推动它的增长：现有产品的地域扩张；国际扩张（主要是通过收购，但公司最近在中国是发起成立）；造势（从产生甚至更多的用户注册来说）；最后，创造新的营销模式。对竞争对手来说，其中三个驱动力量的进入门槛较低，Groupon 争取在关注开发新模式方面作出大胆和有效的决策。

下一步是什么？

从历史上看，小企业每年为美国创造国内生产总值的50%，创造超过75%的就业机会。在过去的十年中，有两个为这些企业的商业底线增值的主要营销平台——黄页和谷歌。作为领先一代的营销平台，黄页是电话业崛起的一个代表，而谷歌的出现则是互联网崛起的一个标志。如 Battelle 等互联网专家们认为，Groupon 有潜力成为新的第三方代理，它能成为融合电话和互联网的平台，并为超越这两个平台增添了多个视角。在2010年，本地在线广告市场规模为14亿美元，并且还有充足的机会进一步壮大，因为当时在美国仍有36%的小型企业连一个网站都没有。此外，本地搜索的支出预计将会从2010年的31亿美元下降到2015年的28亿美元，而对电子邮件的支出预计将在同期增加一倍，属于 Groupon 平台的市场到时候将会毫无疑问地走向成熟。

但无法预料的是，有人怀疑，商家最终是否可能会开始较少地考虑以单种商品为基础的经济，而更多地考虑一些宏观因素，如品牌替换和顾客的终身价值。Groupon 推出 Groupon Stores 和 Groupon Merchant Services 标志着对商家的承诺，但分析师们疑惑接下来会是什么。Groupon 最终将怎样掌控商家和顾客之间的这层关系？它真的希望拥有这种关系吗？

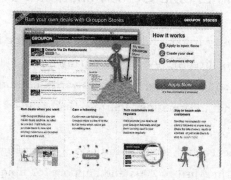

图3

UNIT 23 Hitachi Group Achieves an Integrated Collaboration Environment through E-business

 Text

Summary

Hitachi, Ltd. has kicked off its implementation of Groupmax Collaboration as a company-wide integrated collaboration environment for around 200,000 Hitachi Group employees. By enabling communication beyond the traditional framework of departments and offices, secure information sharing, and a work style independent of time and place, Hitachi has reaped the rewards of TCO optimization through platform integration, in addition to the ability to meet the needs of its customers by facilitating decision-making and creating new insight. With future plans to link to real-time communication technologies such as IP telephony and videoconferencing, Hitachi aims to develop a world-class corporate collaboration environment, and in the process, to revolutionize the work styles of all Hitachi Group employees.

Platform to Enable Cross-Functional Collaboration

These days, the ability to take full advantage of existing knowledge and thereby facilitate decision-making is directly tied to a company's competitive advantage. As such, many companies are starting to make efforts towards building processes to implement flexible collaboration and information sharing that transcends organizational frameworks.

Meanwhile, compliance and security initiatives following the introduction of privacy-protection legislation in April of 2005 and support for ubiquitous work styles regardless of time and place are becoming important topics.

Unit 23 Hitachi Group Achieves an Integrated Collaboration Environment through E-Business

To meet these new business needs, the importance of an IT platform to facilitate conversion to a "cross-functional organization" that seamlessly links individuals, outside of existing organizational hierarchies, as well as to centrally and securely manage the resulting wide array of knowledge gathered, is becoming increasingly clear.

Hitachi's collaboration portal, Groupmax Collaboration, is based on the highly reliable Collaborative E-Business Platform Cosminexus, and provides functionality to realize the vision of a cross-functional organization built around the idea of community.

Here, community means a gathering of problem-oriented people, swapping and sharing information and knowledge, to work towards a common goal.

With Groupmax Collaboration, members can form a community at will, assembling from different organizations and offices, and using functionality, such as mail, electronic forums, and file sharing, provided in a common workplace created for each community. This allows previously scattered information and know-how to be shared in real-time, improving the organization's overall competencies and increasing its business opportunities.

But even with tools intended to maximize an organization's potential, phrases like "collaboration transcending organizations" and "global information sharing" can be but a pipe dream if scalability and operational issues get in the way.

This is why Hitachi, Ltd. has started actual Groupmax Collaboration operation with its employees, one of the largest user pools in the world; to solidify impressive scalability and secure a variety of functional and operational advantages. This involves running a company-wide integrated collaboration environment used by 200,000 of Hitachi Group's total 340,000 employees.

The "IT Infrastructure One Hitachi Initiative" Project: Unifying the Corporate Platform

"The introduction of Groupmax Collaboration is part of the 'IT Infrastructure One Hitachi Initiative' project, an effort to restructure the corporate platform of all Hitachi Group members. The primary goal of the IT Infrastructure One Hitachi Initiative project is to make the company-wide infrastructure both robust and secure through control and consolidation, to achieve better service for its customers by making the most of the knowledge existing between groups." These are the words of Hirotoshi Ise, the main thrust behind the project, and the Senior Engineer of the Network Management Department, part of the E-Platform Promotion Office of the Information Technology Division.

The Hitachi Group IT Platform consists of three parts. The first is the Business Platform, which handles the core competencies of each division, such as Supply Chain Management (SCM) and Digital Engineering (DE). Next is the Management Platform, which is a horizontal, company-wide system for financial affairs, human resources, and resource planning. Finally, the Corporate Platform is responsible for the corporate IT platform, including group-wide authentication and network platforms, as well as telephony and server integration. Groupmax Collaboration is being used as a new "collaboration platform" for this Corporate Platform.

"Even until now, we've used groupware with mail, schedulers, and bulletin boards," continues Ise. "But since the infrastructure of each division was not unified, the way in which we shared information for cross-organizational projects and contacted those with the right specialist know-how and skills was inadequate. From a security and compliance perspective, by aggregating servers and linking to measures outside of IT Infrastructure One Hitachi Initiative such as authentication platforms, we expect a significant impact on efforts for prevention of leaked information and a reliable audit trail. A company-wide implementation of Groupmax Collaboration is one part of efforts to solve these issues."

Supporting Dynamic Discussions and Knowledge Sharing

As the first phase of this project in August of 2004, Groupmax Collaboration was rolled out to around 40,000 employee users at the headquarters and Information & Telecommunications Systems group. Secure access to this new integrated collaboration platform could be performed not just from the office, but also on the road and at home. And in addition to conventional groupware functionality, the electronic forum and file sharing functions allowed members to actively share information and work together, by freely creating communities beyond those of the organization.

In discussing the results of the rollout, Ise went on to say that "In the first four months, more than 800 horizontally organized communities were created, with more than 2,100 electronic forums. Every day, in each community and on each electronic forum, staff members from various sections conducted lively discussions and shared knowledge, and enjoyed the ease in which they could execute cross-organizational projects and even cultural activities between employees." From an operational perspective, a reduction in TCO was achieved by aggregating the servers providing each service (Figure 1).

Communication Beyond Borders and Infrastructures

Just how are these users actually using this new environment? Hikaru Watanabe, who belongs to the Global Business Planning & Operations Division, part of the Information & Telecommunications Systems, explains the state of the organization before

Unit 23 Hitachi Group Achieves an Integrated Collaboration Environment through E-Business

Groupmax Collaboration as follows.

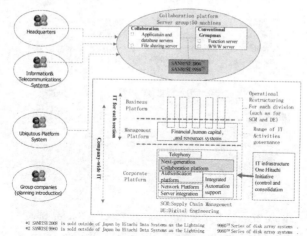

Figure 1 Collaboration platform for 200,000 Hitachi Group employess

"In my division, we are moving forward with global product sales and operations planning for storage, server, and network devices by linking with domestic offices and overseas companies. Of course, our coworkers are based all over the world, in the United States, Europe, China, and Korea, but since the infrastructures of each office were not unified, the exchange of information was limited to e-mail."

With information based on e-mail, there is a limit to how the data can be accumulated and searched, and the risks involved in sharing information, such as handling confidential files over an open network, are significant. Also, disparate infrastructures prevent multiple members from using electronic forums for discussion. But the introduction of Groupmax Collaboration made all the difference.

"First of all," Watanabe continues, "I was quite surprised that I could now create a platform for two-way communication, without even thinking about differences in location or time. Since Groupmax Collaboration is a Web-based application, we did not need to install any software on our computers. As long as you could connect to the intranet, you could access the workplace regardless of your environment, and work without paying attention to differences in time zone. This allows me to join a community, and exchange information or share Microsoft® Excel®, PowerPoint®, or image files in real-time with the other community members. I'm confident that now we have an environment that will allow us to do a lot of the things we have been wanting to do."

The community managed by Watanabe's division has something called a "Global Information Sharing Site", where various weekly and monthly reports for Hitachi headquarters sent in from various overseas locations are maintained in a database. Using the meeting minutes creation functionality from Groupmax Collaboration, notes and ideas related to each piece of information are batch registered, to facilitate data searchability and understanding of overall conditions (Figure 2).

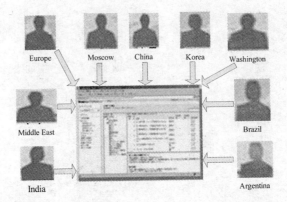

Figure 2 The Global Information Sharing Site of the
Global Business Planning & Operations Division

"Members with access permissions to the related information can share it securely," Watanabe adds, "allowing us to exchange information in real-time. From here, we plan to share information such as Win & Loss analysis related to individual businesses and IT-related demand patterns in each overseas market."

A Simple and Intuitive GUI to Further Raise Adoption Rates

In addition to this site, Watanabe's division has a bulletin-board community for sharing the orders received, report materials, risk contingency information for each country, seminar and training announcements, business trip reports, and operations restructuring plans that are handled by the division, and a community that allows junior team members to solve problems themselves using a database with FAQs for complicated import/export management operations and operation standards. These efforts are helping to stimulate each member to share information, and significantly supporting jump-started communication and business streamlining.

"I didn't expect a Web application to have such a rich GUI," Watanabe adds. While Groupmax Collaboration is a Web application, it achieves the GUI level of a Windows client. The navigation view on the left of the screen can be used to switch user and community workplaces, facilitating operations by allowing quick access to each kind of portlet (such as e-mail, schedules, and electronic forums) and content needed for operation. Also convenient is the e-mail functionality, which allows filtering based on delivery attributes (such as Unread and Urgent), subject, sender, community name, and more. The simplicity, intuitiveness, and usability of the GUI encourages even more use.

In this division, communication is performed currently between around 140 members, spread out across 9 overseas locations, but the division plans to expand future information sharing to other overseas offices and related divisions. In addition to calling on the participation of its business partners and local staff in each office, the division is aiming to make active use of IP telephony and videoconferencing functionality.

In discussing future plans, Watanabe continues, "Because the value added increases with the number of participants, we'd like to continue by increasing our abilities to send and receive information between divisions, and grow with this environment."

Enhanced Security Functionality, Built in

In addition to the above, Groupmax Collaboration is packed with a variety of functionalities and benefits. Mitsuharu Nagayama, Section Manager in the Network Software, part of the Network Application Software Department of the Software Division, had the following to say.

"With regards to Groupmax Collaboration usage within the Global Business Planning & Operation Division, our first priority is to encourage smooth operations through support for globalization, not only by making it easy to switch language settings and time zones, but also by linking to various kinds of operation information accumulated home and abroad."

"Another important feature is support for real-time communication linked to IP telephony and videoconferencing," Nagayama continues. "By linking with CommuniMax, Hitachi's IP telephony solution, we can allow users to use IP telephony simply by clicking another collaboration user's telephone number from a user search window, or hold a real conference while looking over related materials with another remote user, simply by starting videoconferencing from a schedule. We're aiming to continue enhancements to linkage with this kind of real-time communication, as part of our plans for IT Infrastructure One Hitachi Initiative."

In particular, Nagayama emphasizes the significant advantages Groupmax Collaboration enjoys because of its high overall security level. "Most times personal information is leaked, it is due to either error or malicious intent within an organization. With Groupmax Collaboration, access can be managed on a community basis, so that access to information is not permitted for members who do not need access. Also, the existence of a community can be hidden. To prevent information leakage due to files attached to emails, attached files can be stored on a secure file share and accessed by URL from the body of an e-mail, so that information never leaves the organization (Figure 3)."

In addition to this kind of proprietary security functionality, Groupmax Collaboration can also link to Hitachi Open Middleware such as Cosminexus, HiRDB, and Job Management Partner 1, as well as to security-related products, to achieve further enhancements to security and compliance support.

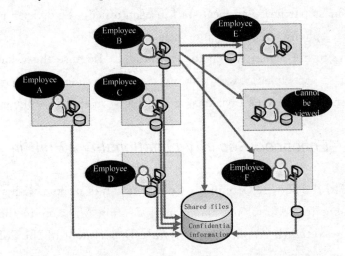

Figure 3 Preventing information leakage from attached files

With the ability to provide integrated know-how about software, hardware, operation and training, Hitachi's total solution is a trusted ally to corporations that are concerned about security risks and leaked information, and are unsure about how to set up a company-wide information sharing system.

In March of 2005, setup was completed for a directory platform and authentication platform to manage the user information of about 200,000 of Hitachi Group's 340,000 employees. With this, company-wide rollout of Groupmax Collaboration is aimed to ramp up quickly by 2007. The goal is a world-class corporate collaboration environment; and by collecting feedback about various know-how and operation techniques, to perfect the functionality, scalability, and reliability of Groupmax Collaboration.

An Example of Using Groupmax Collaboration within Hitach

Each division and section in Hitachi is employing its own techniques to facilitate the rollout of Groupmax Collaboration as an integrated collaboration environment, to streamline operations and improve the quality of the services provided to customers.

The following introduces several such examples. The techniques and know-how gained here will be incorporated as future enhancements and solutions.

Case Study 1

Application to Product Development Operations

Here, electronic forums have been used for each step in discussion solutions for large-scale software development projects, to reduce the number of meetings, and greatly improve efficiency (Figure 4). Also, meeting minutes are taken to record the process of deciding on a specification, so that the process can be used for similar development down the road.

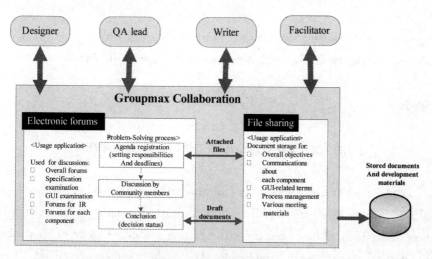

Figure 4 Forum used for each step for large-scale software development projects

Results of application to product development operation:

- Meeting history is logged, to help visualize development operations;
- Forum search functionality is used to enable full-text search, including attached files;
- Reduction in time needed to specify recipients, and prevention of accidental recipient disclosure and specification;
- Accurate status management to facilitate understanding of discussion decision status;
- Data shared within the project is kept up-to-date via file sharing.

Case Study 2

Application to Issue-Oriented Operations

Delivery of an information system is often accompanied by a variety of requirements. While close communication between developers and system engineers is needed to increase the speed and accuracy of related estimates, it is almost impossible for a system engineering division, who handle multiple products from hardware, to hold regular meetings with a given development division. Here, Groupmax Collaboration can be used to start a community for each issue, to facilitate smooth and secure information sharing. This allows estimates to be provided to customers more quickly and accurately.

Results of issue-oriented operations:
- Shared information leakage is prevented and ideas are logged between responsible parties;
- Organization of issue items, to maintain discussion flow;
- Increased security (only certain members can view information).

Case Study 3

Application to Customer IT Solutions

Hitachi is planning to use Groupmax Collaboration to set up "Customer Dot Com", an information-sharing site with hotline functionality for customers with large-scale transaction relationships. The primary feature of this system is to let sales staff and customers contact each other, around the clock. Again, because security is fortified, there is little fear of information leakage.

Results of Hitachi's "Customer Dot Com" site:
- Ability to form secure communities between customers and Hitachi employees;
- Information needed by customers can be provided individually and quickly;
- Knowledge and information is facilitated efficiently for team-selling;
- Customers can request estimates whenever they want (Improved customer satisfaction and more efficient sales efforts from multi-channel customer support).

Words and Expressions

collaboration [kə,læbə'reiʃən]	n.	协作,通敌
implementation [,implimen'teiʃən]	n.	执行
independent [,indi'pendənt]	n.	中立派,无党派者
	adj.	独立自主的,不受约束的
reap [ri:p]	v.	收割,收获
optimization [,ɔptimai'zeiʃən]	n.	最佳化,最优化
integration [,inti'greiʃən]	n.	综合
facilitate [fə'siliteit]	vt.	(不以人作主语的)使容易,使便利,推动,帮助,使容易,促进

Unit 23 Hitachi Group Achieves an Integrated Collaboration Environment through E-Business

insight ['insait]	n.	洞察力,见识
videoconference [ˌvidiəu'kɔnfərəns]	n.	视频会议
functional ['fʌŋkʃənəl]	adj.	功能的
flexible ['fleksəbl]	adj.	柔韧性,易曲的,灵活的,柔软的,能变形的,可通融的
compliance [kəm'plaiəns]	n.	依从,顺从
initiative [i'niʃiətiv]	n.	主动
legislation [ˌledʒis'leiʃən]	n.	立法,法律的制定(或通过)
ubiquitous [ju:'bikwitəs]	adj.	到处存在的,(同时)普遍存在的
seamless ['si:mlis]	adj.	无缝合线的,无伤痕的
hierarchy ['haiərɑ:ki]	n.	层次,层级
swapping ['swæpiŋ]	n.	交换,交换技术
assemble [ə'sembl]	vt.	集合,聚集,装配
	vi.	集合
forum ['fɔ:rəm]	n.	古罗马城镇的广场(或市场),论坛,法庭,讨论会
previously ['pri:vjəsli]	adv.	先前,以前
competency ['kɔmpit(ə)nsi]	n.	资格,能力,[律]作证能力
opportunity [ˌɔpə'tju:niti]	n.	机会,时机
maximize ['mæksmaiz]	vt.	取……最大值,最佳化
potential [pə'tenʃ(ə)l]	adj.	潜在的,可能的,势的,位的
	n.	潜能,潜力,电压
scalability [ˌskeilə'biliti]	n.	可量测性
operational [ˌɔpə'reiʃnəl]	adj.	操作的,运作的
solidify [sə'lidifai]	v.	(使)凝固,(使)团结,巩固
infrastructure ['infrə'strʌktʃə]	n.	下部构造,基础下部组织
unify ['ju:nifai]	vt.	统一,使成一体
primary ['praiməri]	adj.	第一位的,主要的;初步的,初级的;原来的,根源的

robust [rəˈbʌst]	adj.	精力充沛的
consolidation [kənˌsɔliˈdeiʃən]	n.	巩固,合并
horizontal [ˌhɔriˈzɔntl]	adj.	地平线的,水平的
authentication [ɔːˌθentiˈkeiʃn]	n.	证明,鉴定
groupware [ˈgruːpˌwεə]		[计]组件,群件
scheduler [ˈʃedjuːlə]		[计]调度程序,日程安排程序
bulletin [ˈbulitin]	n.	公告,报告
specialist [ˈspeʃəlist]	n.	专门医师,专家
inadequate [inˈædikwit]	adj.	不充分的,不适当的
perspective [pəˈspektiv]	n.	透视画法,透视图,远景,前途,观点,看法,观点,观察
aggregate [ˈægrigeit]	n.	合计,总计,集合体
	adj.	合计的,集合的,聚合的
	v.	聚集,集合,合计
significant [sigˈnifikənt]	adj.	有意义的,重大的,重要的
leak [liːk]	n.	漏洞,漏出,漏出物,泄漏;〈俚〉撒尿
	vi.	漏,泄漏
	vt.	使渗漏
audit [ˈɔːdit]	n.	审计,稽核,查账
	vt.	稽核,旁听
	vi.	查账
trail [treil]	n.	踪迹,痕迹,形迹
	vt.	跟踪,追踪,拉,拖,拖拉,(指植物)蔓生,蔓延,(指人)没精打采地走
dynamic [daiˈnæmik]	adj.	动力的,动力学的,动态的
headquarters [ˈhedˌkwɔːtəz]	n.	司令部,指挥部,总部
conventional [kənˈvenʃnl]	adj.	惯例的,常规的,习俗的,传统的
functionality [ˌfʌŋkʃəˈnæliti]		功能性,泛函性
rollout	n.	首次展示

cultural['kʌltʃər(ə)l]	adj.	文化的
domestic[də'mestik]	adj.	家庭的,国内的,与人共处的,驯服的
accumulate[ə'kju:mjuleit]	v.	积聚,堆积
confidential[kɔnfi'denʃəl]	adj.	秘密的,机密的
disparate['dispərit]	adj.	全异的
adoption[ə'dɔpʃən]	n.	采用,收养
contingency[kən'tindʒənsi]	n.	偶然,可能性,意外事故,可能发生的附带事件
complicated['kɔmplikeitid]	adj.	复杂的,难解的
stimulate['stimjuleit]	v.	刺激,激励
streamline['stri:mlain]	adj.	流线型的
navigation[,nævi'geiʃən]	n.	航海,航空,导航,领航,航行
filtering['filtəriŋ]		过滤,滤除,滤清
intuitive[in'tju(:)itiv]	adj.	直觉的
currently['kʌrəntli]	adv.	普遍地,通常地,现在,当前
participation[pɑ:,tisi'peiʃən]	n.	分享,参与
priority[prai'ɔriti]	n.	先,前,优先,优先权
remote[ri'məut]	adj.	遥远的,偏僻的,细微的
malicious[mə'liʃəs]	adj.	怀恶意的,恶毒的
ramp[ræmp]	n.	斜坡,坡道,敲诈
	vi.	狂跳乱撞,敲诈,蔓延
	vt.	使有斜面,敲诈
logged[lɔgd]	adj.	笨拙的,(树)劈成木材的
visualize['vizjuəlaiz, 'viʒ-]	vi.	显现
	vt.	形象,形象化,想象
recipient[ri'sipiənt]	adj.	容易接受的,感受性强的
	n.	容纳者,容器
disclosure[dis'kləuʒə]	n.	揭发,败露,败露的事情

estimate['estimeit]	v.	估计,估价,评估
	n.	估计,估价,评估
administration[ədminis'treiʃən]	n.	管理,经营,行政部门
trademark['treidmɑ:k]	n.	商标

Notes

(1) Groupmax Collaboration 一种用以协同工作的业务系统
(2) TCO "Total Cost of Ownership"的缩写,总体拥有成本
(3) take full advantage of 充分利用
(4) pipe dream 白日梦
(5) get in the way 妨碍
(6) Supply Chain Management (SCM) 供应链管理
(7) Digital Engineering (DE) 数字化工程
(8) know-how 〈口〉实际知识,技术秘诀,诀窍
(9) From a security perspective 从安全的角度来看
(10) roll out 铺开,低沉地讲出,离开,动身,大量生产,滚出
(11) meeting minutes 会议纪要
(12) the Global Business Planning & Operations Division
全球业务规划及业务分工
(13) GUI [计]图形用户界面
(14) adoption rate 采用率
(15) jump-started 跳跃式展开
(16) value added 附加值
(17) real-time communication 实时沟通
(18) attached file 附加档案

Questions

(1) What's the Groupmax Collaboration?
(2) What factors will affect the Groupmax Collaboration in Hitachi Group?
(3) How can we assess the Groupmax Collaboration?
(4) What are the results of Hitachi Group's using Groupmax Collaboration?
(5) Can you describe the process of Groupmax Collaboration?

Exercises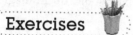

1. Translate the following sentences into Chinese:
(1) But even with tools intended to maximize an organization's potential, phrases like "collaboration transcending organizations" and "global information sharing" can be but a pipe dream if scalability and operational issues get in the way.
(2) From a security and compliance perspective, by aggregating servers and linking to measures outside of IT Infrastructure One Hitachi Initiative such as authentication platforms, we expect a significant impact on efforts for prevention of leaked information and a reliable audit trail.
(3) And in addition to conventional groupware functionality, the electronic forum and file sharing functions allowed members to actively share information and work together, by freely creating communities beyond those of the organization.
(4) With information based on e-mail, there is a limit to how the data can be accumulated and searched, and the risks involved in sharing information.
(5) Delivery of an information system is often accompanied by a variety of requirements. While close communication between developers and system engineers is needed to increase the speed and accuracy of related estimates, it is almost impossible for a system engineering division, who handle multiple products from hardware, to hold regular meetings with a given development division.

2. Translate the following sentences into English:
(1) 日立集团IT平台由三个部分组成。首先是业务平台,处理各部门的核心能力,如供应链管理(SCM)与数字化工程(DE)。其次是管理平台,这是一个水平的全公司系统,用于财务管理,人力资源和资源规划。最后是企业平台,负责公司的IT平台,包括全集团的认证和网络平台,以及电话和服务器整合。
(2) 从业务角度来看,通过聚集服务器提供每一项服务可以降低TCO。
(3) 团队最大化合作使用会议纪要创作功能,与每一项信息相关的笔记和思想都被登记,方便数据搜索能力和了解整体情况。
(4) 除了这种专有的安全功能,团队最大化合作还可以通过链接日立开放式中间件,如Cosminexus,HiRDB和管理工作伙伴1以及与安全有关的产品,达到进一步加强其安全和依从支持的目的。
(5) 日立拟利用团队最大化合作来成立一个"Customer.com"信息交流网站,拥有为大规模交易关系的用户提供热线电话的功能。

Further Reading

You can see the full text in the June 2005 edition of *Hitac*.

For details about Groupmax Collaboration, Cosminexus, HiRDB, or Job Management Partner 1, see their website.

日立集团通过电子商务构筑起了集成协同环境

概　　述

日立有限公司已启动了执行名为"Groupmax Collaboration"（团队最大化合作）的任务，目的是为日立集团旗下大约20万名雇员构筑遍及全公司的集成协同环境。通过跨越传统的部门和办公室框架的壁垒进行沟通，确保安全的信息共享，以及创建独立于时间和空间的工作模式，日立已通过平台整合赢得了TCO最优奖，另外还通过促进决策和创造新的关注点提升满足客户需要的能力。伴随着连通实时通信技术（如IP电话和视频会议）的未来计划，日立的目标是打造一个世界级的企业协作环境，并通过这一过程，改变日立集团所有员工的工作模式。

可实现跨功能协作的平台

现今，充分利用已经存在的知识的能力，进而改进决策，直接决定着一家公司的竞争优势。因此，许多公司已经开始针对建设过程实施灵活的协同和信息共享，以超越现有的组织框架。

与此同时，2005年4月颁布的隐私保护法律的执行和安全议题，以及对不受时间、地点约束的普遍存在的工作模式的支持，都成了重要的课题。

为了满足这些新业务的需求，构建IT平台的重要性变得越来越明显，这一平台有助于转化成"跨功能组织"，它可以无缝地连接个人和现存组织层次的外部，也可以集中和安全地管理由知识集聚所导致的（信息）广泛的分布。

日立公司的协同门户——Groupmax Collaboration，是基于高度可靠的协同电子商务平台Cosminexus，可提供用来实现围绕社区意志而构建的跨功能组织愿景的功能。在这里，社区是指一群以问题为导向的人为了实现一个共同的目标，交换并共享信息和知识。

有了Groupmax Collaboration，大家可以根据意愿形成一个社区，聚集来自不同的组织与机构的人，使用诸如邮件、电子论坛、文件分享等功能，为每一个社区的创造提供一个通用的工作场所。这使得原先分散的信息和技术诀窍可以实时共享，提高了组织的整体竞争力，并增加了商业机会。

但即使有旨在将组织潜力最佳化的工具，如果不解决可延展性和操作问题，实现诸如"协作超越组织"和"全球信息共享"等说法将会是一个白日梦。

这也是为什么日立有限公司已开始与它的员工——世界上最大规模的用户群之一,进行实际的"Groupmax Collaboration"行动的原因,即巩固令人印象深刻的可延展和安全的一系列功能和操作优势。这涉及日立集团34万总雇员中的20万员工在遍及公司范围的集成协同环境下运行业务。

"同一个日立IT基础设施"项目:统一企业平台

"引进Groupmax Collaboration是'同一个日立IT基础设施'项目的一部分,也是努力为重整日立集团所有成员的公司平台。'同一个日立IT基础设施'项目的首要目标是通过在群体间最有效地利用现有的知识,控制和巩固使全公司的基础设施既稳健又安全,达到为客户提供更好服务的目的。"Hirotoshi Ise说,他是项目幕后的主要推动者,也是网络管理部门的高级工程师,同时还是信息技术部电子平台促进办公室的一员。

日立集团IT平台由三个部分组成。首先是业务平台,处理各部门的核心能力,如供应链管理(SCM)与数字化工程(DE)。其次是管理平台,这是一个横向的全公司系统,用于财务事务、人力资源和资源规划。最后是企业平台,负责公司的IT平台,包括全集团的认证和网络平台,以及电话和服务器整合。Groupmax Collaboration则作为该公司IT平台的一个新的"协同平台"。

"虽然到现在,我们已经使用邮件、日程安排程序和电子公告牌等组件,"Ise继续说道,"但由于每个部门的基础设施不统一,导致我们共享跨组织项目信息和接触那些拥有诀窍和技巧的专家的能力不足。从安全和依从的角度来看,通过聚集服务器连接到同一个日立IT基础设施外面的措施,如认证平台,我们希望会对阻止泄漏的信息和发现可靠的审计线索产生重大的影响。在全公司推行Groupmax Collaboration是来努力解决这些问题的一部分。"

支持动态讨论与知识共享

2004年8月,该项目处于第一阶段,Groupmax Collaboration系统从公司总部和信息通信系统集团选择了大约40,000名雇员用户。安全接入这一新的集成协作平台不仅仅局限在办公室,而且可以在路上和家里实现。除了传统的组件功能以外,电子论坛和文件共享功能允许成员积极地交流信息和共同工作,并通过跨越组织而自由创造的社区实现。

在讨论首次展示结果的时候,Ise接着说:"在今年前四个月,已创建了800多个横向有组织的社区,包括2100多个电子论坛。每天在每一个社区和每一个电子论坛里,来自不同部门的工作人员开展热烈的讨论,并分享知识,享受其中的轻松,而且他们可以在员工之间执行跨组织的项目,甚至文化活动。"从业务角度来看,通过聚集服务器提供每一项服务可以降低TCO(见图1)。

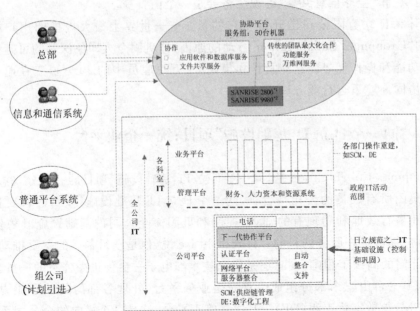

图1 200,000日立集团员工的协作平台

超越边界和基础设施的沟通

如何让这些用户真正地利用好这个新的环境？从属于全球业务规划及业务分工的 Hikaru Watanabe,信息和通信系统部的成员之一,就 Groupmax Collaboration 的组织状态解释如下:

"在我们部门,我们正通过与国内办事处及海外公司联合,朝着全球产品销售和存储、服务器和网络设备的经营规划的方向发展。当然,我们的工人遍布世界各地,有在美国、欧洲、中国和韩国的,但由于每个办事处的基础设施不统一,信息的交流仅限于电子邮件。"

以电子邮件为基础传递信息,存在着数据积累和搜索的局限性,同时信息共享也存在着风险,如在开放的网络上处理机密文件的风险就十分明显。同时,互不相同的设施阻碍多方利用电子论坛进行讨论。但引进 Groupmax Collaboration 就改变了局面。

"首先,"Watanabe 继续说,"曾经对于我来说,可以建立一个平台进行双向沟通,甚至不用考虑地点或时间的不同,是很令人惊讶的。Groupmax Collaboration 是一个基于 Web 的应用,我们不需要在电脑中安装任何软件。只要您能连接到内网上,你就可以进入忽视环境的工作区,工作时也不必关注不同的时区。这使得我可以加入一个社区,实时与其他社团成员交流信息或分享微软®Excel®、PowerPoint®或图片文件。我相信我们现在已经拥有让我们做许多一直想要做的事的环境。"

Watanabe 的部门管理的社区有一种"全球信息共享网站",海外的分支发回总部的周报和月报,都被保存在数据库之中。通过使用 Groupmax Collaboration 会议纪要功能,每一项信息和相关的笔记和创意都予以记录,提高了数据搜索能力和对整体情况的

Unit 23 Hitachi Group Achieves an Integrated Collaboration Environment through E-Business

把握(见图2)。

"成员相关信息的访问权限可以实现安全共享,"Watanabe补充道,"使我们可以进行实时交流信息。今后,我们计划共享信息,如每个海外市场中的单个企业的盈亏分析及IT相关的需求模式。"

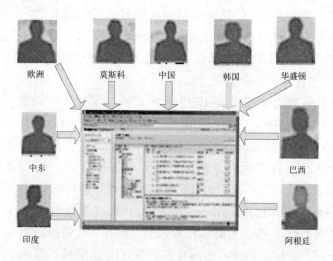

图2　全球业务规划及业务分工的全球信息共享网站

简单而直观的图形用户界面进一步提高采用率

除了这个网站,Watanabe的部门有一个公告板社区,这个社区可以共享收到的订单、报告材料和针对每个国家的风险应急信息、研讨会和培训通知、出差报告和部门处理的业务重组计划、还可以让下级组员利用常见问题解答数据库的输入/输出管理业务和操作标准来解决自己的问题。这些努力都有助于激励每个成员共享信息,重点支持跳跃式展开的沟通和业务精简。

"我没有期望一个Web应用有如此丰富的图形用户界面,"Watanabe补充说。当Groupmax Collaboration应用Web时,它就实现了Windows客户的图形用户界面级。屏幕左边的导航栏可以用来切换用户和社区工作区,操作方便,允许快速进出各种界面(例如电子邮件、日程表和电子论坛),满足运作需求。电子邮件功能也很方便,能过滤基于传递属性(如未看的和紧迫的)、题目、寄件人、社区名字和更多的邮件。简单、直观、可用性的图形用户界面支持更多的用途。

在这个部门,当前实施的是分布于9个海外地区约140名成员之间通信,但该部门计划拓展未来的信息共享给其他海外办事处及相关部门。除要求业务伙伴和当地每个办公室工作人员的参与,该部门旨在积极使用IP电话和电视会议功能。

在谈到未来的计划时,Watanabe继续说道,"因为附加值随参加人数而增加,我们还想通过提高自己的能力继续发送和接收部门之间的信息,并随环境成长。"

增强安全功能,要内嵌其中

除此之外,Groupmax Collaboration 充满了各种功能和效益。Mitsuharu Nagayama,网络软件部的科室经理,软件部下的网络应用软件部的成员之一,说了以下的话:

"至于在全球商业规划与业务分工中 Groupmax Collaboration 的使用,我们的首要目标是要通过支持全球化鼓励平稳操作,不仅使其易于切换语言设置和时区,而且把经营积累的各种资料连接到海内外。"

"另一个重要特点是支持联系到 IP 电话和视频会议的实时沟通,"Nagayama 继续道,"通过同沟通最大化链接,日立的 IP 电话解决方案,我们可以让用户通过从用户搜索窗口点击另一个协作用户的电话号码使用 IP 电话系统,或在浏览相关材料时与另一个远程用户进行实时会话,简单到只要从进度表开始视频会议。我们希望继续加强一种实时通信联系,作为我们对同一个日立 IT 基础设施计划的一部分。"

特别地,Nagayama 强调 Groupmax Collaboration 有着明显优势,由于它具有高度的整体安全水平。"大多数时候个人资料外泄,是由于一个组织内一方的错误或恶意的企图。有了 Groupmax Collaboration,访问可以以社区为基础进行管理,因此,信息的获取是不允许不必要的成员访问的。同时,可以隐藏一个社区的存在。以防止因档案附于电子邮件而使信息泄漏,附加档案可以储存在一个安全的文件共享和通过电子邮件自身的 URL 访问,使信息永远不会离开组织(见图 3)。"

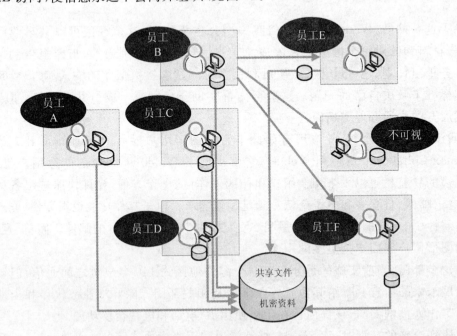

图 3 防止信息泄漏的附加档案

除了这种隐私安全功能,Groupmax Collaboration 还可以通过链接日立开放式中间设备,如 Cosminexus、HiRDB 和管理工作伙伴 1、以及与安全有关的产品,达到进一步加强其安全和依法保护隐私支持的目的。

日立拥有提供软件、硬件的操作和培训的整体的专有技术的能力,其整体解决方案的对象是针对一些值得信赖的盟友企业,它们关心安全风险和资料泄密,但不清楚如何建立一个全公司的信息共享系统。

2005年3月,目录平台和认证平台安装完成后开始管理日立集团的34万员工中20万员工的用户资料。至此,全公司推出Groupmax Collaboration是为了2007年跳跃式上升发展,目标是创造一个世界级的企业协同环境;并通过收集反馈的各种诀窍和操作技巧,完善Groupmax Collaboration的功能性、可伸缩性和可靠性。

日立Groupmax Collaboration的案例

为了精简业务、提高提供给客户的服务质量,日立各部门和科室用自己的技术来协助推展作为一个综合的协作环境的Groupmax Collaboration。

以下介绍几个这样的例子。这里获得的技巧和诀窍将作为今后的改进和解决方案:

案例分析1

产品开发业务的应用

在这,为了减少会议次数和大大提高工作效率,电子论坛已用于讨论解决大型软件开发项目的每一步(见图4)。同时,会议纪要还详细记录了确定一个规格的过程,以供日后参考。

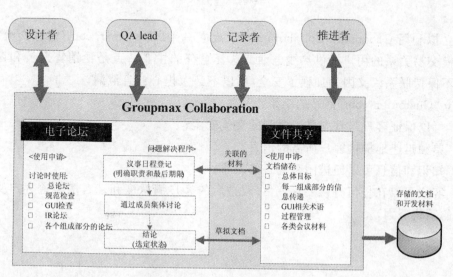

图4 将论坛用于大型软件开发项目的每一步

产品开发业务应用的结果:
- 会议记录在案,使运作过程形象化;
- 论坛搜索功能可用来进行全文搜索,包括附件;

- 减少确认收件人所需时间,防止误发引起的泄密;
- 准确身份管理为便于理解地位决定的讨论;
- 透过档案共享,不断更新项目的共享数据;

案例分析 2

问题导向业务的应用

信息系统的交付,往往伴随着一系列要求。而为了增加速度和准确性的相关估计,与开发商和系统工程师密切沟通是必需的。对于负责处理多种硬件产品的系统工程部门来说,定期与其他开发部门举行例会,几乎完全不可能。在这,Groupmax Collaboration可以用来使社区的每一个问题方便顺利,并保护信息共享。这样系统可允许向客户提供更快捷和准确的信息供其进行评估。

问题导向运营的结果:
- 防止共享信息泄漏,责任方想法均记录在案;
- 组织问题项目用来维持讨论流;
- 加强安全(只有某些成员可查看资料)。

案例分析 3

客户 IT 解决方案的应用

日立拟利用 Groupmax Collaboration 来成立一个"Customer.com"信息交流网站,为大规模交易关系的用户提供热线电话。这套系统的主要特点是让销售人员和客户无时无刻不保持联系。又因为加强了安全,所以不必太担心信息泄漏。

日立"Customer.com"网站的结果:
- 可以保证客户与日立员工之间的交流安全;
- 单独迅速地提供客户所需的信息;
- 知识和信息可以促进团队销售的效率;
- 客户可以在任何时候要求评估(改进后的客户满意度和来自多渠道客户支持的更高效的销售努力)。

CHAPTER 6
E-BUSINESS TECHNOLOGY AND SECURITY ISSUES

电子商务技术与安全

- Some Technology Trends Affecting E-Business
- Usability of the E-Business Web Site
- What is E-Commerce Integration
- E-Business Relies on Security

UNIT 24 Some Technology Trends Affecting E-Business

Text

Without aiming to provide exhaustive or even comprehensive coverage of the issues, the following pages will address some aspects of technology use that have been particularly prominent in the e-business arena in recent months and that will probably influence the development of e-business in coming years.

1. The growth of broadband

The spread of broadband Internet access and related technologies is one reason for Internet traffic rapid growth. The spread of broadband is not only enabling existing Internet users to exchange information more easily, it is also attracting new users. Some operators report that 30 to 50 per cent of their new broadband subscribers have never had an Internet subscription before.

Broadband availability has grown very fast in the past two years. Two dominant technologies have an almost equal share of the world broadband market: DSL (digital subscriber line), with 50 per cent, and cable, with 45 per cent. How will the widespread adoption of broadband influence businesses? Fast Internet access is the main reason for subscribers to switch to broadband technologies. Because data flow faster and users waste much less time waiting for Web pages to download, and because their connections are always on, broadband adopters tend to spend significantly more time online. At the same time, consumers will be able to seek more information, compare more options, or sample digital products.

With regard to broadband's influence on the organization of enterprises or on transactions between businesses, although a number of initiatives aim at building new business models around broadband, no application of it has emerged with an impact on the functioning of markets or on the management of companies that is substantially different from the effects of earlier commercial applications of the Internet. This is not to say that broadband will have no impact on businesses. Businesses buy much more online content than consumers, and broadband makes such content more accessible, easier to use, and therefore more sellable, especially to small and medium enterprises (SMEs). Broadband allows several users to share an Internet connection, which can reduce the cost of every individual connection, an important consideration for SMEs. For larger enterprises, the ability to centralize data and applications in a single storage facility while enabling many users in distant locations to access and use sizeable amounts of information may facilitate the adoption of new forms of organization. Other, broader effects on the economy can also be envisioned. Besides improving access to information society services (e. g. e-health, e-education, e-government) that have indirect but real effects on the productivity of an economy, broadband adoption, like any major new technology, can encourage innovation and thus stimulate economic growth.

2. Security issues

A secure environment is not any more essential for e-business than it is for business in the physical world. Every commercial transaction involves a risk with which participants are normally familiar enough to judge whether the expected returns justify accepting the uncertainty of a potential loss. Even in the presence of considerable risk, if the expected returns are sufficiently high, someone will be willing to take that risk. As e-Business becomes part of the everyday experience of the majority of people, who tend to be more risk-averse than early adopters of technology, security in all its dimensions becomes crucially important. Internet users start to see the Web as a utility that is expected to be operational on a permanent basis and to pose as little risk as water or electricity use.

Internet security problems can take multiple forms: spam, viruses, Web squatting, fraud, copyright violation, denial of service, unauthorized entry into corporate or personal computers and networks (and theft or manipulation of the information stored in them), privacy infringements, and fraud and harassment, among other possibilities. Some of these problems have acquired serious dimensions, and spam (unsolicited e-mail) is now proliferating at an alarming rate. By some estimates, in January 2003 about 25 per cent of all e-mails that circulated on the Internet were unsolicited; by March the percentage was over 36 per cent, and the 50 per cent mark could be reached before the end of 2003. In 2001 the European Commission estimated that spam-related costs amounted to over $9.6 billion worldwide in connection charges alone. Other, more pessimistic estimates put the overall cost of spam to enterprises worldwide in 2003 at $20.5 billion. In addition to spammers operating for financial or other profit, often from offshore ISPs, spam is often used to carry out denial of service attacks. A number of techniques are available to combat spam, although spammers are also becoming increasingly sophisticated. In a growing number of countries, Governments are considering or implementing anti-spam legislation.

Security incidents are not exclusively a problem of developed countries. Several developing countries rank among the countries that were targeted most often in digital attacks in 2002. However, attacks against government sites are less frequent than those against commercial entities, are driven by political factors, and have few economic consequences. Their most important effect may be that the media attention they attract helps undermine public confidence in the Internet in those countries where awareness of and trust in the Internet seem to be less advanced.

Most digital attacks in 2002 originated in a few countries, and 10 of them accounted for 80 per cent of all attacks detected. The United States was at the top of the list, followed by the Republic of Korea, China, Germany and France. Security applications are commonly quoted as one of the areas where CEOs expect major developments in the medium term, and the IT security market is expanding fast. Total sales of IT security software, hardware and services are expected to reach $45 billion by 2006. The development of corporate initiatives in areas such as Web services provides a strong incentive for IT security investment. Reasonable protection against Internet-generated risks can be achieved through a combination of software, hardware and risk management strategies that contemplate all potential sources of liability arising from interactions with customers, workers, suppliers and the general public. Studies based on reported security incidents assess internal threats as being as severe as external ones. In the end, the question of IT security at the firm level is much more a managerial problem than a technical one. It has to do with how penetrable the enterprise wants its business processes to be and how risk management is integrated into those processes. While technology can help reduce those risks and costs, the key to a secure and private online environment is the combination of market efficiency and industry initiatives, political will and an appropriate legal environment.

3. The development of Web services

The concept of Web services refers to automated interaction over the Internet between computers managing different business processes, in such a way that they generate a "grid" of computers in which each machine is able to feed other machines the input they require and/or obtain from them the information it needs. This interaction occurs via software that is designed to use other software. Web services have the potential to significantly improve the efficiency of processes such as inventory control and routine purchasing. In the longer term, their use should extend to other business processes, as they enable seamless, automatic interoperability between the software applications used in running the various aspects of a business as well as with the applications of customers and suppliers.

Beyond that, Web services will be an essential part of an economy in which "communication" between Internet-enabled objects will be increasingly important. Although the main impact of Web services will be in enterprise operations, there are also many possibilities for consumer-oriented applications. For example, Web services could be used to create virtual travel agents that give access to the reservation systems of airlines and railways, car rental companies and hotels, travel-related content providers, and so on.

The potential of Web services to become an important factor of change derives from the fact that they lie at the junction of several strong currents. Some of these currents are changing business organization and interaction, and others could influence the future of computing. The first trend in business organization that influences the development of Web services is the integration of supply chains and the move towards demand chain management. Another factor in the development of Web services is the refocusing of enterprises, particularly larger ones, on those activities and processes that constitute the core of their business, and where their competitive advantage rests. The technology current moving Web services forward is the mounting popularity of distributed computing, an approach in which computing resources are not concentrated in any particular place but pooled together in the network and used when and as needed, thus allowing more efficient allocation of resources.

Words and Expressions

comprehensive [ˌkɔmpriˈhensiv]	adj.	全面的，广泛的
issue [ˈisjuː]	n.	论点，问题
influence [ˈinfluəns]	n.	影响，感化
broadband [ˈbrɔːdbænd]	n.	宽带
operator [ˈɔpəreitə]	n.	工作者，行家，经营者
subscription [sʌbˈskripʃən]	n.	捐献，订金，订阅
adoption [əˈdɔpʃən]	n.	采纳，采用
adopter [əˈdɔptə]	n.	采纳者；接受器
emerge [iˈməːdʒ]	vi.	显现，浮现，显现出来
facility [fəˈsiliti]	n.	设备，工具
envision [inˈviʒən]	vt.	想象，预想

Unit 24 Some Technology Trends Affecting E-Business

innovation [ˌinəuˈveiʃən]	n.	改革,创新
participant [pɑːˈtisipənt]	n.	参与者,共享者
justify [ˈdʒʌstifai]	v.	证明……是正当的
crucial [ˈkruːʃəl]	adj.	紧要关头的,决定性的
spam [spæm]	n.	兜售信息,垃圾邮件
squat [skwɔt]	v.	蹲坐,蹲伏
fraud [frɔːd]	n.	欺骗,欺诈行为
violation [ˌvaiəˈleiʃən]	n.	违背,妨碍,侵害
infringement [inˈfrindʒmənt]	n.	违反,侵权
harassment [ˈhærəsmənt]	n.	折磨
unsolicited [ˌʌnsəˈlisitid]	adj.	未被恳求的,主动提供的
circulate [ˈsəːkjuleit]	v.	流通,(使)循环,(使)传播
offshore [ˈɔ(ː)fʃɔː]	adj.	海外的,国外的
legislation [ˌledʒisˈleiʃən]	n.	立法,法律的制定
contemplate [ˈkɔntempleit]	v.	凝视,沉思,预期,企图
penetrable [ˈpenitrəbl]	adj.	可渗透的,可穿透的
inventory [ˈinvəntri]	n.	详细目录,存货,财产清册,总量
routine [ruːˈtiːn]	n.	例行公事,常规,日常事务
oriented [ˈɔːriənt]	adj.	以……为方向[目的],面向的
reservation [ˌrezəˈveiʃən]	n.	保留,(旅馆房间等)预定,预约
rental [ˈrentl]	adj.	租用的;出租(业)的
junction [ˈdʒʌŋkʃən]	n.	连接,接合,交叉点,汇合处
refocus [riːˈfəukəs]	vt.	使重新聚焦
concentrate [ˈkɔnsentreit]	v.	集中,浓缩

Notes

(1) high-income market   高收入市场,引申为"高端"市场。
(2) Because data flow faster and users waste much less time waiting for Web pages

to download, and because their connections are always on, broadband adopters tend to spend significantly more time online. 这句话包含的两个 because 连接了两个排比句,表示"因为……所以……,因为……所以……"。"adopter"本意是"采纳者;接受器"的意思,但是在这个句子中,后面接的是"花费时间",表示了一个人的动作,因此翻译为"用户"更好。

(3) A secure environment is not any more essential for e-business than it is for business in the physical world. 这里,not more… than 表示"和……一样"。

(4) in the presence of   adv.   在……面前

(5) in all its dimensions   从各方面讲

(6) CEO(Chief Executive Officer)   首席执行官

(7) have to do with   与……相关

(8) in the long term   长期

in the longer term   更长期

(9) as well as   同样,也

(10) consumer-oriented   面向用户的

(11) Another factor in the development of Web services is the refocusing of enterprises, particularly larger ones, on those activities and processes that constitute the core of their business…

refocusing …on   表示重新聚焦在……

distributed computing   分布式计算

分布式计算是一门计算机科学,它研究如何把一个需要非常巨大的计算能力才能解决的问题分成许多小的部分,然后把这些部分分配给许多计算机进行处理,最后把这些计算结果综合起来得到最终的结果。

(12) concentrate in   集于一体

如:Authority was concentrated in the president. 政权集于总统一身。

(13) European Commission   欧盟

Questions

(1) Are broadband network users only in high-income market?

(2) What is the main reason for subscribers to switch to broadband technologies?

(3) Is secure environment important for business in the physical world?

(4) Is Web a utility that is safe like water or electricity use?

(5) Why some offshore ISPs send spam to users?

(6) When two being want to communicate in distance, is Internet needed?

(7) Can you depict the network future for us?

(8) How many technologies are covered in this text?

Unit 24 Some Technology Trends Affecting E-Business

Exercises

1. Translate the following sentences into Chinese:
(1) In the more dynamic economies of the Asia-Pacific region, adoption of e-commerce is more and more perceived by enterprises as the natural future of business.
(2) This being said, since most legitimate industries do not offer extraordinarily high rates of return, a reasonable level of security is needed for the normal conduct of business.
(3) For example, in order to set up a new e-mail account from which to operate, a spammer may use stolen credit card information.
(4) In the end, just as in the physical world an essential function of governments is to maintain peace and security so that citizens can go about their business, so in the digital economy law enforcement agencies will have to adapt to the new commercial environment and ensure the rule of law on the Internet.
(5) As regards data protection and information privacy, few Governments in developing countries have enacted legislation regulating the collection, use, dissemination and protection of the personal data to which business actors have access over the Internet.

2. Translate the following sentences into English:
(1) 宽带业务大发展不仅使宽带运营商看到了希望,同时,它将对整个 IT 产业链产生深远的影响。这对于 IT 企业来说,既是一个巨大的变革和机遇,同时也意味着挑战。
(2) EC(E-Commence)是建立在一个较为开放的网络环境上的(尤其是比互联网更为开放的网络),维护商业机密是 EC 全面推广应用的重要保障。
(3) 宽带互联网的改变不是简简单单地改变网络的速度,它将改变窄带时期的网络信息供应模式,这对于互联网产业来说是一个巨大的变革。
(4) 宽带业务大发展对整个 IT 产业链带来深远的影响,同时,众多的 IT 企业也因此获得了更广阔的发展空间。
(5) 在互联网应用方面,政府部门已陆续建立了自己的 Web 服务器和网站,有的还实现了一些简单的网上业务。

Further Reading

This text is extracted from *E-COMMERCE AND DEVELOPMENT REPORT* 2003 on United Nations Conference on Trade and Development. This third edition of the E-Commerce and Development Report, published by the United Nations Conference on Trade and Development, identifies some of the implications that the growth of the digital economy may have for developing countries. It aims to provide practitioners and policy makers with a better understanding of the options available to them in leading sectors of developing-country economies.

一些影响电子商务的技术趋势

下文将讨论近几个月来在电子商务发展领域特别突出的一些技术应用问题,目的并不是为了详尽或综合性地涵盖各个方面,但这些技术问题可能会在今后几年对电子商务的发展产生影响。

1. 宽带的发展

宽带互联网接入及其相关技术的传播是造成互联网流量快速增长的一个原因。宽带的传播不仅使得现有的互联网用户能够更加容易地交换信息,而且也吸引了新用户。一些操作人员报告,30%～50%的新宽带订购者以前从来没有订购过互联网。

在过去的两年中宽带的可利用性发展很快,两项主要技术几乎占有了世界宽带市场的相同份额:DSL(数字用户线路)宽带占50%,电缆宽带占45%。宽带的广泛采用是怎样影响商业活动的呢? 快速互联网接入是用户转向宽带技术的一个主要原因。因为数据流动更快,用户等待网页下载的时间更少,并且一直处在连接状态,所以宽带使用者乐于花费更多的时间来上网。与此同时,消费者将能够寻找到更多的信息,比较更多的选择,或者体验数字化产品。

关于宽带对企业组织或者在业务间交易产生的影响,尽管很多初创者瞄准于围绕宽带建立新的商业模式,但是还没有出现一种能够影响市场功能或公司管理(与早期的互联网应用效果显著不同)的应用。这并不是说宽带将不会对企业产生影响,事实上,企业比消费者购买了更多的在线内容,宽带使得这些内容更加容易获得,更容易使用,因而更适于销售,对那些中小企业(SME)更是如此。宽带允许多个用户同时共享互联网连接,这样必然会降低单个用户的连接成本,这点同时也被广大中小企业所关注。对更大型的企业来说,将数据和应用集中于一个存储设备,而且让很多远程用户接入并能使用相当大数量的信息,可能会促进一些新的组织形式的采用。另外,对于经济的更广泛的影响是可以想象的。除了丰富进入信息社会服务(如电子健康、电子教育、电子政务)的途径以外,还间接但实实在在地对经济生产力产生了影响,宽带的采用,和任何重大新技术一样,能够鼓励创新和刺激经济的增长。

2. 安全问题

一个安全的环境对电子商务来说和它在现实世界里开展业务一样,都是必需的,每笔商业交易都包含了一种风险,参与者通常对各种风险足够熟悉,来判断预期的回报是否值得接受潜在损失的可能性。即使面临着巨大的风险,但是如果预期回报足够高,那么有人将会愿意冒这个风险。当电子商务成为大部分人的日常生活的一部分,而且这些人比早期网络技术的应用者更能承受风险的时候,从各方面来看安全就会变得至关重要了。互联网用户开始将Web看成一种实用的工具,希望它可以在一个永久性的基础上运作,并且可以像水或电的使用那样,不会对人们造成任何风险。

互联网安全问题可以呈现多种形式:垃圾邮件、病毒、网络入侵、欺诈、侵害著作权、拒绝服务、未经授权进入公司或者个人计算机网络(以及对存储的信息进行偷窃或者操作)、侵犯个人隐私,以及欺诈和其他令人烦扰的行为,还有一些其他的可能性。其中一些问题已经达到了严重的程度,并且垃圾邮件(未被恳求的电子邮件)正在以惊人的速度激增。有人估计,2003年1月,在互联网上流转的邮件中大约25%都是垃圾邮件,到3月,该比例超过了36%,在2003年底前,则可能达到50%。在2001年,欧盟委员会曾评估,在世界范围内仅连接费用方面和垃圾邮件相关的损失总计超过96亿美元。另外,更多的悲观主义者估计垃圾邮件给全世界的企业在2003年带来的全部损失达到了205亿美元。除了一些为了财务或其他利益的垃圾邮件发送者外,其他来自国外的ISP(互联网服务提供商)的垃圾邮件经常执行拒绝服务器正常服务的攻击。尽管垃圾邮件正在变得越来越"先进",但是仍然有很多技术可以用来抗击垃圾邮件。在越来越多的国家,政府正在考虑或者实施反垃圾邮件的立法工作。

安全事故并非是发达国家所独有的问题,许多发展中国家也被列入了在2002年遭受数字攻击最多的国家名单之中。但是,因为出于政治目的而对政府网站进行攻击的频率远小于那些对商业实体的攻击,所以这样的攻击也不致造成大的经济后果。这类攻击最重要的影响可能是用来吸引媒体的注意,以破坏那些互联网的意识和信念都比较薄弱的国家的公众对互联网的信心。

2002年大部分的数字攻击发生在少数国家,其中10个国家占检测到的攻击的80%。美国位居榜首,紧随其后的是韩国、中国、德国和法国。安全应用一般被引证为CEO(首席执行官)希望在任期阶段获得显著进步的一个领域,并且IT安全市场扩展很快。IT安全软件、硬件和业务的总销售预计到2006年可达450亿美元。在诸如网络服务等领域,公司从无到有的发展将会给IT安全投资提供强大的动力。对互联网产生的风险进行合理的保护可以通过联合软件、硬件和风险管理等组合策略实现,而这种组合策略是通过对潜在的来自用户、工人、提供商和普通公众进行交互的所有的可能性进行反复思考后得出的。通过对已报道的安全事故的研究,可以估计出来自内部的威胁与来自外部的一样严峻。最终也可以说,公司级的IT安全与其说是一个技术问题,还不如说是一个管理问题。它与企业想让它的业务流程怎样具有渗透性,并且怎样将风险管理融入到这些过程中去紧密相关。当技术可以帮助减少这些风险和成本的时候,创造一个安全和隐秘的在线环境的关键就是把市场效率和产业动力、政治愿望和一个适合的法律环境结合起来。

3. 网络服务的发展

网络服务(Web services)的概念是指通过互联网在计算机之间管理不同的业务流

程,并实现自动化的交互。这种交互是以产生一种称作计算机"网格"的方式进行工作的,这种"网格"既可以成为其他计算机的输入,也可向其他计算机请求和/或获得它所需要的信息。这种交互通过设计为能够调用其他软件的软件来实现。网络服务具有显著改善诸如存货控制和远程采购等流程效率的潜力。从更长远的角度来看,它们的使用将进一步扩展到其他业务流程,因为它们可以实现应用于一次业务各环节的系统之间无缝隙、自动化的交互操作,也同样适用于客户和供应商间的此类交互操作。

除此以外,网络服务也将成为经济的一个基本的组成部分,在这一经济中,在互联网激活的目标之间实现"通信"将变得日益重要。尽管网络服务的主要影响是在企业运作层面上,但是同样有很多以客户为导向的应用的可能性。比如,网络服务可以被用来建立虚拟旅游代理机构,以准许用户进入航空和铁路公司的订票系统、汽车出租公司、宾馆以及与旅游相关的内容提供商等。

网络服务成为变化的一个重要因素的潜力来自于这样一个事实,即有几种强大的趋势聚集在一起而形成了合力。其中的一些趋势正在改变企业组织和交互性,还有其他的一些趋势将会影响未来的计算。在商业组织中,影响网络服务发展的第一个趋势是供应链集成和转向需求链管理。在网络服务发展中的另一个因素是企业,特别是大型企业,应重新聚焦于能形成它们业务核心的活动和流程中,这是它们的竞争优势所在。向网络服务发展的技术趋势是越来越普及的分布式计算。这种方法并不把计算资源集中在特定的区域,而是在任何需要使用的时候,再通过网络将计算资源聚集在一起,这样就可获得更有效的资源分配。

UNIT 25 Usability of the E-Business Web Site

 Text

Few would deny that the user experience is a critical component of e-business Web site success. Usability testing is one method of assessing the user experience. Usability refers to how easily users can accomplish their tasks. In addition to influencing conversion rates, usability can impact revisit rates, acquisition costs, and order size. Recent estimates indicate that by improving usability, on average, Web sites improved their conversion rates by 100 percent, their traffic by 150 percent and the visitors' use of target features by over 200 percent.

Factor Affecting Usability

There are multiple guidelines for establishing usable Web sites. Among the most important are that Web sites be quick to load, easy to use, searchable, transparent, and consistent.

Quick. A site should be relatively quick to load. One recommendation is that a page take less than 10 seconds to load through a 28.8 modem using a public ISP like AOL or MSN. Waiting for a page to download, however, need not always result in negative Web site evaluations. Managing users' expectations by reducing uncertainty about the wait (e.g., providing a countdown or duration time or informing users that loading a page will require a wait) can help.

Others recommend having small and/or few graphics in order to reduce the download time. Yet graphics as well as the effective use of plug-ins (e.g., Flash, RealOne) can increase users' revisit and purchase intentions by providing an engaging user experience. Rather than adopting a onesite-fits-all approach, companies should allow users to select whether they want a graphics-intensive, flash-enabled, or text site. Indeed, allowing users to customize the Web site experience can elicit such positive results as feelings of alignment with the company and beliefs that it is a trustworthy source.

Regardless of how graphic and technology-intensive the site is, it should also be easy for a user to scan a Web page—this means chunking information into meaningful categories, as well as using light-colored, solid backgrounds. Patterned backgrounds merely compete with the text and graphics for the users' attention. In general, be careful with your page real estate. Avoid crowding the page with information, graphics, and advertisements. It will make the page slow to load and difficult to scan, both of which will likely drive your visitors away.

Easy. The site should reduce the degree to which users must learn how to use it. To gauge how difficult your site is, consider how much you must explain to the user the steps needed to effectively use the site. Although instructions for using the site (e. g. , a frequently-asked-questions (FAQ) page) should be available and clearly visible from every page, you must ask yourself whether the complexities of the site could be reduced. Furthermore, the site should rely on the users' recognizing rather than recalling where features are and what they are. For instance, links to FAQs, the homepage, contact information, and search engine should be available on every page. Otherwise, the user must learn and recall how to find needed information (e. g. , the firm's contact information is available from the home page by clicking on "About Us" and the envelope icon).

Searchable. Navigation consists of interactive tools that allow individuals to move freely through a site at their own discretion through a series of self-initiated searching, accessing, and retrieving activities. Navigational instruments include search engines, search agents, and site indexes. The availability of navigational tools for compiling and sorting information has positive effects on consumers' attitudes, regardless of whether the user has visited the site to browse or to search. Browsers need navigational tools to move fluidly through the site, uninterrupted, whereas searchers need them to find information quickly. Having the tools is not enough, however. For instance, having a search engine is insufficient. It should include simple guided search forms and display the more popular items first. Allowing the user to sort the results by different criteria (e. g. , date, relevance) also facilitates the search process. Furthermore, users often remark that they are "lost" during a Web site visit. To reduce this feeling, each page should show the user where they are (how deep they went into the Web site), where they came from (e. g. , how they got there), and where they can go next (e. g. , at the same level, up a level or even deeper).

Such navigational instruments are especially critical because, by being associated with information access, the Web heightens users' need for understanding, causing them to think more about a product and to want more information about it than they would in traditional media environments. Thus, in addition to having a site rich with information, the site must be easy to search.

Transparent. Transparent Web sites are those that speak the language of their users. One common mistake that disrupts the transparency of a site is to list products by their model numbers. For instance, most people likely do not know the difference between Samsung's HPL6315 and their HPL5025D. However, they likely know the difference between a 63" and a 50" plasma TV. Web sites should also follow conventions that are familiar to users, such as avoiding underlining and icon navigation. On the Internet, underlining represents a hyperlink rather than emphasizing a word. Likewise, icons rarely mean the same thing to all users. There are a few exceptions, such as the company's logo located at the top of the page (often used to redirect the user to the homepage) and a shopping cart (often used for adding something to the cart).

Consistent. The site should look and feel consistent. This includes the size of the pages. If some pages are small (fast to download) and others are large (slow to download), users will feel that they have lost control over the experience. Likewise, the same words, fonts and images should be used throughout the site. Because most Web sites are comprised of pages developed by different people within and outside the company, an inconsistent site is a common usability problem.

The Process of Usability Testing

Testing a site's usability is a relatively simple endeavor. An initial step is to recruit five impartial individuals who are comparable in terms of their age, expertise, Web site proficiency, etcetera. Research has shown that five users find 85 percent of usability problems. At this point, the best course of action is to stop, redesign the site, and conduct another test with five different users. These new users will likely capture many of the remaining problems unidentified from the first round, as well as identify any new problems arising from the redesign.

During the usability test, each individual should view the site alone to avoid contamination. Although many firms conduct these experiments in usability labs, another approach is to observe users in their natural environments. This provides insight into how most users experience the Web site (e.g., through a dial-up connection rather than an internal server and via a smaller monitor). The participant should be given a meaningful task that reflects how people typically use the site. Furthermore, it should be complex enough that it would take at least a few minutes to complete. Examples include researching a product, comparing two products, filling out a form for a newsletter, or purchasing a product.

To assess the users' thought processes as they click through the site, participants should talk aloud. Furthermore, the person administering the test must resist the strong urge to help the user complete their task. Instead, she/he should remain behind the scenes and capture what the users are saying as well as what they are not saying. Are they leaning forward, sighing, and shaking their head? Do they often end up on a page they did not want and need to return to a previous page? How many clicks did it take them to complete the task? From this, look for overall trends and suggest design changes. In the case of Samsung, by promoting this product in offline media, the company should ensure that it is easy to find the product by referring to it on the homepage and making sure that the search engine results contain current pages of it. At the Samsung site, the majority of results were outdated press releases, which are unlikely to meet the needs of the majority of buyers using the search engine. A guided search would help solve this problem. For instance, my search could be limited to products at the site posted in the last year. Consequently, the search engine would do the work for me of filtering out the press releases and other less relevant pages.

Concluding Remarks

Much has been said about satisfying and delighting customers on the Web. Yet, doing so is impossible if the Web site's usability is weak. Highly usable sites are quick to load, easy to use, searchable, consistent, and transparent. Use of graphics and plug-ins can increase the time it takes to load a Web site, but they may be necessary to create an engaging user experience. As broadband adoption increases, concerns about whether users will wait for Web sites to load become less relevant. In the meantime, allowing users to customize the site to their own software, hardware, and information needs should fulfill the goals of satisfying the needs of those with dial-up connections, while also delighting those with broadband access and the desire for more engaging experiences.

Words and Expressions

accomplish [əˈkɔmpliʃ]	vt.	完成,达到,实现
feature [ˈfiːtʃə]	n.	特征,特色,特写,节目,栏目
graphic [ˈɡræfik]	adj.	绘画似的,图解的
engaging [inˈɡeidʒiŋ]	adj.	动人的,有魅力的,迷人的
customize [ˈkʌstəmaiz]	v.	定制,用户化
alignment [əˈlainmənt]	n.	排列,队列,结盟

chunk [tʃʌŋk]	v.	形成块
solid background		一色的背景
pattern ['pætən]	vt.	以图案装饰,模仿,仿制
gauge [geidʒ]	vt.	测量,估量,判断,评价
recall [ri'kɔːl]	v.	记起,想起
icon ['aikɔn]	n.	图标,肖像
browse [brauz]	v.	浏览;吃草,放牧
uninterrupted ['ʌnintə'rʌptid]	adj.	不停的,连续的,未受干扰的,不间断的
heighten ['haitn]	v.	提高,升高
plasma ['plæzmə]	n.	等离子体,等离子区
convention [kən'venʃən]	n.	大会,协定,习俗,惯例
underline [ˌʌndə'lain]	vt.	在……下面划线,作……的衬里,加下划线,强调
hyperlink	n.	超链接
logo ['ləugəu]	n.	标识语
cart [kɑːt]	n.	大车,手推车
	vt.	用车装载
font [fɔnt]	n.	字体,字形,洗礼盘,泉,圣水器
recruit [ri'kruːt]	vt.	使恢复,补充,征募
impartial [im'pɑːʃəl]	adj.	公平的,不偏不倚的
proficiency [prə'fiʃənsi]	n.	熟练,精通,熟练程度
etcetera		=etc.
research [ri'səːtʃ]	vi.	研究,调查
contamination [kəntæmi'neiʃən]	n.	玷污,污染,污染物
dial-up ['daiəlʌp]	v.	拨号(上网)
monitor ['mɔnitə]	n.	班长,监听器,监视器,监控器
	v.	监控

Notes

(1) The text is taken from *The E-Business Review*. The author of the article—Ann Scblosser is an Assistant Professor of Marketing at the University of Washington Business School, she specializes in Internet marketing and consumer behavior, publishing numerous articles for the *Journal of Consumer Research* and the *Journal of Consumer Psychology*. 本文选自《电子商务评论》,作者 Ann Scblosser 是华盛顿大学商学院的助理教授,她专门致力于互联网营销和消费者行为的研究,在《消费者研究》和《消费心理学》等刊物发表了许多论文。

(2) conversion rate   转换率
(3) revisit rate   再次访问率
(4) order size   订单规模
(5) press release   新闻稿
(6) Cf. abbr.   for compare
(7) plug-in   插件程序
(8) Flash   由 macromedia 公司推出的交互式矢量图和 Web 动画的标准。网页设计者使用 Flash 创作出既漂亮又可改变尺寸的导航界面以及其他奇特的效果。
(9) RealOne   一种播放器,可欣赏网上在线音频和视频资料。
(10) at one's own discretion/according to someone's decision   由……自行决定
(11) be comprised of   由……组成
(12) arise from   出现,发生,呈现
(13) lean forward   弯腰向前,探身过去,需要主动参与的
(14) filter out   渗漏,走(泄)漏消息等

Questions

(1) How can we assess the user experience?
(2) Can you describe one of your frustrating experiences concerned with Web Site usability?
(3) What factors will affect usability and a process for assessing and improving Web Site functionality and the user experience?
(4) In the usability testing, what behaviors can reflect the user's thought process?
(5) What are the characteristics of a highly usable site?

Exercises

1. Translate the following sentences into Chinese:

(1) Non-financial entities such as telecommunication and utility companies are also

entering the market, offering payment and other services through their distribution networks and customer relationships.

(2) Driven by advances in communication technology, even trading systems are consolidating and going global.

(3) New electronic systems have lowered the transaction costs of trading and allowed for better price determination because electronic execution and matching techniques reduce the chances of market manipulation.

(4) Because many exchanges are self-regulating organizations, the pressure for change does not usually come from within the industry.

(5) The share of capital raised abroad the traded offshore has increased sharply, especially in emerging markets.

2. Translate the following sentences into English:
(1) 可使用性是指用户能够非常容易地完成他们的任务。
(2) 除了影响转换速度之外,可使用性还影响再访率、购置成本和订单大小。
(3) 几乎每一个上网的用户都有尴尬的用户体验。
(4) 通过提供倒计时器、持续时间,或者通知用户下载页面需要等待等方法来降低等待的不确定性来管理用户期望是有帮助的。
(5) 导航工具包括搜索引擎、搜索代理和站点索引。

Further Reading

You can see the full text in *The User Experience and Web Site Success* by Ann Schlosser on *E-BUSINESS REVIEW*, sponsored by the University of Washington E-Business Program, Fall 2003.

Translation

电子商务网站的可使用性

几乎没有人能够否认用户体验是电子商务网站成功的关键所在。可使用性测试是评价用户体验的一种方法。可使用性是指用户如何能够容易地完成他们的任务。可使用性除了影响转换速度之外,还影响再访率、购置成本和订单规模。新近的估计表明,一般情况下,通过改进网站的可使用性,可以将其转换速度提高一倍,流量提高150%,访问者对目标栏目的使用会超过200%。

影响可使用性的因素

目前有很多建立有效网站的指南,其中最重要的因素是网站能够迅速下载、易于使用、可搜索、透明性和一致性。

迅速。站点能够相对快速地下载。建议使用像 AOL 或者 MSN 的公共 ISP 通过 28.8 K 调制解调器,下载一页花费不到 10 秒的时间。然而,等待网页下载不应该总是导致对网站的否定评价的原因。通过降低等待的不确定性来管理用户期望(例如,提供倒计时器、持续时间,或者通知用户下载页面需要等待)是有帮助的。

为了减少下载时间,有人建议用小的和/或很少的图形。然而图片和插件的有效使用(例如,Flash、RealOne)能通过提供一个动人的用户体验来提高用户的再访率和购买意愿。公司应该允许用户选择是否需要一个具有图形加强、动画激活或者文本功能的站点,而不是采用无所不包的方法。的确,当为用户设计用户化的网站体验时,能对用户产生积极的效果,即感觉与公司结盟并且相信它是一个值得信赖的资源。

不管网站的图形和技术是多么的密集,它都应该是易于浏览的网页——这就意味着要将大量信息适当归类、使用明亮的颜色和一致的背景。要知道,带图案的背景只是为了与吸引用户注意力的文本和图片展开竞争。所以,一般而言,你更应关注网站的真实价值,避免在网页中充斥过多的信息、图形和广告,要不然会使网页下载很慢并且很难浏览,这两者都可能让你的访问者离你而去。

易用。网站应该降低用户必须学习怎样使用它的难度。为了测量你的站点的使用难度,应考虑到你必须向用户解释的有效地使用站点所必需的步骤是多少。虽然使用站点的说明(例如,常见问题解答(FAQ)页)应该在每页都是可用的和清楚可见的,但你必须问你自己是否可以降低站点的复杂性。此外,站点应该依赖于用户的可识别性,而不是让他们回忆在什么地方有什么特征。例如,对常见问题解答的链接、主页、联系方式以及搜索引擎应该在每页上都有。否则,用户必须学习并且回忆怎样找到自己所需要的信息(例如,公司的联系方式可以在主页点击"关于我们"和信封图标获得)。

可搜索性。由交互式工具组成的导航允许个人依照自己的见解通过一系列的自我发起的搜索、存取和检索活动在一个网站自由移动。导航工具包括搜索引擎、搜索代理和站点索引。这种对信息进行编辑和分类的导航工具的可使用性对消费者的态度有积极的影响,不管访问站点的用户是浏览还是搜索。浏览者需要导航工具在站点自由地、不间断地移动,而搜索者需要他们迅速找到信息。但是,仅仅有工具是不够的。例如,只有一个搜索引擎是不够的。它应该包括简单指导搜索表并且首先展示最常用的项目。允许用户按照不同的标准(例如日期、关联性)对结果分类也会使搜索过程变得容易。而且,用户经常谈及他们在访问一个网站时经常会"迷路"。为了减少这种感觉,每页应该显示用户在哪里(他们在网站的何处)、他们从哪里跳转来(例如,他们怎样到达那里的),以及他们下一步能到哪里(例如,在同一层次上、高于这个层次或者更深层次)。

这样的导航工具特别关键。因为,网站通过与信息存取的联系,增加了用户对理解的需要,与在传统的传播媒介环境中相比,客户对有关产品的思考更多,希望了解与它有关的信息也更多。因此,站点除了拥有丰富的信息之外,更要易于搜索。

透明性。透明的网站是那些讲用户语言的站点。破坏网站透明性的一个常见的错误是以它们的型号列举产品。例如,大多数人可能不知道三星电视 HPL6315 和 HPL5025D 之间的差别。但是,他们可能知道在一台 63" 和一台 50" 等离子电视之间的差别。网站也应该遵循为用户所熟知的惯例,例如避免下划线和图标导航。在互联网上,下划线代表的是超链接而不是强调一个词。同样,很少有图标对所有的用户都是同一种意义。有一些例外,如位于网页顶部的公司标识(经常用于把用户再次导向主页)和一辆购物车(经常用于向车内添加东西)。

一致性。网站应该看起来并且感觉起来是一致的,这包括网页的大小。如果一些页面较小(可迅速下载)而其他页面较大(下载缓慢),用户将感到他们已经对体验失去控制。同样,相同的词、字体和图像应该贯穿整个站点使用。因为大多数网站是由公司内部或者外面不同的人开发出来的页面组合而成的,所以,站点风格不一致是一个普遍的可使用性的问题。

可使用性测试的过程

测试站点的可使用性是一次相对简单的工作。第一步是招募就年龄、专长、网站熟练程度等具有可比性的 5 个公平的个体。研究已经显示 5 个用户可发现 85% 的可使用性问题。到这一步,最好的行动步骤就是停止,重新设计站点,并且引导 5 个不同的用户进行另一次试验。这几个新用户将可能发现在第一轮中未辨认出的大部分问题和任何在重新设计中出现的新问题。

在可使用性测试期间,每个人应该单独检查站点以避免相互影响。虽然很多公司在可使用性实验室开展这些实验,但是另一种方法是在自然的环境里观察用户。这为我们提供了洞察大多数用户如何浏览网站的机会(例如,通过拨号连接而不是一台内部的服务器,以及通过一台更小的监视器)。参加者应该分配一个反映人们怎样代表性地使用网站的有意义的任务。而且,这应该是足够复杂的,至少需要几分钟完成。例子包括研究一种产品、比较两种产品、填写一份联络表或者购买一种产品。

为了评价用户通过点击网站时的思考过程,参加者应该高声交谈。而且,管理测试的人必须要忍住帮助用户完成他们任务的强烈欲望。相反,她或他应在幕后捕获用户说了什么和没说什么。他们是否弯腰向前、叹息、摇头?他们经常在他们不想要的一页上结束,并且返回前一页吗?为了完成任务他们点击了多少次?这样,就可以发现一些总的趋势并提出一些设计改进意见。就三星而论,通过在不上网的媒介里推广这种产品,公司应该保证在主页中提及该产品,让访问者能很容易地找到它,并且保证搜索引擎结果包含它的当前页面。如果在三星网站,多数结果是过时的新闻发布,那么这不可能满足多数使用这个搜索引擎的购买者的需要。指导性的搜索将帮助解决这个问题。例如,我的搜寻可能限制在去年网站发布的产品,因此,这个搜索引擎将为我滤出那些新闻发布和其他不那么相关的网页。

结论性评价

　　关于用户对网络的满意和喜悦已经说了很多。然而，如果网站的可使用性差，则要做到让用户满意是不可能的。高质量的可使用性的站点是下载迅速、易于使用、可搜寻、一致和透明的。尽管使用图形和插件程序能增加网站下载的时间，但是它们可能是创造一次吸引用户体验可能性所必需的。随着宽带使用的增加，用户对是否需等待网站下载变得越来越不关心了。同时，允许用户按照自己的软件、硬件和信息需要定制站点，既能实现让那些拨号连接用户满意的目标，更能使那些使用宽带接口并且期望更多动人体验的用户得到愉悦。

UNIT 26 What is E-Commerce Integration

 Text

From a technical perspective, the basic principles of software systems integration are straightforward enough: two or more software programs, or systems, co-operate by one invoking the services of the other. Such integration might take place within a single organization, on a single computer, or involve several computers across a local area network. With business-to-business (B2B) e-commerce integration however, the situation changes, with the software of one business co-operating with that of another across an external network connection. This electronic exchange of messages and documents would, not long ago, have been implemented using Electronic Data Interchange (EDI) business messaging across a private value-added-network (VAN) using leased lines. Now, more commonly, businesses are integrating their software systems by passing messages across the open Internet.

From a business perspective, B2B e-commerce integration means that the application systems of two or more businesses are working together to achieve some common and overarching business goal, such as improved efficiency and reduced delivery times.

The Varieties of E-Commerce

The needs of business and the available technology infrastructure greatly influence the extent and difficulty of the task of integrating business systems. Fundamental issues, such as the degree of business automation common throughout a particular industry sector and the demands of specific trading partners, will have a major impact on e-commerce strategies and how they are realized. There is no single "right" e-commerce strategy; rather there are a number of approaches and trading arrangements that are appropriate for particular businesses at particular times.

These include:
- Simple point-to-point exchanges with one or more pre-established trading partners.
- Opportunistic procurement through a simple connection to one or more trading exchanges.
- As a member of a group of companies forming tighter trading relationships for mutual business advantage, perhaps using common document standards and messaging formats.
- As a member of a sophisticated trading network where B2B relationships are formalized documented as common business processes and automated; new business relationships are then formed dynamically as required.

For many organizations the overriding goal is to use these trading arrangements to improve supply chain integration. The fundamental issues involved are presented below.

Supply Chain Integration

B2B e-commerce changes the nature of business and this impacts heavily all the partners in the supply chain. It is increasingly becoming important for organizations to concentrate on the efficient flow of information, materials and finances from the suppliers to the customers and back again (see Figure 1). Designing efficient business processes throughout the supply chain, and controlling their speed, timing and interaction with one another are crucial factors in a competitive, fast changing electronic marketplace.

Increasingly, the supply chain will cross international boundaries, which brings its own set of challenges and opportunities.

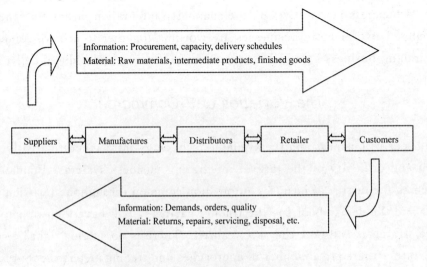

Figure 1　A typical supply chain

In general, bi-directional information, material and finance flows are the key drivers in any supply chain. As shown in Figure 2, a typical business entity in a supply chain can be simplified as a black box connected with three major types of flows. These are procurement (raw materials, goods), finished goods/services, and payment methods. One could also include logistics as a fourth link.

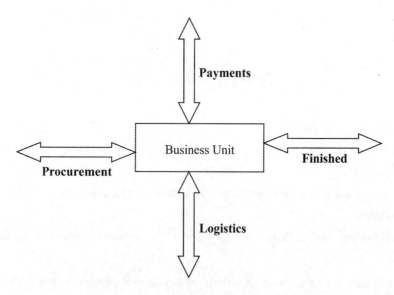

Figure 2 A typical business unit in a supply chain

In an effective B2B e-commerce environment, the supply chain can easily be viewed as a single virtual enterprise, a true value chain in which all resources use Internet technologies to communicate and collaborate effectively, providing and gaining instant access to information. An efficient supply chain can be realized by integrating all its business applications electronically. A complete B2B e-commerce solution can be realized by integrating IT systems at two levels. For any organization, the first level of integration is required with the rest of the internal business, while the second level of integration is required between supply chain partners and customers. Many business customers are shifting purchasing, logistics, and overall supply management to the Internet to shorten supply chains. To this end, it is predicted that within 5 years it is likely that 20% of all business transactions will be carried out electronically.

One of the biggest challenges in any supply chain is getting the right information to the right place at the right time. Traditional supply chains have been dominated by fax and batch information transfers, mechanisms that are faltering under the new requirements for speed, flexibility and ever increasing volumes of data. The key to better supply chain performance is to ensure that all the members of the chain can create, share, and use the information that drives their collective business.

For most organizations, years of accumulating independently developed applications running on a cross-section of hardware systems have resulted in complex and sometimes unwieldy IT environments. The diversity of applications ranges from common packaged desktop software and front-end applications, such as sales force automation, to the enterprise resource planning (ERP) software (e.g., manufacturing, distribution, HR, financial management applications) to custom-developed applications. External systems and technologies encountered through the supply chain further complicate the problem of integrating all of these dissimilar systems. The key to a really efficient supply chain is application integration.

What is Involved?

Application integration involves:
- The transportation and transformation of data between one or more business applications.
- The business rules that govern when this transportation and transformation takes place.
- The integrity constraints that determine the success or failure of the integration.

Business-to-business e-commerce integration could appear in many forms (see Figure 3), including:
- Desktop Integration. Real time integration of data existing in user spreadsheets or other personal productivity software.
- Integration with Electronic Data Input Devices. Real time integration with electronic devices such as bar code and optical scanners, machine tool controllers, point-of-sale systems, etc.
- Front-Office to Back-Office Integration. Synchronizing packaged and custom applications in real time.
- Supply Chain Integration. Connecting partners, vendors and suppliers for greater efficiency.
- Business-to-Business Integration. Extending the enterprise with secure integration to trading partners beyond the firewall.

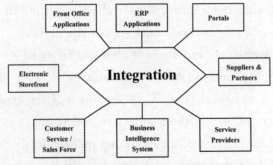

Figure 3　Integrated business-to-business e-commerce

- Enterprise Backbone Integration. Connecting various systems across the extended enterprise.

A complete integration solution requires the following components:
- Broad, reliable, fast and cost-effective connectivity.
- A scalable software and hardware platform.
- Common data standards.
- Reusable integration processes.
- A framework to establish security and trust.

Integration requirements are continuously evolving. For example, there is growing need for the integration of functional behavior of the systems, not just the data alone. The flow of data must be bi-directional and must happen in real time.

How does Technology Support Integration?

The extent and nature of technological support for integration are no less varied than the ways in which individuals, organizations, governments and whole economies conduct business with their partners, suppliers and customers: from humble e-mail systems to the more complex and expensive "enterprise solutions". In the latter category, the predicted growth in B2B e-commerce has attracted the attention of many integration technology vendors. They offer solutions that often feature tried-and-trusted technology but many are also introducing new, additional features that more specifically deal with B2B integration.

The technologies in this space are most generally known as enterprise application integration (EAI) products. Numerous factors have influenced the emergence of EAI market, including the promise of automation, the perceived value-add of e-cusiness integration, mergers and acquisitions, adoption of new technologies, and the need to enhance and control existing business processes. EAI targets the integration of varied types of applications that exist in and between organizations. These include core legacy systems, enterprise resource planning systems, and newer Web-based applications.

One of the leading trends is to deliver pre-built integration solutions. However, there is more to EAI applications than customizable off-the-shelf technology and products. The solution provider must have knowledge of business processes as well as a wide variety of vertical and horizontal applications and technologies. Hence, application integration is not a trivial undertaking. Many vendors are forming alliances to provide complete B2B ecommerce solutions. Some notable specialist EAI vendors are Ariba, Commerce One, and Vitria, who generally provide solutions based on existing middleware and messaging technologies from companies like IBM, Microsoft, TIBCO, BEA Systems, and NEON.

Moreover, there are new technologies that are enabling a new class of "Web Services". In this framework, programmatic interfaces to software within one organization can be used directly by software within another—thus enabling "tight coupling" between software that enacts business services in both. Whilst this has been possible in the past, the new breed of Web services promises to make this type of integration simpler, cheaper and more flexible. For this reason, it has been suggested that they will help SMEs get past some cost & resource barriers that have prevented them from considering integration solutions that feature automated B2B interactions.

Words and Expressions

integration [ˌintiˈgreiʃən]	n.	集成,综合,集成
perspective [pəˈspektiv]	n.	透视画法,透视图,远景,前途,观点,看法,观点,观察
straightforward [streitˈfɔːwəd]	adj.	正直的,坦率的,简单的,易懂的,直截了当的
	adv.	坦率地
lease [liːs]	n.	租借,租约,租赁物,租期,延续的一段时间
	vt.	出租,租出,租得
implement [ˈimplimənt]	vt.	实现,实施,执行
overarch [ˌəuvəˈɑːtʃ]	vt.	在……上做拱形
	vi.	成拱形
infrastructure [ˈinfrəstrʌktʃə]	n.	下部构造,基础下部组织
sophisticated [səˈfistikeitid]	adj.	复杂的,世故的,高度发展的
formalize [ˈfɔːməlaiz]	vt.	使正式,形式化
	vi.	拘泥于形式
dynamical [daiˈnæmikəl]	adj.	动力(学),有力量的
timing [ˈtaimiŋ]	n.	适时,时间选择,定时,调速
logistics [ləˈdʒistiks]	n.	后勤学,后勤
collaborate [kəˈlæbəreit]	vi.	合作,通敌
batch [bætʃ]	n.	(面包等)一炉,一批
falter [ˈfɔːltə]	vt.	支吾地说,结巴地讲出

	vi.	支吾,摇摆,(声音)颤抖
	n.	颤抖,支吾,踌躇
unwieldy [ʌn'wi:ldi]	adj.	笨拙的,不实用的,难处理的,难使用的,笨重的
integrity [in'tegriti]	n.	正直,诚实;完整,完全,完整性
constraint [kən'streint]	n.	约束,强制,局促
scalable ['skeiləbl]	adj.	可攀登的,可升级的
humble ['hʌmbl]	adj.	卑下的,微贱的,谦逊的,粗陋的
	vt.	使……卑下,挫,贬抑
merger ['mə:dʒə]	v.	合并
legacy ['legəsi]	n.	遗留下来的难以处理的东西,遗产,遗赠
opportunistic [ˌɔpətju:'nistik]	adj.	机会主义者的,机会主义的
strategy ['strætidʒi]	n.	策略,战略
procurement [prə'kjuəmənt]	n.	获得,采购,促成
coupling ['kʌpliŋ]	n.	联结,接合,耦合
enact [i'nækt]	vt.	制定法律,颁布(法律),扮演

Notes

(1) CRM：customer relationship management   客户关系管理

(2) ERP：enterprise resource planning   企业资源计划

(3) DRP：distributed resource planning   分销资源计划

(4) HR：human resource   人力资源

(5) SCM：supply chain management   供应链管理

(6) EDI：electronic data interchange   电子数据交换

(7) ATM：asynchronous transfer mode   异步传输技术

(8) EFTPOS：electronic funds transfer at the point of sale   销售点电子化资金转账

(9) Bar code   条形码

(10) EAI：enterprise application integration   企业应用集成

(11) From a business perspective, B2B e-commerce integration means that the application systems of two or more businesses are working together to achieve some common and overarching business goal, such as improved efficiency and

reduced delivery times. 从商业角度看，B2B电子商务集成意味着两家或者更多企业的应用系统协同工作，以达到某些共同的或者更高的目标，比如提高效率、减少交易时间等。

(12) Designing efficient business processes throughout the supply chain, and controlling their speed, timing and interaction with one another are crucial factors in a competitive, fast changing electronic marketplace. 对企业来说，设计贯穿整个供应链的高效业务流程，并控制其速度、安排时间并实现相互之间的交互已成为在竞争激烈、发展迅速的电子化市场中立足的至关重要的因素。

(13) In an effective B2B e-commerce environment, the supply chain can easily be viewed as a single virtual enterprise, a true value chain in which all resources use Internet technologies to communicate and collaborate effectively, providing and gaining instant access to information. 在一个高效的B2B运行环境中，供应链很容易被视为一个单一的虚拟企业。在这一真实价值链中，各种资源运用网络技术提供和获得方便的信息通道，从而进行高效地通信和协同。

Questions

(1) What is e-commerce integration?
(2) How to realize the varieties of e-commerce?
(3) Under a B2B environment, how to realize supply chain integration?
(4) According to the author, what is the key to a really efficient supply chain?
(5) What does application integration involve?
(6) How does technology support integration?

Exercises

1. Translate the following sentences into Chinese:

(1) In the year 2000, the Asia-Pacific region captured 22 percent ($96.8 billion) of the worldwide total B2B spending.

(2) It has been reported that B2B transactions are expected to account for substantial growth of e-commerce in the Asian Pacific region, with the traded value to climb from $39.4 billion in 2000 to more than $338 billion in 2004.

(3) However, elsewhere in the Asia-Pacific region, uptake is marginal, and is likely to remain lower than in neighboring economies.

(4) As the gap widens between whole economies, trading communities and geo-

graphic regions, the phenomenon of the "digital divide" portrays a picture of more sharply fragmented economies.

(5) The social and economic consequences are being addressed in a variety of national and international arenas.

2. Translate the following sentences into English:

(1) 从商业的角度看,电子商业集成可以帮助企业实现更高的目标,比如提高效率、减少交易时间等。
(2) 对于企业来说,没有"唯一"正确的电子商务模式。
(3) B2B 电子商务改变了业务的特征,对交易方式、对整个供应链所涉及的各合作方都产生着重要影响。
(4) 一条高效的供应链可以通过对它所有商业应用进行电子化整合得以实现。
(5) 技术对电子商务集成有着重要支持,并提供了一些特色的解决方案。

Further Reading

You can see the full text in *APEC E-Business: What Do Users Need?* prepared for The APEC Telecommunications and Information Working Group by CSIRO Mathematical and Information Sciences.

Translation

何谓电子商务集成

从技术角度看,软件系统集成的基本原理并不复杂:两个或更多的软件程序或系统,通过相互响应而进行合作。这样的系统集成可以在单一的组织、在某一台电脑上得到实现,也可以通过包括多台微机的局域网实现。然而,随着 B2B 电子商务的整合,情况发生了变化———一家企业的软件系统可以通过外部网络连接与另一企业的软件进行协作。这种信息及文件的电子化交换在不久以前已经借助于电子数据交换技术(Electronic Data Interchange, EDI)的发展而得以实现。它主要是通过租用线路在私营的增值网(VAN)上进行的。现在,更普遍的是,企业正在通过更为开放的国际互联网传递信息,对其软件系统进行整合。

从商业角度看,B2B 电子商务集成意味着两家或者更多企业的应用系统协同工作,以达到某些共同的或者更高的目标,比如提高效率、减少交易时间等。

电子商务多样性

商业需求以及可资利用的技术设施极大地影响着集成业务系统任务的程度和难

度。一些基本的问题,比如跨越一个特定行业部门的业务自动化程度,以及特定贸易伙伴的需求,将对电子商务战略及其如何实现有重要影响。没有"唯一"正确的电子商务战略,而应该说,在特定的时期,对特定的企业来说,有许多合适的途径和贸易安排。这些包括:

- 与一个或多个预先建立起来的贸易伙伴进行单一的点对点式的交易;
- 通过与一个或若干个交易所的一个简单链接进行随机采购;
- 作为公司集团/团体中的一员,为了多边商业利益形成紧密的贸易关系,尽可能使用通用的文档标准和信息格式;
- 作为先进贸易网络中的一员,该网络中 B2B 关系的形成像一般业务流程一样已经文档化并自动化了,而随后新的业务关系有活力地形成将变得十分需要。

对于大多数组织来说,其首要目标是通过应用这些贸易协定去促进供应链整合,这里所涉及的基本问题在下文详细阐述。

供应链集成

B2B 电子商务改变了业务的特征,并对整个供应链所涉及的合作各方都产生着重要的影响。企业专注于从供应商到消费者及其循环着的信息流、物流、资金流的效率已经变得越来越重要(如图 1 所示)。对企业来说,设计贯穿整个供应链的高效业务流程,并控制其速度、安排时间并实现相互之间的交互已成为在竞争激烈、发展迅速的电子化市场中立足的至关重要的因素。

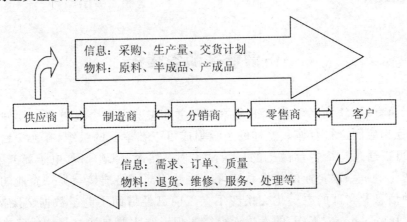

图 1 典型的供应链

越来越明显的是,供应链将穿越国际边界,这将为其自身带来一系列的挑战与机遇。一般来说,双向的信息流、物流和资金流都是供应链的关键驱动力。从图 2 可以看到,在供应链中的一个典型实体可以简化为与"三流"相联系的黑箱:这就是采购(原材料、货物)、终端产品/服务和支付方式。物流可以视为第四个环节包括其中。

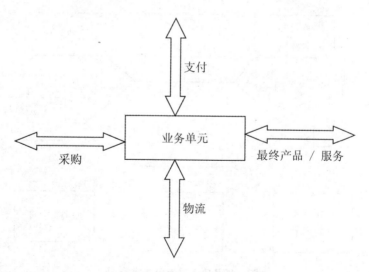

图 2　典型供应链业务单元示意图

在一个高效的 B2B 电子商务运行环境中,供应链很容易被视为一个单一的虚拟企业。在这一真实价值链中,各种资源运用网络技术提供和获得快速方便的信息通道,进行高效地通信和协同。一条高效的供应链可以通过对它的所有商业应用进行电子化整合得以实现。一个完整的 B2B 电子商务解决方案可以通过在两个层次上整合 IT 系统来实现:对任何组织来说,第一层次与该企业内部有关;而第二层次则需要供应链伙伴与客户之间的整合。许多企业客户正在把采购、物流,以及所有供应管理转向互联网来缩短供应链。就这一点来说,据预测,五年内企业所有交易的 20% 将实现电子化。

无论是对于哪一种供应链,最大的挑战都在于如何把适当的信息在适当的时间送到合适的地点。传统的供应链受传真和成批的信息转移控制/影响,在对速度、流动性和数量不断增加的信息的新要求下,这些方式已经逐渐失去了活力。更好的供应链运作的关键因素是确保链上所有成员创造、共享和使用信息,以推动他们共同的业务。

对于大多数企业组织而言,日积月累独立开发的应用软件在跨部门的硬件系统中运行,造成了 IT 环境的复杂化,有时甚至是难以操纵。这种应用程序的多样性体现在从通用的套装桌面软件、前端应用(比如销售力自动化)到企业资源计划(ERP)软件(如:制造、分销、人力资源、财务管理应用等)到客户开发应用软件。企业在供应链中遇到的外部系统和技术使得所有这些不同系统的整合更加复杂化。一个真正有效的供应链的关键是应用程序的整合。

与哪些方面有关?

应用软件整合包括:
- 在一个或多个业务应用系统间实现数据传输与转换;
- 当这种传输与转换发生时应遵循的业务规则;
- 决定整合成败的完整性约束。

B2B 电子商务集成可以有许多形式(如图 3 所示),包括:

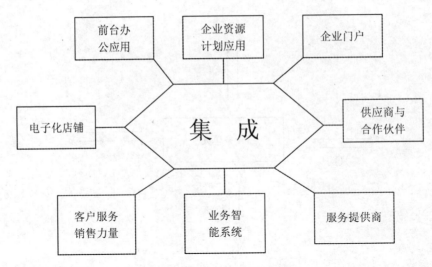

图 3　B2B 电子商务集成示意图

- 桌面整合。实时整合出现在用户空白表格程序或其他个人生产软件中的数据。
- 电子化数据输入设施整合。与电子设备如通过条码、光学扫描、机械工业控制器、销售点系统等进行实时整合。
- 前台办公与后台办公的整合。同步组合和实时定制应用。
- 供应链整合。为了更高的效率,把合作伙伴、卖方、供应商联系起来。
- B2B 方式整合。通过安全整合将企业扩展至防火墙以外的交易伙伴。
- 企业骨架整合。将已经扩展的企业的不同系统链接起来。

一个完整的集成方案需要如下内容:
- 广泛、可靠、快速、低成本、高效率的连接;
- 可扩展的软硬件平台;
- 通用数据标准;
- 可重复使用的集成进程;
- 建立安全与信任的框架。

整合要求在不断地演进。例如,对信息系统功能行为整合的要求正逐步增加,而不仅仅是在数据方面。数据的流动必须是双向的、实时的。

技术如何支持集成

技术对整合支撑的范围和本质,较之于个人、企业、政府部门乃至整个经济体系与它们的合作者、供应商及顾客打交道的方式,都没什么变化:从简单的电子邮件系统到更加复杂昂贵的"企业解决方案"。在后者里,B2B 电子商务预计的增长已经吸引了许多集成技术卖主的注意力。他们提供以尝试—信任为特色的解决方案,但许多人也引入了专门应对 B2B 整合的、新的、额外的特色。

在这一领域中广为熟知的是企业应用集成(EAI)产品。众多因素影响着 EAI 市场的出现和发展。这些因素包括自动化的前景、电子商务整合的增值潜力、合并与收购、新技术的采用,以及提升和控制现有业务流程的需要。EAI 以整合存在于企业内部及企业之间的不同类型的应用程序为目标。这些包括关键性的遗留下来的系统、企业资源计划管理系统,以及新的以网络为基础的应用系统。

　　提供预制的集成方案是其中的一个主流趋势,然而,EAI 应用系统要比可以进行客户化定制的、库存可用的技术和产品多得多。解决方案提供者必须有业务流程知识,以及广泛的纵向和横向应用与多样化的技术。因此,应用整合并不是一项细小的工程。许多卖主组成联盟提供完整的 B2B 解决方案,一些著名的专业 EAI 厂商有 Ariba、Commerce One 和 Vitria,他们通常提供基于 IBM、Microsoft、TIBCO、BEA Systems 和 NEON 等公司提供的中间件和消息技术的解决方案。

　　而且,新技术正在促成一个新的"网络服务"种类。在这种框架中,一个企业针对软件的程序化界面可以直接为另一企业的软件所使用——这就促成了软件间的"紧密结合",使得企业间可以相互服务。尽管这在过去也是可能的,但新出现的网络服务必将使得这种类型的整合更加简单、便宜和更具灵活性。正因为这一点,有人提出这将会有助于中小企业摆脱过去的那些成本及资源方面的障碍,那些障碍曾阻碍了中小企业考虑以自动化的 B2B 交互为特征的集成的解决方案。

UNIT 27 E-Business Relies on Security

Text

E-business security is evolving from the old notion of turning the enterprise into an information fortress to a new, more comprehensive model of privacy and trusted e-business.

The old view of security involved keeping the "bad guys" out by using firewalls, virus protection, and intrusion detection software.

The new view adds the model of trusted e-business: letting the "good guys" in. These good guys are customers, partners, remote employees, or others upon whom your e-Business depends. Giving them access is the very basis of e-business, but allowing partners, customers, and sometimes even competitors inside the e-business infrastructure adds levels of complexity far beyond the traditional model of security. Customer trust depends upon keeping personal information private and secure.

Creating a high-performance e-business security infrastructure demands close coordination of both technical and management policies and procedures. The time and costs associated with monitoring all external connections, internal activities, and vulnerabilities are overwhelming IS departments and corporate executives alike. As a result, many corporations must rethink the overall network strategy and its effectiveness in enabling enterprise-wide business objectives.

When implementing a new security solution, an enterprise must have many goals in mind. These include:

- **Mitigating and managing security risks.** This is the traditional role of security—keeping intruders out and keeping information safe and must be maintained.
- **Privacy—protecting personal and corporate information.** This is one of the biggest changes in the security market: Greater demand to share information with customers and partners is putting new stress on companies to prevent that in-

formation from falling into the wrong hands. Data control and management is a critical issue for corporations. Customer information is a valuable asset and must be protected.

- **Quickly deploying secure e-Business initiatives.** Security solutions must keep time-to-market issues in mind, allowing the e-Business environment to be modified on the fly without compromising security.
- **Reducing ongoing costs of managing and administering security.** Return on investment (ROI) is always a key goal, and many companies consider outsourcing security administration because they can use the latest solutions without buying new products or hiring new expertise.

Security Requirements for E-Business

The security infrastructure needs to have the following basic capabilities:

- **Identification/authentication.** This is the first step of any security and privacy process: being able to tell who users are. Having a security infrastructure that can do this quickly and accurately is necessary for creating a good experience for customers and partners.
- **Authorization.** Once the system determines who users are—and that they are who they say they are—it must provide the correct levels of access to different applications and stores of information.
- **Asset protection.** The system must keep information confidential and private. This has become more difficult in the modern e-business environment, where information is traveling across multiple, often untrusted, networks.
- **Accountability.** This is the ability to keep track of who has done what with what data. E-business solutions also need to ensure that participants in transactions are accountable.
- **Administration.** This involves defining security policies and implementing them consistently across the enterprise infrastructure's different platforms and networks.
- **Assurance.** This demands mechanisms that show the security solutions are working, through methods such as proactive detection of viruses or intrusions, periodic reports, incident recording, and so forth.
- **Availability.** Modern e-businesses must prevent interruptions of service, even during major attacks. This means that the solution must have built-in fault tolerance and applications and procedures to quickly bring systems back online. IT managers must be able to make changes to the system 7×24.

Privacy for E-Business

The whole issue of security in an e-Business environment has evolved to encompass issues of privacy and trust.

Security does not always entail privacy, but privacy requires security. Keeping information confidential requires much more than a technology solution. It is about business policy and the processes they support.

Data privacy is about choice: the freedom of individuals to choose how they wish to be treated by organizations that control data that describes them. Data privacy has emerged as a major societal issue as individuals have begun to question the levels of technological intrusiveness they will tolerate.

Privacy includes several aspects. First and foremost, privacy enables companies to protect personal and organizational assets, such as information about customers and partners; these "good guys" must be let in to access and modify this data, without unauthorized users being able to see it.

Infrastructure and Policy

Security and privacy must be built directly into the infrastructure. Privacy is a matter of policy: determining who can see what within the corporate IT environment. But any privacy policy is only as good as the security infrastructure that backs it up. The security infrastructure is vital to the ongoing relationship with partners and customers.

The combination of security infrastructure and a sound privacy policy creates an environment of trust among partners and other users. This protects not only users but also the enterprises that hold that data—and which could be held liable for its loss.

Businesses can harness their customer's desire for privacy controls into a strategic competitive advantage. On the other hand, a company needs to be aware of the impact of losing control of customer information.

Implementation of E-Business Security

Installing an e-business security solution includes creating a blueprint of security needs, selecting skills and resources, and implementation.

Enterprises should recognize the need to implement security and privacy solutions that can span the end-to-end e-business environment. These systems must provide a range of security controls, including intrusion detection, authentication and authorization tools, vulnerability scanning, incident management, and firewall administration.

The system must take into account data control processes for sensitive information.

This infrastructure must support a comprehensive common security and privacy model that can expand to new applications and resources. This enables companies to lower their total cost of ownership (TCO), focus on their core competencies, and rest assured their networks are maintained with the latest technologies applicable to their particular needs and vertical industry.

Planning: The Blueprint

The first step in the process is creating a blueprint by assessing security needs and determining how to address them. By definition, these needs should align with the company's business objectives. There are several stages in creating this blueprint. The assessment stage establishes a baseline or initial diagnosis of the overall security posture. Within the assessment stage are two main pillars: the technical and the business components.

Technical assessments generally involve two main aspects: a vulnerability assessment to determine system weaknesses and a threat assessment to determine likely threats.

The business assessment can contain the following aspects:

- Physical environment assessment covers the actual office and hardware.
- Incident response assessment reviews the processes necessary to restore functionality in the event of attack or other incident.
- Information protection assessment examines all policies, procedures, and controls with respect to information access and retention.
- A privacy health check will evaluate all of the current processes and procedures, as well as levels of adherence. This check will also evaluate risk of disclosure of confidential data.
- Security awareness assessment of employees.

The next step in the blueprint process is an architectural analysis, which is designed to look at the security solutions already in place and determine what aspects must change. Then the company must create a security strategy plan to implement these changes.

Selection Process for Skills and Resources

Once the security and privacy needs have been outlined, a company needs to determine if it has the necessary skills in-house to implement the blueprint. Some companies will have all the necessary skills in-house, while others must outsource some or all of the implementation.

When looking at possible vendors, which come from many backgrounds, companies must ask and receive answers to the following types of questions:

- Does the service provider have the necessary experience (backed by customer examples and reference accounts) to overcome the security challenges associated with a particular vertical industry or individual business?
- Have the necessary capital investments been made in tools, staffing, global infrastructure, and support?
- Does the service provider have alliances with other key industry players to deliver an integrated security service, or is it operating in a vacuum? Are these just "paper alliances", or are they well coordinated and market tested? If outsourcing with multiple vendors, which vendor would act as the "prime", and would one have contact with the other solutions vendors?
- Is the provider able to not only implement security solutions but also manage them on an ongoing basis if needed?
- Does the provider take into account privacy issues for empowering customers to control their own information? Examples of privacy issues include opt-in or opt-out controls for information gathering, data handling procedures, and data retention standards.

Implementation

Once these questions have been answered, the enterprise enters the implementation stage. On the technical side, a combination of the assessment, architecture analysis, and strategy and planning stages will determine whether the hardware and software requirements are fulfilled.

Consequently, integration best practices involve the creation of a pilot implementation, which can be performance-tested and debugged before migration to the new solution. This practice is designed to limit downtime, complications, or disruption in business service. Testing and debug services will also continue to play a key role in the implementation of information security engagements because the testing data from such services is used to calculate network device management thresholds and performance baselines.

Several human factors should also be considered, such as training, staffing, and processes. A perfectly executed integration of the security system is rendered helpless if the IT staff has no idea how to operate, manage, and maintain the network.

Precisely documented policies, procedures, and specifications, in addition to education and training of IT personnel, are critical success factors.

Conclusion

As security and privacy threats grow in both scope and sophistication, forward-thinking organizations of all shapes and sizes will continue to strengthen their defenses against these threats.

Some organizations will continue to rely on internal systems and resources to manage the "cyber risks" associated with operating in the new economy. Others, however, may lack the training, skills, resources, or interest needed to operate their IT infrastructure securely and will subsequently turn to outside experts for help.

Whether a company looks outside or in-house to implement a new security infrastructure, it must take a series of specific steps. Without following this blueprint, a company cannot hope to create a system that is both secure and up to date, encompassing the divergent needs of greater information sharing and greater privacy.

Words and Expressions

notion ['nəuʃən]	n.	概念,观念,想法,意见
fortress ['fɔːtris]	n.	堡垒,要塞
comprehensive [ˌkɔmpri'hensiv]	adj.	全面的,广泛的
overwhelming [ˌəuvə'welmiŋ]	adj.	压倒性的,无法抵抗的
intruder [in'truːdə]	n.	入侵者
deploy [di'plɔi]	v.	展开,配置
multiple ['mʌltipl]	adj.	多样的,多重的
proactive [ˌprəu'æktiv]	adj.	(心理)前摄的
encompass [in'kʌmpəs]	v.	包围,环绕,包含或包括某事物
entail [in'teil]	v.	使必需,使蒙受,使承担,遗传给
societal [sə'saiətəl]	adj.	社会的
harness ['hɑːnis]	vt.	治理,利用,上马具,披上甲胄
install [in'stɔːl]	v.	安装,安置,使就职
vulnerability [ˌvʌlnərə'biləti]	n.	弱点,攻击
vertical ['vəːtikəl]	adj.	垂直的,直立的,顶点的,[解]头顶的

baseline ['beislain]	n.	基准,控制点,[计]基线
posture ['pɔstʃə]	n.	(身体的)姿势,体态,状态,情况,心境,态度
retention [ri'tenʃən]	n.	保持力
outline ['autlain]	v.	描画轮廓,略述,外形,要点,概要
debug [di:'bʌg]	vt.	调试,改正有毛病部分
threshold ['θreʃhəuld]	n.	开始,开端,极限,门槛;门口,起点;最低限度
render ['rendə]	vt.	呈递,归还,着色,汇报,致使,放弃,表演,实施
sophistication [səˌfisti'keiʃən]	n.	世故,复杂性,强词夺理
divergent [dai'və:dʒənt]	adj.	分歧的

Notes

(1) The text is adapted from *Intergrated E-Business Security: Widening the Community, but Controlling the Access*, which is a research published as part of an information service also available by subscription from IDC, providing written research, analyst-on-call, e-flashes, telebriefings and conferences.

(2) evolve from　　由……进化

(3) on the fly　　在飞行中,不工作,闲混

(4) keep track of　　明了

(5) align with　　与……结盟

(6) pilot implementation　　试执行

Questions

(1) What is the difference between the old and new notion of e-business security?

(2) What goal must an enterprise have in mind when implementing a new security solution?

(3) What is the relationship between privacy and security?

(4) What is the privacy and what is the most important aspect of it?

(5) What should we pay attention to in implementing security and privacy solutions?

Exercises

1. Translate the following sentences into Chinese:
(1) Charging higher interest rates may not, however, be in the interests of the banks because low-risk borrowers, who are most likely to repay loans, are driven from the market.
(2) The forces of rapid globalization and technological change have largely driven recent trends in financial services.
(3) The production and export of agricultural commodities from developing countries deserve attention because of the central role that these commodities play in the economies of those countries.
(4) Cross-border capital flows have been the most important financial service delivery mechanism.
(5) Over the years, a number of policies and strategies have been adopted at the national and international levels to help producers receive higher export prices so as to sustain production and promote overall economic development.

2. Translate the following sentences into English:
(1) 我们应该将客户信任建立在对私人信息的私密性和安全性的基础上。
(2) 技术和管理策略、方法的紧密配合是建立一个高效率的电子商务基础设施所必需的。
(3) 数据控制和管理对公司而言是一个十分关键的环节。
(4) 安全性和私密性必须直接建立在安全设施基础上。
(5) 安全基础设施对于维护现有的客户和合作伙伴的关系是至关重要的。

Further Reading

You can visit www.IDC.com to learn more about IDC's subscription and consulting services.

Translation

电子商务依赖于安全性

电子商务安全正在从"把企业转变成一个信息堡垒"的旧观念向新的、更具包容性的隐私和可信任的电子商务模型演进。

旧的安全保护措施包括使用防火墙将"不怀好意的人"挡在外面、采用病毒保护方案以及应用入侵检测软件。

新的观点引入了电子商务的信任模型：让"好人"进来。这里的"好人"指的是客户、合作伙伴、远程雇员或者其他任何电子商务所依赖的个体。让"好人"能够访问系统是电子商务最基本的条件，但是允许合作伙伴、客户，有时甚至你的竞争对手进入电子商务系统，将会带来许多远超出传统安全模型之外的复杂性。客户信任建立在个人隐私保护和安全上。

构建一个高绩效的电子商务安全基础框架（或体系），需要包括技术与管理制度和程序的紧密配合。由于需要监控所有的外来链接、内部交互活动以及系统本身弱点所造成的相关时间和成本的耗费，这已经把信息安全(IS)部门和公司相关的执行人员压得喘不过气来，所以，许多公司在实现企业商业目标时必须重新考虑整体网络策略和有效性。

在实施一个新的安全解决方案时，一个企业必须牢记多个方面的目标。这些目标包括：

- **减轻和管理安全风险**。这是安全的传统角色——拒入侵者于门外，同时保证信息的安全性，并且必须长期坚持。
- **私密性——保护个人和企业信息**。这是安全市场的重大变化之一：与客户和合作伙伴共享信息的更大需求，在如何防止这些信息被恶意利用方面，给公司带来了新的压力。对公司而言，数据控制和管理是一个很棘手的问题。客户信息是一份很有价值的资产，必须得到严格的保护。
- **快速部署安全电子商务行动**。安全解决方案必须牢记"时间即市场"的思想，应允许电子商务环境在不被抱怨安全性的前提下，能够对系统进行在线实时的更新。
- **降低运行中管理和监控安全的成本**。投资回报率(ROI)总是一个关键的目标，许多公司考虑将安全管理的职能外包，因为这样可以及时采用最新的安全措施，而不必去购买新的安全设备或者雇佣新的安全专家。

电子商务的安全需求

安全基础设施需要具有以下基本功能：

- **身份认证/实名认证**。这是实施任何安全和隐私方法的第一步，目的是要能够识别出用户是谁。一个能够快速而准确地进行身份/实名认证的安全基础设施对给客户和合作伙伴留下一个愉快的经历是必需的。
- **授权**。一旦系统识别出用户的身份——也就是说他们确实与其所表明的身份相一致，那么系统就应该向其提供相应级别的进入不同的信息应用和存储系统的权限。
- **资产保护**。系统必须保持信息的机密性和隐私性。这对现代电子商务环境而言是比较困难的，因为在电子商务环境中，信息是通过多重的，有时甚至是不可确信的网络环境传播的。
- **责任性**。这是一种跟踪用户对数据处理记录的能力。电子商务解决方案也需要确保交易的参与者是能够承担责任的。
- **执行**。这涉及定义安全策略以及在不同的平台和网络的企业基础设施上始终如一地实施这些策略。
- **保证**。这要求有一个能够表明安全解决方案正在运作的机制,如通过对病毒或者入侵的前向探测、定期报告、事件记录等。
- **有效性**。现代的电子商务系统必须防止服务中断这种情况的发生,哪怕是在受到重大打击时也要如此。这就是说,安全解决方案必须要有内置的容错,以及应用系统与程序的在线快速恢复能力。IT 经理必须能够对系统进行 7×24[①] 的调整。

电子商务的私密性

完整的电子商务环境的安全体系已经演进到必须把隐私和信任问题考虑在内的阶段。

安全性并不总牵涉到私密性,但是私密性却要求得到安全保证。保持信息的机密性比一个技术解决方案的要求要高得多,它关系到业务的政策以及它们所支持的程序。

数据隐私实际上是一个选择问题:每个个体都有选择的自由,即有权要求那些掌控有关他们信息的机构按照自己的意愿进行信息的处理。由于公众个体开始质疑他们到底能够承受多大程度上的技术入侵,数据私密性已经作为一个主要的社会问题出现。

隐私包括几个方面:第一也是最重要的,隐私应能确保企业能够保护个人和组织的财产,比如客户和合作伙伴的信息;这些"好人"应能允许进入访问并能修改相关数据信息,同时保证未被授权的使用者看不到这些数据。

基础架构与政策

安全性和私密性必须直接建立在基础架构上。私密性是一个政策问题:明确在企业 IT 环境下谁具有相应的浏览什么内容的权限。但是,任何私密性政策最多只能达到安全基础架构所支持的安全性的程度。安全基础架构对于维护现有的客户和合作伙伴的关系是至关重要的。

安全基础架构与完善私密性政策的结合,在商业伙伴和其他用户之间建立起了一个相互信任的环境。这样的方式,不仅保护了用户,同时也保护了那些拥有数据的企业,这就可让企业对数据的丢失承担责任。

一方面,企业可以把满足客户对私密性控制的需求转变为一种战略上的竞争优势,另一方面,企业也必须意识到失去对客户信息的控制所产生的影响。

电子商务安全的实施

实施一个电子商务安全解决方案包括:规划安全需求的蓝图、选择相应的技能和资

[①] 每周 7 天,每天 24 小时。

源,并组织实施。

企业应该认识到这样一种需求,即可以执行跨越端到端的电子商务环境的安全性和私密性解决方案的需求。这些系统必须提供一系列的安全控制,包括入侵检测、认证和授权工具、攻击扫描、事件处理和防火墙监控。对于敏感信息,系统还必须考虑相应的数据控制程序。

这种基础架构必须支持全面通用的安全和隐私模型,以扩展新的应用和资源。这样可使企业进一步降低它们的总拥有成本(TCO),集中关注它们的核心竞争力,并让它们确信无疑地认识到,它们的网络是采用最新的技术维护的,可用来满足它们的特定需求和从生产到销售的行业需要。

计划:蓝本

程序的第一步是要通过评估安全需求和确定实现安全需求的方案以制定出蓝本。根据定义,安全需求应该与企业的商业目标一致。制订蓝皮书有几个步骤:在评估阶段,应确定一个关于全面的安全状况的基准或初步的诊断。在评估阶段主要有两个支柱:一个是技术成分,另一个是业务成分。

技术评估通常涉及两个主要方面:确定系统脆弱性的缺陷评估和决定类似威胁的威胁评估。

业务评估则包括以下几个方面:
- 覆盖实际办公和硬件设施的物理环境评估;
- 检测必要流程的事件响应评估,以确保在遇到攻击事件或其他不测时能恢复功能;
- 信息保护评估要检查所有的政策、程序以及有关信息接入和保留的控制;
- 隐私的健康性检查,以评估当前所有的处理流程和程序,并坚持相同的水平进行,这一检查也将评估泄露机密数据的风险;
- 雇员的安全意识评估。

制订蓝皮书的第二个步骤是架构分析。它是设计用来检测已经实施了的安全解决方案,并且确定哪些方面还需要改进的。之后,企业就必须制订安全策略计划去实施这些改进。

技能和资源的选择程序

一旦大致勾勒出了安全和私密性需求,一个公司就要决定在公司内部是否有足够的技术能力来实现这个蓝图。一些公司将在内部拥有所有必需的重要的技术能力,与此同时,其他一些公司必须外包部分或者全部的实施以实现计划。

在考虑来自不同背景的可能提供商时,公司必须提出以下各类问题,并要能够得到相应的答案:
- 服务提供者是否具有必要的经验(由客户案例和参考报道支持)来克服与特定

的纵向性行业和单个企业相关的安全性挑战？
- 在工具开发、员工、全球基础设施建设和支持方面是否具有足够的资金投入？
- 服务提供者是否和其他关键行业主导者联合起来提供一个集成化的信息安全服务，或者还是处在隔绝状态中运作？这些仅仅是"纸上谈兵式的联盟"，还是已经合作良好并得到了市场的检验？如果把业务外包给多个提供商，那么哪个服务商能够扮演"主角"？一个销售商是否能和其他解决方案提供商保持联系？
- 服务提供商是否具有不仅能够实施安全解决方案，而且还能够在需要的时候在正在运行的系统上进行管理？
- 服务提供商是否通过授权给顾客来控制他们信息的方法来考虑私密性问题？私密性问题的例子包括信息收集的流入与流出控制、数据处理程序和数据存储标准。

实　　施

一旦这些问题得到解决，企业便进入实施阶段。从技术角度讲，评估、结构分析、策略及计划阶段的结合将决定硬件和软件需求是否得以实现。

因此，最优实践的集成牵涉到创立一个试执行的过程，该过程为在正式实施一个新的解决方案之前能够检测绩效并进行调试。这一做法是设计用来限制停工时间、降低复杂性或预防商业服务的中断。测试和调试服务将继续在信息安全方面扮演重要角色，因为来自于这些服务的测试数据用来计算网络设计的管理门槛和绩效基准。

许多人为因素也应该被考虑到，如：培训、员工配置和流程。如果IT人员不知道如何运行、管理和维护网络，那么一个再完美的安全系统实施集成也是徒劳无益的。

除了对IT人员的教育和培训之外，详细准确的文档化的政策、程序和说明文件都是成功的关键因素。

结　　论

随着安全性和隐私的威胁在范围和复杂程度上的不断增加，各种类型和规模的作出超前思考的组织，将会继续强化它们对这些威胁的防御能力。

一些机构将继续依赖内部系统和资源来监控在新经济下运营的相关的"网络风险"。但是，其他的一些机构可能缺乏安全运作他们的IT基础架构所需要的培训、技能、资源或兴趣，最终只能转向外部专家寻求帮助。

一个公司不管是通过外部还是内部实行一种新的安全基础架构，都必须实行一系列特定的步骤。如果不依照这一蓝本，一个企业就不能指望建立起这样一个既安全又能实时更新，还能满足更加多样化的信息共享和更高级别隐私需求的系统。

ChAPTER 7
COMPREHENSIVE ISSUES ABOUT E-BUSINESS

电子商务综合

- E-Supply Chain Management: Prerequisites to Success
- The Features, Applications and Trends of M-Commerce
- International Taxation of E-Commerce
- E-Business and Government Promotion of International Trade
- The Role of Knowledge Management in Building E-Business Strategy

UNIT 28

E-Supply Chain Management: Prerequisites to Success

Where's the Payoff?

Where does the Internet enhance the creation of value? Is it just a vehicle of convenience to shop, check stock prices, send e-mail, and rummage through various websites? Web-based marketing and catalog sites have become very familiar communication mechanisms between prospects, customers and suppliers. The self-service web sites that provide for unassisted sales are significant in sales volume, but the fastest growing and highest volume by far is business-to-business transactions in supply chains. Internet capabilities already have, and will continue, to fundamentally change business-to-business supply chain models.

Be assured that e-Supply chains are making, and will go on making, inroads into manufacturing, like no technology ever seen before, in terms of the number of companies who will voluntarily and involuntarily adopt e-Supply Chain Management. The fact is, you will have to rapidly evolve to the e-Supply Chain in the near future or be left behind because the old ways of communicating and transmitting information are plainly no longer fast or cost effective because new standards of performance have developed.

Big Company Influence

Some of the most influential business leaders have made some very bold statements about the Internet and e-commerce. For example, many companies have launched very aggressive e-commerce initiatives—so aggressive, in fact, that one CEO publicly stated "…all of our suppliers will supply us on the Internet or they won't do business with us." Now that is a statement that will give many a supplier heartburn.

There is no doubt about the heavy emphasis on e-commerce and e-supply chain activities. Large staffs, big information technology investments and other resources have been deployed to create sophisticated e-supply chains. The scope of these e-supply chains will include everything from product development, supply chain management, marketing, sales and accounting activities. Suppliers, regardless of size, should have received the signal loud and clear... the e-Supply Chain has arrived.

Even more intriguing is the rapid evolution of the digital marketplace which allows buyers and sellers to transact in a single intelligent, multidimensional marketplace that connects multiple trading exchanges. This allows buyers to consolidate orders from multiple vendors and subsequently provide for the effective integration of the final logistical activities. Putting intelligence into super portals so customers can get their information their way is essential.

As you can see, the larger company adopters will create huge ripple effects into their smaller company supply bases. Your best choice—Be Prepared.

Transformation is Needed

Management, across all industries, will need to embrace collaboration with customers and suppliers in the planning and replenishment process. As customers and suppliers band together in mutually beneficial partnerships, the need for better supply chain management processes and systems is very evident and a very high business priority.

For many companies, it has become clear that a supply chain that flows information and material best can be a significant competitive differentiator. Improving supply chain management is getting lots of attention because forward-thinking managements know it is the best strategy to increase market share, reduce costs, minimize inventories and, of course, improve profits. In many industries, market share will be won and lost based on supply chain performance.

With the stakes so high, there is a frenzy of activity along the supply chain front. Executives are assessing how their companies do business, especially in supply chain activities. They often find dysfunctional sets of policies, processes, systems and measurements. And these exist at all points in the supply chain, including business partners. The existence of a "company of silos" becomes apparent and, most importantly, a new clarity of needs and goals emerges for supply chain management. There is a need to transform from dysfunctional and un-synchronized decision-making—which results in disintegrated and very costly supply activities—to a supply chain that performs in such a way that it is one of the company's competitive advantages.

Prerequisites to Success

Effectively integrating the information and material flows within the demand and supply process is what supply chain management is all about. In most companies, however, two major and very interdependent issues must be simultaneously addressed. The first deals with delivering products with customer-acceptable quality, with very short lead times, at a customer-acceptable cost—while keeping inventories throughout the supply chain at a minimum. The second issue, which tends to be less understood and accepted, is the need for high quality, relevant and timely information that is provided when it needs to be known. For many customers and manufacturers, business processes and support systems will not measure up to the task of quickly providing planning and execution information from the marketplace to production and onto vendors so that the customer's objectives are consistently met. The fact is, most information supplied is excessive, often late and frequently inaccurate.

For many companies, the nagging question about superior supply chain management remains, "What is it going to take to get ahead and stay ahead of our competition?" The answer to that question is, of course, "plenty," but successful extended enterprises share some characteristics.

As always, the challenge for top management is setting the right priorities, allocating appropriate resources and, of course, achieving the required results. Complicating the challenge is the enormous risk of not keeping pace in the marketplace, which can result in driving your customers into the waiting, open arms of your more aggressive competitors. The impact of a lost customer on revenue and profit are compounded by the costs a company will incur to recapture or replace lost customers.

The E-Supply Chain

High speed, low cost, communication and collaboration with your customers and suppliers are critical success factors to more effectively manage your supply chain. Then, the e-supply chain is very likely in your future. The very essence of supply chain management is effective information and material flow throughout a network of customers and suppliers. The potential for improved productivity, cost reduction and customer service are enormous. Of course, the benefits are based on effectively employing the right processes and supporting information technology. This is a higher priority than ever before. Providing the right amount of relevant information to those who need to know it, when they need to know it is, in fact, effective supply chain management from an information point of view.

Good supply chain practitioners know that information should be passed on only to those who need to know it, in the form they need to have it. Demand information, inventory positions, order-fulfillment, supply management and a whole host of other information exchange activities will change how we sell products, supply products and make and receive payments for goods and services. The e-supply chain will have customers and suppliers seamlessly linked together, throughout the world, exchanging information almost instantly.

Fast access to relevant supply chain information can pay-off handsomely in lower costs, less inventory, higher quality decision-making, shorter cycle times and better customer service. One of the biggest cost savings is in the overhead activity associated with lots of paperwork and its inherent redundancies. The non-value added time of manual transaction processing can instead be focused on higher revenue creation activities without proportional increases in expense. The result in cycle time compression, lower inventories, decision-making quality, reduced overhead costs, among other benefits makes e-supply chain management a highly desirable strategy. Supply chain processes can be more streamlined and efficient than could have been imagined just a few years ago. For many companies, more effective supply chain management is where the profit and competitive advantages will emerge and be sustained.

Developing an E-Supply Chain Strategy

E-supply chain management significantly changes the way in which business does business. As a result, management needs to change how they view and serve markets. Yesterday's methods are no longer sufficient, especially for those companies seeking to increase market share. As more and more companies evolve new chain models, management is compelled to take the right actions or risk being left behind. However, the question is—will the actions taken produce the desired results?

supply chain management systems will be substantially altered in terms of strategy, process, and system. Mistakes here could prove very costly in the near-and longer terms. E-supply chain management has redefined and will continue to redefine how companies will compete for customers. While the internet offers some exciting opportunities to improve supply chain management effectiveness by lowering costs and increasing the speed of order-to-delivery, it is by no means the first step on the right path to having highly competitive e-supply chain capabilities.

Just throwing more software at the problem is not the answer to the core issues of supply chain management. Although software is needed, it is very necessary to define the process of information flow that will activate material flow at the right time. Lessons learned by early adopters of new technologies is that overzealous adoption of those technologies without a carefully planned strategy can prove very costly, especially when the target is missed, or worse, not defined in the first place.

Words and Expressions

prerequisite [ˌpriːˈrekwizit]	n.	先决条件
	adj.	首先必备的
payoff [ˈpeiˌɔːf]	n.	决定因素,成功,结局,付工资
enhance [inˈhɑːns]	vt.	提高,增强
rummage [ˈrʌmidʒ]	v.	到处翻寻,搜出,检查
mechanism [ˈmekənizəm]	n.	机构,机制,机械装置
prospect [ˈprɔspekt]	n.	潜在顾客,希望,勘探
fundamentally [fʌndəˈmentəli]	adv.	基础地,根本地
inroad [ˈinrəud]	n.	攻击,袭击,减少
bold [bəuld]	adj.	大胆的
launch [lɔːntʃ]	v.	开办,发动,发起,投入,开始
initiative [iˈniʃiətiv]	n.	动议,主动
heartburn [ˈhɑːtbəːn]	n.	心痛,嫉妒
sophisticated [səˈfistikeitid]	adj.	复杂的,精密的,老练的
intriguing [inˈtriːgiŋ]	adj.	引起兴趣的,迷人的
multidimensional [ˌmʌltidiˈmenʃənl]	adj.	多面的,多维的
consolidate [kənˈsɔlideit]	v.	巩固
vendor [ˈvendɔː]	n.	卖主
logistical [ləuˈdʒistikəl]	adj.	物流的
portal [ˈpɔːtəl]	n.	门户,入口
ripple [ˈripl]	n.	波纹
	v.	起波纹
replenishment [riˈpleniʃment]	n.	补给,补充
differentiator [ˌdifəˈrenʃiˌeitə]	n.	区分者,微分器
boardroom [ˈbɔːdruːm]	n.	会议室,交换场所

stake [steik]	n.	柱,赌注,利益
frenzy ['frenzi]	n.	狂暴,狂怒
dysfunctional [dis'fʌŋkʃənəl]	adj.	功能紊乱的
nagging ['nægiŋ]	adj.	唠叨的,挑剔的
compound ['kɔmpaund]	v.	混合,配合
collaboration [kəlæbə'reiʃən]	n.	协作,合作
employ [im'plɔi]	v.	雇用,使用
practitioner [præk'tiʃənə]	n.	从业者,开业者

Notes

(1) The author of the article—R. Michael Donovan is a management consultant and partner in supply chain Performance Partners in Framingham, Massachusetts. His firm specializes in supply chain Management, Cycle time and Inventory Reduction, ERP Performance Improvement, Manufacturing Strategy, Flow Manufacturing and Strategic Planning. 本文作者 R. Michael Donovan 是一位管理咨询师,也是一家总部位于马萨诸塞州的 Framingham 供应链绩效咨询公司的合伙人。他的公司致力于供应链管理、周期时间、库存减少、ERP 绩效提高、管理战略、工作流管理及战略规划方面的咨询。

(2) make inroads into   侵袭,侵入
(3) leave behind   留下,遗留,超过
(4) forward thinking   前瞻性思考
(5) lead time   订货至交货的时间
(6) measure up to   符合,达到,够得上
(7) get ahead   (使)走在前面,进步,获得成功
(8) incur to   招致
(9) by no means   决不

Questions

(1) What can fundamentally change business-to-business supply chain models?
(2) What does the e-supply chain include?
(3) Why are we in urgent need of better supply chain management Processes and systems?

(4) What makes it is necessary to transform from dysfunctional and unsynchronized decision-making to a supply chain?

(5) Can you tell me the definition of supply chain Management?

(6) What suggestions can you make to develop an e-supply chain strategy?

Exercises

1. Translate the following sentences into Chinese:

(1) The supply chain is made up of all the activities that are required to deliver products to the customer—from designing products to receiving orders, procuring materials, marketing, manufacturing, logistics, customer service, receiving payment and so on.

(2) Anyone, anything, anywhere that influences a product's time-to-market, price, quality, information exchange, delivery, among other activities is part of the supply chain.

(3) Consider that e-supply chain management is digitally connecting the entire world into one big (very big) network of supply chain.

(4) The growth estimates for the next few years for business-to-business e-commerce are astounding.

(5) More than likely, your company has many internal information and material flow process problems to solve before going external.

2. Translate the following sentences into English:

(1) 到目前为止,在供应链中增长最快、销售额最大的是企业与企业间的交易。

(2) 互联网已经并将继续从根本上改变企业与企业间供应链模型。

(3) 一个企业必须加快发展电子化供应链,否则它将在很多方面被落在后面。

(4) 供应商,不管其规模大小,都应该意识到——电子化供应链时代已经到来。

(5) 在客户和供应商网络中形成富有效率的信息流和物流是供应链管理的本质。

Further Reading

You can read the latest book of the author *Strengthening Manufacturing's Weak Links*, or you can get other educational material through the web-site www.rmdonovan.com.

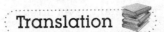

电子化供应链管理：成功的先决条件

决定因素在何处？

互联网在哪些方面提高价值的创造力呢？难道它仅仅是一个购物、查询股票价格、发送电子邮件和通过各种不同的网站到处搜索的一种媒介物吗？基于网络的营销和产品目录站点已经发展成为在潜在客户、客户和供应商之间非常熟悉的沟通机制。提供独立销售服务的自助销售网站，它的销售量是可观的，但到目前为止，在供应链中增长最快、销售额最大的仍是企业与企业间的交易。互联网的容量已经并将继续从根本上改变企业与企业之间的供应链模式。

毫无疑问，就那些自愿或不自愿采用电子化供应链管理的企业而言，电子化供应链作为一种前所未有的技术正在并将持续地对制造业带来冲击。事实上你不得不在不远的将来向电子化供应链演进，否则将会落伍，因为在新的绩效标准下，传统的交流和信息传递方式无论在速度上还是在成本上都已经不占优势。

大公司的影响力

一些最具影响力的企业领导已经就互联网和电子商务做出了一些非常大胆的陈述。比如，许多公司已经开展了非常有进取性的电子商务动议——这样的进取性已经在现实中有所体现，一位首席执行官公开地宣称"……我们的全部供应商将会在互联网上向我们供货，否则他们就不能与我们开展业务了。"尽管这只是一个表态，但已经给很多供应商带来不小的压力。

毋庸置疑，电子商务和电子化供应链活动已广受重视，大量的人员、巨大的信息技术投资和其他的资源已经配置到开发先进的电子化供应链的各个环节了。这些电子化供应链的范围将包括产品开发、供应链管理、营销、销售和财务活动的每个方面。供应商，不管其规模大小，都应该接受这一清晰响亮的信号——电子化供应链时代已经到来了。

但更吸引人的是数字化市场的快速崛起，它允许买卖双方在单个智能化的、多维的、能够连接多种交易体系进行交易。这使得买方能把若干卖主的订单合并起来，随后为最终的物流活动提供有效的整合。其中必不可少的一环是将智能化的信息放在超级门户中，以便客户能以更便捷的方式取得其所需的信息。

正如你所看到的一样，实施电子化供应链的比较大的公司将对其下游的供应商产生的影响是巨大的。最好选择就是——时刻作好准备。

转型是必要的

跨越所有产业的管理在计划的制订和补充过程中,需要加强与客户和供货商之间的协调合作。由于客户和供应商是一种捆绑型的互惠互利的伙伴合作关系,因此,对优化供应链管理流程和系统的需求是十分明确的,必须把它放在企业优先考虑的位置。

对许多公司而言,能使信息和原材料最佳流动的供应链是这个公司最具竞争力的优势,这一点已变得很清晰了。因为具有超前思想的管理层认为供应链管理是增加市场份额、降低成本、最大限度地降低存货,以致提高利润的最好策略,所以提高供应链管理水平正在得到广泛的关注。在许多行业中,供应链的绩效将直接决定市场份额的得失。

由于投资如此可观,因此在供应链前端有一些狂乱的活动。经理们正在评价他们的公司如何开展业务,尤其是在供应链活动中。他们经常发现系列政策、流程、系统和评价的功能不全。而且这些问题存在于供应链的每一个环节中,包括业务伙伴在内。"竖塔型公司"的存在变得显而易见,更重要的是,一个全新的和一个思路清晰的目标应该出现在供应链管理中。公司从残缺的和非同步的决策(这些决策往往使供应链管理毫无建树并且造价高昂)向电子化供应链转变,这将成为公司的竞争优势之一。

成功的先决条件

在需求和供给实现的过程中有效地整合信息流和物流是供应链管理的全部工作。但是,在绝大多数的公司中,两个主要的、相互依赖的问题一定要同时得到处理。第一个问题是在非常短的时间内生产出使客户满意的质优价廉的产品——同时还要保证在整个供应链中存货量最少。第二个问题似乎更加难以理解和接受,就是要在客户需要获知信息的时候,公司能够提供高质量的、相关的和实时的信息。当然,对于许多客户和制造商而言,其业务流程和支持系统都将不能胜任这样的工作,即快速提供从市场到生产再到销售这样从头到尾一直满足客户目标的计划和执行信息。实际上,公司提供的大部分信息都是冗余的,并且常常是滞后的,不准确的频率也较高。

对许多公司而言,关于卓越供应链管理的一个令人困惑的问题是,"我们怎样获得成功并且在竞争中保持领先地位?"当然,问题的答案有"很多",但是,成功扩展的企业有一些共同特点。

一如既往地,对高层管理的挑战是设定正确的优先权、合理配置资源,当然,还要获得预期的效果。促使挑战趋于复杂化的因素是不能与市场保持同步的巨大风险,这将导致你的客户陷入等待之中,使他们投向你的强大的竞争者。失去一个客户对一个公司收入和利润的影响,是由公司想方设法重新获得流失客户(或发展新客户所需)的成本来衡量。

电子化供应链

高速度、低成本、与你的客户和供应商沟通和合作是更有效管理你的供应链成功与否的关键性因素。因而,电子化供应链很有可能在你的未来实现。供应链管理的本质是在客户和供应商网络中产生高效的信息流和物流。提高生产率、降低成本和提升客户服务质量的潜力是巨大的。当然,利益是建立在有效地采用合适的流程和支持信息技术的基础之上的,这一点比以往任何时候都具有更高的优先权。实际上,从信息的角度来看,有效的供应链管理就是向那些需要获知信息的人在他们需要的时候提供合适数量的相关信息。

良好的供应链实践者深知,信息应该只传递给那些需要获知信息的人,而且信息传递的形式也要符合他们的需要。信息需求、库存状况、订单执行情况、供应链管理和大量其他信息交换活动将会改变我们的售货方式、供货方式和为产品及服务的付费方式。电子化供应链将会使遍及世界各处的客户和供应商无缝隙地连接在一起,近乎实时地交换信息。

在低成本、少库存、高质量决策、短周期和良好的客户服务体系中,快速获取相关供应链信息的能力可以应付自如。成本最大的节省是避免了许多与管理活动相关的大量纸质工作以及与其相关的人浮于事的现象。纸质化交易过程中无价值的额外时间不再被虚度,转而投向可以创造高额利润的相关活动,但相应的支出却没有增加。与其他的益处相比,循环周期的压缩、更低的库存、决策的质量、经常性管理费用的减少加上其他的利益使得电子化供应链管理成为一个高度可取的策略。供应链流程比数年以前想象的更加流畅和更富有效率。对于许多公司而言,更有效的供应链管理存在于利润和竞争同时凸显并且持续下去。

发展电子化供应链策略

电子化供应链管理显著地改变了企业开展业务的方式,以管理者需要改变他们看待市场和为市场服务的方式。尤其对于那些努力增加市场份额的公司而言,过去的方法显然已不能满足需要。当越来越多的公司发展新的供应链模式时,管理者将不得不采取有效行动,否则就有被淘汰的风险。然而,存在的问题是,所采取的行动能否带来预期的结果?

供应链管理系统将会在战略、流程和系统方面作根本性改变。从近期和更长的一段时间来看,重组过程中出现的错误的代价是高昂的。电子化供应链管理已经并将继续重新定义公司如何争夺客户。尽管互联网通过降低成本、提高订单传递速度在提高供应链管理效率方面创造了许多激动人心的机会;但是它绝不是向具有高度竞争力的电子化供应链道路上迈出的第一步。

仅仅在相关问题上投入更多的软件并不是供应链管理的核心所在。虽然软件是必需的,但是给信息流的过程作出恰当的定义是非常必要的,这有助于在恰当的时间激活物流系统。从新技术的早期采用者那里得到的教训是:如果没有周密的计划和战略而过分热心地采用这些新技术,那么必将付出沉重的代价,特别是在目标迷失的时候,而更糟糕的是,在一开始的时候就没有定义明确的目标。

UNIT 29 The Features, Applications and Trends of M-Commerce

 Text

Main Features of M-Commerce

M-commerce represents the extension of e-commerce to a mobile environment. The main types of e-commerce—B2B, B2C, B2G and P2P—remain. In developing countries mobile business applications, especially when used by small and medium-sized enterprises in remote areas, may become a key method for reaching potential customers, and are expected to be highly important features of m-commerce. Most m-commerce is B2C where micro-purchases are involved. Larger transactions continue to be conducted using the usual e-commerce methods.

The surge in mobile handset use throughout the world, the dramatic growth of the Internet, and the proliferation of PDA (personal data assistants) are expanding the e-commerce market in which m-commerce is expected to flourish. A number of unique advantages of m-commerce have been identified:

- **Immediacy.** Consumers are constantly moving, working, commuting, traveling, socializing and shopping. M-commerce lets them buy goods and services as soon as the need arises.
- **Connectivity.** Users sharing a common location or interest can be instantly connected via text messaging and mobile chat capabilities. Advertisers can use such access to promote products and make special offers with the expectation that subscribers will answer and listen to their messages.
- **Localization.** With the deployment of positioning technologies, such as the global positioning system (GPS), companies can know users' whereabouts and will be able to offer goods and services specific to their location.

- **Data portability.** Users can store profiles of products, company addresses, information about restaurants and hotels, banking details, payment and credit card details, and security information, and access these when needed for purchases or for making contact, all from their mobile handsets.

Internet use has been dependent on personal computers (PCs) and a fixed-line network. And the growth of the Internet drives e-commerce. Consequently, until the advent of mobile telephone, e-commerce has been dependent on expensive infrastructure and equipment. Today, however, there is a growing convergence of the Internet and mobile communication. Handsets are acquiring functionalities that were limited to desktop PCs only a few years ago. Many are already running slimmed-down versions of PC operating systems and applications, and the difference between future handheld and desktop devices is likely to be related to the ergonomics of the physical user interface that will be designed to serve a particular purpose, rather than lack of processing power, memory or network accessibility.

The burning question for companies that have grown dependent on the Internet as a business vehicle is whether mobile telephony will result more in B2C applications than in B2B applications. It is impossible on the basis of existing experience to extrapolate what will happen in the years ahead. As regards B2B, there is little evidence that companies will change their purchasing practices because of m-commerce. The short-term potential for m-commerce growth resides with the one billion mobile telephone users, who could supplement existing B2C e-commerce with m-commerce. There is rapid growth in micro-payments for small items and information services. The key to increasing traditional B2C purchases such as banking transactions and to trading in securities through m-commerce is the implementation of payment systems that are low-cost and customer-friendly.

M-Commerce Applications and Trends

Mobile telephone customers in many developed countries are starting to use handsets to make purchases from retail stores, conduct personal banking and make travel reservations, as well as to view sports and news programmes, and search the Web. mobile service providers allow both prepaid and post-paid account subscribers to register and link their cash/debit cards with mobile phone subscription accounts. This allows subscribers to conduct mobile transactions for services and goods offered through their particular mobile service provider, for example topping up of prepaid accounts and purchase of theatre tickets. Certain commercial activities using SMS, such as hotel and restaurant reservations, could eventually lead to a growth in m-commerce applications. The following discussion takes a more detailed look at several promising applications.

1. SMS

Since 1992, SMS has allowed people to send and receive text messages using their mobile phones. Each message can contain up to 160 alphanumeric characters. SMS is the backbone of m-commerce today. One of the greatest concentrations of SMS users is in Singapore, where 52 percent of phone users utilize SMS more than once a day. SMS use in Australia, China and the Philippines is reported to be almost as high. The global average, however, is 23 percent.

SMS is said to offer a practical alternative for those who do not have a computer. A mobile short message is actually much cheaper than a telephone call. SMS accounts for a growing portion of mobile telephone revenues, since for every call made on a mobile phone, an average of 10 short messages are sent.

2. Micro-payments

M-commerce offers vast opportunities to make micro-purchases easier. These can be as simple as buying from a vending machine, paying a parking meter or purchasing gasoline. Among the most widespread m-commerce applications using SMS, is making payments through post-paid accounts linked to debit cards. In the case of subscriptions to information services, the mobile service provider charges the customer through monthly bills. However, in many developing countries a shortage of consumer credit systems and the lack of automated payment systems that can be conveniently used for wireless electronic payments are hampering advancement of m-commerce. Micro-payments and settlements via wireless are growing rapidly in a number of developed countries.

3. Financial Services

A wide variety of mobile payment and settlement methods are currently used in various countries.

Saving time, simplicity and speed of payments are the main advantages of mobile settlements. The following characteristics are listed in order of importance:
- Payments;
- Rapid payment;
- Record of payment provided;
- Less cash to carry around;
- Signature not required.

A number of concerns still exist and demonstrate the novelty of mobile settlements and people's lack of awareness about how to take advantage of them. The main concerns are:

- Difficulty in making a payment or a financial transaction;
- Risk to the confidentiality of personal data;
- Difficulties in processing payments, including loss of payments;
- Problems stemming from the loss of a mobile device, which someone might find and use to make illegal purchases.

Mobile banking is still hampered by the requirement for standardized payment cards and online systems. There has been more success with securities trading, however, where investors can buy and sell shares using their mobile handsets. Other areas are opening up—for example, insurance, where potential customers can receive offers and submit personal details for premium quotes by insurers, all with their mobile phones.

4. Logistics

The potential of mobile communications for generating greater efficiency in transport and logistics is widely acknowledged. The movement of goods within developing countries, as well as with regard to imports/exports, has traditionally been slow and inefficient owing to a lack of modern logistics systems. ICTs have become the key to achieving efficient logistics. Logistics costs in developed countries add about 12 percent to the retail cost of a product, whereas in developing countries this may be as high as 20 percent.

Transport and logistics will clearly benefit from the introduction of wireless services and, in doing so, expand m-Commerce. Wireless data access will make it possible to follow goods movements throughout the supply and value chain. With the growing use of information technologies in cargo booking, tracking, clearance and delivery by major shipping lines, as well as in customs clearance, ports, warehouses and stock points, external and internal trade will become more efficient.

The challenge lies in the introduction of hardware, software and networking which are costly and require technical expertise to operate. Trackability and traceability need to be ensured through interfacing technologies such as ID chips and bar codes. Mobile communications devices will then help link-up the supply chain.

Transport is typically multimodal, ranging from rail-water-air-shipping to express delivery services. The introduction of intelligent transport services further increases the value of mobile communications in the logistics supply chain, in particular for support services such as pick-up and delivery of goods.

5. Information Services

News, weather reports, and traffic and map information have increasingly become the services most sought after by mobile telephone subscribers.

Value added text messaging is the use of SMS to provide a content service or product to the consumer at a premium price. The value added to the text message by the application or the content contained therein is assumed to be above and beyond that of a standard text message and the consumer knowingly consents to be billed for that added value.

6. Wireless CRM Services

Customer relationship management (CRM) services usually consist of a set of methodologies, software and Internet capabilities that are coordinated and co-integrated and whose purpose is to help an enterprise manage its relationships with customers. Company activities can be very varied and may not always be managed in a coordinated way from a customer-centric point of view. The advantages for consumers of having better coordination between, say, research and development, manufacturing and after-sales services may translate for the company into marketable value-added or increased competitiveness. Much of any commercial organization's activities, including business operations and customer servicing, falls within the scope of CRM.

Mobile technology is starting to emerge as the newest value-added feature for CRM. Three levels of benefits are expected:

- Wireless CRM enables greater mobilization of the sales force, replacing periodic data synchronization with real-time information concerning products, client status, purchase history, inventory levels, product vendor information, order tracking and related data. The sales force will also have wireless financial transaction capabilities, shortening the sales cycle and increasing enterprise responsiveness.
- Wireless CRM facilitates a higher level of customer support by providing additional contact channels for clients seeking information or technical assistance. By extending customer data to mobile devices, the enterprise enables its support staff to better anticipate and respond to customer issues and enables customers to take advantage of self-service support and transactions via their mobile phones or PDAs.
- Location-based marketing will be an extension of current marketing automation and customer analysis systems. These emerging applications are expected to stimulate m-commerce by extrapolating location-specific buying behavior to provide information to mobile device users.

7. Other Mobile Services

M-commerce opens up a myriad of options for new electronic services. These include making appointments, voting, applications for membership or membership renewal and entitlement cards, and alarm systems. Norway provides an excellent example of this diversity of m-commerce.

A survey of frequently purchased items in the Republic of Korea found buying habits similar to those in Japan. About 12 percent of mobile subscribers indicated that their main preferences are buying movie tickets, cosmetics, banking, audio-visual and electronics products.

Words and Expressions

represent [ˌriːpriˈzent]	vt.	表现,描绘,声称,象征,扮演,回忆,再赠送,再上演
	vi.	提出异议
remote [riˈməut]	adj.	遥远的,偏僻的,细微的
transaction [trænˈzækʃən]	n.	办理,处理,会报,学报,交易,事务,处理事务
surge [səːdʒ]	n.	急剧上升,激增
	vi.	汹涌,澎湃,振荡,滑脱,放松
	vt.	使汹涌奔腾,急放
handset [ˈhændset]	n.	电话听筒,手机,手持机
proliferation [prəuˌlifəˈreiʃən]	n.	增殖,分芽繁殖,激增,扩散
PDA (abbr., Personal Digital Assistant)		个人数字助理
flourish [ˈflʌriʃ]	vi.	繁荣,茂盛,活跃,手舞足蹈,兴旺,处于旺盛时期
	vt.	挥动,夸耀
	n.	茂盛,兴旺,华饰,繁荣
immediacy [iˈmiːdiəsi]	n.	直接
advertiser [ˈædvətaizə]	n.	登广告者,广告客户
access to		有权使用
localization [ˌləukəlaiˈzeiʃən]	n.	地方化,局限,定位
portability [ˌpɔːtəˈbiləti; ˌpɔrtəˈbiləti]	n.	可携带,轻便
infrastructure [ˈinfrəˌstrʌktʃə]	n.	下部构造,基础下部组织
convergence [kənˈvəːdʒəns]	n.	集中,收敛
ergonomics [ˌəːgəuˈnɔmiks]	n.	人类工程学,生物工程学,工效学

Unit 29 The Features, Applications and Trends of M-Commerce

interface ['intə(ː),feis]	n.	分界面,接触面,界面
accessibility [,æksesi'biliti]	n.	易接近,可到达的
burning question		目前最吸引人的问题,亟待解决的问题
telephony [ti'lefəni]	n.	电话学,电话,电话制造
extrapolate [eks'træpəleit]	v.	推断,外推
as regards	adv.	至于,关于
reside [ri'zaid]	vi.	居住
item ['aitem, 'aitəm]	n.	(可分类或列举的)项目、条款,(消息、情报等的)一则,一条
securities [si'kjuəritiz]	n.	有价证券
as well as	adv.	也,又
debit ['debit]	n.	借方,借
	vt.	记入借方
top up	v.	加满,充值
promising ['prɔmisiŋ]	adj.	有希望的,有前途的
alphanumeric [,ælfənjuː'merik]	adj.	有希望的,有前途的
backbone ['bækbəun]	n.	脊椎,中枢;骨干,支柱;意志力,勇气,毅力,决心;广域网中的一种高速链路
revenue ['revinjuː]	n.	收入,国家的收入,税收
vending machine	n.	自动售货机
parking meter	n.	停车计时器(以硬币付费)
subscription [səb'skripʃn; səb'skripʃən]	n.	预订,订购
hamper ['hæmpə]	v.	妨碍,牵制
novelty ['nɔvəlti]	n.	新奇事物,文中指创新性
insurer [in'ʃuərə]	n.	保险业者,保险公司
confidentiality	n.	机密性
logistics [lə'dʒistiks]	n.	后勤学,后勤,指物流
cargo book		(租船代理人的)货物登记册

customs clearance		清关,海关放行
warehouses ['wɛəhaus]	n.	仓库,货栈,大商店
	vt.	贮入仓库,以他人名义购进(股票)
trackability [ˌtrækə'biliti]	n.	(唱机、唱针或唱头的)跟踪能力
traceability [ˌtreisə'biləti]	n.	可描绘,可描写,可追溯
knowingly ['nəuiŋli]	adv.	有意地,心照不宣地
consent to	v.	同意,答应
methodology [ˌmeθə'dɔlədʒi]	n.	方法学,方法论
synchronization [ˌsiŋkrənai'zeiʃən]	n.	同一时刻,同步
stimulate ['stimjuleit]	vt.	刺激,激励
	v.	刺激,激励
cosmetic [kɔz'metik]	n.	化妆品
	adj.	化妆用的

Notes

(1) In developing countries mobile business applications, especially when used by small and medium-sized enterprises in remote areas, may become a key method for reaching potential customers, and are expected to be highly important features of m-commerce. 在发展中国家,使用移动电子商务,尤其是偏远地区的中小企业使用移动电子商务,很可能会成为其联系潜在客户的一个主要方法,同时也被认为是移动电子商务的非常重要的特征。

(2) Many are already running slimmed-down versions of PC operating systems and applications, and the difference between future handheld and desktop devices is likely to be related to the ergonomics of the physical user interface that will be designed to serve a particular purpose, rather than lack of processing power, memory or network accessibility. 许多已经可以运行PC操作系统的精简版本和应用程序、未来移动电话和桌面设备之间的不同将不是缺乏处理能力、存储和网络接入功能,而可能是与有形的用户界面有关的人类工程学。

(3) Mobile telephone customers in many developed countries are starting to use handsets to make purchases from retail stores, conduct personal banking and make travel reservations, as well as to view sports and news programmes, and search the Web. 许多发达国家移动电话用户开始使用移动终端向零售商店订

购商品、处理自己的银行账户、进行旅行预订,还可以观看体育和新闻节目、上网浏览。

(4) This allows subscribers to conduct mobile transactions for services and goods offered through their particular mobile service provider, for example topping up of prepaid accounts and purchase of theatre tickets. 这使得用户可以借助于特定移动业务提供商处理所提供的业务进行移动交易获得商品与服务,比如预付费账户的充值和剧院订票。

(5) However, in many developing countries a shortage of consumer credit systems and the lack of automated payment systems that can be conveniently used for wireless electronic payments are hampering advancement of m-commerce. 尽管如此,在许多发展中国家,消费者信用体系的匮乏和能被方便地用来进行无线电子支付的自动支付系统的不足正在阻碍移动电子商务的进步。

(6) By extending customer data to mobile devices, the enterprise enables its support staff to better anticipate and respond to customer issues and enables customers to take advantage of self-service support and transactions via their mobile phones or PDAs. 通过扩展客户数据到移动设备,企业能够使售后服务的员工对客户问题有更好的预期和响应,并能使客户利用他们的手机或者PDA来获得自助服务支持并进行交易。

Questions

(1) What is the main feature of m-commerce?
(2) Give us a introduction on SMS.
(3) How is micro-payment developed?
(4) Can financial service in m-commerce be popularized? What's the challenge?
(5) What is m-commerce's application in logistics?
(6) What is e-commerce's contribution to CRM? What are the benefits expected?
(7) What is your point on the application and trend of m-commerce?

Exercises

1. Translate the following sentences into Chinese:

(1) The most common definition of m-commerce is the buying and selling of goods and services using wireless handheld devices such as mobile telephones or personal data assistants (PDAs).

(2) The introduction of wireless communications has not only expanded telephony in many developing countries, but also introduced wireless data services which are essential for conducting m-commerce.

(3) For many people in developing countries, mobile handsets may be the first and main access route to information and communication technologies (ICT), the Internet and e-commerce technologies.

(4) The challenge is to provide access to the global telecommunications system for a significant number of citizens in developing countries.

(5) Mobile communications may be the technology that overcomes the barriers constituted by the high cost of installing fixed-line infrastructure that developing countries continue to encounter.

2. Translate the following sentences into English:
(1) 移动电子商务表现为电子商务向移动环境的扩展。
(2) 移动服务提供商现在已经向客户提供文本短消息、彩信、新闻、天气预报和交通等方面的信息服务。
(3) 无线服务的引入将使运输和物流部分获益明显。
(4) 可以预见,在发展中国家,由于低廉的运营成本,电信运营商将继续快速增加移动用户数量。
(5) 许多发达国家的移动电话用户开始使用手机从零售商那里订购商品。

Further Reading

This text is selected from *E-Commerce and Development Report*: 2002, issued by UN.

移动电子商务的特征、应用与趋势

移动电子商务的主要特征

移动电子商务代表电子商务向移动环境的扩展。电子商务的主要类型——B2B、B2C、B2G 和 P2P 将继续存在。在发展中国家,使用移动电子商务,尤其是偏远地区的中小企业使用移动电子商务,很可能会成为其联系潜在客户的一个主要方法,同时也被认为是移动电子商务的非常重要的特征。大多数的移动电子商务是 B2C 型的,包含小额购买。较大额度的交易则继续采用常规的电子商务方式进行。

世界范围内手机用户数与互联网的急速增长、个人数字助理(PDA)使用的快速扩散不断拓展电子商务市场,移动电子商务前景一直被看好,其一系列的独特优势表现为:
■ **即时性**。消费者经常活动、工作、交流、旅行、社交及购物,移动电子商务使他们在需求产生的时候就可以进行购物和享受服务。
- **连通性。**同一地区有相同兴趣的用户可以方便地通过文本消息和移动聊天的方式相互联通,广告商可以通过这种途径促销商品,提供特殊优惠,以期望订阅者做出回应并接受他们的信息。
- **定位。**借助于定位技术,比如全球定位系统(GPS),企业可以识别出用户的位置,将能根据他们的位置提供特定的服务。
- **数据便携性。**用户可以保存商品外形、公司地址、饭店和宾馆的信息、银行细目、支付和信用卡详情以及安全信息,同时这些都可以在他们需要购物或者签订合同时通过移动终端获得。

互联网的使用依赖于个人电脑(PC)和固定网络,互联网的增长也驱动了电子商务,因此,在移动电话的出现之前,电子商务一直都是受制于昂贵的基础设施和设备。但是今天,互联网越来越与移动通信相结合,移动终端电话正在取得那些几年前只是局限于台式个人电脑才有的若干功能。许多已经可以运行 PC 操作系统的精简版本和应用程序,未来移动电话和桌面设备之间的不同将不是缺乏处理能力、存储和网络接入功能,而可能是与有形的用户界面有关的人类工程学。

对于依赖互联网作为商务工具的公司来说,最亟待解决的问题是移动电话是否能够在 B2C 应用方面有比 B2B 应用方面更好的效果。以现有的经验来推断未来几年将要发生的事是不可能的。对 B2B 而言,几乎没有迹象表明这些公司会因移动电子商务而改变它们的采购方式。移动电子商务的短期潜力存在于 10 亿移动电话用户身上,他们可能以移动电子商务来补充现有的 B2C 电子商务。小宗购物和信息服务等小额支付领域也有了快速的增长。增加传统 B2C 消费(比如利用移动电子商务实现的银行交易)以及证券交易的关键在于使用低成本、用户界面友好的支付系统。

移动电子商务应用和趋势

在许多发达国家移动电话用户开始使用移动终端从零售商店订购商品、处理自己的银行账户、进行旅游预订,还可以观看体育和新闻节目、上网浏览。移动业务提供商允许预付费和后付费用户注册其银行现金/信用卡账户与手机账户绑定,这使得用户可以借助于特定移动业务提供商所提供的业务进行移动交易获得商品与服务,比如预付费账户的充值和剧院订票。某些商业活动使用 SMS,比如预订宾馆和餐馆,会最终引起移动电子商务的增长。下面将详细研究一些有前途的移动应用业务。

1. SMS

从 1992 年开始 SMS(手机短信)就可以让人们使用他们的手机发送和收取文本信息,每个消息可以达到容纳 160 个字符。SMS 是当今移动电子商务的支柱。SMS 使用者最集中的地区之一是新加坡,在那儿有 52% 的电话用户每天使用 SMS 一次以上。据报道,在澳大利亚、中国和菲律宾差不多也有这么高的比率,尽管全球平均水平是 23%。

SMS 被认为是无电脑者的较实际选择,一个手机短信实际上比电话低廉了许多。

SMS 收入也是移动业务收入中正在增长的一部分,因为每发生一个移动语音业务的同时,就会有约 10 条短信被发送。

2. 小额支付

移动电子商务可以使小额支付进一步简化,使其简单得如同在自动售货机上购物、支付停车费用或者是购买汽油。在众多利用 SMS 进行移动应用的业务之中,小额支付是通过连接到信用卡的后付费账户来支付费用的。如果是订阅信息服务,那移动业务提供商通过客户的每月账单收取费用。尽管如此,在许多发展中国家,消费者信用体系的匮乏和能被方便地用来进行无线电子支付的自动支付系统的不足,正在阻碍移动电子商务的进步。基于无线的小额支付和结算正在很多发达国家快速增长。

3. 金融服务

各种各样的移动支付和结算方法当前在不少国家已得到使用。
省时、简便、快捷是移动结算的主要优势,下面按重要性列出了一些特征:
- 付款
- 快速支付
- 提供支付记录
- 携带更少量的现金
- 无须签名

目前仍还有一些疑问存在,表明移动支付的创新性以及人们对其缺乏了解。主要的疑问是:
- 进行支付和金融交易的困难性
- 个人数据保密的风险
- 处理支付,包括支付损失的困难
- 移动设备丢失带来的问题,某些人可能会得到它并利用它做一些非法的交易

移动银行因需要标准支付卡和在线系统而受到制约,但是证券交易已经有了更大的成功,投资者可以使用他们的手机买卖股票。其他领域也正在开放,比如保险,潜在的客户可以完全通过手机来接受报价,并通过手机提交给保险人做保险报价所需要的详细个人资料。

4. 物流

众所周知,移动通信有提高运输和物流效率的潜力,在发展中国家,包括进出口在内的货物流动,传统上由于缺乏现代物流系统造成速度缓慢和效率低下。信息通信技术已经成为达到高效物流的关键,发达国家的物流成本使一种产品零售成本增加大约12%,然而在发展中国家这可能高达 20%。

运输和物流将因引入无线服务而获得明显的效益,同时,移动电子商务也会得到扩展。无线数据接入使得沿着供应链和价值链追踪货物成为可能,随着信息技术逐渐应用于主要航线的货物登记、跟踪、票据交换结算和交付等环节,以及在清关、港口、仓库、

存货等领域,内部的和外部的交易将都变得更加有效率。
　　困难在于引进硬件、软件和网络,因为这些东西不但昂贵,而且需要技术专家操作。可跟踪性与可追溯性需要通过像 ID 芯片和条形码这样的接口技术来得以确保,移动通信设备随后将有助于把供应链连接起来。
　　运输具有典型的多样性,从铁路、水路、空中、海运到快递,智能运输服务的引入提高了移动通信在物流供应链方面的价值,尤其是在支持服务,比如提取和交付货物服务。

5. 信息服务

　　新闻、天气预报、交通和地图信息已经逐渐成为移动电话用户最为追捧的业务。
　　增值文本信息利用 SMS 向用户提供内容服务或产品并加收额外费用。增值的文本消息由于包含应用与服务内容在其中,因而其价值高于并超过普通标准文本信息,消费者也理解地认同应为增值部分而额外付费。

6. 无线 CRM 服务

　　客户关系管理(CRM)服务通常由一套协调和整合的方法论、软件和互联网所组成,其目的是帮助企业管理与客户的关系。公司活动能会纷繁复杂,可能会做不到事事以客户为中心进行协调管理。对消费者来说,在研究和开发、制造和售后服务之间的更好的协调是一种优势,而且这种优势对公司而言可以转换成可市场化的价值增值和竞争力提升。任何一个商务组织的许多活动,包括商务运作和客户服务,都可以包括在 CRM 范围内。
　　移动技术开始为 CRM 呈现出最新的增值特征,预计将有三个层面的收益:
- 无线 CRM 使销售力量有更大的移动性,并以实时信息取代定期的数据同步,包括产品信息、客户资料、购买记录、存货情况、销售商信息、订单跟踪和相关数据。销售力量也将拥有无线财务处理能力,缩短了销售周期,提高了企业的响应能力。
- 无线 CRM 通过为需要信息查询和技术协助的客户提供了另一个联系渠道,使客户支持达到一个更高的水平。通过扩展客户数据到移动设备,企业能够使售后服务的员工对客户问题有更好的预期和响应,并能使客户利用他们的手机或者 PDA 获得自助服务支持并进行交易。
- 基于位置的市场营销将是当前营销自动化和客户分析系统的扩展。这些正在出现的应用有望通过推断特定区域的购买行为,提供信息给移动设备用户,以刺激移动电子商务的发展。

7. 其他移动服务

　　移动电子商务为新兴的电子服务提供了无数选择,包括约会、投票、会员申请或者会员更新和会员卡、警报系统。挪威在移动电子商务的多样性方面提供了一个极好的例子。
　　对韩国经常购买小件商品的消费者的调查发现韩国的购买习惯和日本很相似,大约 12% 的手机用户指出他们主要通过手机来购买电影票、化妆品、银行服务、视频和电子产品。

UNIT 30 International Taxation of E-Commerce

Text

Imagine for a second, that you have developed and own a terribly smart web site which may sell electronically distributed products to many people. Let's call your web site wizzkidd.com. You have read Seth Godin's "Unleashing the Idea Virus" (www.ideavirus.com) and you are convinced that your web site will be visited by many customers from all over the world who will have to pay for the electronically downloaded products they get. Unlike so many other web sites yours has been set up to generate some revenue in excess of expenses.

You may wonder how you are taxed on the revenues which may be generated by your web site. Let us further suppose that you sit somewhere in the U.S. (personally I favour Ann Arbor, Michigan) and that you have decided to run your business as a sole proprietorship. For a web site to be made available on the Internet it has to be hosted on a web server. Let's suppose that you have found such nearby web server and that you have gone around all the legal nitty gritties so that you can get started. Congratulations!

Please don't stop reading if your are Swiss resident engaged in electronic distribution of products designated for U.S. customers. Reversing the fact pattern does not alter the results which will be described below.

1. Income Tax

As you will have customers around the world and as you will be receiving money from all over the world, you may thus wish to know something on how your e-commerce revenues will be taxed. I am assuming that you are a U.S. resident and hence subject to U.S. income tax on your worldwide income. As you have set up an e-commerce you will be allowed to account for your expenses and will be taxed on a net income basis. As every good citizen you either prepare your own tax return or you may have your tax return prepared by a local accountant.

You may have many customers in such countries as e. g. Switzerland and you may wonder what happens to your income from abroad. How does Switzerland as a source country tax the payments Swiss customers will make to you. In this context it may be important to know that between the U. S. and Switzerland there is a double taxation treaty which determines which one of the two countries has the first right to tax certain income items. Such treaties exist between all industrialized nations. Their sole purpose is to have both treaty countries sharing in the taxation of revenues rather than to have both countries imposing tax as they deem fit. If we assume 20 industrialized nations which do have treaties with all other industrialized nations than that makes 450 treaties.

All these 450 treaties are based on a single model convention which has been designed by the OECD, the Paris based "Organisation for Economic Cooperation and Development".

The OECD has done a lot of work in order to free e-commerce from interposed income and/or withholding taxes. The most significant task undertaken by the OECD concerned the treatment of transactions involving the download of digital content, including software copies, data, images, text and video.

It is in this context that the OECD has determined that e-commerce is a digital delivery and thus not any different from a physical delivery. From a tax point of view it does not matter whether a book is delivered to you physically or downloaded via the Net. In both instances your cash remuneration constitutes business income which is not subject to tax in the source country. In essence you may thus be receiving income from all over the world. Because such income qualifies as business income it will not be subject to any foreign withholding tax. If your Swiss customer pays an invoice of 100 you will be receiving 100 (minus bank charges). So far so good.

2. Permanent Establishment

One of the very fundamental principles of international taxation concerns so called permanent establishments. If you have permanently established yourself in another country (in our example that would be Switzerland) you will be subject to income tax in that other country. So the one thing you don't want to have is a permanent establishment in any other country. The term permanent establishment is as old as international taxation is. It stems from the time where one shipped widgets, tomatoes and spare parts across country boundaries. The fundamental principles thus say that you will only have a permanent establishment in another country if you have a physical presence there. In essence this means that you will not have a permanent establishment in another country unless you have offices and employees in that other country.

As you are working from your home in Ann Arbor, Mich. and as you are distributing your web site services throughout the world by using your nearby web host, there is no need for you to have offices and employees abroad. The OECD has determined that a mere virtual presence such as the one which you are creating by your web site is simply not enough for you to be permanently established abroad. As you will not be maintaining a permanent establishment is Switzerland, the 100 paid by your Swiss customer will find their way to Ann Arbor free and clear of foreign income and/or withholding taxes. So far so good.

As far as income taxes are concerned you have to keep three principles in your mind. Where-ever you are a resident of this will be the country where you will be subject to tax on your worldwide income. E-commerce will generate business profits which are not subject to tax abroad even if the payment comes from abroad. Thirdly, you will be present throughout the world without thereby, however, creating any permanent establishments abroad. This is pretty hot stuff, which makes your situation much better than the one of e.g. a car distributor.

3. Moving Residence

So if you are a U.S. citizen you can go to other countries where you pay less income taxes than in the U.S. but in essence this does not matter, because a U.S. citizen remains subject to U.S. tax regardless where he resides. If you are a U.S. citizen and you would move from Ann Arbor to a place in Switzerland you will finally end up paying as much taxes as if you would stay where you are. This lesson is, however only applicable to U.S. citizens and green card holders.

If you are not a U.S. citizen (or a holder of a U.S. green card) then you may consider to relocate your residence to a country where you pay less taxes than in the U.S. This brings us to a fourth and final principle of international income taxation. The principle says that no matter where you reside try to be a resident of a country which has a treaty with the U.S. Let us assume that you are residing somewhere in Switzerland and you have your main e-commerce market in the U.S. Let us further assume that you have no offices and employees in the U.S. but have hired the services of numerous U.S. resident consultants to put together your web site. According to U.S. domestic tax Law, the IRS will tax your U.S. source income if you are engaged in U.S. trade or business.

The mere fact that you employ U.S. consultants to hit U.S. customers in the U.S. market may cause your being engaged in U.S. trade or business. So what you want is to make sure that you are residing in a country with which the U.S. entertains a double taxation treaty. Why? Because the treaty contains the old permanent establishment principle which requires a fixed place of business, i.e. offices and employees of your own in the other country. This means that the engaged in U.S. trade or business principle will not apply for as long as you can claim treaty protection. Countries which are not linked with the U. S. with any double taxation treaty are sometimes referred to as "off shore" (the Caymans, the Bahamas, you name it). So the forth lesson would be: do not go offshore but make sure that you operate your e-commerce business in a treaty protected fiscal environment.

4. Value Added Tax

The income tax side of your equation is thus pretty straight forward. What else do you have to keep in mind. In the EU and in many other countries like e. g. Switzerland there is a Value Added Tax System in place ("VAT"). The EU and other countries who apply VAT are giving a great deal of thought on how to go about e-commerce. So far only one thing has become clear: digital deliveries will not generate any business income but qualify as vatable service instead.

In general, cross-boarder transactions are either subject to a system which incorporates the place of origin ("Ursprungslandprinzip") or on a system which incorporates the place of destination ("Bestimmungslandprinzip"). The place of destination system means that imports of goods and services are subject to VAT whereas the export of any such good or service is zero-rated, i. e., it is entitled to input VAT credits despite the fact that there is no tax on the export.

As far as e-services and digital deliveries are concerned the EU will be adopting a place of destination tax system. Sooner or later there will thus be a consumer tax applicable to electronic distributed imports and the still open question is how to impose such tax on the ultimate consumers. Such tax is being referred to as a "reverse charge" because normally VAT is charged to the Distributor and not to the ultimate consumer, whereas in the case of electronic distributed imports the tax will be charged directly on the ultimate consumer.

It will take one or maybe two more years before an effective system is in place. For the time being you can note that as an e-commerce merchant you have nothing to fear from VAT simply because the system has not been perfected as yet.

The EU is however working on an amendment of its Sixth VAT Directive. Non-EU-Member States such as e. g. Switzerland will have to align their own VAT system in order not to have any competitive disadvantages vis à vis the EU.

As your Swiss customers will be importing electronic distributed products from a country which is not an EU Member State, they will be treated as persons who import vatable services. They will not only have to pay you 100, but they will—at some future stage—also be subject to an import VAT. Said VAT will range from 7.6% (in the case of Switzerland) to 22% (in the case of France) according to where your European customer will be a resident of. Although said VAT will not be charged to you (as the U. S.

distributor) but on your EU resident customers instead (if your customer is a business he may even claim an input VAT deduction), such tax will clearly put you at a competitive disadvantage, because the same VAT will not apply, if electronic distributed products are being distributed within the EU.

5. Conclusion

As far as income taxes and withholding taxes are concerned the system is pretty transparent. There are no foreign taxes if you are a resident of Ann Arbor Michigan and receive payments from your Swiss customers. You can also reverse the fact pattern and assume that you are a Swiss resident receiving income from U.S. customers. The result will be the same, i.e. there will not be any U.S. taxes on the payments made to a Swiss resident who distributes his products by using the Internet.

Although the European VAT systems are not as yet ready to impose a consumer tax, it is likely that such tax will be implemented within a short period of time. It will have a significant impact on internet products distributed throughout Europe by persons or business which are not residents in an EU Member State or an other European country.

Words and Expressions

unleash [ˈʌnˈliːʃ]	v.	释放
convince [kənˈvins]	vt.	使确信,使信服
generate [ˈdʒenəˌreit]	vt.	产生,发生
revenue [ˈrevinjuː]	n.	收入,国家的收入,税收
sole [səul]	n.	脚底,鞋底,基础
	adj.	单独的,唯一的
	v.	换鞋底
proprietorship [prəˈpraiətəʃip]	n.	所有权
nitty [ˈniti]	adj.	多虱卵的,〈口〉愚蠢的,笨的
gritty [ˈgriti]	adj.	有砂砾的,坚韧不拔的
designate [ˈdezigneit]	v.	指明,指出,任命,指派
reverse [riˈvəːs]	n.	相反,背面,反面,倒退
	adj.	相反的,倒转的,颠倒的
	vt.	颠倒,倒转

assume [əˈsjuːm]	vt.	假定,设想,采取,呈现
hence [hens]	adv.	因此,从此
alter [ˈɔːltə]	v.	改变
impose [imˈpəuz]	v.	征税,强加;以……欺骗
deem [diːm]	v.	认为,相信
convention [kənˈvenʃən]	n.	大会,协定,习俗,惯例
interpose [ˌintə(ː)ˈpəuz]	v.	提出
withhold [wiðˈhəuld]	v.	使停止,拒给,保留,抑制
significant [sigˈnifikənt]	adj.	有意义的,重大的,重要的
transaction [trænˈzækʃən]	n.	办理,处理;会报,学报;交易,事务,处理事务
remuneration [riˌmjuːnəˈreiʃən]	n.	报酬
constitute [ˈkɔnstitjuːt]	vt.	制定(法律),建立(政府),组成,任命
essence [ˈesns]	n.	基本,[哲]本质,香精
permanent [ˈpəːmənənt]	adj.	永久的,持久的
widget [ˈwidʒit]	n.	小器具,装饰品
virtual [ˈvəːtjuəl, -tʃuəl]	adj.	虚的,实质的;[物]有效的,事实上的
reside [riˈzaid]	vi.	居住
fiscal [ˈfiskəl]	adj.	财政的,国库的,会计的,国库岁入的
ultimate [ˈʌltimit]	adj.	最后的,最终的,根本的
amendment [əˈmendmənt]	n.	改善,改正
align [əˈlain]	v.	使结盟,使成一行
transparent [trænsˈpɛərənt]	adj.	透明的,显然的,明晰的
implement [ˈimplimənt]	n.	工具,器具
	v.	贯彻,实现;执行

Notes

(1) in this context　　在……的背景/条件下

(2) be subject to 受支配,从属于,可以……的,常遭受……
(3) in essence 本质上,大体上,其实
(4) stem from 来自或起源于某事物;由某事物造成
(5) in the case of 在……的情况
(6) the Caymans 开曼群岛
(7) the Bahamas 巴拿马群岛

Questions

(1) How are you taxed on the international income?
(2) If you are a Swiss resident, how does Swiss as a source country tax the payments you make?
(3) What do you think of permanent establishment?
(4) What tax will you refer to if you are an American?
(5) According to added value tax, what will Non-EU-Member States such as e.g. Switzerland do in order not to have any competitive disadvantages vis à vis the EU?

Exercises

1. Translate the following sentences into Chinese:

(1) As you will have customers around the world and as you will be receiving money from all over the world, you may thus wish to know something on how your e-commerce revenues will be taxed.

(2) Their sole purpose is to have both treaty countries sharing in the taxation of revenues rather than to have both countries imposing tax as they deem fit. If we assume 20 industrialized nations which do have treaties with all other industrialized nations than that makes 450 treaties.

(3) As you will not be maintaining a permanent establishment is Switzerland, the 100 paid by your Swiss customer will find their way to Ann Arbor free and clear of foreign income and/or withholding taxes. So far so good.

(4) Let us further assume that you have no offices and employees in the U.S. but have hired the services of numerous U.S. resident consultants to put together your web site.

(5) Such tax is being referred to as a "reverse charge" because normally VAT is charged to the Distributor and not to the ultimate consumer, whereas in the case of electronic distributed imports the tax will be charged directly on the ultimate consumer.

2. Translate the following sentences into English:

（1）因为你已经创立了电子商务企业,你就可以自理费用开支,且只对净收益征税。作为一个好公民,你要么自己报税,要么通过本地会计师报税。

（2）从税务的角度来看,一本书是通过物理传输还是网上下载没有什么两样。在这两种情况下,你的现金报酬构成了营业收入,在源国家是不需要交税的。

（3）实质上就是说,除非你在其他国家有办事处和雇员,否则你在另一个国家是不能有一个常设机构的。

（4）因为该条约包含旧的常设机构原则,其中规定要有固定的营业地点,即在其他国家有自己的办事处和员工。

（5）目的地系统是指进口货物和服务应缴纳增值税,而出口任何这类物品或服务是零税率,即尽管没有进口税,它有权实行增值税。

（6）这种税将让你处于明显不利的竞争地位,因为如果电子分布式产品在欧盟内流通的话,同样的增值税将不再适用。

Further Reading

In modern times, the trades among countries over the world are of high frequency and then there comes some issues, such as taxation payments. The extract tells of the relevant issues on international taxation of e-commerce.

Translation

电子商务的国际税收

想一想,你开发和拥有一个属于自己的十分奇妙的网站,它向人们出售分布式的电子产品。我们不妨称你的网站为 wizzkidd.com。如果你看过 Seth Godin 的"释放思想病毒"(www.ideavirus.com),并确信你的网站会被世界各地的人们点击访问,他们将需要付费下载他们所需要的电子软件,那么与许多其他网站不一样的是,你已经建立了一个收入大于支出的网站。

你可能不知道你该如何为你的网站收入交纳税费。让我们进一步假设你处在美国的某处(我个人建议密歇根的安·阿伯),并决定开始创业,且是个人独资企业。要使一个网站能够在互联网上使用,必须有一台网络服务器作为主机。我们再假定你已经在附近找到了服务器,并且已经看过了所有相关的法律法规,那么,祝贺你,你可以开始创业了。

如果你是瑞士居民,且从事专为美国消费者设计的产品的电子分销,那么请不要停止阅读。改变论据并不能改变下文要提到的结论。

1. 所得税

既然你的顾客遍布全球,你就会赚取世界各地的钱,那么你可能就想了解各国对电子商务收入是如何征税的。假设你是一个美国居民,那么你的全球收入应根据美国所得税征收。因为你已经创立了一家电子商务企业,你就可以自理费用开支,且只有净收益会被征税。作为一个好公民,你要么自己报税,要么通过本地会计师报税。

在瑞士这样的国家你可能有很多客户,也很想知道你来自国外的收入都会发生什么,作为源国家,瑞士是如何对瑞士顾客给你创造的财富收入征税的。这里,了解美国和瑞士之间有一个双重课税条约是很重要的,它决定了谁对某些收入项目享有第一征税权。在所有的工业化国家都存在这样的协议。它们的目的是使协议的双方共享税收收入,而不是每个国家征收它们自己认为合适的税费。如果我们假设20个工业化国家与所有其他工业化国家之间都存在协议,那么就是存在着450个协议。

这450个协议都是基于一个单一的模式公约,它由巴黎的"经济合作与发展组织"(OECD,简称经合组织)所设计。

经合组织也做了很多工作,将电子商务自中间业务收入和/或截留税款中释放出来。关注数字类下载的交易处理是经合组织承担的最重要的任务,包括软件、数据、图片、文章和录像的下载。

正是在这一背景下,经合组织已将电子商务确定为是以数码方式交货的,因而与实物交付没有什么差别。从税务的角度来看,一本书是通过物理传输还是网上下载没有什么两样。在这两种情况下,你的现金报酬构成了营业收入,在源国家这是不需要交税的。大体上这样你就可以获得来自世界各地的收入。因为这种收入属于营业收入,就不会受到任何外国的代扣税。如果你的瑞士顾客自付100的发票,你就会收到100(减去银行手续费)。到现在为止,这一直都不错。

2. 常设机构

国际税收一个十分基本的原则就是关于所谓的常设机构。如果你在另一个国家已经设立了常设机构(在这里我们说的是瑞士),那么你就要交纳这个国家的所得税。因此,你肯定不希望在任何国家拥有常设机构。常设机构一词与国际税收一样的古老,它起源于那个时代人们跨国运送小器具、西红柿和零件。因而,基本原则就是,如果你在本国有实体店,在另一个国家你只能有一个常设机构。实质上就是说,除非你在其他国家有办事处和雇员,否则你在另一个国家是不能有常设机构的。

当你在密歇根安·阿伯的家里工作时,当你使用附近的网络主机向世界各地提供网站服务时,你没有必要在海外拥有办公室和雇员。经合组织认为如果仅仅有一个虚拟的存在,比如一个由你的网站所创造的,这还不足以在海外设立常设机构。正如你不会在瑞士维持一个常设机构。瑞士顾客付给你的100会自己到达安·阿伯,完全免除外汇收入和/或截留税款。到现在为止,这一直都不错。

对于所得税而言,你必须记住三个原则。第一,你是哪个国家的居民,你的全球收入就会按哪个国家的所得税被征收。第二,电子商务所创造的营业利润,不交纳国外的税,即使支付款来自国外。第三,你将出现在世界各地,但因此就不用在国外设立任何常设机构了。这是十分神奇的,它使得你比汽车经销商的情况要好很多。

3. 移动居留

如果你是美国公民,你可以去其他国家,在那里你可以支付比在美国更少的所得税。但实质上,这并不打紧,因为一个美国公民无论他居住在哪里仍然要受到美国税制的约束。如果你是一个美国公民,并打算从安·阿伯搬到瑞士的某个地方去,你最终会发现你支付的税费和在其他地方是一样的。然而这一经验教训只适用于美国公民和绿卡持有者。

如果你不是美国公民(或美国绿卡持有者),那么你可以考虑把你的居住地移到另一个国家,在那里你可以支付比在美国更少的税费。这里就需要谈到第四条也是最后一条国际收入税收原则。原则上说无论你在何处居住,都要尝试成为一个与美国有贸易协议的国家的居民。我们假设你居住在瑞士某处,且美国是你的主要电子商务市场。我们进一步假设,你在美国没有办公室和雇员,但雇用众多的美国驻地顾问撰写你的网站。根据美国国内税法,如果你从事美国贸易或业务,美国国税局将对你的美国源收入征税。

针对美国市场上的客户,你聘请美国顾问,这样就可能导致你从事相关的美国贸易或业务。那么,你要的就是确保你居住在这样一个国家,美国与其有双重课税条约。为什么?因为该条约包含旧的常设机构原则,其中规定要有固定的营业地点,即在其他国家有自己的办事处和员工。这意味着只要你能要求条约保护,从事美国贸易或业务的原则将不适用。那些与美国没有任何双重课税条约联系的国家有时被称为"境外"(开曼群岛、巴哈马群岛,凡是你想得起的)。做出来的教训是:不要去境外,但要确保你的电子商务业务在有条约保护的财政环境中运行。

4. 增值税

除了自我因素,个人所得税是十分直截了当的,没有什么要你谨记在心。在欧盟和许多其他国家,比如瑞士,有一种增值税制度("VAT")。欧盟和其他适用增值税的国家对如何去做电子商务都给予了大量关注。到目前为止,只有一件事情十分清楚:数字传输不会带来任何业务收入,但相对取得了增值服务的资格。

一般来说,跨国交易要么服从于包括源产地的系统,要么建立在目的地系统之上。目的地系统是指进口货物和服务应缴纳增值税,而出口任何这类物品或服务是零税率,即尽管没有出口税,它有权实行增值税。

对于电子服务和数字交付而言,欧盟将采取目的地税务制度。因而迟早会有一种适用于电子分布式进口的消费税,而且还有一个未解决的问题,即如何向最终消费者征税。这个税种被称为"反向收费",因为通常增值税是向经销商而不是最终消费者征收的,然而在涉及电子分布式进口时,最终消费者是直接征税对象。

一个有效的监管制度至少要花一到两年的时间才能切实可行。就目前而言,你可以看到,作为一个电子商务贸易商,你不用害怕增值税,因为该系统至今还不完善。

欧盟正致力于第六增值税指令修正案。非欧盟成员国,如瑞士,将不得不调整自己的增值税制度,以避免对欧盟有任何不利的竞争。

当你的瑞士客户将从一个非欧盟成员国引进电子分布式产品时,他们将被当作是进口增值服务的人。他们不仅要支付给你100,而且在将来的某个阶段也会支付进口增值税。根据你的欧洲顾客是哪国居民,上述增值税将分布在7.6%(如瑞士)至22%(如法国)之间。上述增值税不会向你征收(如美国分销商),而是转向你的欧盟常住居民用户(如果你的客户是一门生意,他甚至要求进项税额抵扣)。这种税将让你处于明显不利的竞争地位,因为如果电子分布式产品在欧盟内流通的话,同样的增值税将不再适用。

5. 结论

所得税和代扣税款方面的制度是相当透明化的。如果你居住在密歇根的安·阿伯,并且从瑞士顾客那儿获得了收入,那么你将没有外来税费。您还可以扭转事实的格局。再假设你是一个瑞士居民,并从美国客户那儿获得收入,结果将是一样的。也就是说,一个瑞士居民通过因特网派发宣传他的产品也无须接受美国的征税。

虽然欧洲的增值税制度尚未准备开征消费税,但很可能这种税将在很短的时间内得到实施。它将对在欧洲流通的因特网产品有重大影响。这些产品靠各地的人或者营业所分散到欧洲各地,这些人不是欧盟成员国或其他欧洲国家的居民。

UNIT 31

E-Business and Government Promotion of International Trade

Text

We can draw some lessons from recent experience with e-business in the CAFTA region. To stimulate e-business, developing countries need to build and strengthen institutional capacities and public-private communication, promote the development of network infrastructure, find ways to make hardware and software more available, invigorate the development of local talent, eliminate legal and regulatory barriers, and place government agencies online.

1. Build and Strengthen Institutional Capacity

Many governments in the CAFTA region and elsewhere have hastily undertaken ICT initiatives better suited to the private sector, while the private sector waits for the public sector to eliminate obstructions to innovation, investment, and growth. Yet e-government and e-business initiatives can be transformational only if embraced jointly by public and private leadership. Credible channels for public-private cooperation and communication are rare, yet e-government and e-business strategies alike require such channels to meet the challenge of global competition and generate sound priorities for national action. This has been the key to success in Canada, Chile, Singapore, Korea, and other countries.

2. Promote Network Infrastructure

Extend Coverage. Governments should promote the creation of voice and data networks with extensive geographical coverage. Where private telecommunications providers compete for business, regulators should require them to subsidize some level of connectivity in even the remotest areas ("universal service", including public telephony) as a condition of participation in the market. That agriculture and tourism, two of the largest contributors to international commerce in Central America and other regions, are often in remote areas makes this extension of connectivity especially important.

Control Costs. Regulators should ensure that the costs of basic voice or data transmission services are kept low to prevent "digital divides" in access to networks between the rich and the poor. They should also promote regulations and market conditions that favor reasonable prices for, and proliferation of, newer services such as high-speed dedicated "broadband" connectivity and "Voice over Internet Protocol" (VoIP). With these services, local businesses can participate in nationwide or even international exchange of high volumes of voice and data transmissions at manageable prices.

Assign Frequency Bands Efficiently. Likewise, regulators should promote the use of wireless transmission (cellular telephony, wireless broadband), since the cost of extending wireless coverage is far lower than the cost of extending wire and cable networks. Successful growth in wireless telecommunications requires that the government efficiently manage the assignment of frequency bands in the electromagnetic spectrum. Inefficient management is a source of constant friction and frustration in Central American countries.

Ensure Reliability. Frequent loss of service, chronic network congestion, transmission errors, and slow resolution of these problems can prove fatal for e-commerce, especially when local businesses trade with customers in developed countries who expect them to be constantly and reliably available. To help ensure reliability, regulators need to require telecommunications providers to maintain certain levels of network availability, limit numbers of transmission errors, and improve response times to customer complaints. In truly competitive markets, the ability of customers to move from one provider to another is especially effective at guaranteeing network reliability, as well as reasonable costs and wide availability.

Concentrate Telecommunications. Where it is not possible to provide first-class connectivity throughout a country, it is reasonable to concentrate intensive telecommunications use in a single location, such as free trade zones, industrial or technology parks, industry clusters, or even office centers. Concentration allows one or a few high-speed, very reliable network connections to serve multiple businesses involved in international commerce.

3. Make Computers and Software More Available

Governments are not as involved in providing computers, operating systems, and applications as they are in providing telecommunications services, but they can and frequently do help make computers more available. They create "telecenters" in underprivileged or remote areas so residents can use Internet-connected computers at subsidized rates. (All Central American governments sponsor telecenters, and Honduras is a world leader in innovative strategies in this field.) They also negotiate the donation of refurbished computers with organizations in other countries, mount national initiatives to provide state-backed financing for inexpensive computers (e.g., Costa Rica's Programa Acceso), provide individual loans on reasonable terms through government development banks, and manage import taxes and tariffs to make the purchase of imported computers and software possible for a wide range of citizens.

In addition, governments in developing countries (though not Central American countries) often promote the use of open-source software, thereby helping businesses avoid license fees and discouraging software piracy. Savings from open-source software, however, may not be as great as expected because support services for the software do have a cost, and technicians trained in the software may be harder to find or more expensive than persons trained in licensed software. The threat of losing business has forced some large software providers to lower licensing costs in some larger developing countries.

4. Promote ICT Skills in the Current and Future Workforce

Governments should do everything possible to promote the use of information and communication technologies, starting with formal primary education. Students should learn how to type, use a mouse, manage files, navigate the Internet, etc. while using computers and the Internet in as many activities as possible. This will make them aware of how technology can help them reach their goals and broaden their horizons.

Here, the most common barrier is the scarcity of computers and Internet connections in public schools. In Costa Rica, the Central American leader in computer use in public schools, 46 percent of primary school students have access to computers in school, and 29 percent have access to the Internet. In other Central American countries, these figures are below 5 percent. Governments in the region must make enormous efforts to improve school access if their citizens are to participate readily in a globalized society.

Governments can also promote ICT skills by supporting technical schools and technical certification programs offered by hardware and software vendors. Educational partnerships, such as that between the Costa Rican Chamber of Software Producers and local universities, can quickly produce workers with the skills necessary to conduct programming for local and foreign customers. Businesses in developed countries are increasingly interested in outsourcing ICT skills such as programming.

5. Resolve Legal and Regulatory Issues

Pass "Digital Signature" Laws. Commercial agreements are increasingly developed and finalized in digital formats. Developing countries need to pass laws recognizing "digital signatures" on electronic documents as legally binding evidence of identity and intent. Drafts of laws have been submitted to legislatures in most Central American countries, but none have been passed, and some have been withdrawn for revisions. This is not necessarily a bad thing because many drafts were based on obsolete approaches that should not be enshrined in law. Here, progress requires keeping legislators abreast of technological trends.

Respect IP Rights. Developing countries that are not signatories to various international agreements to respect intellectual property rights, or that do not make credible efforts to prosecute violations of these agreements, put their businesses at a competitive disadvantage in pursuing international commerce in "information economies". Foreign customers will be reluctant, for example, to contract services such as industrial design, research and development, or programming to businesses in developing countries if local workers are free to make use of the results for their own purposes. Central American countries are almost uniformly signatories of all major agreements and treaties in this area, though implementation and enforcement capacity varies widely.

Protect Privacy and Data. Developing countries must establish standards and laws for the protection of privacy and security of data. Without such standards and laws, the ability of developing countries to benefit from the outsourcing of processing of financial, medical or tax information will be jeopardized. Such information must remain confidential, especially when "identity" theft has become rampant in developed countries. This is an area where regional and international cooperation is critical.

Weigh the Costs and Benefits of Taxing Electronic Commerce. Several Central American governments are considering taxing Internet commerce. The potential loss of revenue represented by not taxing such commerce must be weighed against the possibility that taxing it will stifle innovation and growth. No decisions have been reached on taxation, which is complicated by the practical challenges posed by gathering information on the sale of "digital goods" (music, computer programs, consulting reports) to foreign customers.

6. Devise Programs to Promote ICT Use in International Commerce

All national governments in Central America have programs to promote ICT use—a vital step in facilitating the commercial use of ICTs. But no program has aimed to improve international commerce through ICTs, nor have any produced the results that programs in Ireland, India, and Singapore have. This may be due mostly to lack of financial resources and concrete action plans.

Other popular programs for improving the competitiveness of local businesses through use of ICTs are notable for their absence in Central America: promotion of knowledge-intensive business clusters; formation of ICT-related trade or industry associations; grants, subsidies, or tax concessions to stimulate technological innovation; and support for quality certification programs, such as those of the International Standards Organization (ISO) or the Capability Maturity Model (CMM), in ICT industries, among others.

7. Put Government Functions Online

Placing customs paperwork and forms online will facilitate international trade that uses ICTs. Most Central American countries have elementary forms with searchable texts available as downloadable PDFs (e. g. , www. hacienda. go. cr/aduanas, www. centrex. gov. sv, www. seadex. org. gt). Some agencies in charge of export promotion and foreign trade also use websites to make commercial opportunities visible to foreign customers (e. g. , Guatemala's www. seadex. org. gt and Costa Rica's www. marketplacecostarica. com).

8. Consider a Range of Other Incentives

To jumpstart e-business, governments can provide many other incentives:
- Subsidies or programs that support enterprise digitization.
- Public procurement portals with the payment component available to the private sector.
- Alternative dispute resolution centers for online disputes.
- Seal of trust programs (e. g. , Better Business Bureau online).
- Online Invoice programs.

Central American governments are capable of creating and maintaining sophisticated online systems, as the existence of their world-class state Internet banking applications, financial intranets, and government procurement sites show. This same capability must now be directed toward the facilitation of export activities if these countries are to participate effectively in global trade.

Words and Expressions

infrastructure [ˈinfrəˈstrʌktʃə]	n.	基础设施
initiative [iˈniʃiətiv]	n.	主动
invigorate [inˈvigəreit]	v.	鼓舞
coverage [ˈkʌvəridʒ]	n.	覆盖
proliferation [prəuˌlifəˈreiʃən]	n.	增殖

telecentre		n.	远程通信中心
subsidize ['sʌbsidaiz]		v.	资助,津贴
underprivileged [ˌʌndə'prividʒd]		adj.	穷困的
enshrine [en'ʃrain]		vt.	铭记
piracy ['paiərəsi]		n.	侵犯版权,非法翻印
outsourcing ['autˌsɔːsiŋ]		n.	[商]外部采办,外购
legislature ['ledʒisˌleitʃə]		n.	立法机关,立法机构
signatory ['signətəri]		n.	签名人,签字者
sophisticated [sə'fistikeitid]		adj.	老练的
procurement [prə'kjuəmənt]		n.	获得,取得

Notes

(1) CAFTA: Central America Free Trade Agreement 中美洲自由贸易协定
(2) VoIP: Voice over Internet Protocol 一种由 IP 网络传送话音的技术服务。
(3) ISO: International Organization for Standardization 国际标准化组织,主要提供质量认证服务。
(4) CMM: Capability Maturity Model 软件能力成熟度模型

Questions

(1) In order to stimulate e-business, what do developing countries need to do?
(2) What are the problems to prevent the development of e-commerce?
(3) How to make computers and software more available?
(4) What should governments and students do in order to promote e-commerce?
(5) What can we do to resolve legal and regulatory issues?

Exercises

1. Translate the following sentences into Chinese:
(1) Yet e-government and e-business initiatives can be transformational only if embraced jointly by public and private leadership.
(2) Regulators should ensure that the costs of basic voice or data transmission

services are kept low to prevent "digital divides" in access to networks between the rich and the poor.

(3) Successful growth in wireless telecommunications requires that the government efficiently manage the assignment of frequency bands in the electromagnetic spectrum.

(4) Governments are not as involved in providing computers, operating systems, and applications as they are in providing telecommunications services, but they can and frequently do help make computers more available.

(5) No decisions have been reached on taxation, which is complicated by the practical challenges posed by gathering information on the sale of "digital goods" (music, computer programs, consulting reports) to foreign customers.

2. Translate the following sentences into English:
(1) 各国政府应推动建立具有广泛的地域范围的语音和数据网络。
(2) 在这里,公立学校最常见的障碍是缺少电脑和网际互联网络的连接。
(3) 因为许多草案是基于过时的做法,所以不应被写入法律。
(4) 发展中国家必须为隐私保护和数据安全建立标准和法律。
(5) 把报关文件及表格放在网上将方便利用信息通信技术的国际间贸易。

电子商务与政府对国际贸易的促进

我们可以从中美洲自由贸易协定区(the CAFTA region)最近的电子商务发展经历中得到一些教训。为了刺激电子商务,发展中国家必须做到:建立和加强制度上的能力以及公共和私营部门之间的沟通,促进网络基础的发展,设法让硬件和软件更容易获得,鼓励本地人才的开发,消除法律和监管障碍,使政府机构在线。

1. 建立和加强制度上的能力

在中美洲自由贸易协定区和其他地区,许多国家政府都急切地开发信息通信技术(ICT)举措以使其更适合私营部门,与此同时,私营部门亟待公共部门消除阻碍改革、投资和经济增长等方面的障碍。然而面向电子政务和电子商务方向的转型,只有当由公共和私营部门领导共同认同时,才能得以推进。尽管电子政务和电子商务战略都需要合作和沟通的可靠渠道,以应付全球竞争的挑战和为国家行动创造良好的优先权,但是当今公共和私营部门的合作和沟通的可靠渠道还十分稀少。加拿大、智利、新加坡、韩国以及其他一些国家成功的关键就是解决了这一瓶颈问题。

2. 推进网络基础设施建设

扩大覆盖面。各国政府应推动建立具有广泛地域范围的语音和数据网络。在私营电信运营商为业务而开展竞争的地方,监管机构应该要求他们对某种程度的连通提供补贴,即使在最偏远的地区也不例外("普遍服务",包括公共电话),以作为参与市场的条件。农业和旅游业,这两个是中美洲与其他地区国际贸易的最大贡献者,往往集中在偏远地区,使得这种广泛的连接显得特别重要。

控制成本。管理者应该确保基本话音或数据传输服务的成本都保持在低水平上,以出现防止富人和穷人进入网络的"数字鸿沟"。还应促进有助于新的服务(比如高速专用"宽带"的连接和"基于互联网的语音协议"(VoIP))形成合理的价格和增值等推广的法规和市场条件。有了这些服务,本地企业可以以可控的价格参与全国甚至国际间的高容量的语音和数据传输交换。

高效分配频段资源。同样,由于延伸无线覆盖的成本远远低于延长有线及电缆网络的成本,因此监管机构应促进无线传输手段(移动通信、无线宽带)的利用。无线通信的成功增长,需要政府有效管理电磁频谱频率波段的分配。在中美洲国家,管理不善是摩擦和挫折不断发生的原因。

确保可靠性。频繁的服务损失、慢性网络拥塞、传输错误和缓慢解决问题的能力,这些问题很可能成为电子商务的致命伤,尤其是当地企业与发达国家的客户进行贸易时,这些客户期待他们能够随时随地进行可靠的联系。为了确保可靠性,监管者要求电信服务供应商维持一定水平的网络可用性,限制发送错误次数,并在最短的时间内解决客户的投诉。在真正的竞争性市场环境里,客户从一个运营商转向另一个运营商的可能性对保证网络的可靠性,以及合理的成本和广泛的可用性是极为有效的。

集中通信。当在整个国家不可能提供一流的通信服务时,在个别地方诸如自由贸易区、工业区或科技园区、产业集群,甚至办公中心,集中利用集约电信是合理的。集中允许一个或几个高速、很可靠的网络连线来处理国际贸易中的多种业务服务问题。

3. 使计算机和软件更有效

政府不像提供电信服务那样提供电脑、操作系统和应用系统,但他们能够并且经常可以做一些有助于电脑更容易获得的事。它们在穷困或者偏远地区创建"远程通信中心",使那儿的居民能以优惠的价格用互联网来连接他们的电脑。(所有中美洲国家政府都赞助远程通信中心,在这个领域,洪都拉斯的创新战略世界领先。)他们还同在其他国家的组织商谈捐赠整修电脑,越来越多的国家主动提供国家支持的资金购买低价电脑(例如,哥斯达黎加的"Acceso"项目),通过政府发展银行和管理的进口税和关税,以合理的条件提供个人贷款下,使更多的公民能够买到进口电脑和软件。

此外,发展中国家政府(虽然不是中美洲国家)经常推广使用开放源码软件,从而帮助企业免除特许费和令人烦恼的盗版软件的侵扰。然而从开放源码软件中得到的收益可能不会像预期的那么多,因为这些软件的支持服务也是有花费的,并且这类软件的受训技术人员可能比授权软件的受训人员更难找到或代价更为高昂。失去业务的威胁已迫使一些大型软件供应商在一些较大的发展中国家降低许可证费用。

4. 在当前和今后的工作中推动信息通信技术技能

政府要千方百计地促进信息和通信技术的使用,并从正规的小学教育起步。在尽可能多地用电脑和因特网行动,同时,学生应学习如何打字、如何使用鼠标、如何管理文档,以及如何浏览因特网等。这将使他们认识到技术如何能帮助他们实现自己的目标,开阔他们的眼界。

在这里,公立学校里遇到的最大障碍是缺少电脑和网际互联网的连接。哥斯达黎加的公立学校电脑普及率在中美洲国家处于领先地位,但也只有46%的小学生在学校能够接触电脑,29%能上网。在其他中美洲国家,这些数字均低于5%。为使它们的公民更容易地接触全球化社会,这些地区的各国政府必须作出巨大努力以改善学校电脑的使用。

政府还可以通过对由硬件和软件供应商提供的技术学校和技术认证项目提供支持,以促进信息通信技术技能的发展。建立教育伙伴关系,比如哥斯达黎加软件制造商会与当地大学之间的结盟,可以很快培养出有技能的工人,这些技能对承担本地和外国客户的项目是必要的。对诸如编程这样的信息通信技术技能进行外包表现出越来越浓厚的兴趣。

5. 解决法律和规章问题

通过"数字签名"的立法。 商业协议正日益发展并以数字化格式定稿。发展中国家需要在电子文件上通过法律认可的"数字签名",作为具有身份和意愿法律约束力的证明。大部分中美洲国家法律草案已提交给议会,但没有获得通过,并且有的修订本已经撤销。这不一定是坏事,因为许多草案是过时的,不应被写入法律。在这里,所取得的进展要求立法者跟上科技发展趋势。

尊重知识产权。 发展中国家中那些没有成为各种旨在保护知识产权的国际协议的签约国,或者没有做出令人信服的、起诉违反这些协议的努力的国家,使它们的企业在"信息经济"时代从事国际商务时处于竞争劣势。例如,如果发展中国家当地工人个个假公济私,国外客户将不愿意与之签订诸如工业设计、研究开发等劳务合同以及业务项目。虽然在这方面实施和执行能力大相径庭,但是中美洲国家几乎都在所有主要的协议和条约上签字了。

保护隐私权和数据。 发展中国家必须为隐私保护和数据安全建立标准和法律。如果没有这样的标准和法律的约束力,发展中国家从"外购"的金融、医疗或税务信息处理中获益的能力将处于危险境地。这类信息必须保密,尤其是在冒充"身份"的盗窃者在发达国家已经猖獗的时候。这个领域的区域和国际合作是至关重要的。

衡量成本和电子商务征税效益。 不少中美洲国家政府正在考虑征收因特网商务税收。必须在没有征收此种商业税收所带来的潜在的税收损失与征税将会扼杀创新和增长的可能性之间进行权衡。由于是否征税尚未作出决定,这使得向外国客户出售"数字化产品"(如音乐、电脑程序、咨询报告)收集信息成为非常复杂的现实挑战。

6. 制订计划以促进信息通信技术在国际贸易中的使用

中美洲的所有国家都打算促进信息通信技术的使用——这是促使信息通信技术商业化的关键一步。但没有任何项目旨在通过信息通信技术改善国际商贸,也没有看到诸如爱尔兰、印度和新加坡已经取得成效的项目成果。这可能主要因为缺乏资金和具体的行动计划。

其他一些通过利用信息通信技术提高本地企业竞争力的受欢迎的项目,在中美洲也有明显的缺失,这需要:促进知识密集的企业群的形成;组建信息通信技术相关商业或行业协会;通过资助、补贴或减税来刺激技术创新;在信息通信技术产业以及其他相关产业支持质量认证项目,比如国际标准组织(ISO)和软件能力成熟度模型(CMM)。

7. 让政府职能上网

把报关文件及表格放在网上将有利于国际间贸易利用信息通信技术。大部分中美洲国家已基本形成可检索文本作为可下载的 PDF 格式获得(例如,www.hacienda.go.cr/aduanas、www.centrex.gob.sv、www.seadex.org.gt)。一些负责促进出口和外贸的机构还利用网站(例如危地马拉的 www.seadex.org.gt 和哥斯达黎加的 www.marketplacecostarica.com)使外国客户可以看到商业机会。

8. 考虑到其他一系列激励措施

政府可以提供许多其他的激励措施促使企业开展电子商务:
- 提供补贴或制订计划支持企业向数字化方向发展;
- 具备支付功能的公共采购入口可以供私营部门使用;
- 为解决在线纠纷提供可选择的纠纷解决中心;
- 给可信任的项目提供印证(例如,更好的在线商务办公署);
- 建立在线开具发票业务。

中美洲政府有能力建立和维护一套复杂的联机系统,因为它有着世界级的国家互联网银行应用系统、金融内联网以及政府采购站点展示等。如果这些国家决心有效地参与全球贸易,就必须拥有同样的能力来直接简化出口活动。

UNIT 32 The Role of Knowledge Management in Building E-Business Strategy

E-business strategy is a roadmap to guide the organizations to a correct selection of both tools and solutions to achieve the organizations' goals and context of applications on internet. Building (Creating) e-business strategy is Information Technology (IT) project. The vital goal of building e-business strategy is to address the way of how Internet technologies can support the organization and give competitive advantages through the configuration of its available resources to meet the needs of the market and customers, as well as support the Customer Relationship management (CRM) and supply chain management (SCM). Organizational Knowledge Base is one of the essential components for building successful e-business strategy project in any firm, because it contains data, information and a set of knowledge assets about the firm. Thus, the firm must depend on and use this source as an elementary step to perform some of the strategy tasks easily and efficiently. Creating e-business strategy based on four stages: ① Initiate, ② Diagnose, ③ Breakout, and ④ Transition.

Knowledge Resource in e-Business Strategy

Organizational knowledge base means Explicit Knowledge available in the firm and tacit knowledge (e.g. Managerial Expertizes, experiences which reside in the minds of its owners) should be used in those stages in order to help the project stakeholders to participate and perform all e-business strategy tasks efficiently.

Formulating new e-business strategy for any organization is a duty of high-level management (Executive Managers), to allocate the required resources to carry out the project successfully. Resources are as follows:

(1) Tangible Resources, e.g. Mainframe.
(2) Intangible Resources, e.g. Knowledge Assets.
(3) Human Resources (HR), e.g. Web Designer.

The most valuable required intangible resource for strategies is knowledge. In e-business, knowledge also is the most strategically important resource, such as products' specifications, trademarks, production and operations management expertizes customer and supplier relationships records, organization culture, policy, and reputation.

An Overview of Knowledge management in e-Business

E-business is wide term means the use of all IT capabilities in business, it does not mean only buying and selling (e-commerce), it also includes other business processes such as serving customers/suppliers and managing their relationships electronically (e-CRM), managing all supply activities till delivering products/services to customers (e-SCM), internal communication between employees and external collaboration with other business partners. Obviously, all those activities are intangible assets, which mean that e-business solutions concentrate on the management of knowledge (intangible assets). E-business strategy based on group work of different levels of management and organization departments, the shared factor which integrate them together is knowledge.

Why Knowledge management?

Because the flood of huge quantity of information through the organization about its business processes, rules, relationships. Many organizations are suffering from the information overload, and looking for suitable representation of information (knowledge) to benefit typically. In e-business strategies, there are a lot of possible opportunities as well as risks that should be critically identified before creating the strategy. Leveraging knowledge is one of the success factors for e-business strategy as a new economy. E-business strategy has multi challenges to efficient and effective sources of KM:

- In the context of CRM, it gives perceptive meaning that enables the organization knows more about its customers, suppliers, and partners, and their relationships, and linkages with the organization.
- In the context of SCM, enables the organization knows what materials available, what is required, how the organization operates these materials, how it delivers the products/services (distribution channels), how it markets and serves the customers.
- KM links all project stakeholders and management levels together, and supports the team work by sharing the experiences and expertizes.
- KM processes organize, distribute, filter, and store a huge amount of organization's data, information, and knowledge in distributed knowledge base which resides in different locations. This knowledge supports the decision making

process and improve the project performance.

Benefits of KM Tools into E-Business Information management

KM tools are all technologies and resources that enable the knowledge transfer, generation, and codification. It does not mean that all KM tools are computer-based applications; knowledge can be transferred via phone calls. The following are possible benefits of KM tools for e-business information management:

1. Organize and Evaluate Customers' and Suppliers' Requirements and Relationships (Customers-Suppliers Oriented Trends)

Questionnaires as a tool for gathering data and information are one of the common methods to get information. But getting information is nothing new to organizations. The classification and evaluation processes are based on all gathered information from customers, suppliers, and partners such as satisfaction, suggestions, recommendations, and requirements. Knowledge Base System (KBS) is KM tool to organize a collection of information and evaluate them in such way to be "knowledge".

The importance of this process is to enable the organization to respond and make correct decisions toward the customers' or suppliers' demands. This is the first step for organization changes "new strategy".

For example, after classifying the knowledge related to customers' feedbacks, the organization found out that, customers do not receive up-to-date information about new products, prices, and offers. That would make the organization think about "new marketing" tool to improve the promotion, such as e-brochures or e-mail marketing.

2. Support the Decision Making Process (Forecast)

KBS for existing customers and suppliers helps the organization to keep update their needs (Declarative Knowledge), as well as benefit from the internet technologies as KM tool such as search engines, also capable the organization to capture more information about the market competition, new customers' demands, customer's demographics, competitors, etc. (Behavioral Knowledge).

3. Filter and Store All Organization's Knowledge in Knowledge Repository (Organizational Trends)

Knowledge repository stores the processed information that are captured, organized, filtered, and evaluated and save them as knowledge, as well as store all knowledge that are related with other organization's strategies such as marketing strategy and Information System (IS) strategy. Knowledge repository makes the process simple for employees to save, retrieve, access, and organize all knowledge.

These three benefits prepare the basic infrastructure to formulate e-business strategy, and identify where we can practically benefit from knowledge in the building process. They show KM value chain components begin from creation to storage and distribution of knowledge.

The Contribution of KM in E-Business Strategy Stages

There are numbers of well-known international organization integrate KM in e-Business activities such as Sun Microsystems. As mentioned before, building e-business strategy is based on four stages as follows:

1. Initiate Stage

The objectives of this stage are:
- Outline project scope.
- Identify project stakeholders.
- Determine project schedule.

Project scope and schedule tasks deal with data and information nothing tangible "no deliverables", they are about prediction and general study. KM has extremely significant contribution for these two tasks because both depend on gathered data/information "Declarative Knowledge" about customers and suppliers, as well as "Behavioral Knowledge" about organization documents, market competition, and prediction for deliverables. All these tasks can be performed effectively by the following KM tools:
- Organizational knowledge base.
- Knowledge mining.
- Knowledge determination.

2. Diagnose Stage

The purpose of this stage is to find out strengths, weaknesses, opportunities, and threats (SWOT) of the current business strategy, which can be done by:
- Analyzing the organization position among its competitors, and
- Revises the current strategy in order to understand the current relationships between the organization and its suppliers and customers.

To analyze and assess the current organization position there are some analytical tools can be used that enable the firm to assess its position. Small-size firms can use industry analysis, medium/large-size can use supply chain analysis. For customers'-suppliers' relationships there is a tool called Customer/Supplier Life Cycle enable the firms to evaluate its relationships.

All tasks in this stage need organizational knowledge base and knowledge repository to be carried out, because they are about the current state of the organization which means no need for gathering data/information and no predictions as well for the future behavior.

3. Breakout Stage

The objective of this stage is to derive a new strategy (e-breakout strategy) from the overall business strategy to match the organization goals. E-business strategy could be dependent or independent on other organization's strategy. That is why it is recommended to understand the relationship between the proposed e-business strategy and other adopted strategies before creation. New e-business strategy should be ready to form based on (Diagnose Stage) the assessment of organization strategy and (SWOT) analysis of its position, these both are intellectual assets of the organization.

The derivation process of the new strategy is duties of project manager for allocating staff, distributing tasks, identifying IT requirements, adding/deleting new features to optimize the corporate overall business strategy, satisfy SWOT deficiencies. Furthermore, the responsibilities of the project manager deal directly with the human dynamics of the corporation and concerned on the required technology. In conclusion, building e-business strategy is about converting the corporation's intellectual assets (Knowledge) into a new roadmap of what the corporation needs to do, by re-arranging the corporate business strategy based on IT infrastructure. The main role of Chief Knowledge Officer (CKO) is to convert knowledge into valuable profit by managing and controlling the corporation's intellectual assets. Therefore, CKO can be e-business strategy project manager.

4. Transition Stage

In this stage, the firm has to implement the proposed roadmap of the new strategy. Transition means that the firm will move from current state to the proposed state, this movement will be supported by new resources and capabilities.

In this case, it is recommended for firms to carry out gap analysis in order to avoid the changes, risks, and conflicts between the current and new strategy to understand and identify the differences between them.

The key role of KM in this stage is vital and valuable. KM is necessary to measure the organization's ability for implementing the new strategy. Knowledge as intangible resource of the organization comprise of organization's culture, policy, business processes, and HR experiences, will enable the corporation to assess itself by assessment tools (e. g. risk or change readiness analysis) to know if the corporation has the ability to cope with the changes of the new strategy, and able to alter or not, and critically determine all areas of changes in order to manage these changes. CKO can conduct the evaluation process of the corporation and diagnose risk and opportunities of the new strategy.

Conclusion

The innovation of information technologies in business is forced the organization to adopt new strategies to enable the real time optimization of the value chain. Building e-business strategy and plans should be derived from the business objectives, culture, policy, and current strategies (knowledge resources).

From effective knowledge management, the organization can build suitable e-business strategy, as well as control the organization changes, evaluate and estimate the cost/benefit/risk of the project (e-business strategy); CKO can lead the e-business strategy project as a project manager.

Managing knowledge should be based on technology platforms to provide the sharing and exchange processes. Therefore knowledge management is a combination of human resources, technology resources, and information resources.

In conclusion, knowledge management does not exist in specific organizational position or management level, KM can be found in the overall corporate strategy, organization objectives, business operations, and people.

Words and Expressions

configuration [kənˌfigju'reiʃən]	n.	构造,形状;外貌,轮廓
explicit [iks'plisit]	adj.	详述的,明确的;不含糊的
tacit ['tæsit]	adj.	缄默的,不说话;默许的
formulate ['fɔːmjuleit]	vt.	构想出,规划;确切的阐述
tangible ['tændʒəbl]	adj.	明确的,确凿的;有形的
intangible [ɪn'tændʒəbəl]	adj.	难以捉摸的,难以理解的
expertise [ˌekspəˈtiːz]	n.	专门知识或技能
leverage ['liːvəridʒ]	vt.	促使……改变
questionnaire [ˌkwestiə'nɛə]	n.	调查表,问卷
filter ['filtə]	vt.	透过,过滤
deliverable [di'livərəbl]	adj.	可交付的,可交付使用的

Unit 32 The Role of Knowledge management in Building E-Business Strategy

declarative [diˈklærətiv]	adj.	宣言的,公布的
revise [riˈvaiz]	vt.	修订,修改
intellectual [ˌɪntiˈlektjuəl]	adj.	智力的;理智的,善于思维的
implement [ˈimplimənt]	vt.	使生效,贯彻,执行

Notes

(1) The vital goal of building e-business strategy is to address the way of how Internet technologies can support the organization and give competitive advantages through the configuration of its available resources to meet the needs of the market and customers, as well as support the Customer Relationship management (CRM) and supply chain management (SCM). 构建电子商务战略的重要目标是解决因特网技术如何支撑组织利用其现有资源配置的竞争优势来满足市场和客户的需求,以及如何解决客户关系管理(CRM)和供应链管理(SCM)等方面的问题。

(2) KBS for existing customers and suppliers helps the organization to keep update their needs (Declarative Knowledge), as well as benefit from the internet technologies as KM tool such as search engines, also enable the organization to capture more information about the market competition, new customers' demands, customer's demographics, competitors, etc. (Behavioral Knowledge). 现有客户和供应商的 KBS 有助于组织不断更新它们的需求(公开性的知识),以及从作为 KM 工具,如搜索引擎的互联网技术中收益,同时,使组织能够捕捉到更多的有关市场竞争、新客户需求、客户特征、竞争对手(行为知识)方面的信息。

(3) Knowledge repository stores the processed information that are captured, organized, filtered, and evaluated and save them as knowledge, as well as store all knowledge that are related with other organization's strategies such as marketing strategy and Information System (IS) strategy. 知识仓库存储经捕获、组织、筛选和评估并已经作为知识保存的处理过的信息,同时存储和组织战略相关的知识,如营销战略和信息系统(IS)战略。

(4) KM has extremely significant contribution for these two tasks because both depend on gathered data/information "Declarative Knowledge" about customers and suppliers, as well as "Behavioural Knowledge" about organization documents, market competition, and prediction for deliverables. 对于这两项任务, KM 具有极其显著的贡献,因为这两项任务都取决于收集到的数据/有关客户和供应商"概述性知识"信息,以及有关组织文件、市场竞争、交付预测的"行为知识"。

Questions

(1) What dose Organizational knowledge base mean?
(2) What knowledge resources does e-business strategy include?
(3) In business management, why should we introduce KM?
(4) What are the possible benefits of KM tools for e-business information management?
(5) To perform all those tasks in Initiate stage, which KM tool should we take?

Exercises

1. Translate the following sentences into Chinese:
(1) Knowledge management (KM) comprises a range of strategies and practices used in an organization to identify, create, represent, distribute, and enable adoption of insights and experiences.
(2) Knowledge management efforts typically focus on organizational objectives such as improved performance, competitive advantage, innovation, the sharing of lessons learned, integration and continuous improvement of the organization.
(3) Knowledge Sharing remains a challenging issue for knowledge management, and while there is no clear agreement barriers may include time issues for knowledge works, the level of trust, lack of effective support technologies and culture.
(4) It was suggested that many current interpretations of knowledge management are based on an outdated model of business strategy and may have adverse implications for e-business performance.
(5) Better and accurate understanding of the strategic relevance of knowledge and knowledge management is expected to contribute to more effective e-business strategies that result in sustained business performance.

2. Translate the following sentences into English:
(1) 从企业的竞争优势来看,知识将是形成竞争优势的主要来源。
(2) 知识管理是个手段,不是目的,目的就是提高机构的智力或公司智商。
(3) 知识管理的出发点是把知识作为企业最重要的资源,最大限度地利用知识作为提高企业竞争力的关键。
(4) 目前对知识管理的理解很多是基于过时的商务模型,这会对电子商务产生负面影响。
(5) 从本质上讲,电子商务战略是商业驱动,而不是由信息技术来驱动的。

Unit 32　The Role of Knowledge management in Building E-Business Strategy

Further Reading

This text is submitted toUSAID/EGAT/TI byNathan Associates Inc. TCB Project, about lessons from the CAFTA Region.

Translation

知识管理在构建电子商务战略中的作用

　　电子商务战略是引导组织在管理工具和解决方案方面作出正确选择的一个路线图，以期在互联网应用背景下实现组织的目标。构建（创立）电子商务战略是信息技术（IT）中的项目。构建电子商务战略的重要目标是解决因特网技术如何支撑组织利用其现有资源配置的竞争优势来满足市场和客户的需求，以及如何解决客户关系管理（CRM）和供应链管理（SCM）等方面的问题。组织知识库（OKB）包含数据、信息和与公司有关的一系列知识资产，它是任何一家公司成功建立电子商务战略项目的重要组成部分之一。因此，公司必须依赖这些资源并且将其当作基本的步骤以便简单和高效地执行一些战略任务。创建电子商务战略基于四个阶段：① 启动；② 诊断；③ 突破；④ 转型。

电子商务战略中的知识资源

　　组织知识基础是指公司中可获得的显性知识和隐性知识（如存在个人头脑中的管理专业知识、经验）应该在哪些阶段中得到合理利用，以利于项目的利益相关者有效地参与和执行所有的电子商务战略任务。
　　对于任何组织来说，制定新的电子商务战略是高层管理（执行经理）的任务，如分配所需资源，以便成功地开展项目。资源如下：
　　（1）有形资源，如主机。
　　（2）无形资源，如知识资产。
　　（3）人力资源，如网页设计师。
　　电子商务战略所需的最宝贵的无形资源是知识。在电子商务中，知识也是最重要的战略性资源，如产品的规格、商标、生产和运营管理的专业知识、客户和供应商关系记录、组织文化、政策和声誉等。

电子商务中知识管理概述

　　电子商务广义上是指商务中IT技术的使用，它并不仅意味着购买和销售（电子商务），还包括其他业务流程，比如服务于客户/供应商并且管理他们之间关系的电子化客户关系管理(e-CRM);管理所有的供应活动,直至产品/服务到达客户手中的电子供应链管理(e-SCM)以及内部员工之间的沟通和与其他业务伙伴之间的协作。显然,所有这些活动都是无形资产,这意味着电子商务解决方案应专注于知识管理(无形资产)。电子商务战略以不同的管理层次、组织部门的团队合作以及知识整合的共享因素为基础。

为什么要应用知识管理

由于与组织业务流程、规则和关系相关的信息数量十分巨大,许多组织都面临信息超载,企图寻找合适的信息(知识)的典型并从中获益。在电子商务战略中,创建战略之前,有很多可能的机会以及风险需要仔细认真地识别。利用知识是电子商务作为一种新的经济模式成功的因素之一。电子商务战略在知识管理(KM)中资源的有效性方面面临众多挑战:

- 在 CRM 的背景下,它给出了明确的定义,使组织更加了解客户、供应商和合作伙伴以及它们之间的关系及其和组织之间的联系。
- 在 SCM 的背景下,使组织了解什么材料是可得的、什么是组织需要的、组织如何运行这些材料、如何传输产品/服务(分销渠道)以及它是如何推广和服务客户的。
- KM 将所有项目的利益相关者和管理层联系在一起,并通过分享经验和专业知识来支撑团队的工作。
- KM 流程在不同地点的分布式的数据库中组织、分配、过滤和存储大量的组织数据、信息和知识。这些知识支持决策过程,提高项目绩效。

电子商务信息管理中运用 KM 工具的益处

KM 工具包含知识转化、产生和编撰的所有技术和资源。它并不意味着所有的 KM 工具都是基于计算机的应用,知识同样可以通过电话进行转移。以下是 KM 可能给电子商务信息管理带来的好处:

1. 组织和评估客户和供应商的需求以及他们之间的关系(客户-供应商导向发展趋势)

问卷调查作为收集数据和信息的工具,是获得信息的最常用方法之一。但得到的信息对组织来说没有什么新意。分类和评估过程基于所有从客户、供应商和合作伙伴收集过来的信息,比如满意度、建议、提议和需求。知识库系统(KBS)是组织信息的收集,并以"知识"这样的方式来评估这些信息的 KM 工具。

这一进程的重要性是使组织能够回应并且针对客户和供应商的要求作出正确的决策。这是组织变革"新战略"的第一步。

例如,将与用户反馈意见相关的知识分类后,组织就会发现,客户未能获得有关新产品、价格和供货的最新信息。这将会使该组织考虑"新营销策略"工具来改善推广,如电子手册或电子邮件营销。

2. 支持决策过程(预测)

现有客户和供应商的 KBS 有助于组织不断更新它们的需求(公开性的知识),以及从作为 KM 工具,如搜索引擎的互联网技术中收益,同时,使组织能够捕捉到更多的有关市场竞争、新客户的需求、客户特征、竞争对手(行为知识)方面的信息。

3. 在知识仓库中过滤和存储所有组织知识(组织趋势)

知识仓库存储经捕获、组织、筛选和评估并作为知识保存的处理过的信息,同时存储和组织战略相关的知识,如营销战略和信息系统(IS)战略。知识仓库使得员工保存、检索、访问和组织所有知识等过程都变得相对简单。

这三个益处为制定电子商务战略准备了基础设施,并找出构建过程中我们能从知识中受益的地方。他们展现了从创建到知识存储和分配的 KM 价值链组件。

KM 在电子商务战略阶段的贡献

根据已有大量的知名国际组织在电子商务活动中集成的 KM 系统,如 Sun 系统,再结合前面讲述的内容,构建电子商务战略基于如下四个阶段:

1. 启动阶段

这一阶段的目标是:
- 概述项目范围;
- 确定项目的利益相关者;
- 确定项目进度表。

在这一阶段,项目的范围和计划任务主要处理数据和信息,没有实际的成果,主要进行预测和一般性的研究。对于这两项任务,KM 具有极其显著的贡献,因为这两项任务都取决于收集到的数据/有关客户和供应商"概述性知识"方面的信息,以及有关组织文件、市场竞争、交付预测的"行为知识"。所有这些任务都可以通过以下 KM 工具有效地执行:
- 组织的知识基础;
- 知识挖掘;
- 知识决策。

2. 诊断阶段

本阶段的目的是找出目前组织战略的优势、劣势、机会和威胁(SWOT 分析),可以通过以下两个方面实现:
- 分析组织在所有竞争者中的地位;
- 修改当前的战略,以了解组织和其供应商、客户之间的关系。

有一些分析工具可以用来分析和评估组织当前的地位,使公司能够评估其地位,小型公司可以使用行业及市场分析,中等/大型公司可以使用供应链分析。对于客户-供应商关系,有一个叫做客户/供应商生命周期模型的工具可以使公司评估其关系。

在这个阶段的所有任务,需要组织知识基础和知识资源库,因为它们是该组织目前的状态,这意味着没有必要收集数据/信息以及同样对未来的行为没有预测。

3. 突破阶段

这个阶段的目标是能够从整体组织战略中得出一个新的电子战略(e 突围策略)来匹配组织目标。电子商务战略可以依赖也可以独立于其他组织的战略,这就是为什么要用它来理解经提议的电子商务战略和其他在创造之前所采取的战略之间的关系。新的电子商务战略应以(诊断阶段)组织战略评估和定位分析(SWOT 分析)构成为基础,这些都是组织的知识资产。

新战略的推导过程是项目经理的任务,分配工作人员、分发任务、确定 IT 需求、增加/删除新的功能来优化组织的整体经营战略、弥补 SWOT 分析法的不足。此外,项目经理直接处理该公司的人员流动和所需的相关技术等问题。总之,基于 IT 基础设施来重新安排组织的经营战略,构建电子商务战略,是该公司的知识资产(知识)转换成一个什么样的公司所必须做的。首席知识官(CKO)的主要作用是通过管理和控制组织的知识资产来将知识转化成宝贵的利润。因此,CKO 可以担任电子商务战略项目经理。

4. 转型阶段

在这个阶段,公司已经开始实施新战略提议的路线图。转型意味着公司将从目前的状态过渡到建议的状态中,新的资源和能力将支持这种过渡。

在这种情况下,建议公司进行差异性分析以避免变化、风险以及现有的和新战略之间的冲突,来理解并识别它们之间的不同。

KM 在这个阶段的主要作用是极为重要和宝贵的。KM 在衡量组织实施新战略的能力方面是非常有必要的,知识作为组织的无形资源,包括组织的文化、政策、业务流程、人力资源经验,将使公司有能力通过评估工具来评估它们自身,以了解自身是否有能力应对新战略的变化、能否改变以及批判性地决定各个领域的变化,从而能管理这些变化。CKO 能够领导公司的评估过程和诊断新战略的风险和机会。

结　　论

组织信息技术的创新使得组织不得不采用新战略来实现价值链的实时优化,构建电子商务战略和规划应该源于组织的经营目标、文化、政策和当前战略(知识资源)。

从有效的知识管理中,组织可以建立合适的电子商务战略,以及控制组织变化、评价和评估项目成本/效益/风险(电子商务战略);CKO 可以作为项目管理来领导电子商务战略项目。

知识管理应该基于技术平台来提供共享和交换过程,因此知识管理是人力资源、技术资源和信息资源的一个集成。

总之,知识管理不存在于特定的组织位置或管理层次,KM 可以在整体组织战略、组织目标、业务运行和人员中得以体现。

Appendix

E-Business Terms Explanations

（电子商务术语解释）

Below you'll find a short list of the most common Internet and e-business terms. If you're looking for an acronym or term that's not on this list, check out www. whatis. com or www. webopedia. com, two online dictionaries for Internet technology users.

以下是一些常见的互联网和电子商务术语。如果在这里找不到你想要的首字母缩略词或术语，你可以到为互联网用户服务的两个在线字典 www. whatis. com 和 www. webopedia. com 上查询。

B2C (Business to Consumer) The exchange of goods and services between businesses and consumers. In Internet terms, B2C is also known as "e-tailing" which is short for electronic retailing and refers to the selling of retail goods on the Internet.

企业对消费者电子商务 是指企业和消费者之间商品和服务的交换。电子商务术语中，B2C 指电子零售，即在因特网上进行商品零售。

Bandwidth Literally, the width of a band of electromagnetic frequencies. This is the data that flows along a given transmission path. Both digital and analog signals have a bandwidth. Bandwidth usage on the Internet increases with the amount of data transmitted or received. In terms of e-commerce application, when choosing a web hosting service a user must consider how their website will function, how much bandwidth they require, and how their web hosting provider can service their bandwidth needs.

带宽 从字面意义上理解，它指的是电磁频率带的宽度。这里指沿着特定传输路径流动的数据，无论是数字还是模拟信号都有一个带宽。随着互联网上传输量和接收量的增加，带宽的使用也不断增多。提到电子商务交易，在选择主页时，用户必须考虑到网站的功能、带宽的要求以及网络主机提供商怎样才能适合带宽的要求。

Browser A software application used to search information posted on the World Wide Web. The two most common applications are Netscape and Internet Explorer.

浏览器 它是用来搜索万维网上信息的一种应用软件。Netscape 和 Internet Explorer 是两种最常见的应用软件。

Content management System   An administrative software system that enables a user to add or change content on a website.
内容管理系统   管理软件系统使得用户能够添加或更改网站内容。

DSL（Digital Subscriber Line）   A technology designed to bring high-bandwidth information to homes and small businesses over ordinary copper telephone lines.
数字用户线路   指的是通过普通电话线将高频带宽连接到家庭或小型企业中去的一项技术。

E-Business   The use of Internet technologies to conduct or facilitate business.
电子商务   利用互联网技术管理和完善商务活动。

E-Commerce   The trading of goods and services over the Internet.
电子商贸   在互联网上进行商品和服务的交换。

Extranet   An intranet that is partially accessible to outsiders. As a business tool, it can allow secure access to customers, suppliers and other key business partners through the use of a username and password.
外联网   指的是部分对外开放的企业内联网。作为商业工具，外联网允许可靠的客户、供应商和其他重要商业伙伴通过用户名和密码登录。

Firewall   A system designed to prevent unauthorized access to or from a private network. Firewalls are frequently used to prevent unauthorized Internet users from accessing private networks connected to the Internet, especially intranets.
防火墙   防火墙是用来阻止非法用户访问私人网站的系统。它经常被用来阻止未经授权的互联网用户访问接入到互联网上的私人网站，特别是企业内联网。

Home Page   The main page of a website that users first see when they connect to a website.
主页   一个网站的主要部分，用户登录网站后首先看到的网页。

HTML（Hypertext Markup Language）   A "code" used to build web pages. A common language used to share data over the web.
超文本标识语言   是一种建立网页的"代码"，它是网络中共享数据的一般语言。

Hyperlinks   Embedded "connections" in web pages that allow users to "jump" from page to page anywhere on the Internet.
超链接   网页之间的内部"连接"，它允许用户无论在互联网的何处都能实现从一个网页跳转到另一个网页上去。

Internet   The decentralized global network of computers, routers and cable connections that enable millions of the world's computers to "talk" to each other as long as they are both connected to the Internet.

互联网　是允许数百万的连接到互联网的全球计算机通过主机、路由器和电缆连接实现相互"对话"的分散的全球网络。

Intranet　A private internal network that uses Internet technology to connect users. It provides a secure connection protected by a firewall, and allows access only to those of the same company or organization.

内联网　是使用互联网技术与用户联系的私人内部网络。它提供一个受防火墙保护的可靠连接，只允许公司或组织内部成员访问。

ISP（Internet Service Provider）　Also called Internet Access Provider. An organization that provides access to the Internet either digitally or via analog for a monthly fee.

互联网服务提供商　也称"网络访问提供者"。它通过数字或模拟信号提供进入互联网的通路，按月收取费用。

P2P（Peer to Peer）　A form of file sharing communications in which each participant has the same capabilities and either party can initiate a communication session. PayPal is an example of a P2P payment system.

P2P（对等网络）　一种文件共享通信的形式，每一参与者具有相同的权利，每一方都能发起通信会议。PayPal是P2P支付系统的例子。

Client/Server　A form of file sharing communications in which one program, the client, makes a service request from another program, the server, which fulfills the request. Most often used in a network of computers, as the client/server model provides a convenient way to interconnect programs that are distributed efficiently across different locations. Online banking services are an example of client/server communication.

客户机/服务器　文件共享通信的一种类型，客户在一个程序中提出服务请求，另一个程序下的服务器满足这一要求。它是计算机网络中最常用的一种模式，因为这一模式给程序在不同站点之间有效分布，程序间相互连接提供了便捷的方法。在线银行服务就是使用客户机/服务器的例子。

Server　A network device that provides services to client PCs, for example file access, print spooling or remote execution.

服务器　一种网络设备，给客户个人计算机提供服务，如文件接入、打印暂存和远程执行等。

Splash Page　An introductory page before a home page that acts as a curtain to a website. Usually holds little information and is mainly used for graphic illustration.

醒目页面（形象页面）　主页前面的介绍性网页，起着网站的"门帘"作用。通常含有较少的信息，主要用图例说明。

URL（Uniform Resource Locator） The alpha-numeric address used to locate a website.
统一资源定位器　指定站点位置，由文字和数字组成的地址。

VoIP（Voice over IP：voice delivered using the Internet Protocol） A set of hardware and software that allows users to use the Internet as a transmission device for ordinary telephone calls. A major advantage of VoIP and Internet telephony is that it avoids the tolls charged by ordinary telephone service. A major disadvantage is that currently it does not offer the same level of quality as direct telephone service connections.
基于互联网协议的语音信息传输服务　一组允许用户将因特网当作传输工具进行普通电话呼叫的硬件和软件。VoIP 和 Internet 通信的主要优点在于它消除了普通电话服务的费用。主要缺陷在于目前的因特网通话服务质量不如直接电话服务连接好。

Web Host An organization that provides users who do not have their own web servers with server space to "park" their website and allow others to view it over the Internet. ISPs also host websites and those such as AOL, will allow subscribers a small amount of server space to host.
虚拟主机　是给没有网络服务器的用户提供服务器空间供他们"安置"网站并允许其他人上网浏览的系统。ISP 也往往是虚拟主机站点，比如 AOL，为用户提供较小量的服务器空间以安放数。